The Amazing Adventures of
THE ESCAPIST™

VOLUME 1

Based on *The Amazing Adventures of Kavalier & Clay* by Michael Chabon

Wraparound Cover Art by Chris Ware

DARK HORSE BOOKS™

CONTENTS

CONTENTS

INTRODUCTION

by Michael Chabon

I STILL REMEMBER THE FIRST *ESCAPIST* COMIC I EVER CAME ACROSS.
It appears to have been one of the later Fab Comics issues, from 1968, though I did not discover it until four or five years later, at the bottom of a box of old comics passed along to me by my cousin Arthur when he went off to college. It contained a story in which the Escapist fell prey to a villain named the Junkman, who employed an "atom spike" to administer a dose of "superjunk" that first plunged the Escapist into a deep coma and then subjected him to an endless string of unbearable nightmares. All I can really remember about the story — but I have never forgotten it — is a single, stunning panel (possibly drawn by Neal Adams). It depicted the Escapist, in his simple blue costume, in the disturbing, inspiring, and surrealistic act of *escaping from his own head.*

That single panel, it seems to me, perfectly expresses the appeal not only of the Escapist, Master of Elusion, but of the entire genre of comic books from which, as from a great dreaming forehead, he sprang. Escape and escapism, in art and literature, have received a bad name. It was given to them, I believe, by the very people who forged the locks and barred the windows in the first place.

Twenty years would pass before I encountered the Escapist again. By then — at the end of 1995 — I had begun actively to research the novel that would become *The Amazing Adventures of Kavalier & Clay.* As I made my way through the literature—from *The Steranko History of Comics* to Bob Harvey's *The Art of the Comic Book* — I was intrigued by hints and references, here and there, to "the great lost superhero of the Golden Age," and in time decided to make that character, and his youthful creators, the subject of my fictional history.

The Golden Age Escapist, as published from 1940 to 1954 by Sheldon Anapol's Empire Comics, turned out to be the easiest to track down. After Sheldon Anapol settled the famous lawsuit with DC Comics, and ceased publication of his flagship title, the history of the Escapist grew Byzantine and sketchy. During the Golden Age, the Escapist and his Kavalier & Clay-created cohorts were ubiquitous in the druggists' and candy stores of America; after 1954 the Escapist began a fugitive and phantom career, surfacing, disappearing, reappearing, the Sasquatch of comics, often stumbled upon, never quite caught on film. I can't tell you how many people have described, after hearing about my cousin Artie's box of comics, their own chance, not-to-be-repeated encounters with an *Escapist* comic book over the years; how they came across a tattered book featuring the Score Comics or Hi-Tone Comics or Fab Comics version of the character, loved it, and were never able to locate another.

Now, thanks to the determination of the dedicated archivists at Dark Horse Comics, the generosity of the Kavalier and Clay estates, and the implacable scholarship of Kevin McCarthy, widely acknowledged to be the world's leading expert in "Escapistry," the entire patchwork epic of the Escapist is being reassembled for your reading pleasure. Future issues of *The Amazing Adventures of the Escapist* will continue to feature stories culled from every epoch of the Escapist's strange and checkered history, as well as the best of the secondary Kavalier & Clay characters — Luna Moth, Kid Vixen, Mr. Machine Gun among them — and samples of the later comics work done, separately and together, by Sam Clay and Joe Kavalier. I hope that they bring all the reading pleasure that bad luck and good lawyers have so long conspired to deny you.

The Passing of the Key

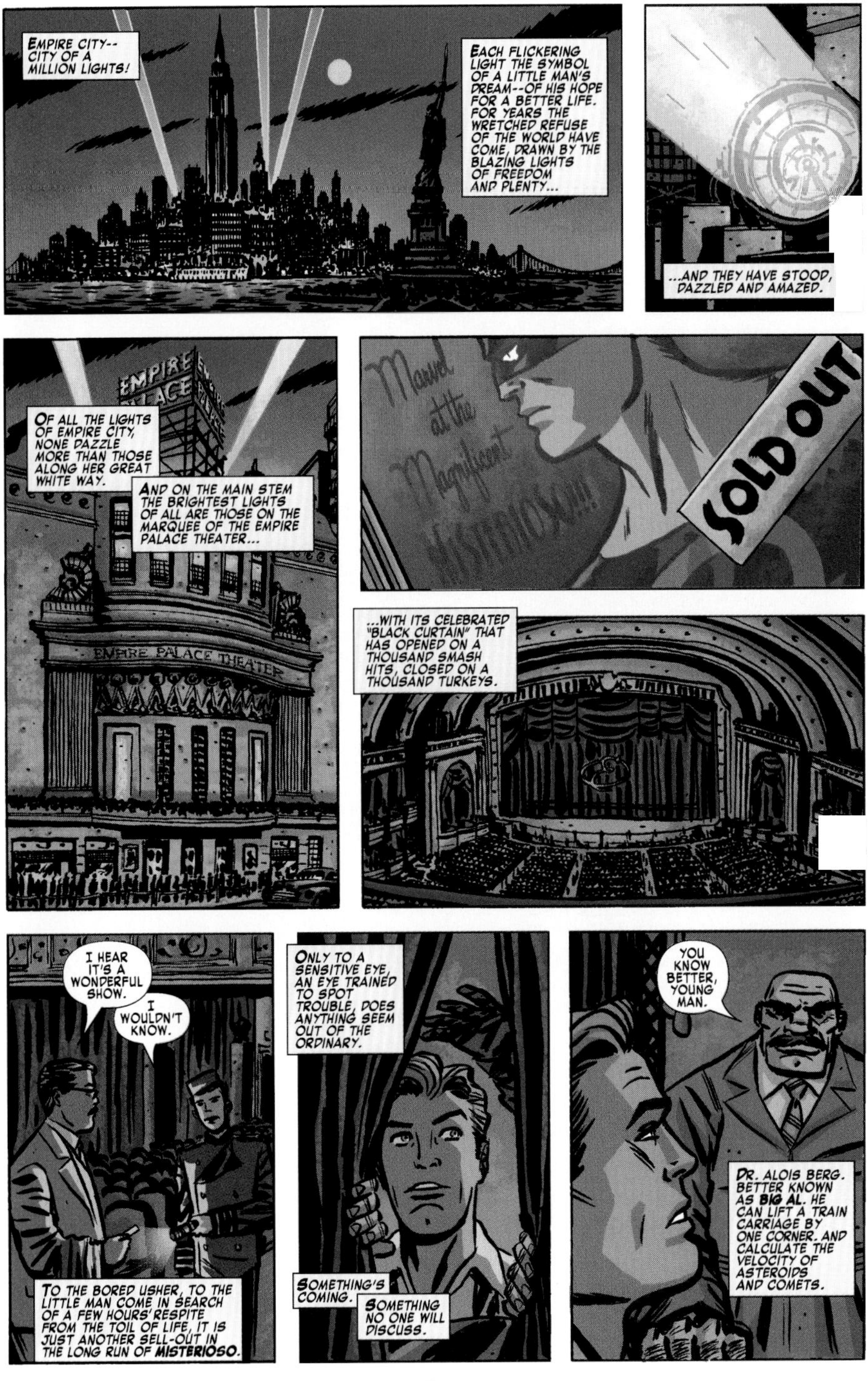

EMPIRE CITY-- CITY OF A MILLION LIGHTS!
EACH FLICKERING LIGHT THE SYMBOL OF A LITTLE MAN'S DREAM--OF HIS HOPE FOR A BETTER LIFE. FOR YEARS THE WRETCHED REFUSE OF THE WORLD HAVE COME, DRAWN BY THE BLAZING LIGHTS OF FREEDOM AND PLENTY...
...AND THEY HAVE STOOD, DAZZLED AND AMAZED.
EMPIRE PALACE
OF ALL THE LIGHTS OF EMPIRE CITY, NONE DAZZLE MORE THAN THOSE ALONG HER GREAT WHITE WAY.
AND ON THE MAIN STEM THE BRIGHTEST LIGHTS OF ALL ARE THOSE ON THE MARQUEE OF THE EMPIRE PALACE THEATER...
EMPIRE PALACE THEATER
Marvel at the Magnificent
SOLD OUT
...WITH ITS CELEBRATED "BLACK CURTAIN" THAT HAS OPENED ON A THOUSAND SMASH HITS, CLOSED ON A THOUSAND TURKEYS.
I HEAR IT'S A WONDERFUL SHOW.
I WOULDN'T KNOW.
TO THE BORED USHER, TO THE LITTLE MAN COME IN SEARCH OF A FEW HOURS' RESPITE FROM THE TOIL OF LIFE, IT IS JUST ANOTHER SELL-OUT IN THE LONG RUN OF MISTERIOSO.
ONLY TO A SENSITIVE EYE, AN EYE TRAINED TO SPOT TROUBLE, DOES ANYTHING SEEM OUT OF THE ORDINARY.
SOMETHING'S COMING.
SOMETHING NO ONE WILL DISCUSS.
YOU KNOW BETTER, YOUNG MAN.
DR. ALOIS BERG. BETTER KNOWN AS BIG AL. HE CAN LIFT A TRAIN CARRIAGE BY ONE CORNER. AND CALCULATE THE VELOCITY OF ASTEROIDS AND COMETS.

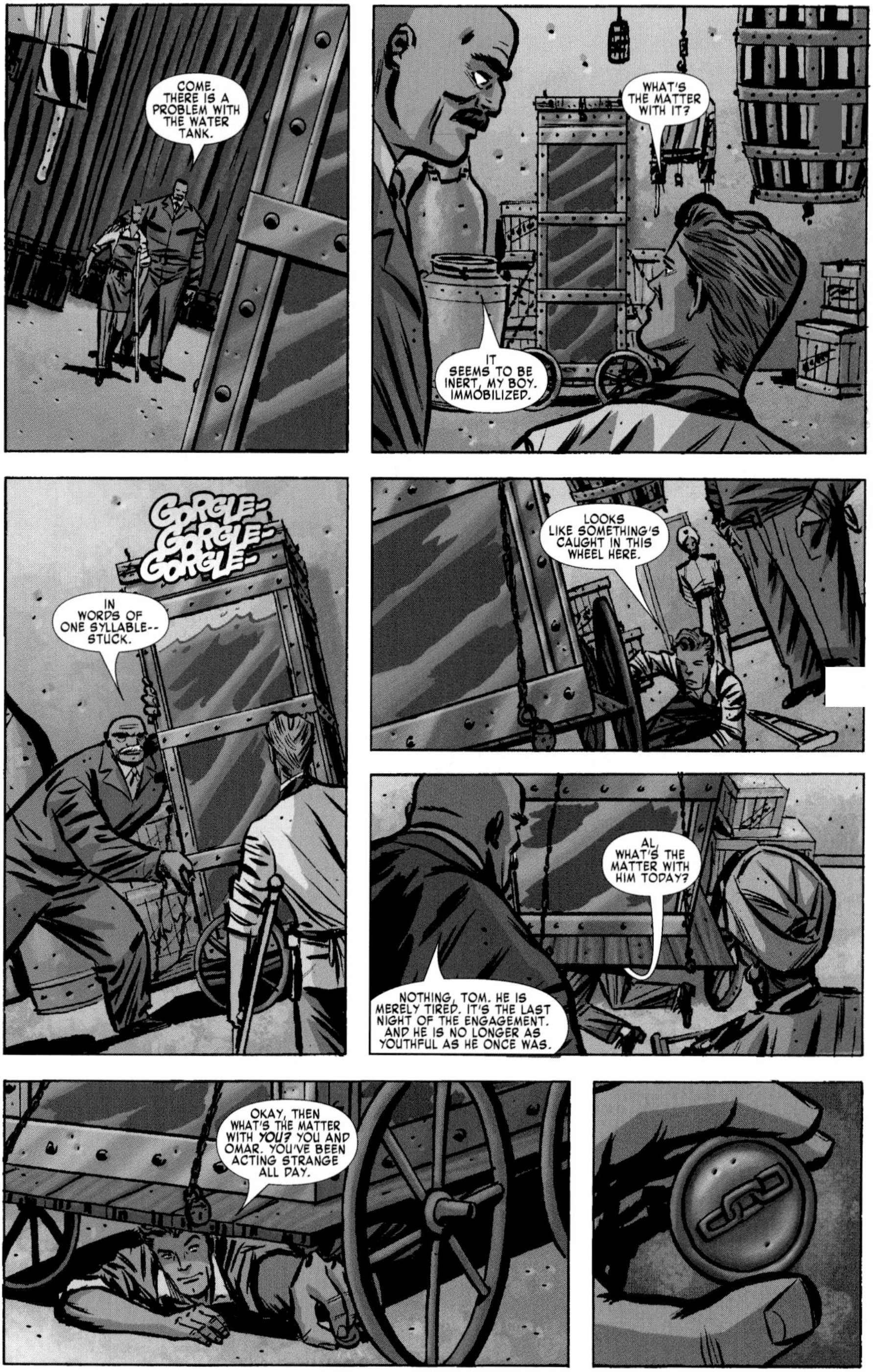
COME. THERE IS A PROBLEM WITH THE WATER TANK.
WHAT'S THE MATTER WITH IT?
IT SEEMS TO BE INERT, MY BOY. IMMOBILIZED.
GORGLE-GORGLE-GORGLE-
IN WORDS OF ONE SYLLABLE--STUCK.
LOOKS LIKE SOMETHING'S CAUGHT IN THIS WHEEL HERE.
AL, WHAT'S THE MATTER WITH HIM TODAY?
NOTHING, TOM. HE IS MERELY TIRED. IT'S THE LAST NIGHT OF THE ENGAGEMENT. AND HE IS NO LONGER AS YOUTHFUL AS HE ONCE WAS.
OKAY, THEN WHAT'S THE MATTER WITH *YOU?* YOU AND OMAR. YOU'VE BEEN ACTING STRANGE ALL DAY.

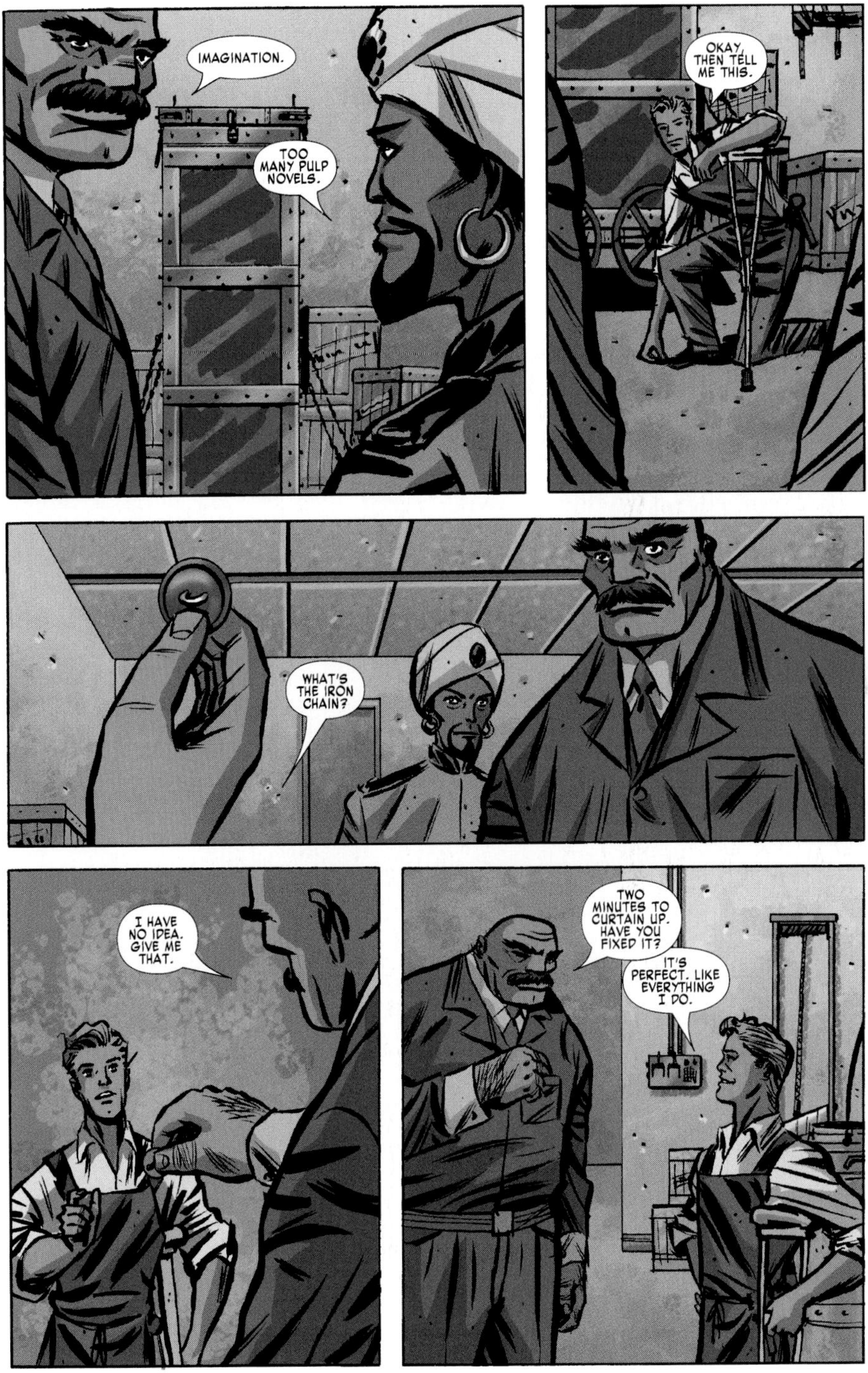
IMAGINATION.
TOO MANY PULP NOVELS.
OKAY, THEN TELL ME THIS.
WHAT'S THE IRON CHAIN?
I HAVE NO IDEA. GIVE ME THAT.
TWO MINUTES TO CURTAIN UP. HAVE YOU FIXED IT?
IT'S PERFECT. LIKE EVERYTHING I DO.

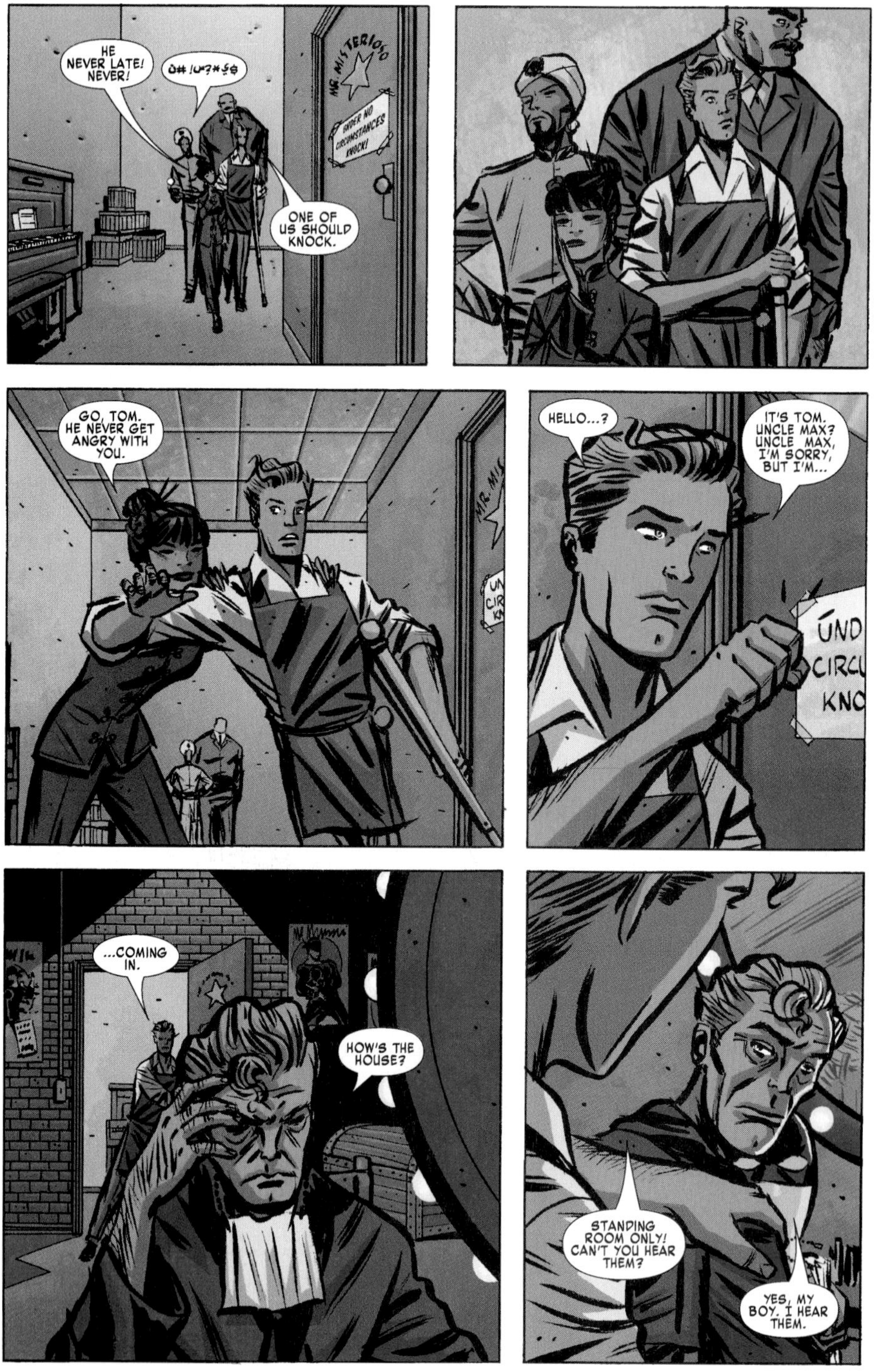
HE NEVER LATE! NEVER!
MR. MISTERIOSO
UNDER NO CIRCUMSTANCES KNOCK!
ONE OF US SHOULD KNOCK.
GO, TOM. HE NEVER GET ANGRY WITH YOU.
HELLO...?
IT'S TOM. UNCLE MAX? UNCLE MAX, I'M SORRY, BUT I'M...
...COMING IN.
HOW'S THE HOUSE?
STANDING ROOM ONLY! CAN'T YOU HEAR THEM?
YES, MY BOY. I HEAR THEM.

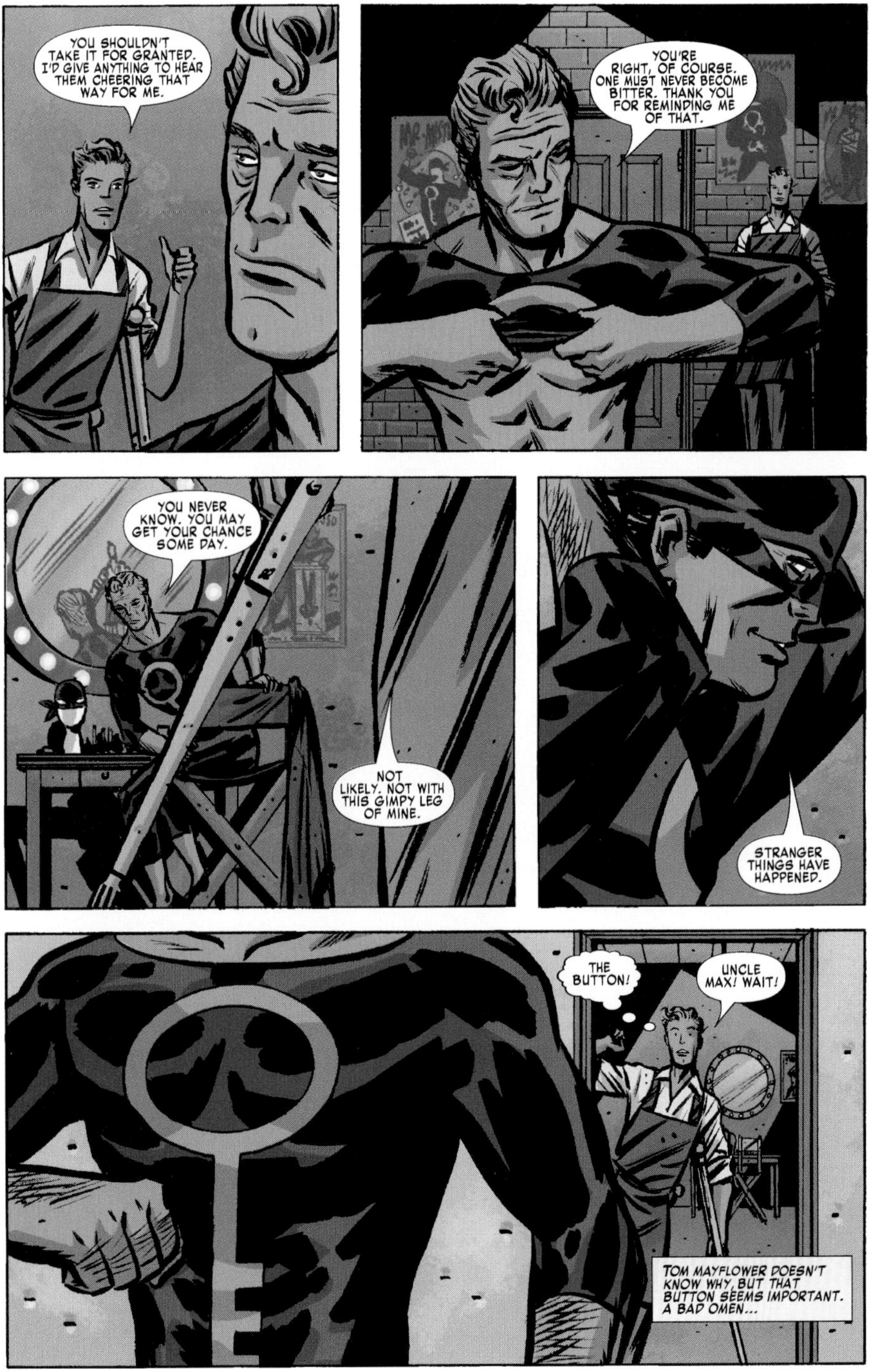
YOU SHOULDN'T TAKE IT FOR GRANTED. I'D GIVE ANYTHING TO HEAR THEM CHEERING THAT WAY FOR ME.
YOU'RE RIGHT, OF COURSE. ONE MUST NEVER BECOME BITTER. THANK YOU FOR REMINDING ME OF THAT.
YOU NEVER KNOW. YOU MAY GET YOUR CHANCE SOME DAY.
NOT LIKELY. NOT WITH THIS GIMPY LEG OF MINE.
STRANGER THINGS HAVE HAPPENED.
THE BUTTON!
UNCLE MAX! WAIT!
TOM MAYFLOWER DOESN'T KNOW WHY, BUT THAT BUTTON SEEMS IMPORTANT. A BAD OMEN...

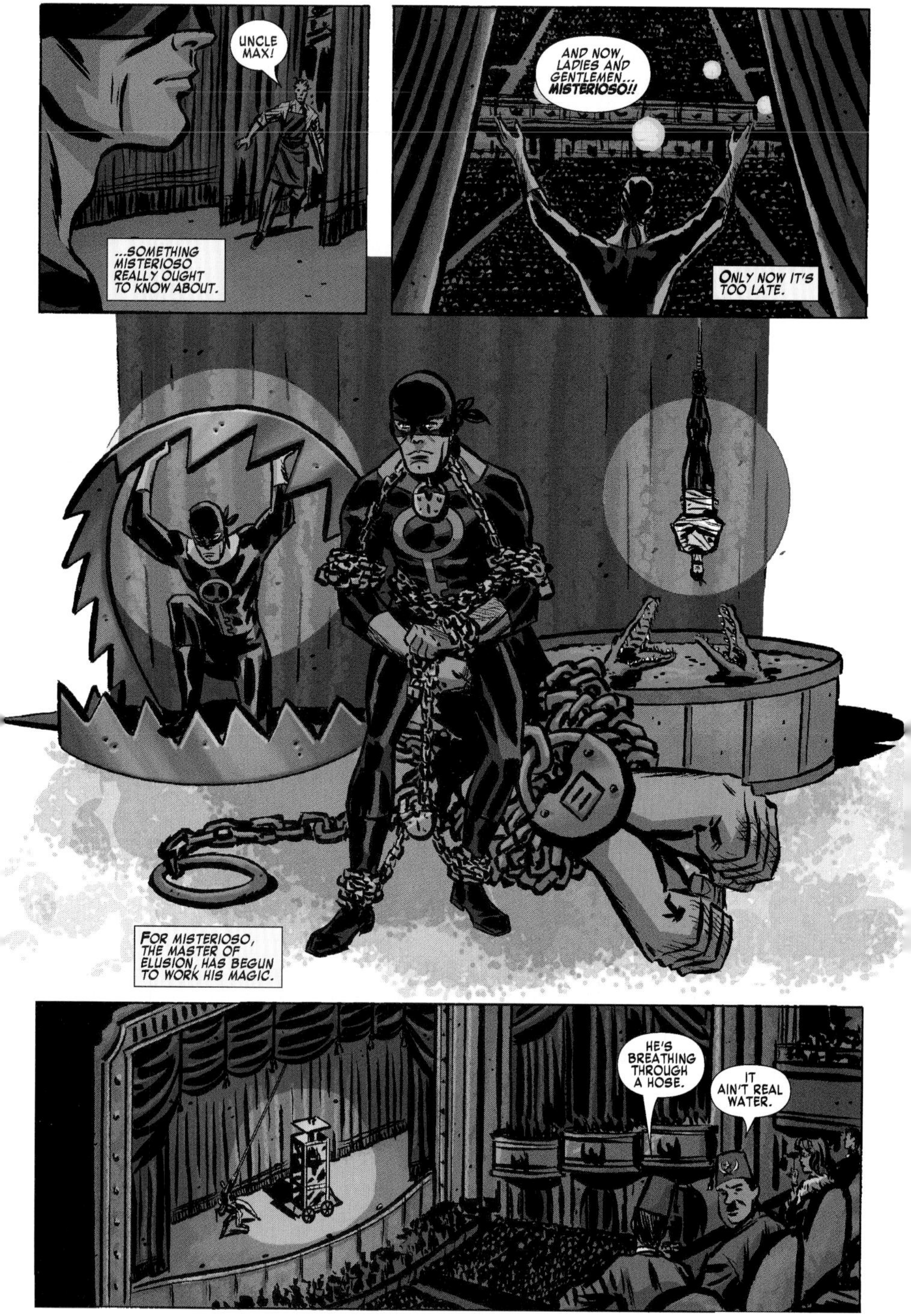
UNCLE MAX!
...SOMETHING MISTERIOSO REALLY OUGHT TO KNOW ABOUT.
AND NOW, LADIES AND GENTLEMEN... MISTERIOSO!!
ONLY NOW IT'S TOO LATE.
FOR MISTERIOSO, THE MASTER OF ELUSION, HAS BEGUN TO WORK HIS MAGIC.
HE'S BREATHING THROUGH A HOSE.
IT AIN'T REAL WATER.

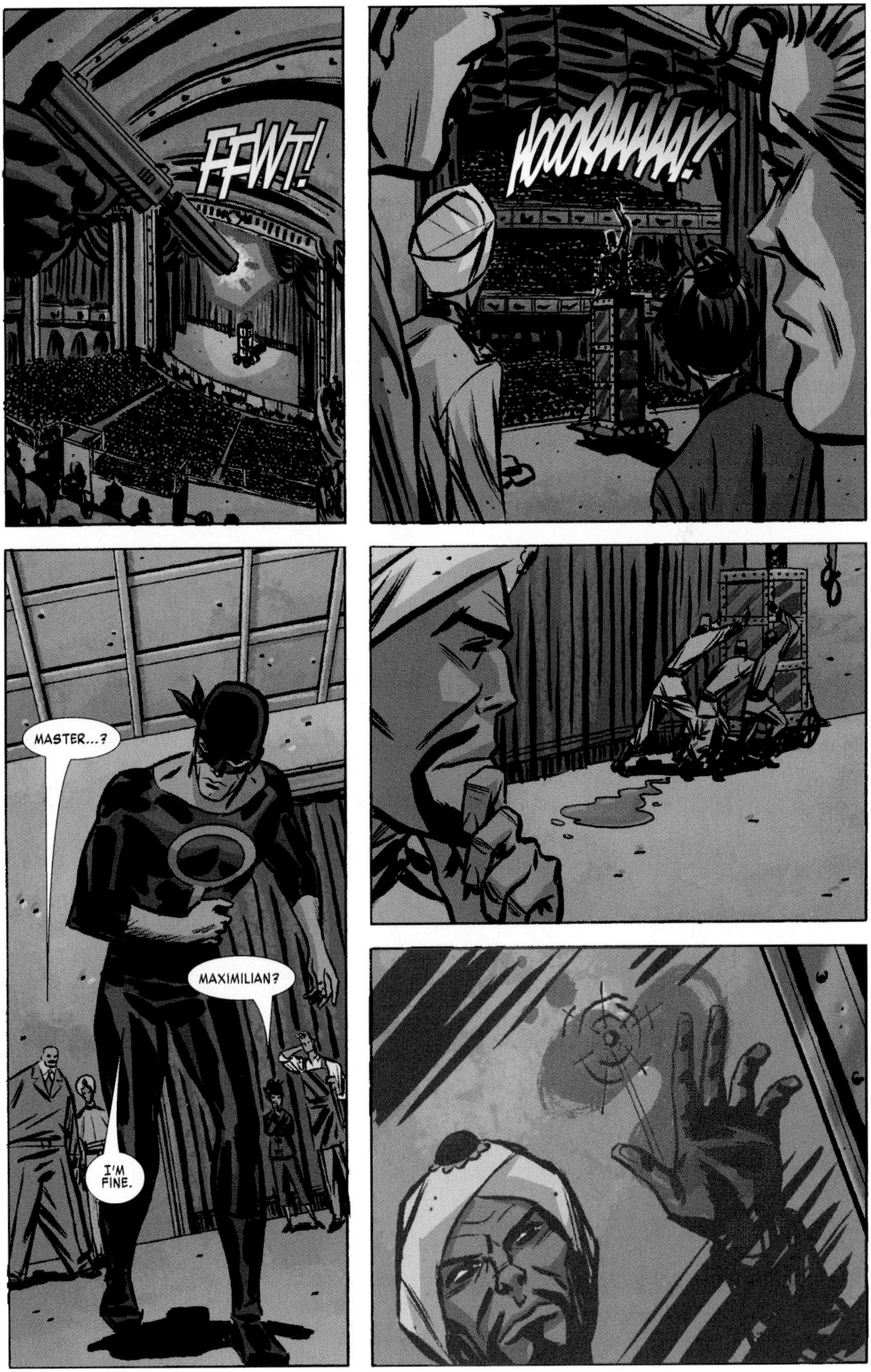
FFWT!
HOOORAAAAAY!!
MASTER...?
MAXIMILIAN?
I'M FINE.

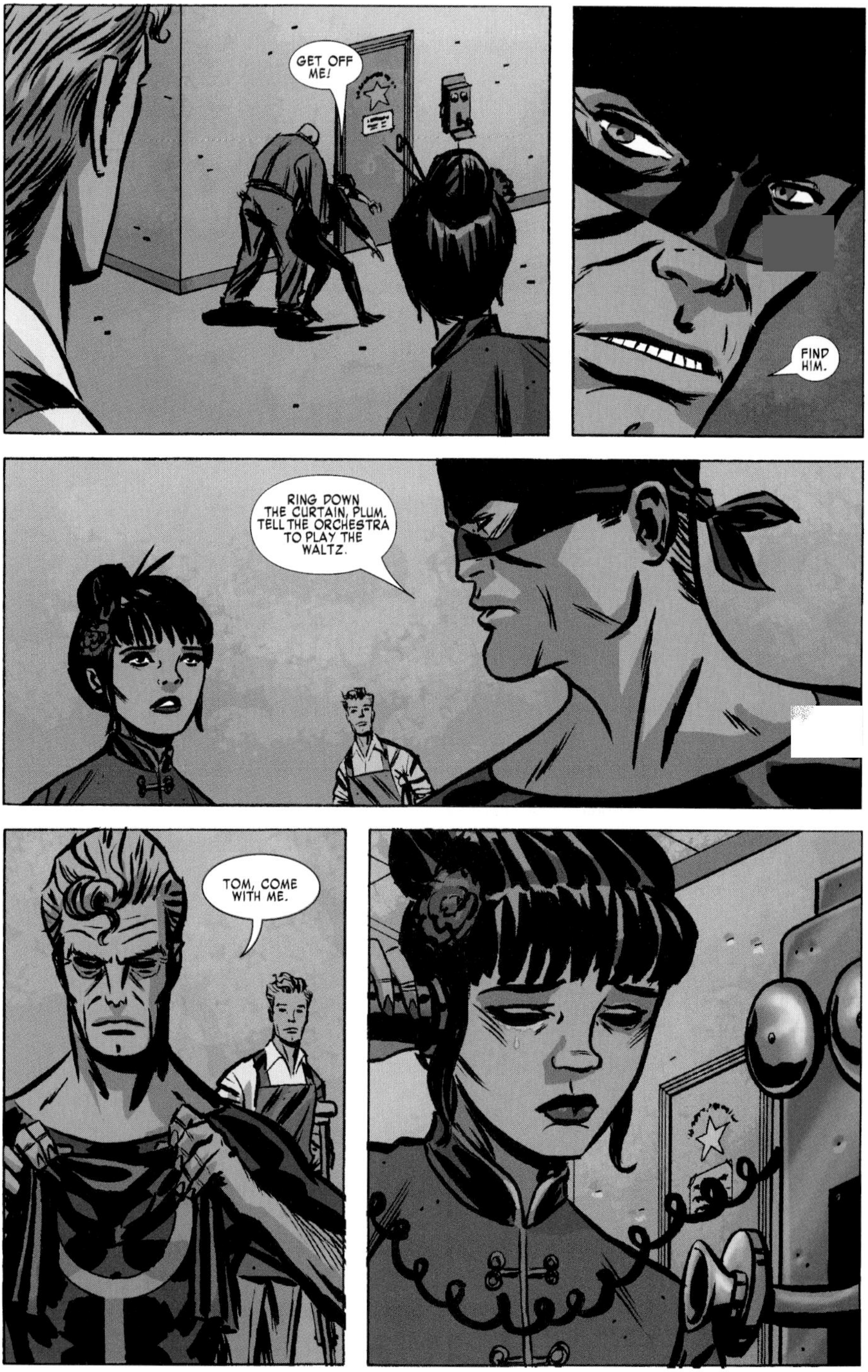
GET OFF ME!
FIND HIM.
RING DOWN THE CURTAIN, PLUM. TELL THE ORCHESTRA TO PLAY THE WALTZ.
TOM, COME WITH ME.

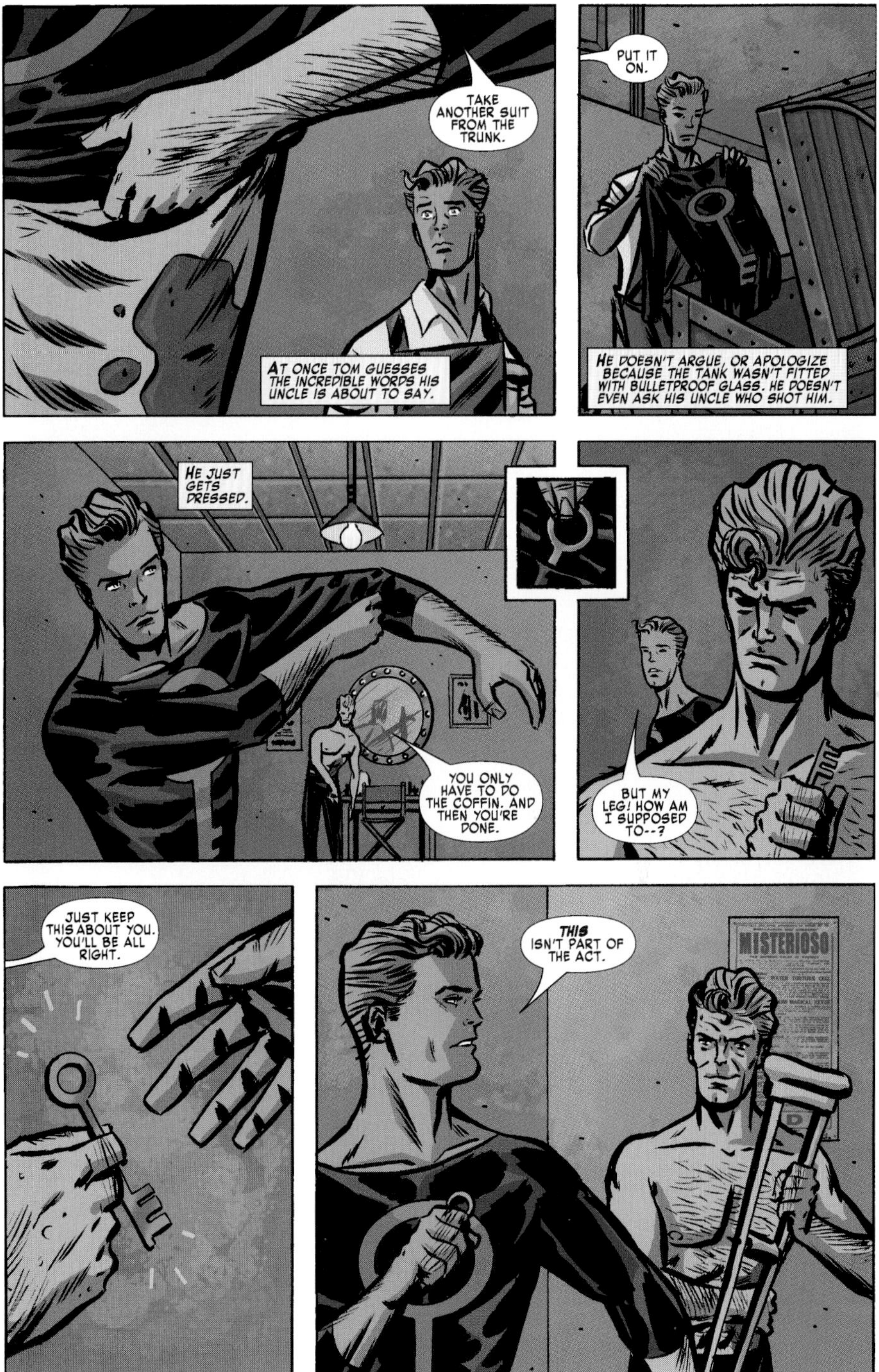
TAKE ANOTHER SUIT FROM THE TRUNK.
AT ONCE TOM GUESSES THE INCREDIBLE WORDS HIS UNCLE IS ABOUT TO SAY.
PUT IT ON.
HE DOESN'T ARGUE, OR APOLOGIZE BECAUSE THE TANK WASN'T FITTED WITH BULLETPROOF GLASS. HE DOESN'T EVEN ASK HIS UNCLE WHO SHOT HIM.
HE JUST GETS DRESSED.
YOU ONLY HAVE TO DO THE COFFIN. AND THEN YOU'RE DONE.
BUT MY LEG! HOW AM I SUPPOSED TO--?
JUST KEEP THIS ABOUT YOU. YOU'LL BE ALL RIGHT.
THIS ISN'T PART OF THE ACT.
MISTERIOSO

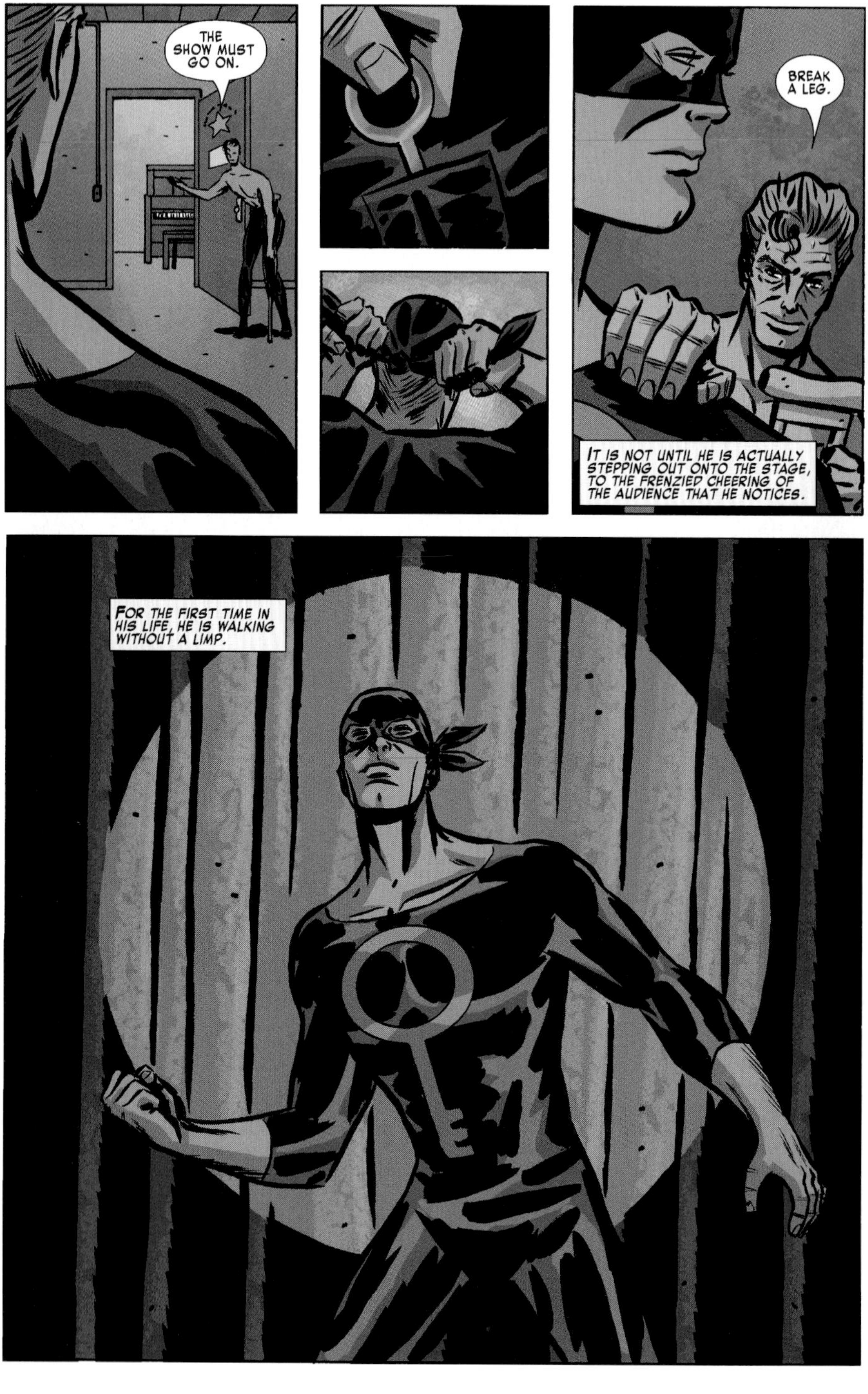
THE SHOW MUST GO ON.
BREAK A LEG.
IT IS NOT UNTIL HE IS ACTUALLY STEPPING OUT ONTO THE STAGE, TO THE FRENZIED CHEERING OF THE AUDIENCE THAT HE NOTICES.
FOR THE FIRST TIME IN HIS LIFE, HE IS WALKING WITHOUT A LIMP.

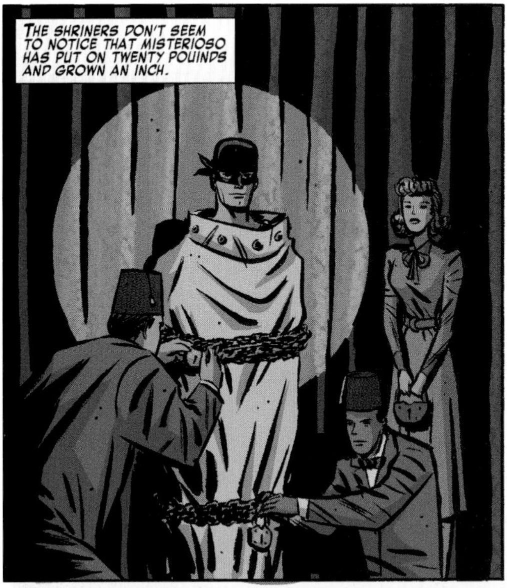
THE SHRINERS DON'T SEEM TO NOTICE THAT MISTERIOSO HAS PUT ON TWENTY POUINDS AND GROWN AN INCH.

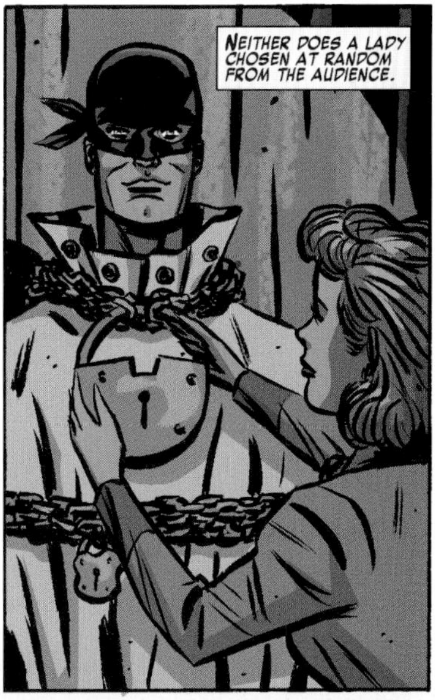
NEITHER DOES A LADY CHOSEN AT RANDOM FROM THE AUDIENCE.

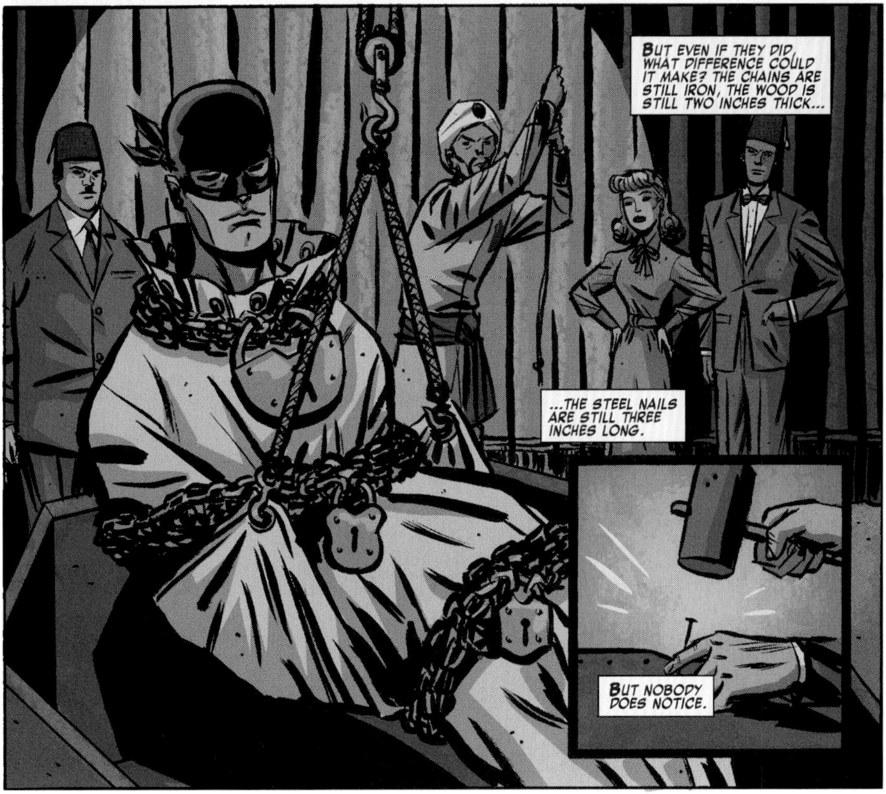
BUT EVEN IF THEY DID, WHAT DIFFERENCE COULD IT MAKE? THE CHAINS ARE STILL IRON, THE WOOD IS STILL TWO INCHES THICK...
...THE STEEL NAILS ARE STILL THREE INCHES LONG.
BUT NOBODY DOES NOTICE.

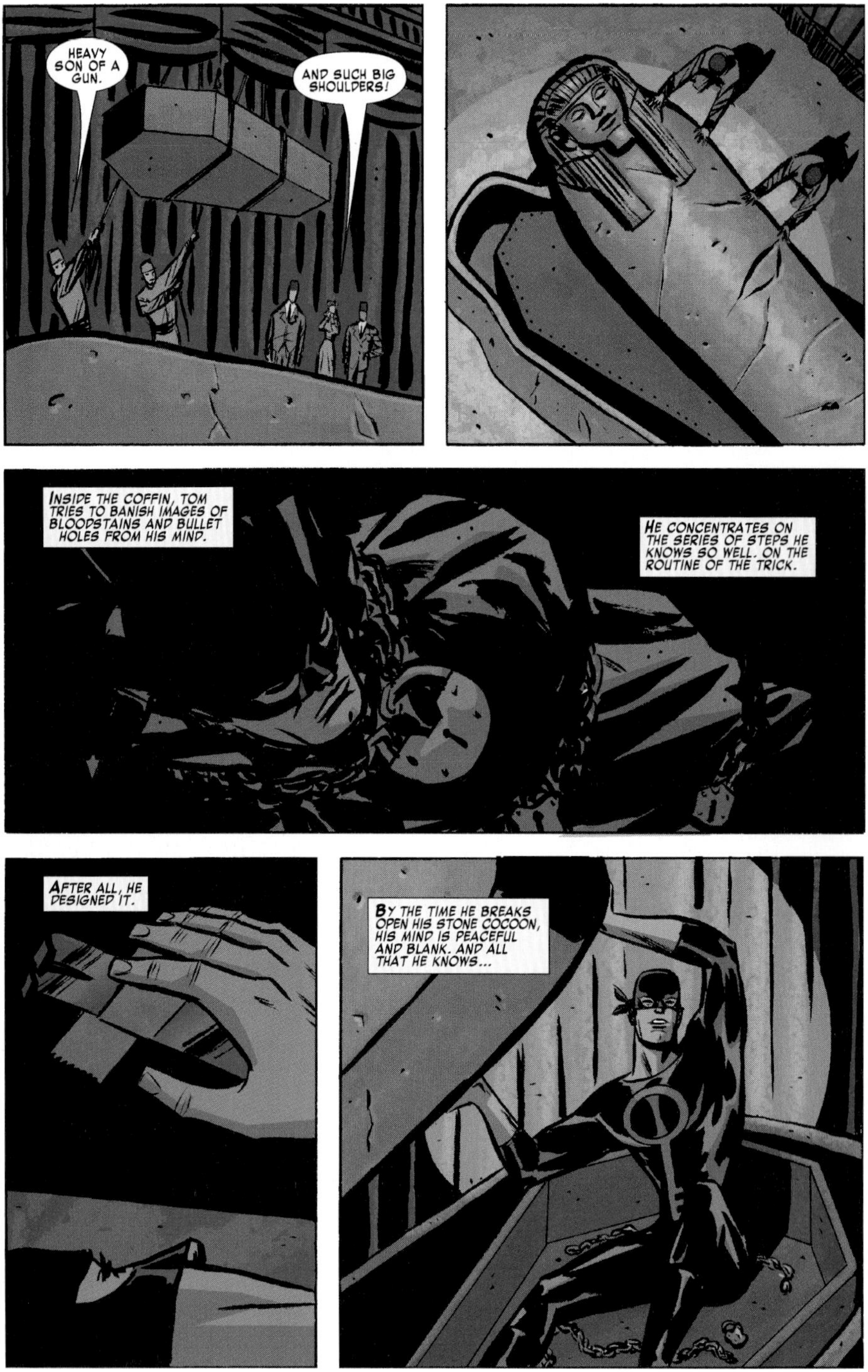
HEAVY SON OF A GUN.
AND SUCH BIG SHOULDERS!
INSIDE THE COFFIN, TOM TRIES TO BANISH IMAGES OF BLOODSTAINS AND BULLET HOLES FROM HIS MIND.
HE CONCENTRATES ON THE SERIES OF STEPS HE KNOWS SO WELL. ON THE ROUTINE OF THE TRICK.
AFTER ALL, HE DESIGNED IT.
BY THE TIME HE BREAKS OPEN HIS STONE COCOON, HIS MIND IS PEACEFUL AND BLANK. AND ALL THAT HE KNOWS...

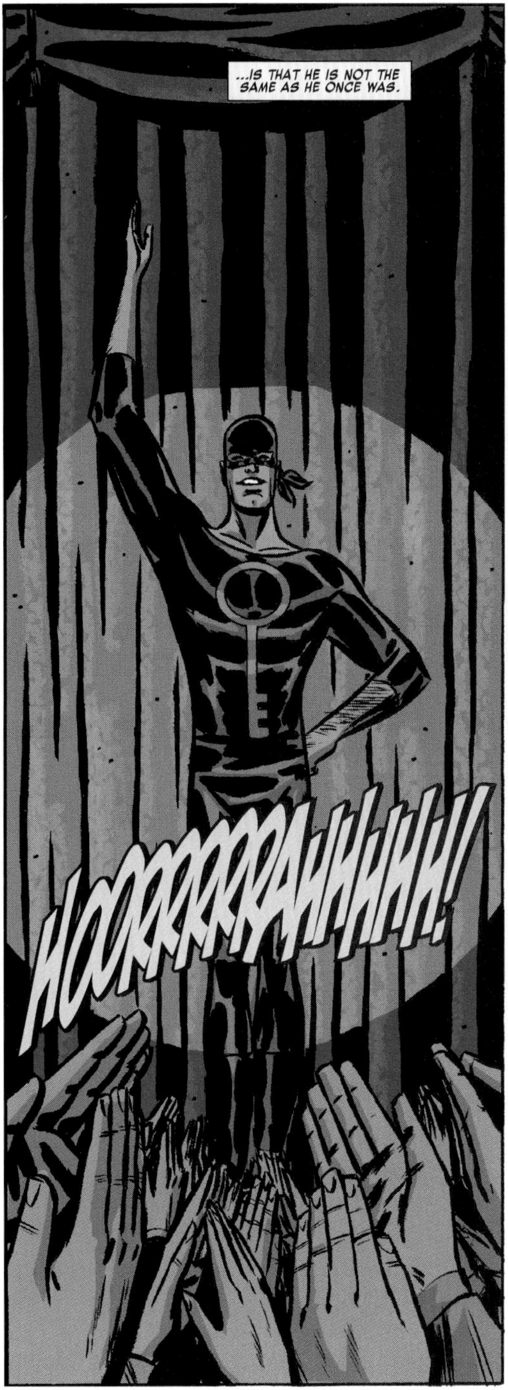
...IS THAT HE IS NOT THE SAME AS HE ONCE WAS.
HOORRRRRAHHHHHH!

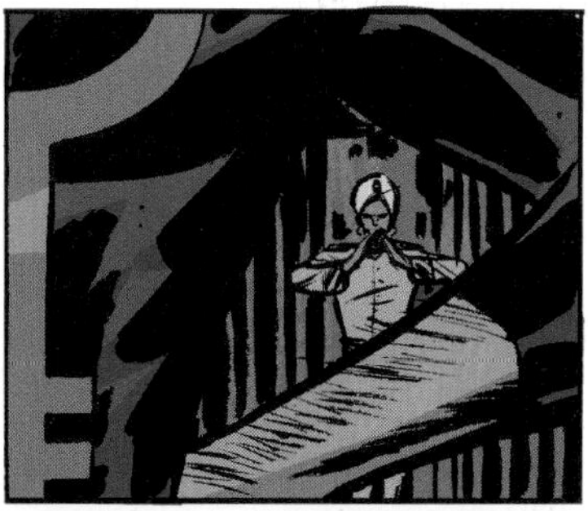

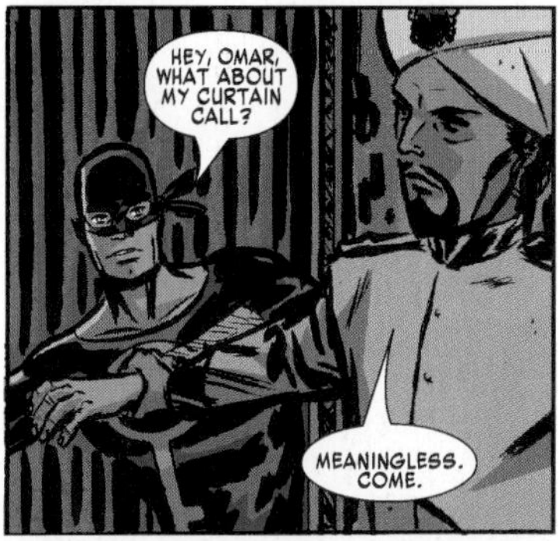
HEY, OMAR, WHAT ABOUT MY CURTAIN CALL?
MEANINGLESS. COME.

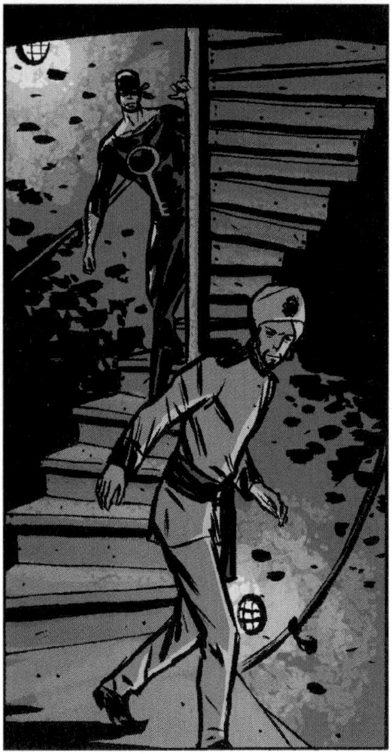

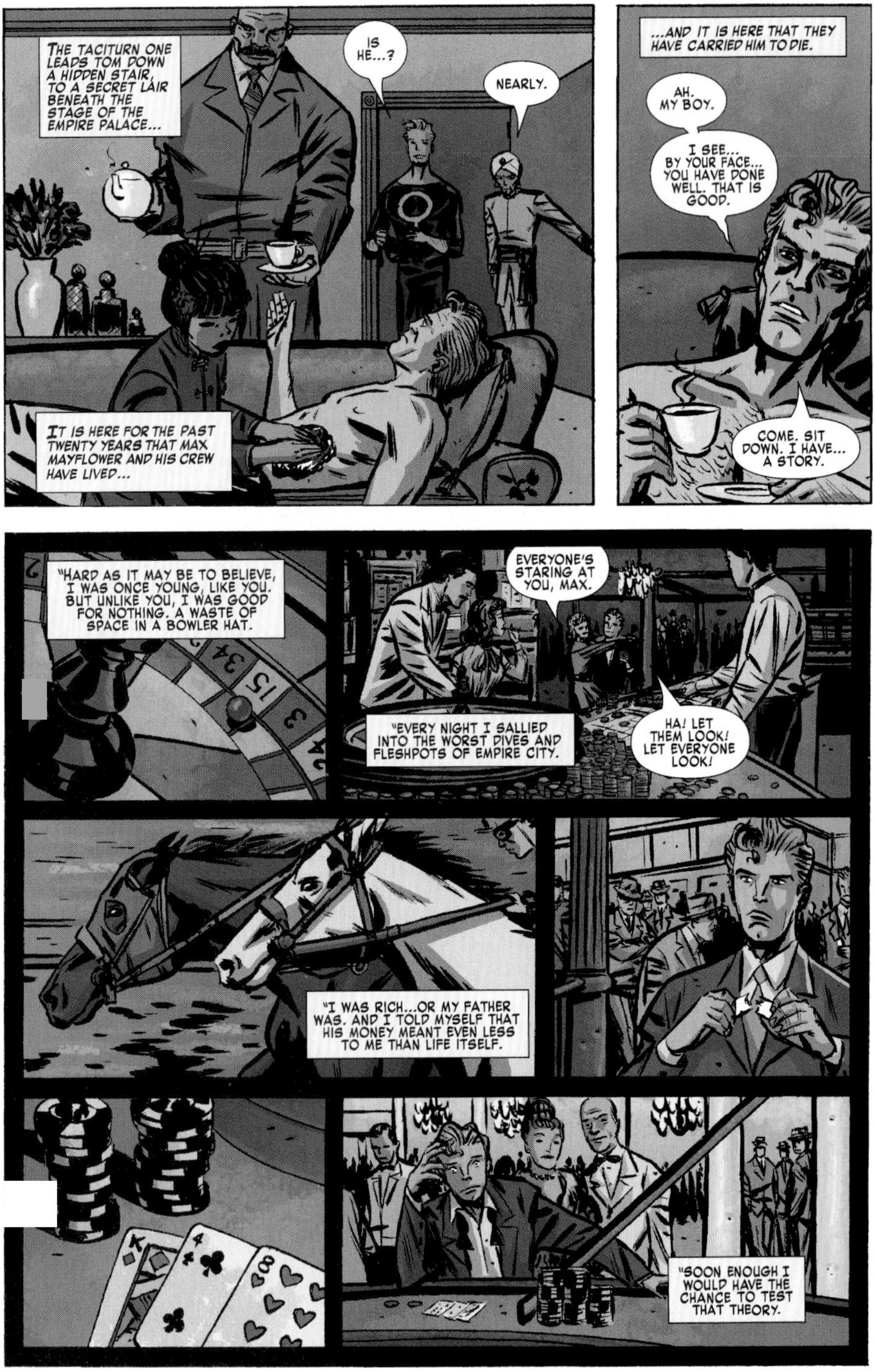
THE TACITURN ONE LEADS TOM DOWN A HIDDEN STAIR, TO A SECRET LAIR BENEATH THE STAGE OF THE EMPIRE PALACE...
IS HE...?
NEARLY.
IT IS HERE FOR THE PAST TWENTY YEARS THAT MAX MAYFLOWER AND HIS CREW HAVE LIVED...
...AND IT IS HERE THAT THEY HAVE CARRIED HIM TO DIE.
AH. MY BOY.
I SEE... BY YOUR FACE... YOU HAVE DONE WELL. THAT IS GOOD.
COME. SIT DOWN. I HAVE... A STORY.
"HARD AS IT MAY BE TO BELIEVE, I WAS ONCE YOUNG, LIKE YOU. BUT UNLIKE YOU, I WAS GOOD FOR NOTHING. A WASTE OF SPACE IN A BOWLER HAT.
EVERYONE'S STARING AT YOU, MAX.
"EVERY NIGHT I SALLIED INTO THE WORST DIVES AND FLESHPOTS OF EMPIRE CITY.
HA! LET THEM LOOK! LET EVERYONE LOOK!
"I WAS RICH...OR MY FATHER WAS. AND I TOLD MYSELF THAT HIS MONEY MEANT EVEN LESS TO ME THAN LIFE ITSELF.
"SOON ENOUGH I WOULD HAVE THE CHANCE TO TEST THAT THEORY.

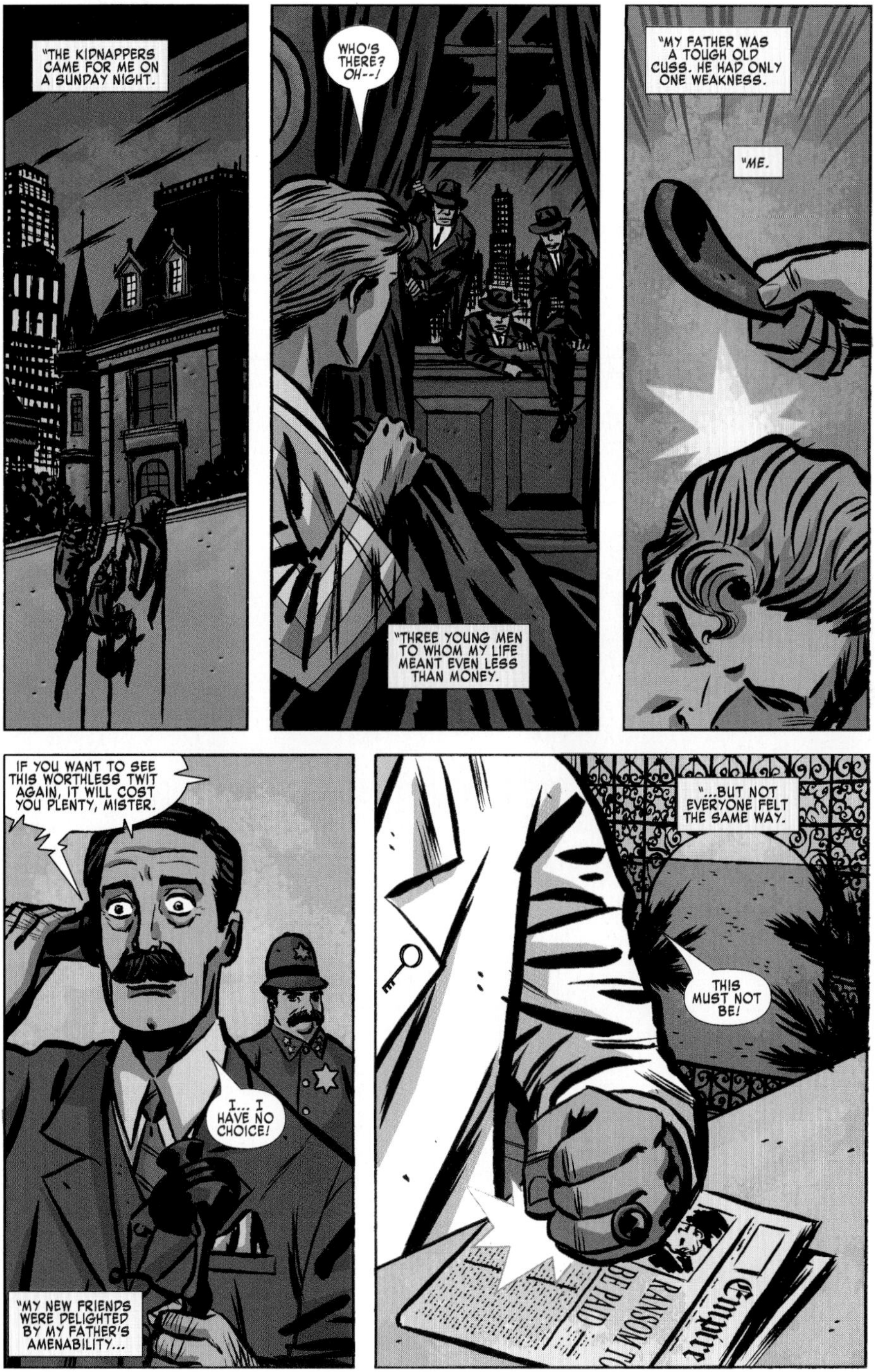
"THE KIDNAPPERS CAME FOR ME ON A SUNDAY NIGHT.
WHO'S THERE? OH--!
"THREE YOUNG MEN TO WHOM MY LIFE MEANT EVEN LESS THAN MONEY.
"MY FATHER WAS A TOUGH OLD CUSS. HE HAD ONLY ONE WEAKNESS.
"ME.
IF YOU WANT TO SEE THIS WORTHLESS TWIT AGAIN, IT WILL COST YOU PLENTY, MISTER.
I... I HAVE NO CHOICE!
"MY NEW FRIENDS WERE DELIGHTED BY MY FATHER'S AMENABILITY...
"...BUT NOT EVERYONE FELT THE SAME WAY.
THIS MUST NOT BE!
Empire
RANSOM TO
BE PAID

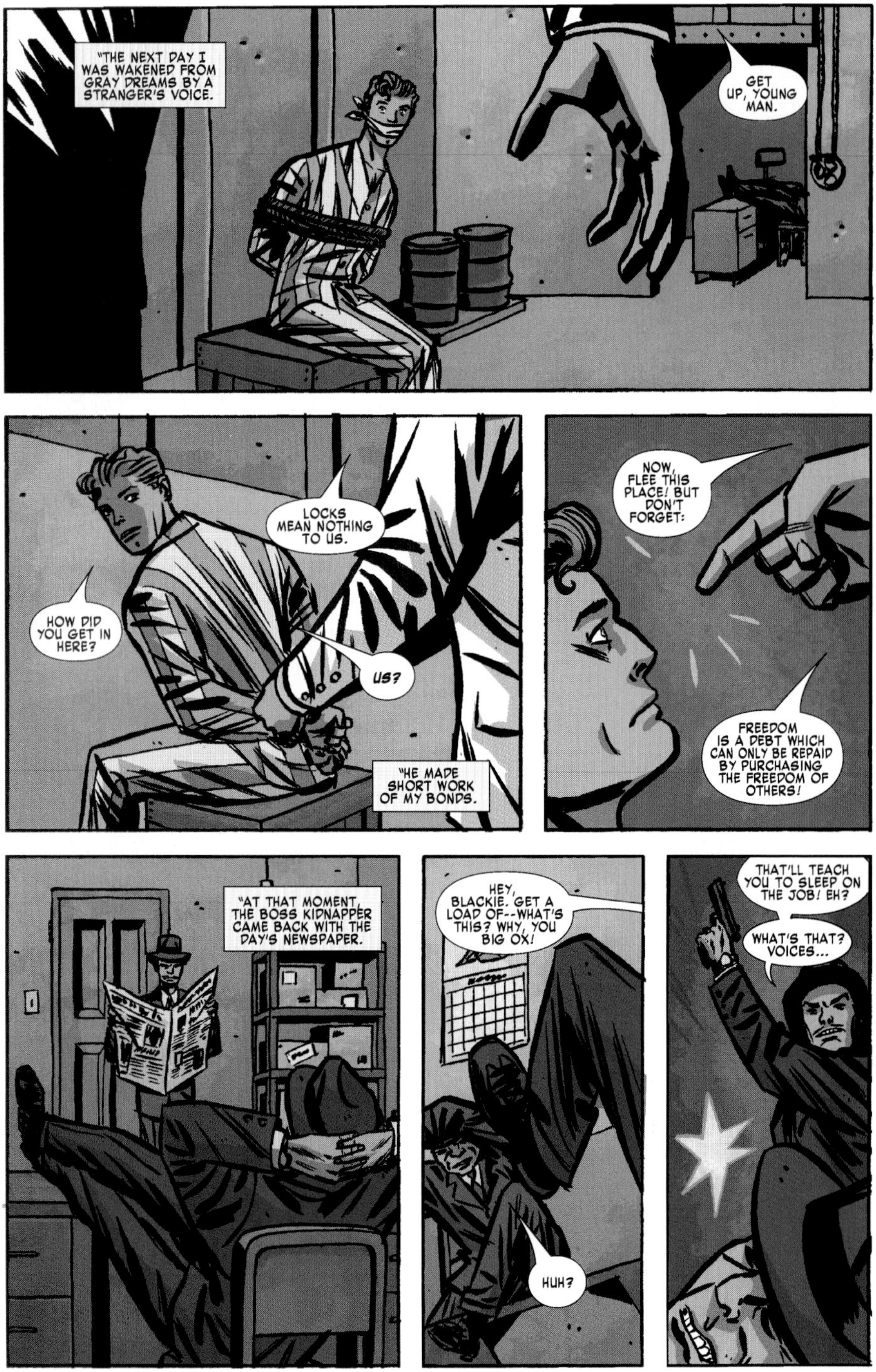
"THE NEXT DAY I WAS WAKENED FROM GRAY DREAMS BY A STRANGER'S VOICE.
GET UP, YOUNG MAN.
LOCKS MEAN NOTHING TO US.
HOW DID YOU GET IN HERE?
US?
"HE MADE SHORT WORK OF MY BONDS.
NOW, FLEE THIS PLACE! BUT DON'T FORGET:
FREEDOM IS A DEBT WHICH CAN ONLY BE REPAID BY PURCHASING THE FREEDOM OF OTHERS!
"AT THAT MOMENT, THE BOSS KIDNAPPER CAME BACK WITH THE DAY'S NEWSPAPER.
HEY, BLACKIE. GET A LOAD OF--WHAT'S THIS? WHY, YOU BIG OX!
HUH?
THAT'LL TEACH YOU TO SLEEP ON THE JOB! EH?
WHAT'S THAT? VOICES...

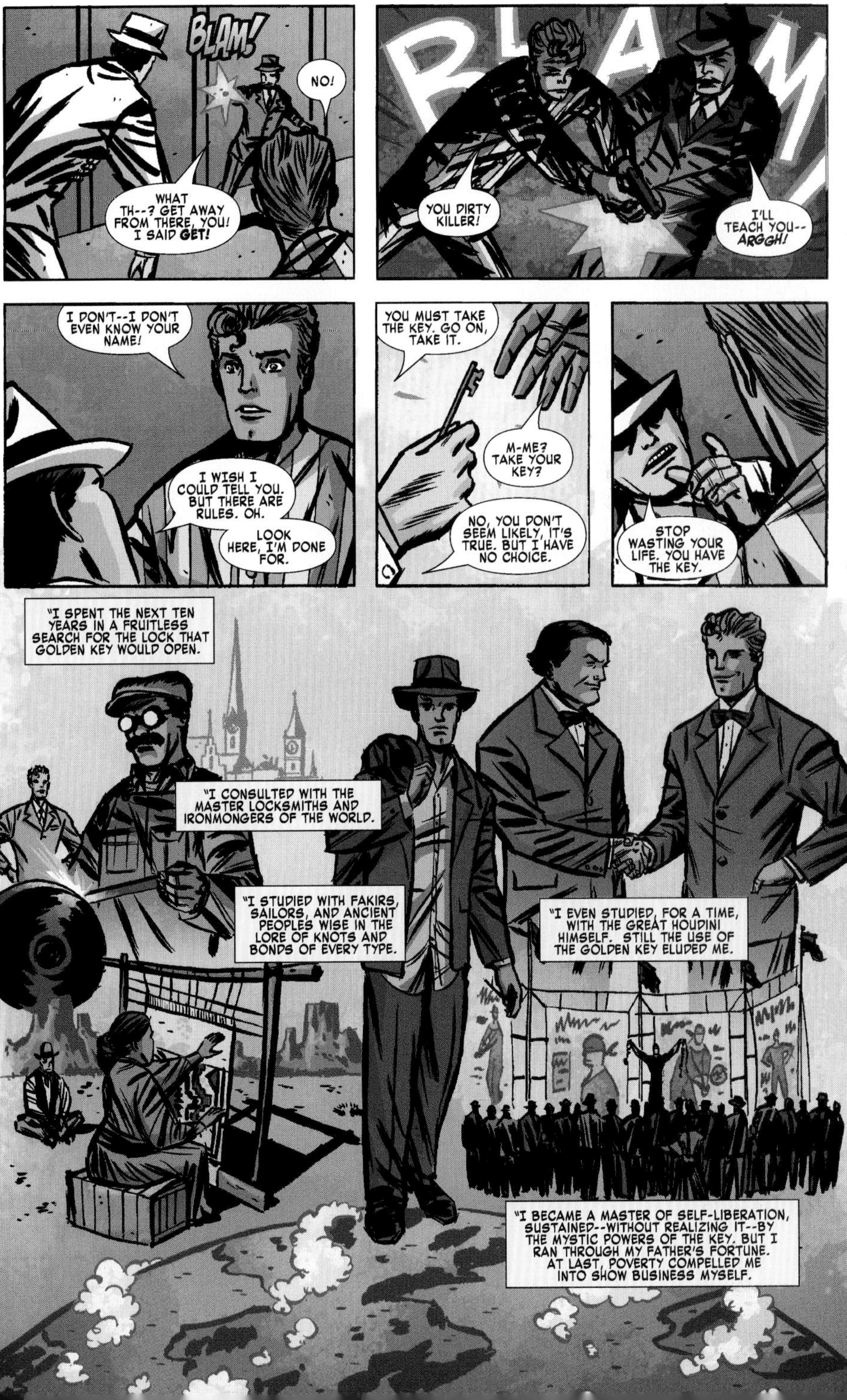
BLAM!
NO!
WHAT TH--? GET AWAY FROM THERE, YOU! I SAID **GET!**
BLAM
YOU DIRTY KILLER!
I'LL TEACH YOU-- **ARGGH!**
I DON'T--I DON'T EVEN KNOW YOUR NAME!
I WISH I COULD TELL YOU. BUT THERE ARE RULES. OH.
LOOK HERE, I'M DONE FOR.
YOU MUST TAKE THE KEY. GO ON, TAKE IT.
M-ME? TAKE YOUR KEY?
NO, YOU DON'T SEEM LIKELY, IT'S TRUE. BUT I HAVE NO CHOICE.
STOP WASTING YOUR LIFE. YOU HAVE THE KEY.
"I SPENT THE NEXT TEN YEARS IN A FRUITLESS SEARCH FOR THE LOCK THAT GOLDEN KEY WOULD OPEN.
"I CONSULTED WITH THE MASTER LOCKSMITHS AND IRONMONGERS OF THE WORLD.
"I STUDIED WITH FAKIRS, SAILORS, AND ANCIENT PEOPLES WISE IN THE LORE OF KNOTS AND BONDS OF EVERY TYPE.
"I EVEN STUDIED, FOR A TIME, WITH THE GREAT HOUDINI HIMSELF. STILL THE USE OF THE GOLDEN KEY ELUDED ME.
"I BECAME A MASTER OF SELF-LIBERATION, SUSTAINED--WITHOUT REALIZING IT--BY THE MYSTIC POWERS OF THE KEY. BUT I RAN THROUGH MY FATHER'S FORTUNE. AT LAST, POVERTY COMPELLED ME INTO SHOW BUSINESS MYSELF.

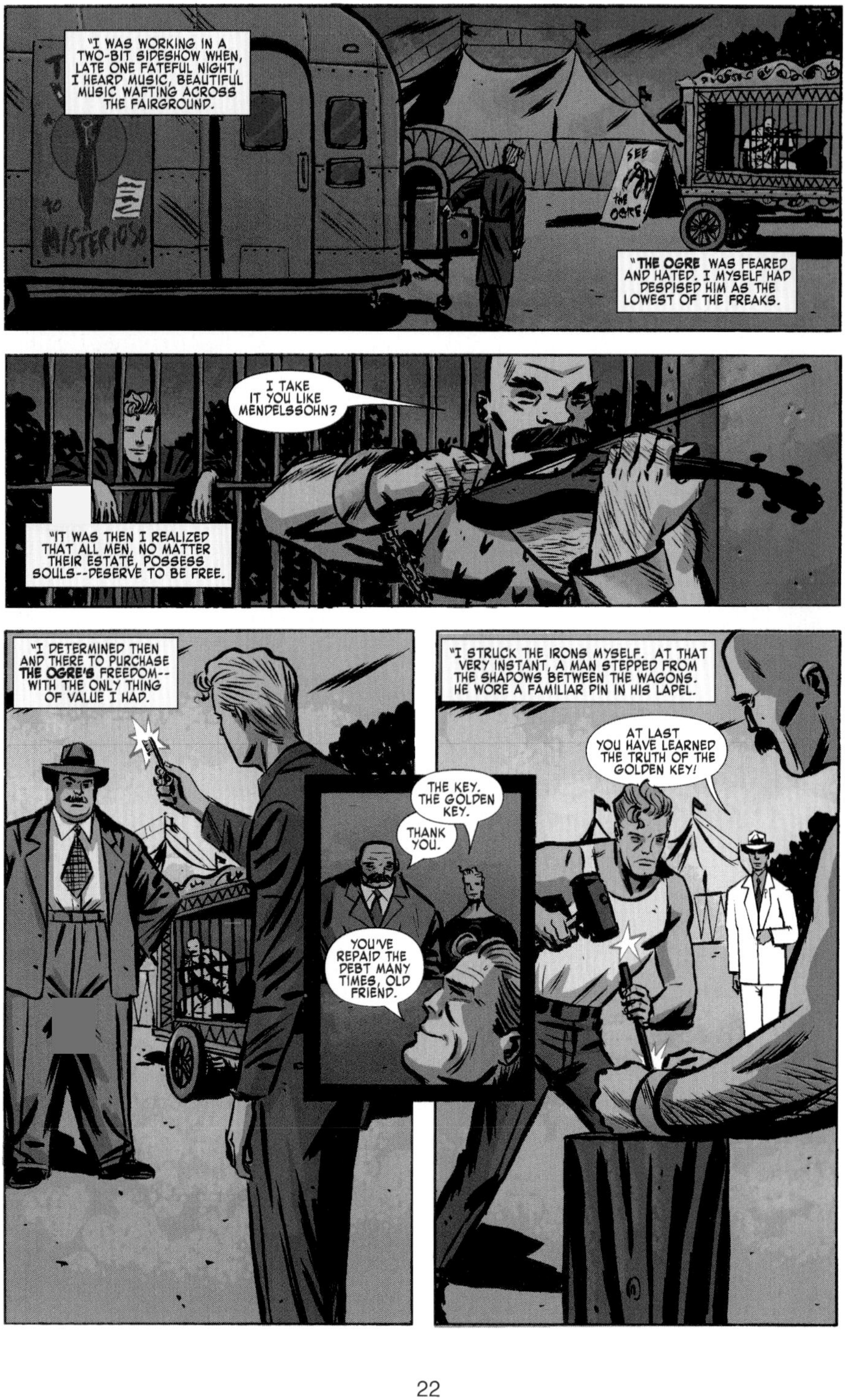
"I WAS WORKING IN A TWO-BIT SIDESHOW WHEN, LATE ONE FATEFUL NIGHT, I HEARD MUSIC, BEAUTIFUL MUSIC WAFTING ACROSS THE FAIRGROUND.
"THE OGRE WAS FEARED AND HATED. I MYSELF HAD DESPISED HIM AS THE LOWEST OF THE FREAKS.
I TAKE IT YOU LIKE MENDELSSOHN?
"IT WAS THEN I REALIZED THAT ALL MEN, NO MATTER THEIR ESTATE, POSSESS SOULS--DESERVE TO BE FREE.
"I DETERMINED THEN AND THERE TO PURCHASE THE OGRE'S FREEDOM--WITH THE ONLY THING OF VALUE I HAD.
THE KEY. THE GOLDEN KEY.
THANK YOU.
YOU'VE REPAID THE DEBT MANY TIMES, OLD FRIEND.
"I STRUCK THE IRONS MYSELF. AT THAT VERY INSTANT, A MAN STEPPED FROM THE SHADOWS BETWEEN THE WAGONS. HE WORE A FAMILIAR PIN IN HIS LAPEL.
AT LAST YOU HAVE LEARNED THE TRUTH OF THE GOLDEN KEY!

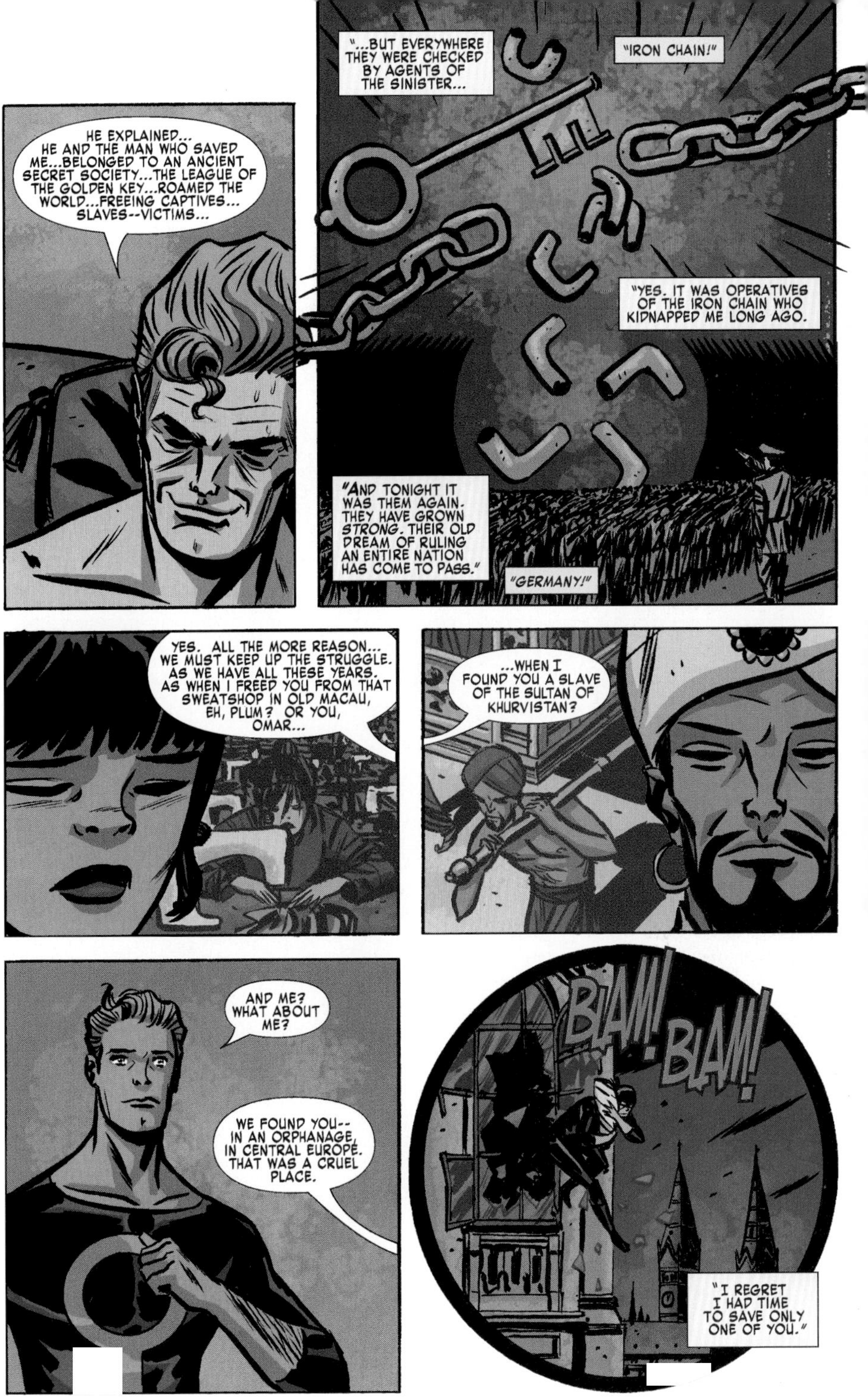

HE EXPLAINED... HE AND THE MAN WHO SAVED ME...BELONGED TO AN ANCIENT SECRET SOCIETY...THE LEAGUE OF THE GOLDEN KEY...ROAMED THE WORLD...FREEING CAPTIVES... SLAVES--VICTIMS...
"...BUT EVERYWHERE THEY WERE CHECKED BY AGENTS OF THE SINISTER...
"IRON CHAIN!"
"YES. IT WAS OPERATIVES OF THE IRON CHAIN WHO KIDNAPPED ME LONG AGO.
"AND TONIGHT IT WAS THEM AGAIN. THEY HAVE GROWN STRONG. THEIR OLD DREAM OF RULING AN ENTIRE NATION HAS COME TO PASS."
"GERMANY!"
YES. ALL THE MORE REASON... WE MUST KEEP UP THE STRUGGLE. AS WE HAVE ALL THESE YEARS. AS WHEN I FREED YOU FROM THAT SWEATSHOP IN OLD MACAU, EH, PLUM? OR YOU, OMAR...
...WHEN I FOUND YOU A SLAVE OF THE SULTAN OF KHURVISTAN?
AND ME? WHAT ABOUT ME?
WE FOUND YOU-- IN AN ORPHANAGE, IN CENTRAL EUROPE. THAT WAS A CRUEL PLACE.
BLAM! BLAM!
"I REGRET I HAD TIME TO SAVE ONLY ONE OF YOU."

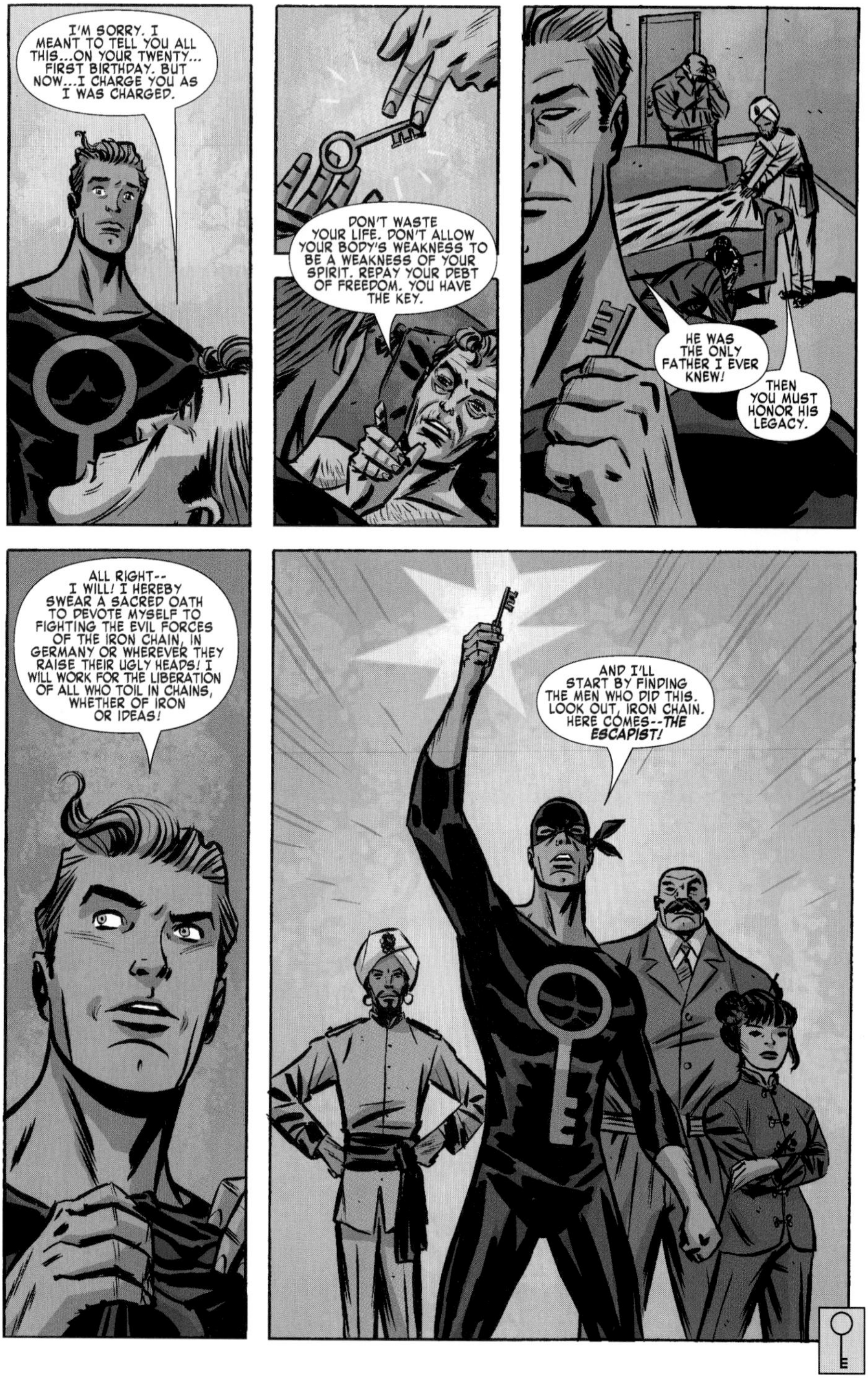
I'M SORRY. I MEANT TO TELL YOU ALL THIS...ON YOUR TWENTY... FIRST BIRTHDAY. BUT NOW...I CHARGE YOU AS I WAS CHARGED.
DON'T WASTE YOUR LIFE. DON'T ALLOW YOUR BODY'S WEAKNESS TO BE A WEAKNESS OF YOUR SPIRIT. REPAY YOUR DEBT OF FREEDOM. YOU HAVE THE KEY.
HE WAS THE ONLY FATHER I EVER KNEW!
THEN YOU MUST HONOR HIS LEGACY.
ALL RIGHT-- I WILL! I HEREBY SWEAR A SACRED OATH TO DEVOTE MYSELF TO FIGHTING THE EVIL FORCES OF THE IRON CHAIN, IN GERMANY OR WHEREVER THEY RAISE THEIR UGLY HEADS! I WILL WORK FOR THE LIBERATION OF ALL WHO TOIL IN CHAINS, WHETHER OF IRON OR IDEAS!
AND I'LL START BY FINDING THE MEN WHO DID THIS. LOOK OUT, IRON CHAIN. HERE COMES--THE ESCAPIST!

ESCAPISM 101

The tangled and glorious history of one of the comics' greatest characters.

by Malachi B. Cohen

Reprinted from the pages of *The Comics Journal*, with the kind permission of Messrs. Gary Groth and Kim Thompson, proprietors.

"To all those who toil in the bonds of slavery and the shackles of oppression, he offers the hope of liberation and the promise of freedom! Armed with superb physical and mental training, a crack team of assistants, and ancient wisdom, he roams the globe, performing amazing feats and coming to the aid of those who languish in tyranny's chains! He is — the Escapist!"

WITH THESE STIRRING WORDS, rippling in a banner across the splash page of the first issue of *Amazing Midget Radio Comics* (January 1940), was launched one of the longest and most checkered careers in comics. Over the next sixty years, the man who made cheating death both an art and a mission would find himself repeatedly trapped in the figurative lockbox of oblivion, bound in the ropes of legal machinations and buffeted by the whims of the marketplace, only to leap free, time and time again, reborn, renewed, and ready to wow another generation of admiring fans.

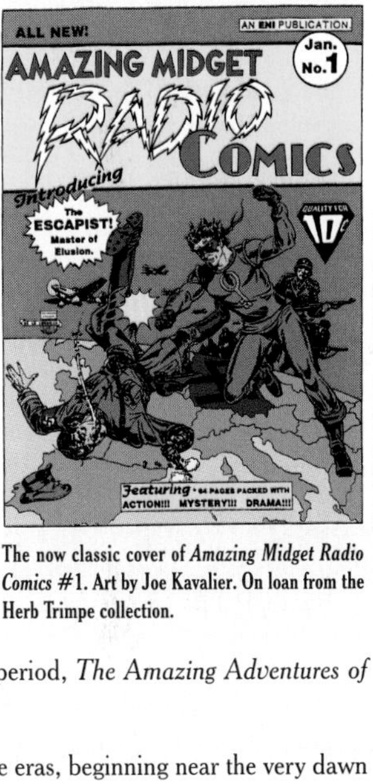
ALL NEW!
Jan. No.1
AMAZING MIDGET
RADIO
COMICS
Introducing
The ESCAPIST! Master of Elusion.
10¢
Featuring
ACTION!!! MYSTERY!!! DRAMA!!!

The now classic cover of *Amazing Midget Radio Comics* #1. Art by Joe Kavalier. On loan from the Herb Trimpe collection.

The author of the present monograph has attempted to trace the thorny, at times wildly ramifying path of that career, taking note not merely of the shifts and dodges of the Escapist's legal fortunes but also of the way the character has changed, evolved, at times regressed, along with the medium of comics itself. In doing so, extensive use has been made of court documents and interviews, as well as of secondary materials, in particular Michael Chabon's detailed if somewhat hyperbolic and unreliable documentation of the period, *The Amazing Adventures of Kavalier & Clay*.

The history of the Escapist divides, more or less neatly, into five eras, beginning near the very dawn of comic book superhero history, with:

I
The Empire Comics Era
January 1940 - April 1954

Empire Comics was founded in October 1939, when Mr. Sheldon Anapol merged his Empire Novelties, Inc., the nation's seventh-largest wholesaler and retailer of cheap novelties, with Racy Publications, Inc., a third- or perhaps fourth-rate publisher of pulp magazines owned by Mr. Jack Ashkenazy, Anapol's brother-in-law. Initially they published only one title, *Amazing Midget Radio Comics*, later shortened to *Radio Comics*. Eventually they expanded to some forty-seven titles, including, at the peak, around 1946, eight titles featuring the adventures of the Escapist and allied characters.

In 1946, Ashkenazy sold his interest in Empire to his brother-in-law and founded Pharaoh House, a third- or perhaps fourth-rate publisher of comic books.

The Empire Era can itself be usefully broken down into three distinct periods:

The First Empire:
January 1940 - April 1942

This period covers the classic run of stories by the artist/writer team of Kavalier & Clay, beginning with the origin story in *Amazing Midget Radio Comics #1*. [See "The Passing of the Key" in this volume.] Chabon argues strongly that the work of this period, in particular after issue number 19 of *Radio Comics*, was heavily influenced by Kavalier & Clay's repeated self-exposure to that revolutionary work of cinema genius, *Citizen Kane*. As he puts it:

> The sudden small efflorescence of art, minor but genuine, in the tawdry product line of what was then the fifth- or sixth-largest comic book company in America has usually been attributed to the potent spell of *Citizen Kane* acting on the renascent aspirations of Joe Kavalier. But without the thematic ban imposed by Sheldon Anapol at the behest of Parnassus Pictures — the censorship of all storylines having to do with Nazis (Japs, too), warfare, saboteurs, fifth columnists, and so on — which forced Sammy and Joe to a drastic reconsideration of the raw materials of their stories, the magical run of issues that commenced with *Radio Comics #19* and finished when Pearl Harbor caught up to the two-month Empire lead time in the twenty-first issue of *Triumph Comics* (February 1942) looks pretty unlikely. In eight issues apiece of *Radio*, *Triumph*, *All Doll*, and the now-monthly *Escapist Adventures*, the emphasis is laid, for the first time, not only on the superpowered characters — normally so enveloped in their inevitable shrouds of bullets, torpedoes, poison gases, hurricane winds, evil spells, and so forth, that the lineaments of their personalities, if not of their deltoids and quadriceps, could hardly be discerned — but also, almost radically for the comic book of the time, on the ordinary people around them, whose own exploits, by the time hostilities with Germany were formally engaged in the early months of 1942, had advanced so far into the foreground of each story that such emphasis itself, on the everyday heroics of the "powerless," may be seen to constitute, at least in hindsight, a kind of secret, and hence probably ineffectual, propaganda. There were stories that dealt with the minutiae of what Mr. Machine Gun, at home in the pages of *Triumph*, liked to call "the hero biz," told not only from the point of view of the heroes but from those of various butlers, girlfriends, assistants, shoe-shine boys, doctors, and even the criminals. There was a story that followed the course of a handgun through the mean streets of Empire City, in which the Escapist appeared on only *two pages*. Another celebrated story told the tale of Luna Moth's girlhood, and filled in gaps in her biography, through a complicated series of flashbacks narrated by a group of unemployed witches' familiars, talking rats and cats and reptilian whatsits, in a "dark little hangout outside of Phantomville." And there was "Kane Street," focusing for sixty-four pages on one little street in Empire City, as its denizens, hearing the terrible news that the Escapist lies near death in the hospital, recall in turn the way he has touched their lives and the lives of everyone in town (only to have it all turn out, in the end, as a cruel hoax perpetrated by the evil Crooked Man).

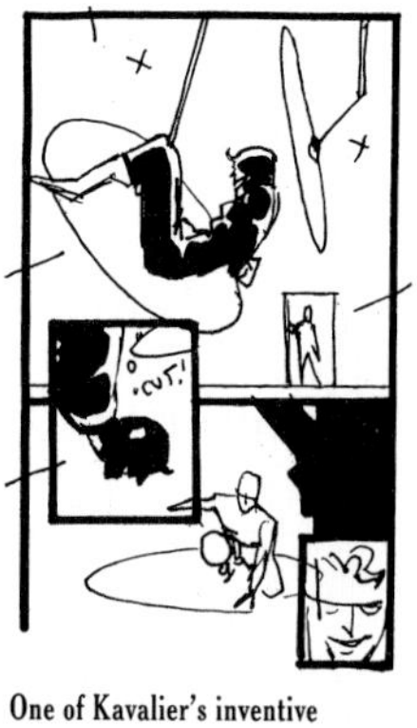
CUT!

One of Kavalier's inventive thumbnail breakdowns. From the collection of Shawn Martinbrough.

All of these forays into chopping up the elements of narrative, in mixing and isolating odd points of view, in stretching, as far as was possible in those days, under the constraints of a jaded editor and of publishers who cared chiefly for safe profit, the limits of comic book storytelling, all these exercises were, without question, raised far beyond the level of mere exercise by the unleashed inventiveness of Joe Kavalier's pencil. Joe, too, made a survey of the tools at hand, and found them more useful and interesting than he ever had before. But the daring use of perspective and shading, the radical placement of word balloons and captions, and above all the integration of narrative and picture by means of artfully disarranged, dislocated panels that stretched, shrank, opened into circles, spread across two full pages, marched diagonally toward one corner of a page, unreeled themselves like the frames of a film — all these were made possible only by the full collaboration of writer and artist together.

The Second Empire
May 1942 - May 1943

For a year following Joe Kavalier's enlistment in the Navy and the subsequent exhaustion of the stockpile of Kavalier & Clay stories, Sam Clay continued to script all of the Escapist stories. Though some have noted a slight flagging in invention after Kavalier's departure, the level of storytelling remains high, and the artwork, though scattershot, benefits from the talents of a number of talented journeymen, including Bill Everett and Sam Glanzman.

The Third Empire
May 1944 - May 1954

In this third and longest period, following Sam Clay's avowedly permanent but effectively rather brief departure from the comics business, literally dozens of different writers and artists handled the character. Careful research and interviews by the author have revealed that among those working at Empire over this decade, many of whom may have or almost certainly did work on the Escapist books, were the aforementioned Everett and Glanzman, Mac Raboy, Mort Meskin, and John Severin.

Chabon characterizes this period in the history of the character as follows:

> In later years, in other hands, the Escapist was played for laughs. Tastes changed, and writers grew bored, and all the straight plots had been pretty well exhausted. Later writers and artists, with the connivance of George Deasey, turned the strip into a peculiar kind of inverted parody of the whole genre of the costumed hero. His chin grew larger and more emphatically dimpled, and his muscles hypertrophied until he bulged, as his post-war arch-foe Dr. Magma memorably expressed it, "like a sack full of cats." Miss Plum Blossom's ever-ready needle was pressed into providing the Escapist with a Liberacean array of specialized crime-fighting togs, and Omar and Big Al began to grumble openly about the bills their boss piled up by his extravagant expenditures on supervehicles, superplanes, and even a "handcarved ivory crutch" for Tom Mayflower to use on big date nights. The Escapist was quite vain; readers sometimes caught him stopping, on his way to fight evil, to check his reflection and comb his hair in a window or the mirror of a drugstore scale. In between acts of saving the earth from the evil Omnivores, in one of the late issues, #130 (March 1953), the Escapist works himself into quite a little lather as he attempts, with the help of a lisping decorator, to redo the Keyhole, the secret sanctum under the boards of the Empire Palace. While he continued to defend the weak and champion the helpless as reliably as ever, the Escapist never seemed to take his

A jaunty and rather dapper Tom Mayflower, circa 1946. Courtesy of the Eric Wight archives.

adventures very seriously. He took vacations in Cuba, Hawaii, and Las Vegas, where he shared a stage at the Sands Hotel with none other than Wladiu Liberace himself. Sometimes, if he was in no particular hurry to get anywhere, he let Big Al take over the controls of the Keyjet and picked up a movie magazine that had his picture on its cover. The so-called "Rube Goldberg plots," in which the Escapist, as bored as anyone by the dull routine of crimebusting, deliberately introduced obstacles and handicaps into his own efforts to thwart the large but finite variety of megalomaniacs, fiends, and rank hoodlums he fought in the years after the war, in order to make things more interesting for himself, became a trademark of the character: he would agree with himself beforehand, say, to dispatch some particular gang of criminal "barehanded," and only to use

The hypertrophied muscle-bound clown, circa 1954. From the Kyle Baker collection.

his by now vastly augmented physical strength if one of them uttered some random phrase like "ice water," and then, just after he was almost licked and the weather too cold for anyone ever to ask for a glass of ice water, the Escapist would hit on a way to arrange things so that inexorably the gang ended up in the back of a truck full of onions. He was a superpowerful, muscle-bound clown.

The Third Empire came to an abrupt end in April 1954. Nervous about the plummeting sales of the Escapist titles (and of superhero comics in general), troubled by his (correct) premonition of an impending loss in *DC v. Empire*, and fearing fallout from *Seduction of the Innocent* and the Kefauver hearings, Sheldon Anapol killed the three surviving Escapist titles. The next day, the New York Court of Appeals handed down its ruling in favor of DC Comics.

Soon after, Joe Kavalier purchased Empire Comics from Sheldon Anapol, but not before Anapol, in a characteristic move, had sold the rights to the entire Empire superhero stable, including the Escapist and Luna Moth, to DC. Kavalier continued to publish under the Empire Comics name, with an entirely new line of "Adult Interest" comics.

II
The Score Comics Era
June 1954 - November 1959

Shortly after DC acquired the rights to the Escapist and the rest of the Empire superheroes, one of Harry Donenfeld's nieces announced her impending marriage. Her intended was Marvin "Lucky" Lemberg, a man of no great ability or intelligence, and very little in the way of luck. It was felt in the family that suitable employment ought to be found for Lemberg, and when he evinced an interest in comic books (especially those drawn by Matt Baker) it was proposed and arranged that the old Empire stable be "spun off" and established at a new company, partially controlled by DC, which the new publisher, Mr. Lemberg, fatally named Score Comics.

Production problems, distribution problems, personnel problems, and, above all, Mr. Lemberg's own long-standing problems with alcohol, gambling, and the former Miss Donenfeld hampered Score from the start. His artists, working to suit Lemberg's own taste, constantly fell afoul of the new Comics Code Authority. In a little over five years Mr. Lemberg had so encumbered Score with entanglements, lawsuits, and creditors (some with rumored ties to the Profaci and Gambino crime families) that DC found it expedient to divest itself of all its holdings in the company, and its copyrights, lest its own

28

sterling empire be tarnished by association. Lucky Lemberg's publishing career met an inglorious and unfortunate end with a five-year term at Sing Sing, and the Escapist and his costumed cohorts lapsed into a gray-lit realm of uncertain ownership, competing publishers, and general lack of interest.

Nonetheless, during this period some excellent stories appeared, written and drawn by a number of interesting people, some DC veterans or future DC stalwarts, among them Murphy Anderson, Jack Cole, Frank Frazetta, Bob Powell, Robert Kanigher, Edmond Hamilton, Otto Binder, Jerry Siegel, Ramona Fradon, Joe Maneely, Dick Ayers, and, some have argued, Steve Ditko.

The stories during the Score Era tend, roughly, to fall into three categories:

1) "Tough Guy" stories, often emphasizing a) the workings and operations of the entire Escapist team, generally in a noirish world of lowlifes and gangsters, and b) the breasts of Miss Plum Blossom.

2) "Puzzler" stories, Houdini-esque variations on the locked-room mystery, in which a seemingly impossible escape is effected by ingenious means which have been carefully laid out beforehand, and just as carefully concealed, from the reader. This type of story was a favorite of the great Hamilton, who wrote nearly two dozen of them.

3) Weird stories emphasizing the occult connections of the Escapist and the world of magic in which the League of the Golden Key operates. The Escapist featured in these stories is often pointed to as a precursor of Marvel's Doctor Strange.

III
The Wild Years
Roughly 1960 - 1968

During this woolly and fascinating period, with the copyright on the Escapist thrown into confusion, five separate publishers brought out competing versions of the character.

These varied wildly in tone, quality, approach, and personnel, with occasional bright spots, in particular the Fab Comics run of late '65-'68, with the fledgling Steranko and Neal Adams and a top-of-his-game post-Marvel Ditko taking interesting whacks at the character.

Fab Comics pursued an approach to the character centered around show-stopping artwork, while the battered remnant of Score Comics churned out poorly printed, badly lettered, juvenile (but withal entertaining) crap. Big Top Comics and Hi-Tone Comics (some have argued they were in fact the same entity operating under separate names) purveyed barely recognizable, in-name-only versions of the character, intended chiefly to capitalize on all the confusion.

The most interesting incarnation of the Escapist during this wide-open period, perhaps, was the short-lived version produced by Conquaire Comics, publishing arm of Conquaire Grooming Products, manufacturers of hair-care and skin-care products for African-Americans, and somehow or other another of Lucky Lemberg's many creditors. For an all too brief run of five issues, the first of which predated Marvel's Black Panther (who debuted in *Fantastic Four #52*, July 1966) by a month, the streets of Empire City were prowled by a black Escapist whose unique, historically based twist on the theme of enslavement and liberation remains a personal favorite of the author's.

This chaos, however, could not continue, and in 1968, the greeting-card and poster publisher Gerald Sunshine, Lemberg's largest single creditor, succeeded in securing copyright to the Escapist and the other old Empire characters (by this point completely neglected and abandoned). Having won this victory, the owner and founder of Sunshine Cards celebrated by immediately ceasing production of all Escapist comic books while he pursued ambitious but illusory television, film, and theme park concepts, all of which in the end failed to pan out (though rumors persist of an hour-long pilot *Escapist* TV show, shot for ABC for the fall of 1970).

IV
The Sunshine Comics Years
1972 - 1976

In 1972, Gerald Sunshine died, and control of Sunshine Media Group passed to his son Danny. Danny Sonnenschein, then 21, was a lifelong fan of the Escapist and a protegé of Sam Clay's, and seized the opportunity to revive and restore the character to some of its former glory. A product of his era, Danny Sonnenschein also hoped to make the character of the Escapist "relevant" and expressive of the "nitty gritty."

The 1974 re-design of The Escapist, by Howard Chaykin. Courtesy of the artist.

This venture lasted for three and a half years. Production budgets were tight; Sonnenschein experimented heavily with black-and-white and magazine-format books. And while the Sunshine distribution network was extensive, it proved difficult to sell "gritty" comic books through suburban greeting card stores. Nonetheless some of the top early-'70s talent, including Gerber, Englehart, O'Neil, Rogers, Wrightson, Kaluta, Chaykin, etc., worked for Sunshine. In 1976, Sunshine Media Group was acquired by the giant Omnigrip Corporation, its staff fired, and its operations shut down. For the Escapist, apart from one reprinting, by a tiny press, of classic Kavalier & Clay material, a period of nearly eight years of total obscurity followed.

V
The Escapist Comics Era
1984 - Present

In 1984, seeking to make itself more attractive to merger partners, Omnigrip sold off a number of its small, unproductive, or irrelevant holdings. These included, of course, the by now tattered and forgotten line of costumed superhero characters, most of them the brainchildren of Joe Kavalier and Sammy Clay, their glory days far behind them.

One person, however, had not forgotten the Escapist and his band: Danny Sonnenschein. After the collapse of the Sunshine Comics venture he had dabbled in a number of activities, one of which proved lucrative enough to enable him, when the opportunity arose, to repurchase the old Empire characters from Omnigrip, at a bargain price. With the balance of his personal fortune he set about acquiring the rights to all the prior versions and incarnations of the character. Reconstituting himself as publisher of Escapist Books in 1985, he initially intended only to create a kind of grand archive of the Escapist, and his series of hardbound, high-quality reproductions from that era, though difficult to find now, are considered definitive.

With the birth of the independent comics scene in the late '80s, Sonnenschein saw the opportunity to revive the characters he loved, and in 1991, under the imprint of Escapist Comics, he launched the first issue of *New Adventures of the Escapist*, updating the character and his cohorts, raising the quality of the writing and the level of realism in the treatment both of the world of performing magic and the nature of evil, and exploring the ambiguous nature of the League of the Golden Key itself.

"ARE YOU NOW OR HAVE YOU EVER BEEN..."

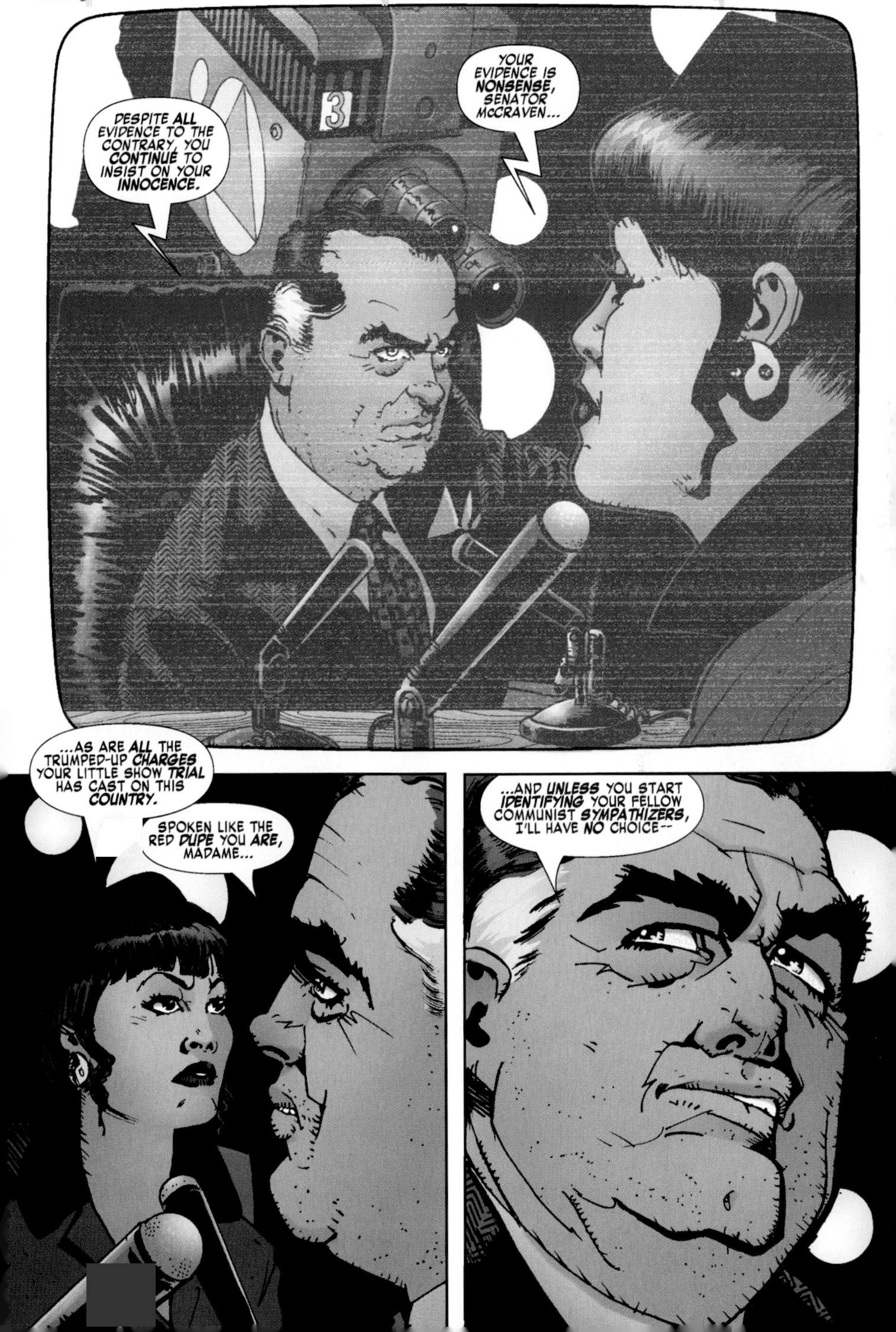
DESPITE ALL EVIDENCE TO THE CONTRARY, YOU CONTINUE TO INSIST ON YOUR INNOCENCE.
YOUR EVIDENCE IS NONSENSE, SENATOR McCRAVEN...
...AS ARE ALL THE TRUMPED-UP CHARGES YOUR LITTLE SHOW TRIAL HAS CAST ON THIS COUNTRY.
SPOKEN LIKE THE RED DUPE YOU ARE, MADAME...
...AND UNLESS YOU START IDENTIFYING YOUR FELLOW COMMUNIST SYMPATHIZERS, I'LL HAVE NO CHOICE--

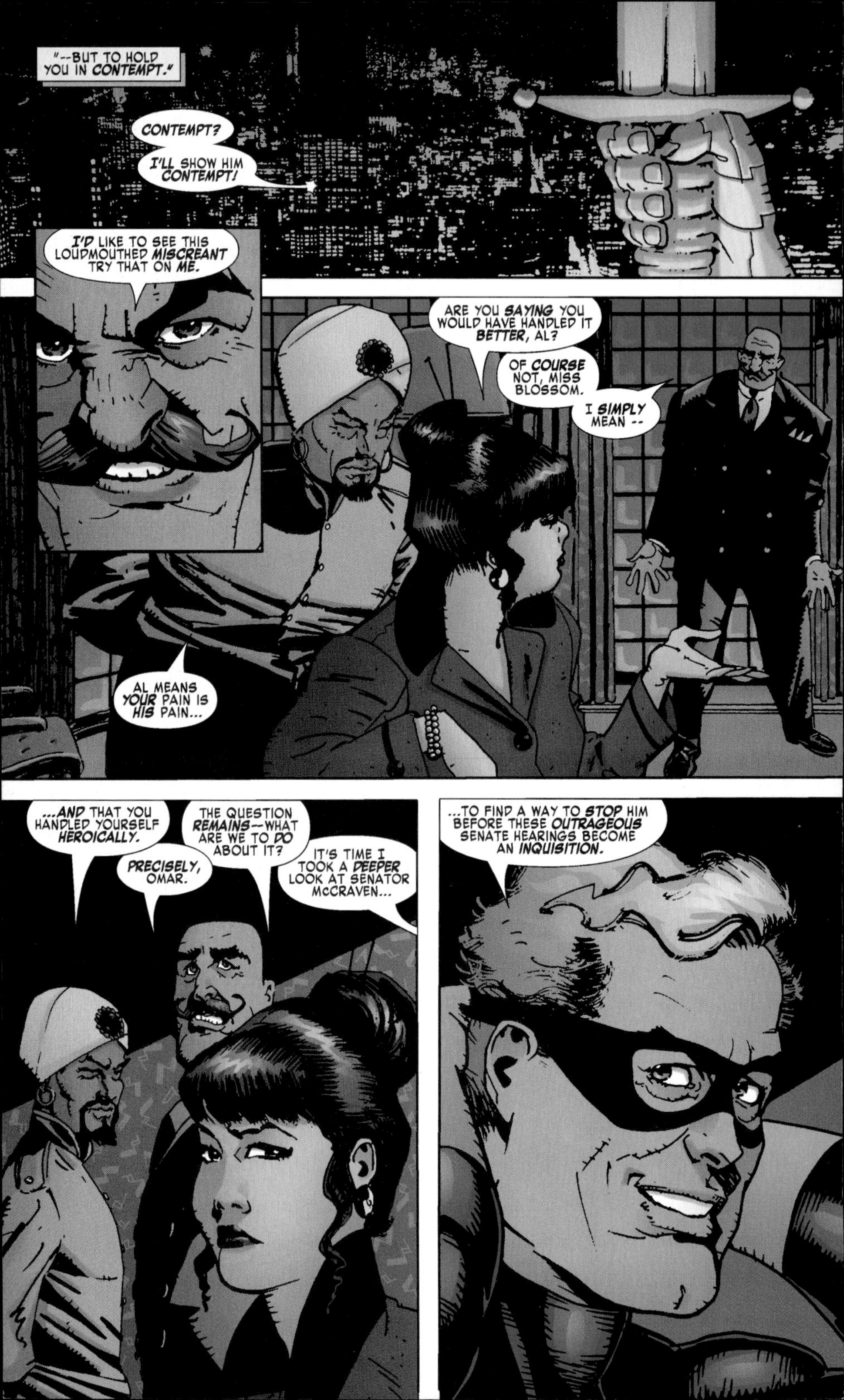
"--BUT TO HOLD YOU IN CONTEMPT."
CONTEMPT?
I'LL SHOW HIM CONTEMPT!
I'D LIKE TO SEE THIS LOUDMOUTHED MISCREANT TRY THAT ON ME.
ARE YOU SAYING YOU WOULD HAVE HANDLED IT BETTER, AL?
OF COURSE NOT, MISS BLOSSOM.
I SIMPLY MEAN --
AL MEANS YOUR PAIN IS HIS PAIN...
...AND THAT YOU HANDLED YOURSELF HEROICALLY.
PRECISELY, OMAR.
THE QUESTION REMAINS--WHAT ARE WE TO DO ABOUT IT?
IT'S TIME I TOOK A DEEPER LOOK AT SENATOR McCRAVEN...
...TO FIND A WAY TO STOP HIM BEFORE THESE OUTRAGEOUS SENATE HEARINGS BECOME AN INQUISITION.

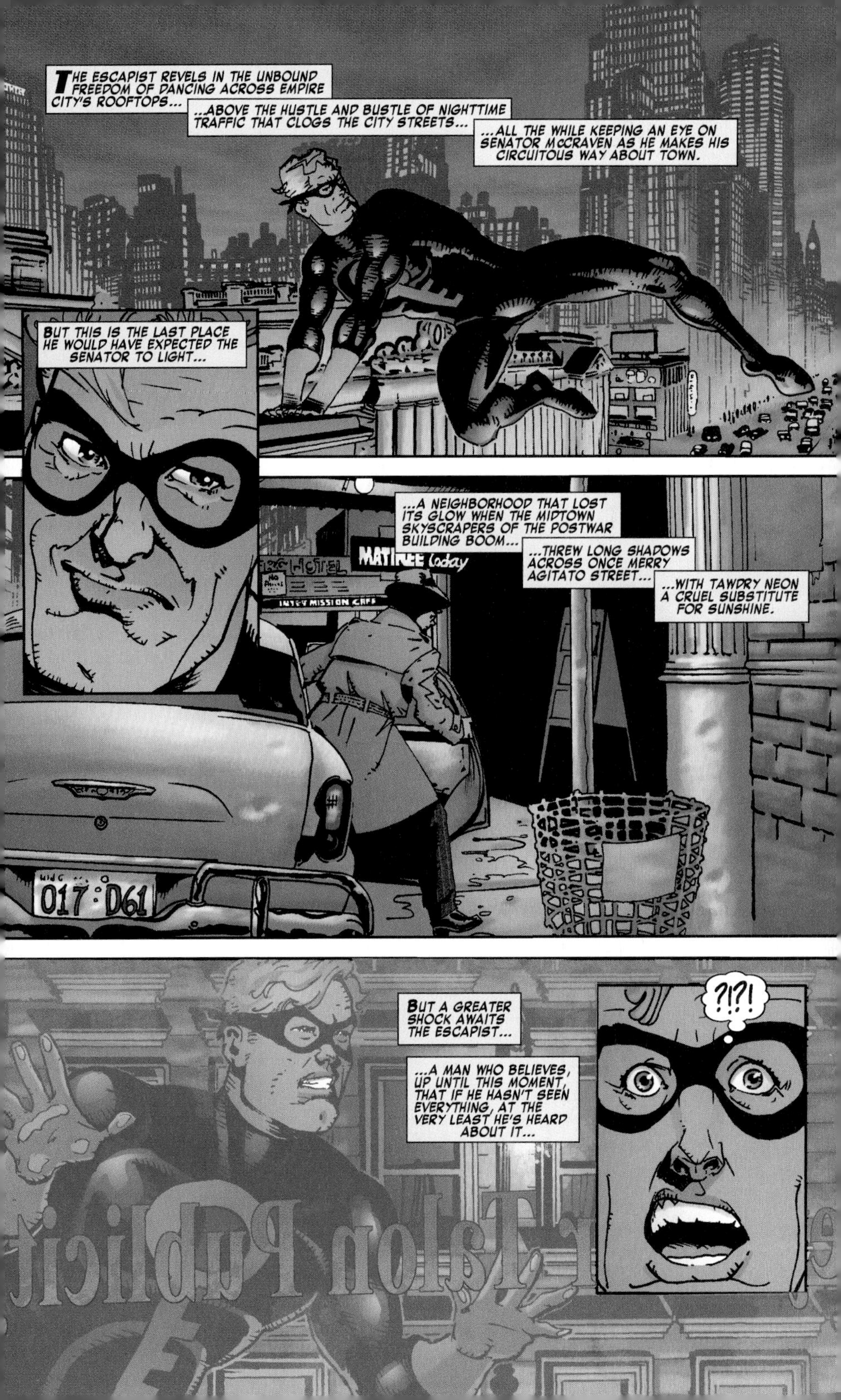
THE ESCAPIST REVELS IN THE UNBOUND FREEDOM OF DANCING ACROSS EMPIRE CITY'S ROOFTOPS...
...ABOVE THE HUSTLE AND BUSTLE OF NIGHTTIME TRAFFIC THAT CLOGS THE CITY STREETS...
...ALL THE WHILE KEEPING AN EYE ON SENATOR McCRAVEN AS HE MAKES HIS CIRCUITOUS WAY ABOUT TOWN.
BUT THIS IS THE LAST PLACE HE WOULD HAVE EXPECTED THE SENATOR TO LIGHT...
...A NEIGHBORHOOD THAT LOST ITS GLOW WHEN THE MIDTOWN SKYSCRAPERS OF THE POSTWAR BUILDING BOOM...
...THREW LONG SHADOWS ACROSS ONCE MERRY AGITATO STREET...
...WITH TAWDRY NEON A CRUEL SUBSTITUTE FOR SUNSHINE.
MATINEE today
017 D61
BUT A GREATER SHOCK AWAITS THE ESCAPIST...
...A MAN WHO BELIEVES, UP UNTIL THIS MOMENT, THAT IF HE HASN'T SEEN EVERYTHING, AT THE VERY LEAST HE'S HEARD ABOUT IT...
?!?!

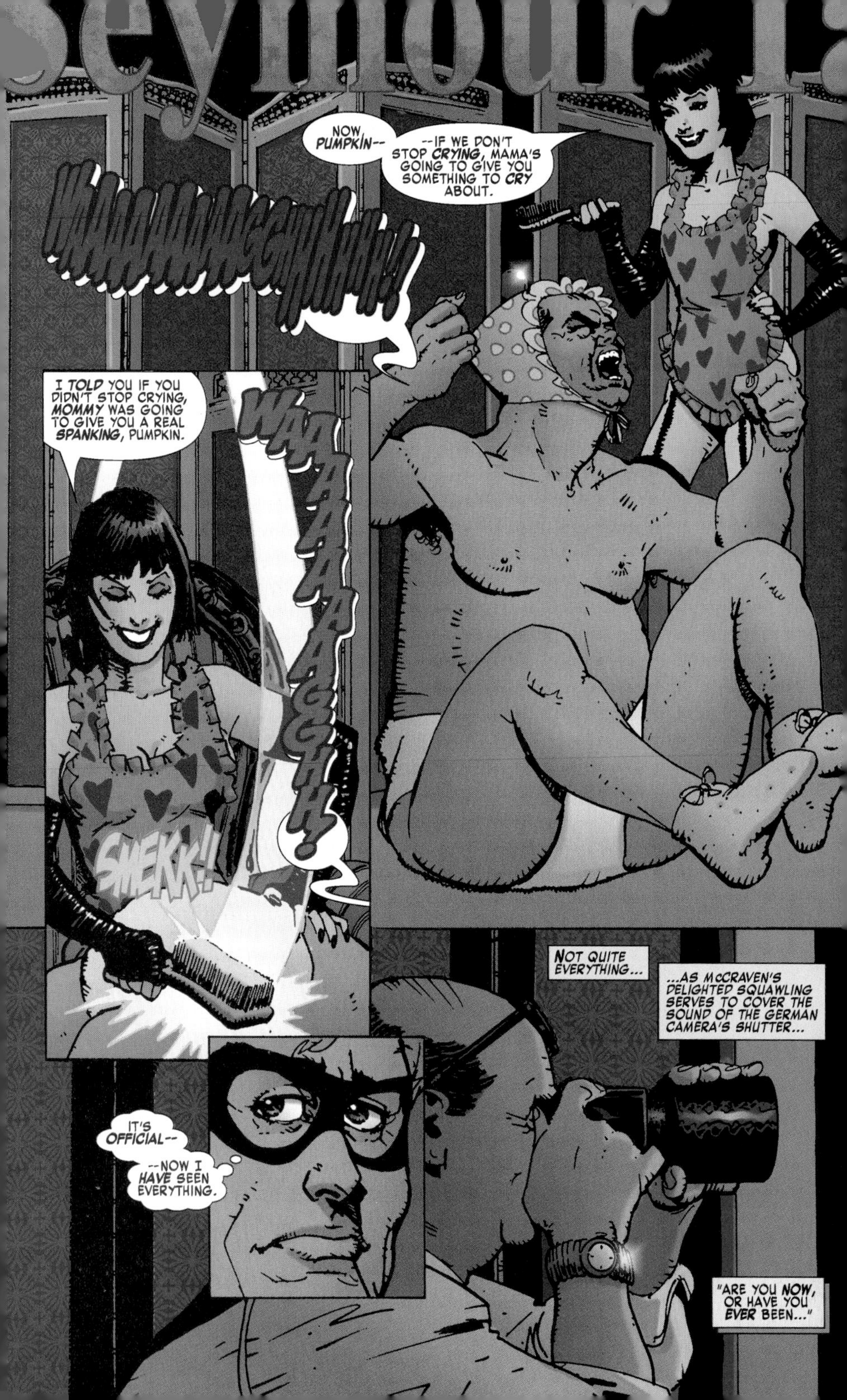

NOW PUMPKIN--
--IF WE DON'T STOP CRYING, MAMA'S GOING TO GIVE YOU SOMETHING TO CRY ABOUT.
I TOLD YOU IF YOU DIDN'T STOP CRYING, MOMMY WAS GOING TO GIVE YOU A REAL SPANKING, PUMPKIN.
SMEKK!!
NOT QUITE EVERYTHING...
...AS McCRAVEN'S DELIGHTED SQUAWLING SERVES TO COVER THE SOUND OF THE GERMAN CAMERA'S SHUTTER...
IT'S OFFICIAL--
--NOW I HAVE SEEN EVERYTHING.
"ARE YOU NOW, OR HAVE YOU EVER BEEN..."

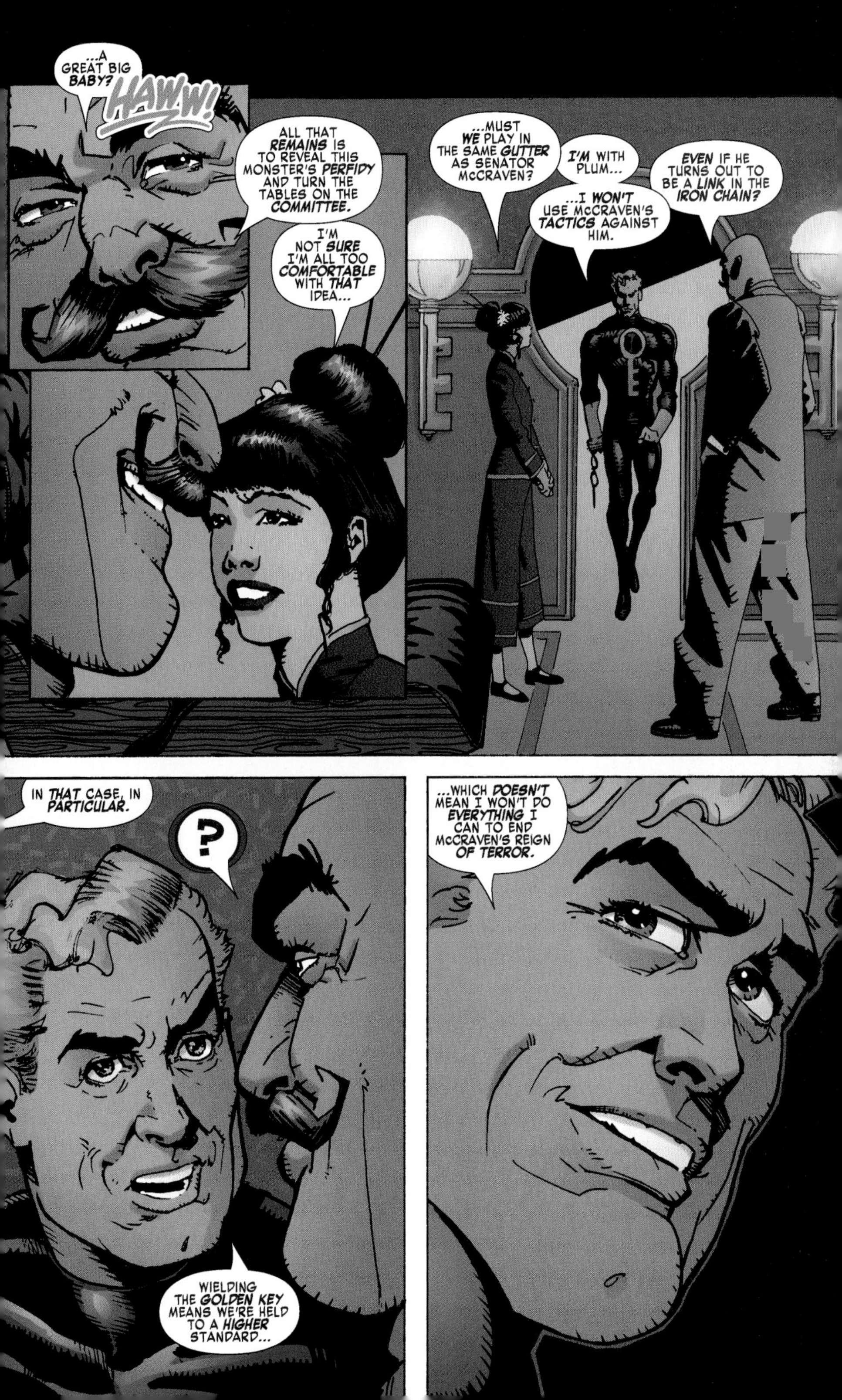
...A GREAT BIG BABY?
HAWW!
ALL THAT REMAINS IS TO REVEAL THIS MONSTER'S PERFIDY AND TURN THE TABLES ON THE COMMITTEE.
I'M NOT SURE I'M ALL TOO COMFORTABLE WITH THAT IDEA...
...MUST WE PLAY IN THE SAME GUTTER AS SENATOR McCRAVEN?
I'M WITH PLUM...
...I WON'T USE McCRAVEN'S TACTICS AGAINST HIM.
EVEN IF HE TURNS OUT TO BE A LINK IN THE IRON CHAIN?
IN THAT CASE, IN PARTICULAR.
?
WIELDING THE GOLDEN KEY MEANS WE'RE HELD TO A HIGHER STANDARD...
...WHICH DOESN'T MEAN I WON'T DO EVERYTHING I CAN TO END McCRAVEN'S REIGN OF TERROR.

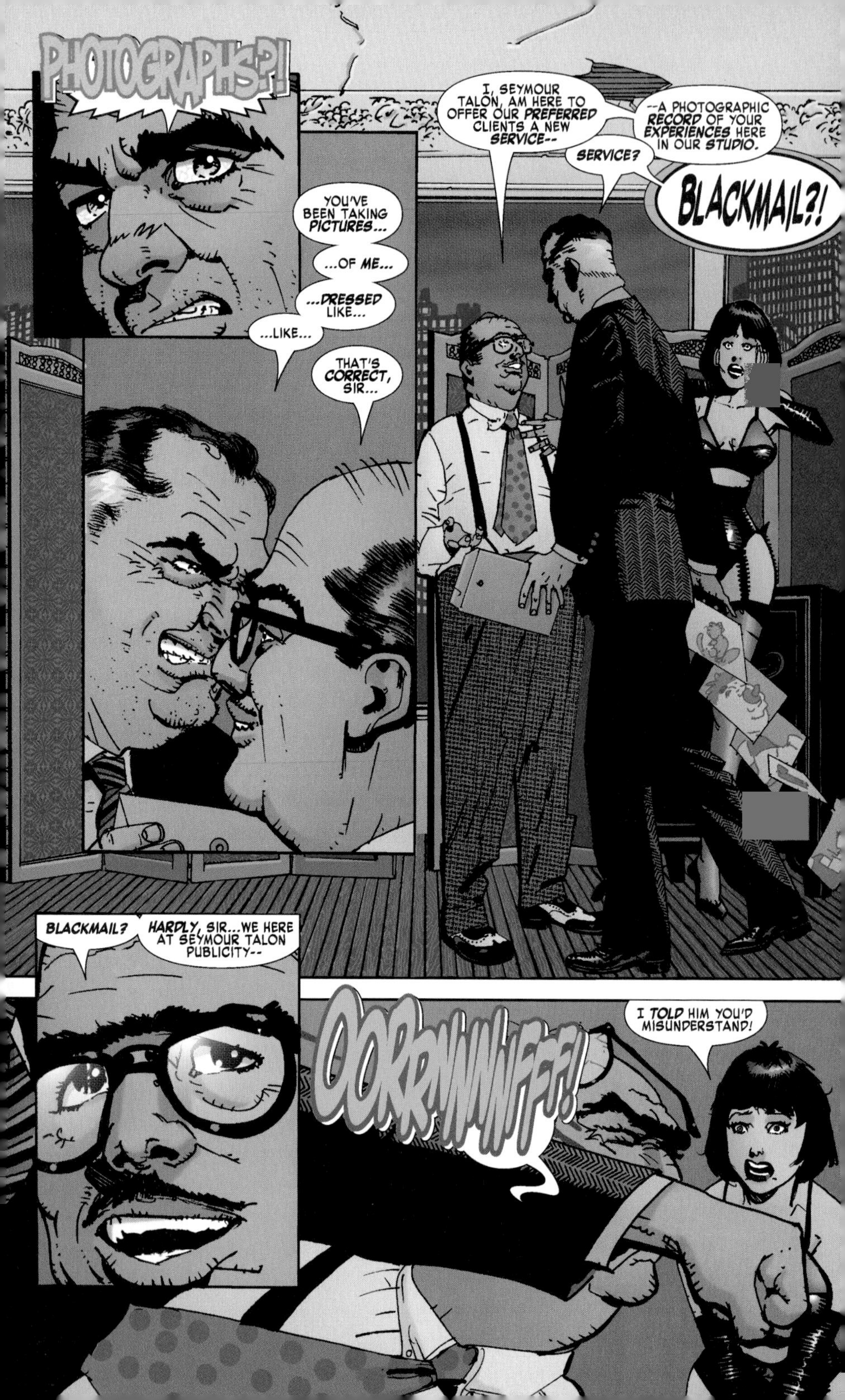
PHOTOGRAPHS?!
YOU'VE BEEN TAKING PICTURES...
...OF ME...
...DRESSED LIKE...
...LIKE...
THAT'S CORRECT, SIR...
I, SEYMOUR TALON, AM HERE TO OFFER OUR PREFERRED CLIENTS A NEW SERVICE--
--A PHOTOGRAPHIC RECORD OF YOUR EXPERIENCES HERE IN OUR STUDIO.
SERVICE?
BLACKMAIL?!
BLACKMAIL?
HARDLY, SIR...WE HERE AT SEYMOUR TALON PUBLICITY--
OORRNNNNFFF!
I TOLD HIM YOU'D MISUNDERSTAND!

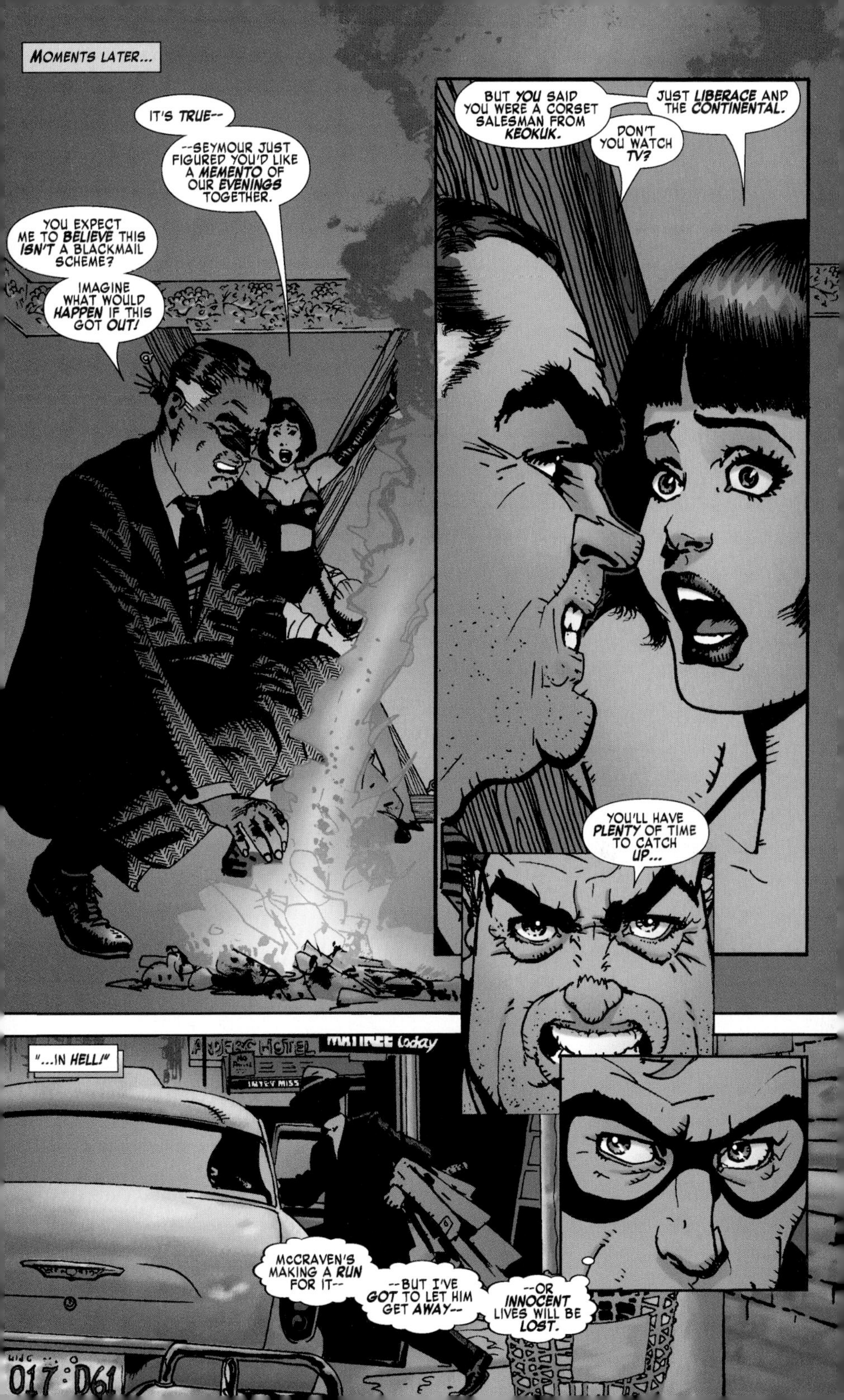
MOMENTS LATER...
IT'S TRUE--
--SEYMOUR JUST FIGURED YOU'D LIKE A MEMENTO OF OUR EVENINGS TOGETHER.
YOU EXPECT ME TO BELIEVE THIS ISN'T A BLACKMAIL SCHEME?
IMAGINE WHAT WOULD HAPPEN IF THIS GOT OUT!
BUT YOU SAID YOU WERE A CORSET SALESMAN FROM KEOKUK.
DON'T YOU WATCH TV?
JUST LIBERACE AND THE CONTINENTAL.
YOU'LL HAVE PLENTY OF TIME TO CATCH UP...
"...IN HELL!"
MATINEE today
McCRAVEN'S MAKING A RUN FOR IT--
--BUT I'VE GOT TO LET HIM GET AWAY--
--OR INNOCENT LIVES WILL BE LOST.

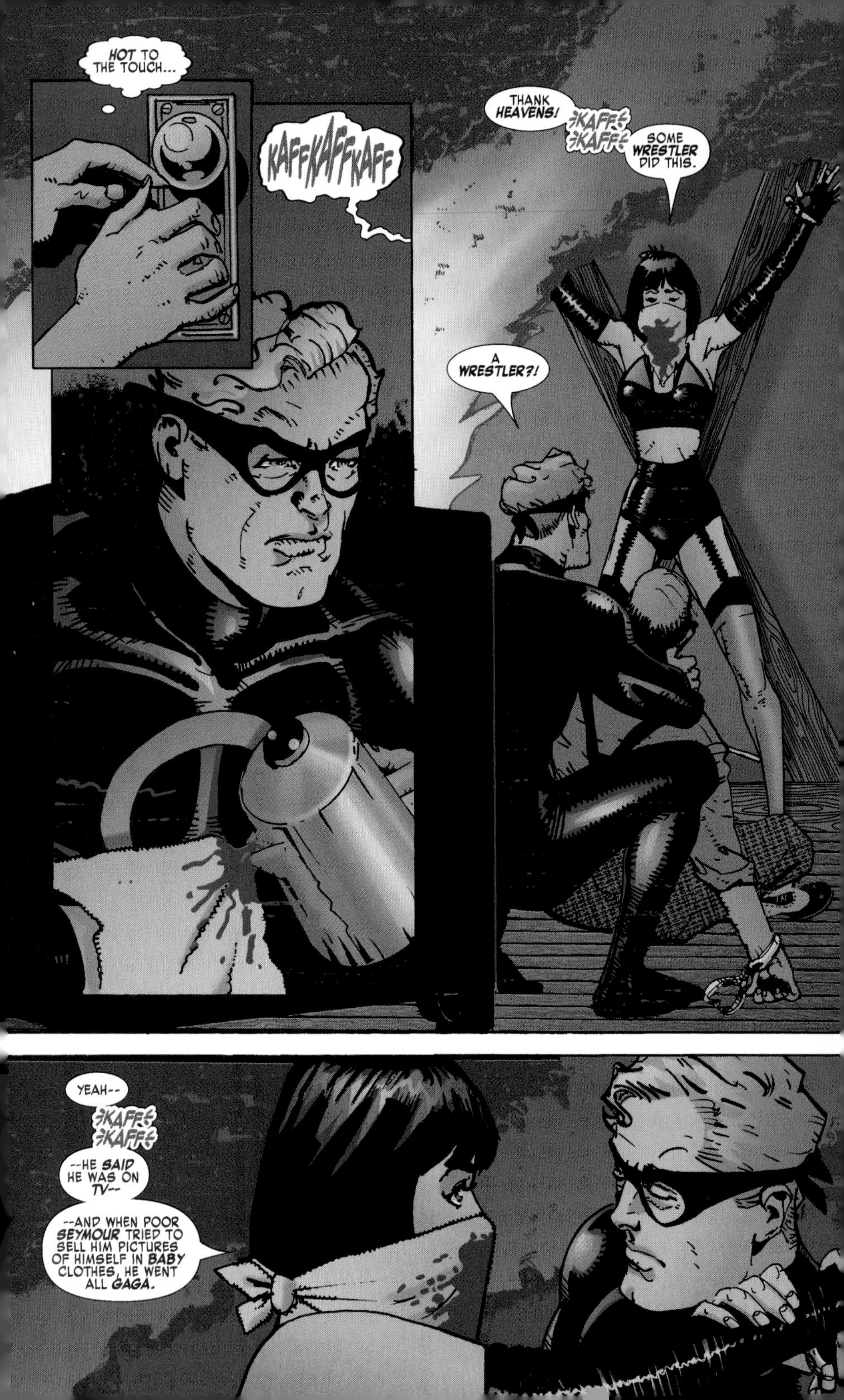
HOT TO THE TOUCH...
KAFFKAFFKAFF
THANK HEAVENS!
KAFF KAFF
SOME WRESTLER DID THIS.
A WRESTLER?!
YEAH--
KAFF KAFF
--HE SAID HE WAS ON TV--
--AND WHEN POOR SEYMOUR TRIED TO SELL HIM PICTURES OF HIMSELF IN BABY CLOTHES, HE WENT ALL GAGA.

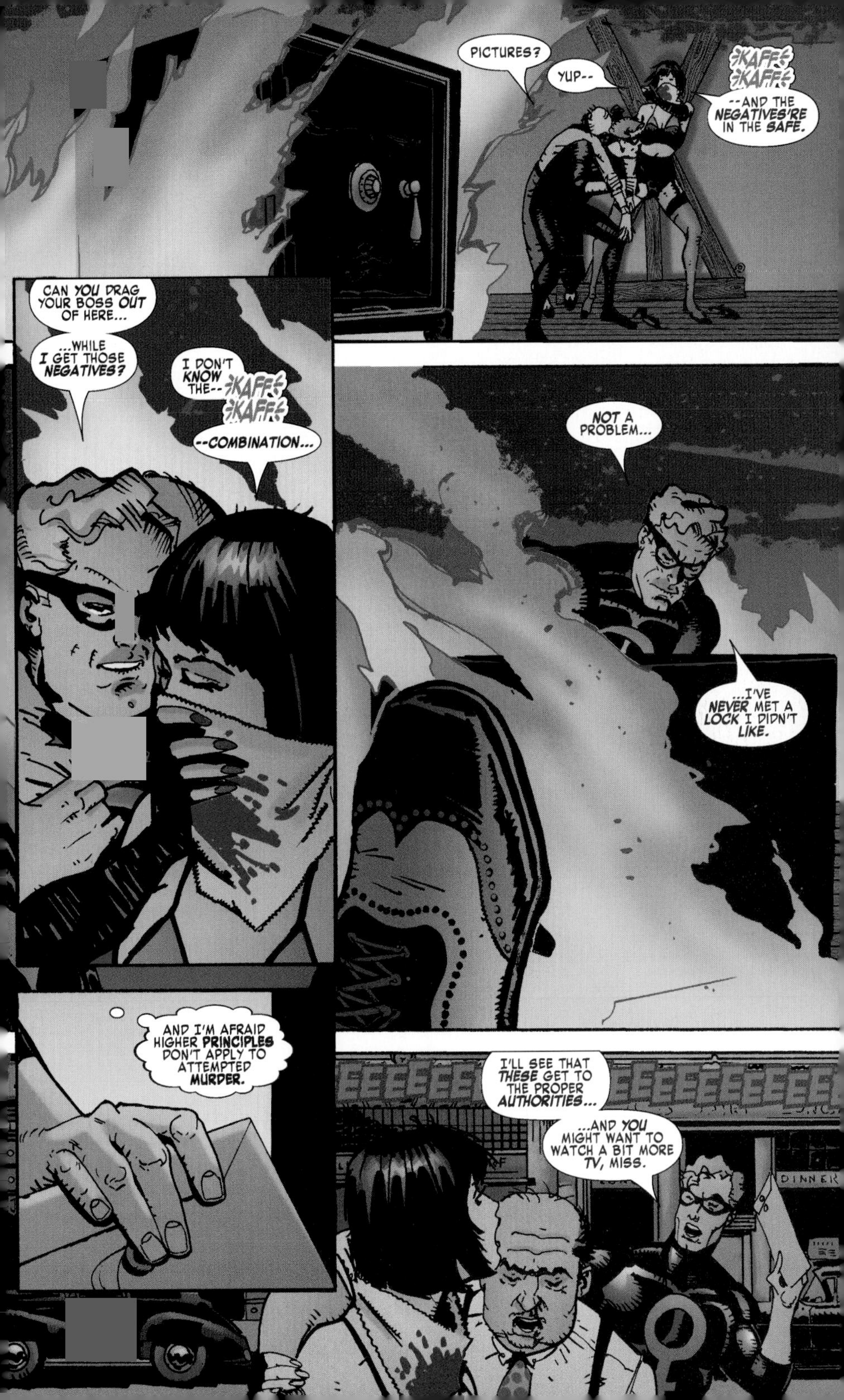
PICTURES?
YUP--
KAFF KAFF
--AND THE NEGATIVES'RE IN THE SAFE.
CAN YOU DRAG YOUR BOSS OUT OF HERE...
...WHILE I GET THOSE NEGATIVES?
I DON'T KNOW THE--
KAFF KAFF
--COMBINATION...
NOT A PROBLEM...
...I'VE NEVER MET A LOCK I DIDN'T LIKE.
AND I'M AFRAID HIGHER PRINCIPLES DON'T APPLY TO ATTEMPTED MURDER.
EEEEEE EEEEEEEEE
I'LL SEE THAT THESE GET TO THE PROPER AUTHORITIES...
...AND YOU MIGHT WANT TO WATCH A BIT MORE TV, MISS.
DINNER

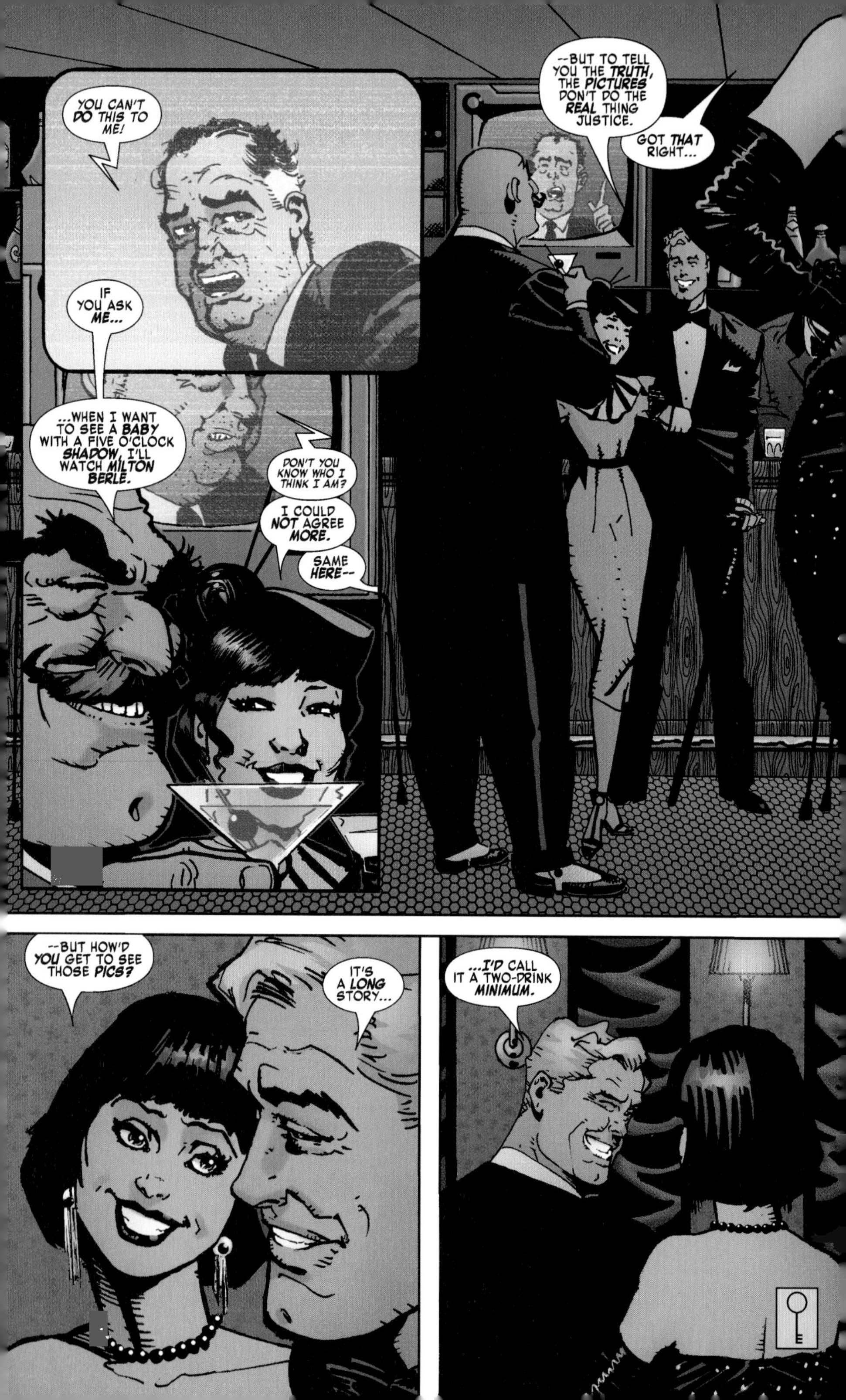
YOU CAN'T DO THIS TO ME!
IF YOU ASK ME...
...WHEN I WANT TO SEE A BABY WITH A FIVE O'CLOCK SHADOW, I'LL WATCH MILTON BERLE.
DON'T YOU KNOW WHO I THINK I AM?
I COULD NOT AGREE MORE.
SAME HERE--
--BUT TO TELL YOU THE TRUTH, THE PICTURES DON'T DO THE REAL THING JUSTICE.
GOT THAT RIGHT...
--BUT HOW'D YOU GET TO SEE THOSE PICS?
IT'S A LONG STORY...
...I'D CALL IT A TWO-DRINK MINIMUM.

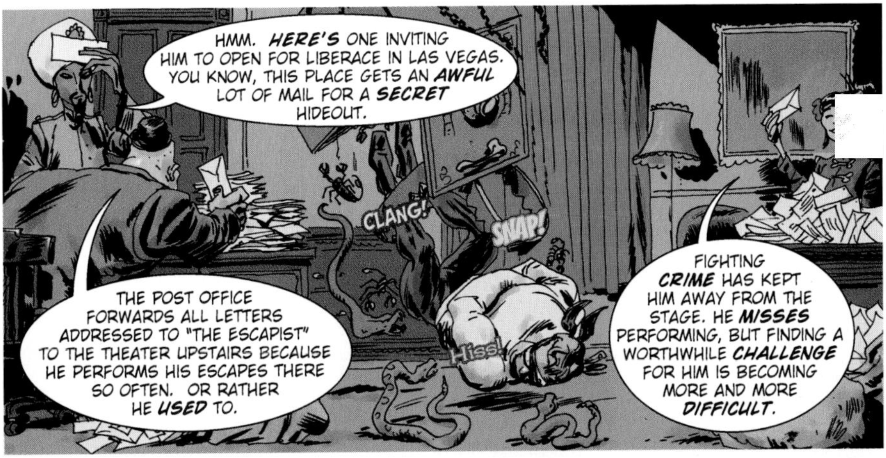
HMM. HERE'S ONE INVITING HIM TO OPEN FOR LIBERACE IN LAS VEGAS. YOU KNOW, THIS PLACE GETS AN AWFUL LOT OF MAIL FOR A SECRET HIDEOUT.
CLANG!
SNAP!
HISS!
THE POST OFFICE FORWARDS ALL LETTERS ADDRESSED TO "THE ESCAPIST" TO THE THEATER UPSTAIRS BECAUSE HE PERFORMS HIS ESCAPES THERE SO OFTEN. OR RATHER HE USED TO.
FIGHTING CRIME HAS KEPT HIM AWAY FROM THE STAGE. HE MISSES PERFORMING, BUT FINDING A WORTHWHILE CHALLENGE FOR HIM IS BECOMING MORE AND MORE DIFFICULT.

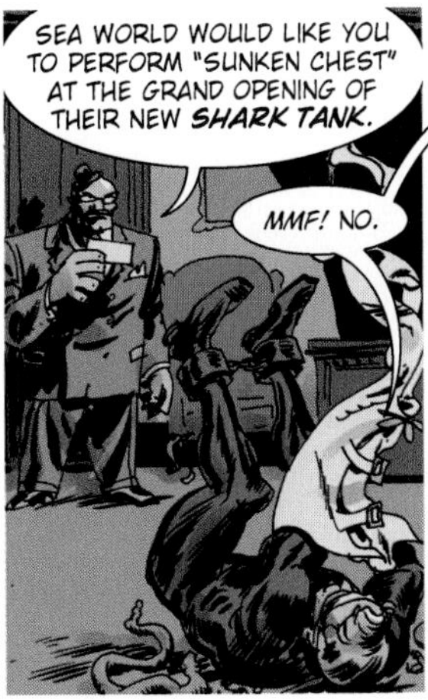
SEA WORLD WOULD LIKE YOU TO PERFORM "SUNKEN CHEST" AT THE GRAND OPENING OF THEIR NEW SHARK TANK.
MMF! NO.

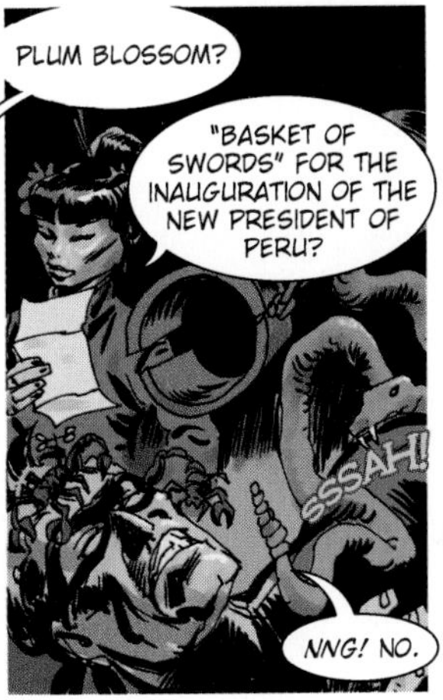
PLUM BLOSSOM?
"BASKET OF SWORDS" FOR THE INAUGURATION OF THE NEW PRESIDENT OF PERU?
SSSAH!
NNG! NO.

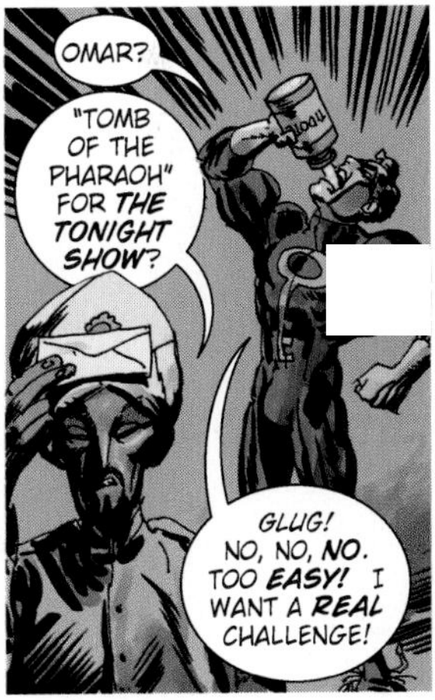
OMAR?
"TOMB OF THE PHARAOH" FOR THE TONIGHT SHOW?
GLUG! NO, NO, NO. TOO EASY! I WANT A REAL CHALLENGE!

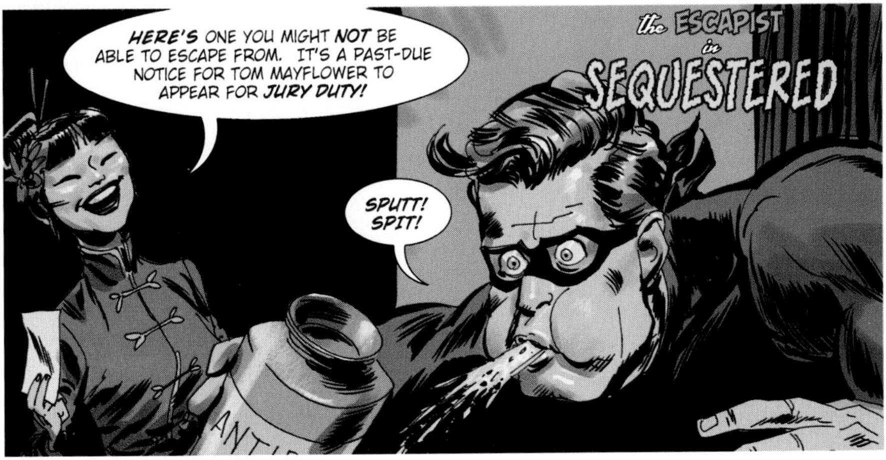
the ESCAPIST in SEQUESTERED
HERE'S ONE YOU MIGHT NOT BE ABLE TO ESCAPE FROM. IT'S A PAST-DUE NOTICE FOR TOM MAYFLOWER TO APPEAR FOR JURY DUTY!
SPUTT! SPIT!

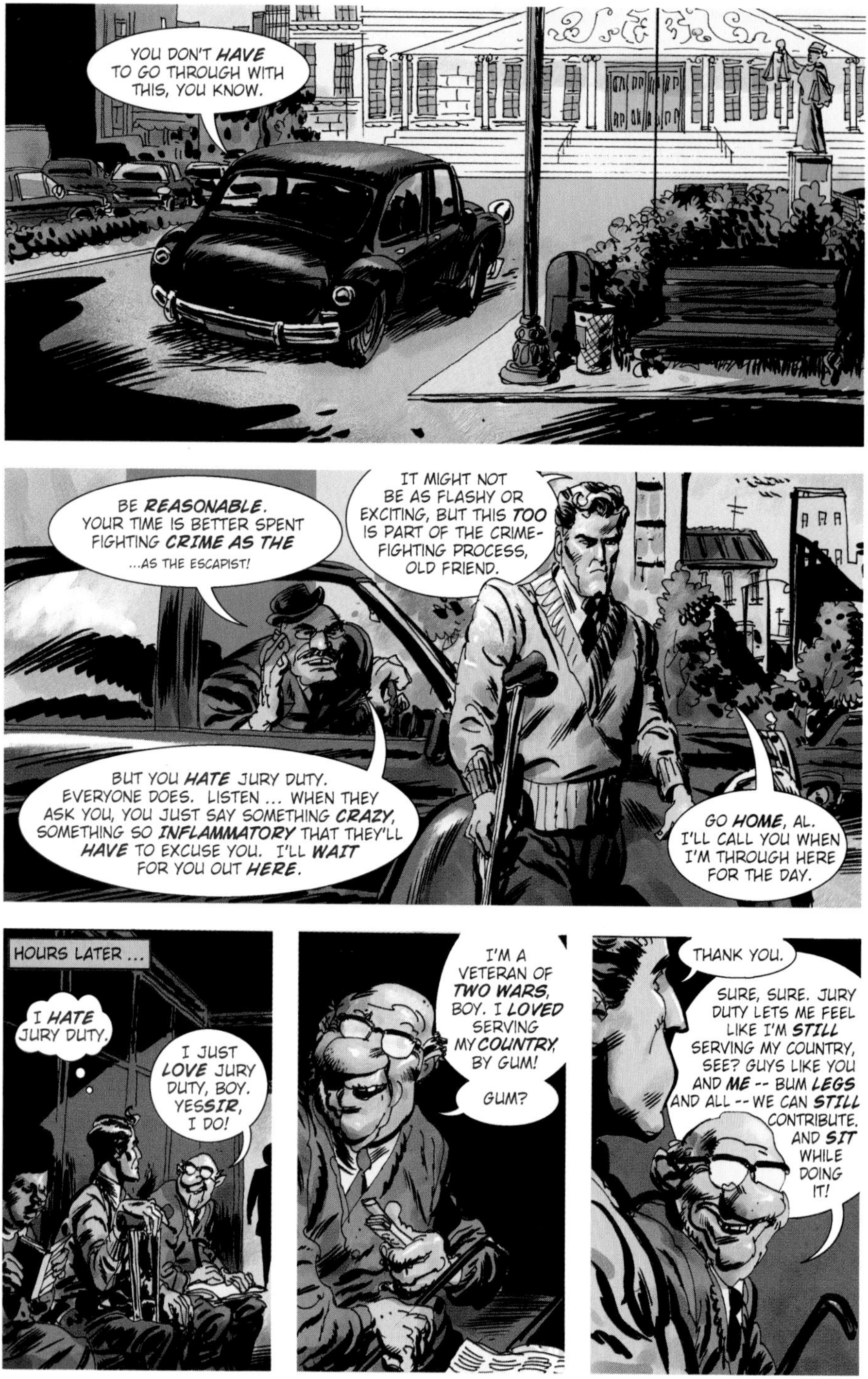
YOU DON'T HAVE TO GO THROUGH WITH THIS, YOU KNOW.
BE REASONABLE. YOUR TIME IS BETTER SPENT FIGHTING CRIME AS THE ...AS THE ESCAPIST!
IT MIGHT NOT BE AS FLASHY OR EXCITING, BUT THIS TOO IS PART OF THE CRIME-FIGHTING PROCESS, OLD FRIEND.
BUT YOU HATE JURY DUTY. EVERYONE DOES. LISTEN ... WHEN THEY ASK YOU, YOU JUST SAY SOMETHING CRAZY, SOMETHING SO INFLAMMATORY THAT THEY'LL HAVE TO EXCUSE YOU. I'LL WAIT FOR YOU OUT HERE.
GO HOME, AL. I'LL CALL YOU WHEN I'M THROUGH HERE FOR THE DAY.
HOURS LATER ...
I HATE JURY DUTY.
I JUST LOVE JURY DUTY, BOY. YESSIR, I DO!
I'M A VETERAN OF TWO WARS, BOY. I LOVED SERVING MY COUNTRY, BY GUM!
GUM?
THANK YOU.
SURE, SURE. JURY DUTY LETS ME FEEL LIKE I'M STILL SERVING MY COUNTRY, SEE? GUYS LIKE YOU AND ME -- BUM LEGS AND ALL -- WE CAN STILL CONTRIBUTE. AND SIT WHILE DOING IT!

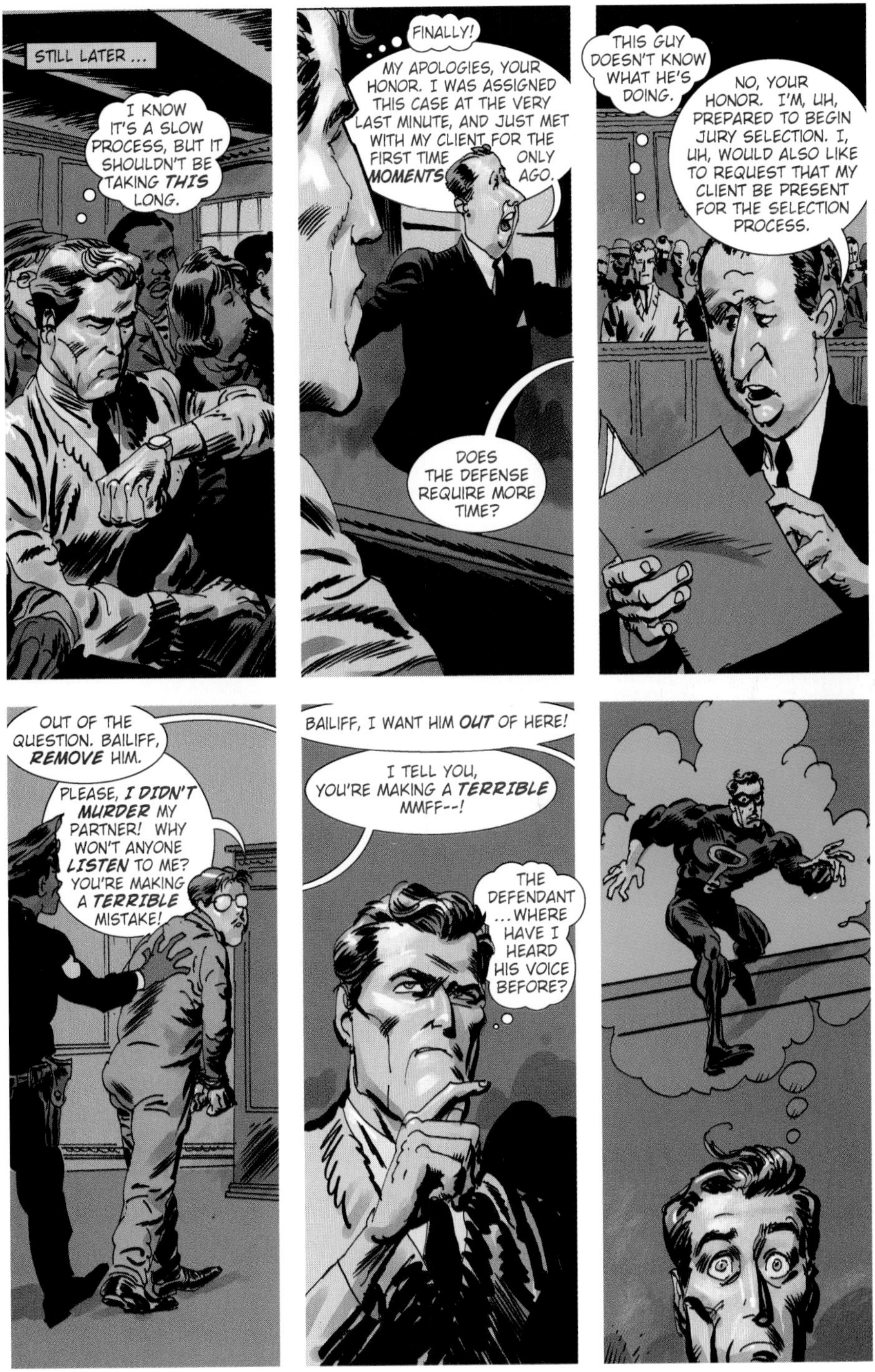

STILL LATER ...
I KNOW IT'S A SLOW PROCESS, BUT IT SHOULDN'T BE TAKING THIS LONG.
FINALLY!
MY APOLOGIES, YOUR HONOR. I WAS ASSIGNED THIS CASE AT THE VERY LAST MINUTE, AND JUST MET WITH MY CLIENT FOR THE FIRST TIME ONLY MOMENTS AGO.
DOES THE DEFENSE REQUIRE MORE TIME?
THIS GUY DOESN'T KNOW WHAT HE'S DOING.
NO, YOUR HONOR. I'M, UH, PREPARED TO BEGIN JURY SELECTION. I, UH, WOULD ALSO LIKE TO REQUEST THAT MY CLIENT BE PRESENT FOR THE SELECTION PROCESS.
OUT OF THE QUESTION. BAILIFF, REMOVE HIM.
PLEASE, I DIDN'T MURDER MY PARTNER! WHY WON'T ANYONE LISTEN TO ME? YOU'RE MAKING A TERRIBLE MISTAKE!
BAILIFF, I WANT HIM OUT OF HERE!
I TELL YOU, YOU'RE MAKING A TERRIBLE MMFF--!
THE DEFENDANT ...WHERE HAVE I HEARD HIS VOICE BEFORE?

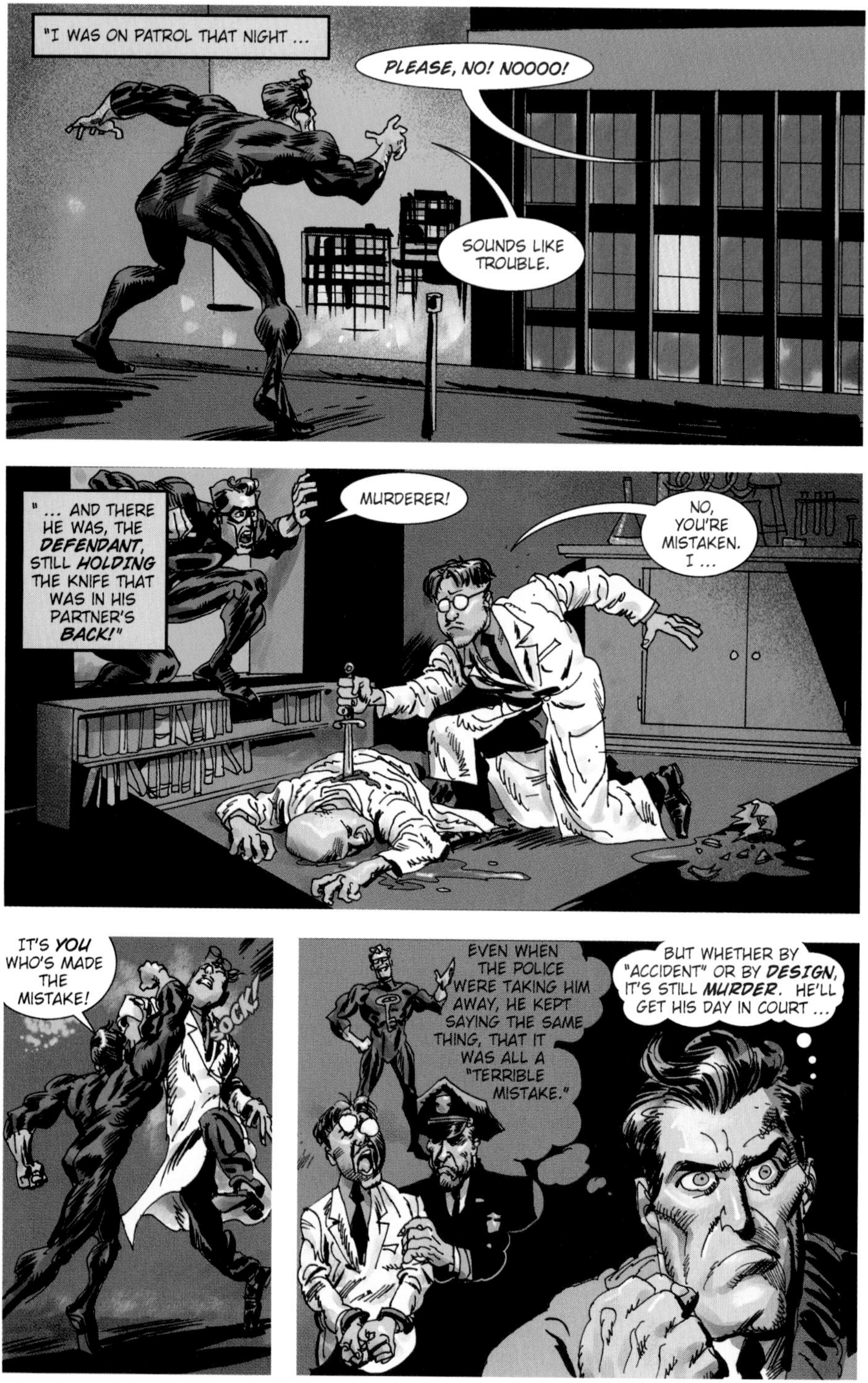
"I WAS ON PATROL THAT NIGHT ...
PLEASE, NO! NOOOO!
SOUNDS LIKE TROUBLE.
" ... AND THERE HE WAS, THE ***DEFENDANT***, STILL ***HOLDING*** THE KNIFE THAT WAS IN HIS PARTNER'S ***BACK!***"
MURDERER!
NO, YOU'RE MISTAKEN. I ...
IT'S ***YOU*** WHO'S MADE THE MISTAKE!
SOCK!
EVEN WHEN THE POLICE WERE TAKING HIM AWAY, HE KEPT SAYING THE SAME THING, THAT IT WAS ALL A "TERRIBLE MISTAKE."
BUT WHETHER BY "ACCIDENT" OR BY ***DESIGN***, IT'S STILL ***MURDER***. HE'LL GET HIS DAY IN COURT ...

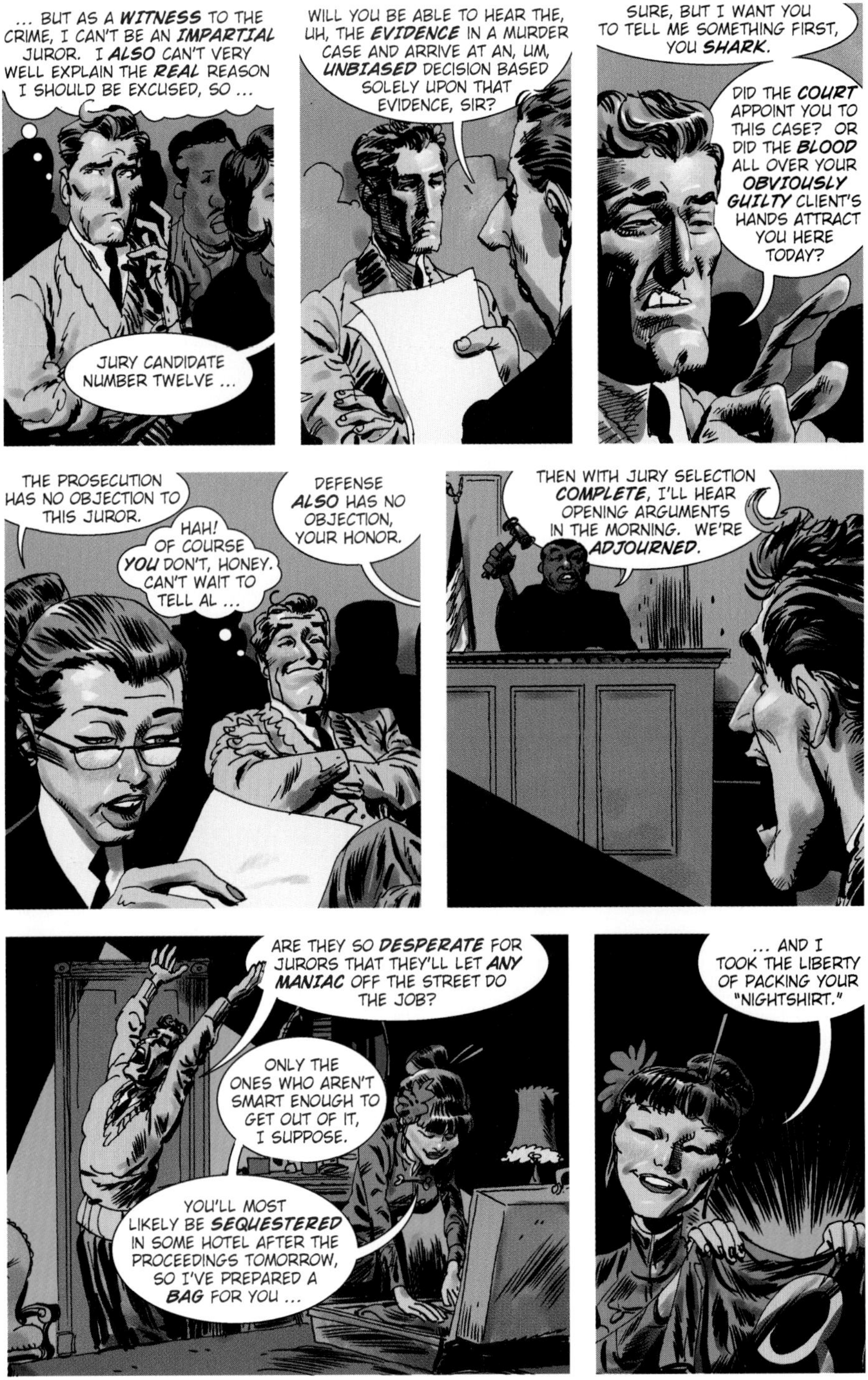

... BUT AS A WITNESS TO THE CRIME, I CAN'T BE AN IMPARTIAL JUROR. I ALSO CAN'T VERY WELL EXPLAIN THE REAL REASON I SHOULD BE EXCUSED, SO ...
JURY CANDIDATE NUMBER TWELVE ...
WILL YOU BE ABLE TO HEAR THE, UH, THE EVIDENCE IN A MURDER CASE AND ARRIVE AT AN, UM, UNBIASED DECISION BASED SOLELY UPON THAT EVIDENCE, SIR?
SURE, BUT I WANT YOU TO TELL ME SOMETHING FIRST, YOU SHARK.
DID THE COURT APPOINT YOU TO THIS CASE? OR DID THE BLOOD ALL OVER YOUR OBVIOUSLY GUILTY CLIENT'S HANDS ATTRACT YOU HERE TODAY?
THE PROSECUTION HAS NO OBJECTION TO THIS JUROR.
HAH! OF COURSE YOU DON'T, HONEY. CAN'T WAIT TO TELL AL ...
DEFENSE ALSO HAS NO OBJECTION, YOUR HONOR.
THEN WITH JURY SELECTION COMPLETE, I'LL HEAR OPENING ARGUMENTS IN THE MORNING. WE'RE ADJOURNED.
ARE THEY SO DESPERATE FOR JURORS THAT THEY'LL LET ANY MANIAC OFF THE STREET DO THE JOB?
ONLY THE ONES WHO AREN'T SMART ENOUGH TO GET OUT OF IT, I SUPPOSE.
YOU'LL MOST LIKELY BE SEQUESTERED IN SOME HOTEL AFTER THE PROCEEDINGS TOMORROW, SO I'VE PREPARED A BAG FOR YOU ...
... AND I TOOK THE LIBERTY OF PACKING YOUR "NIGHTSHIRT."

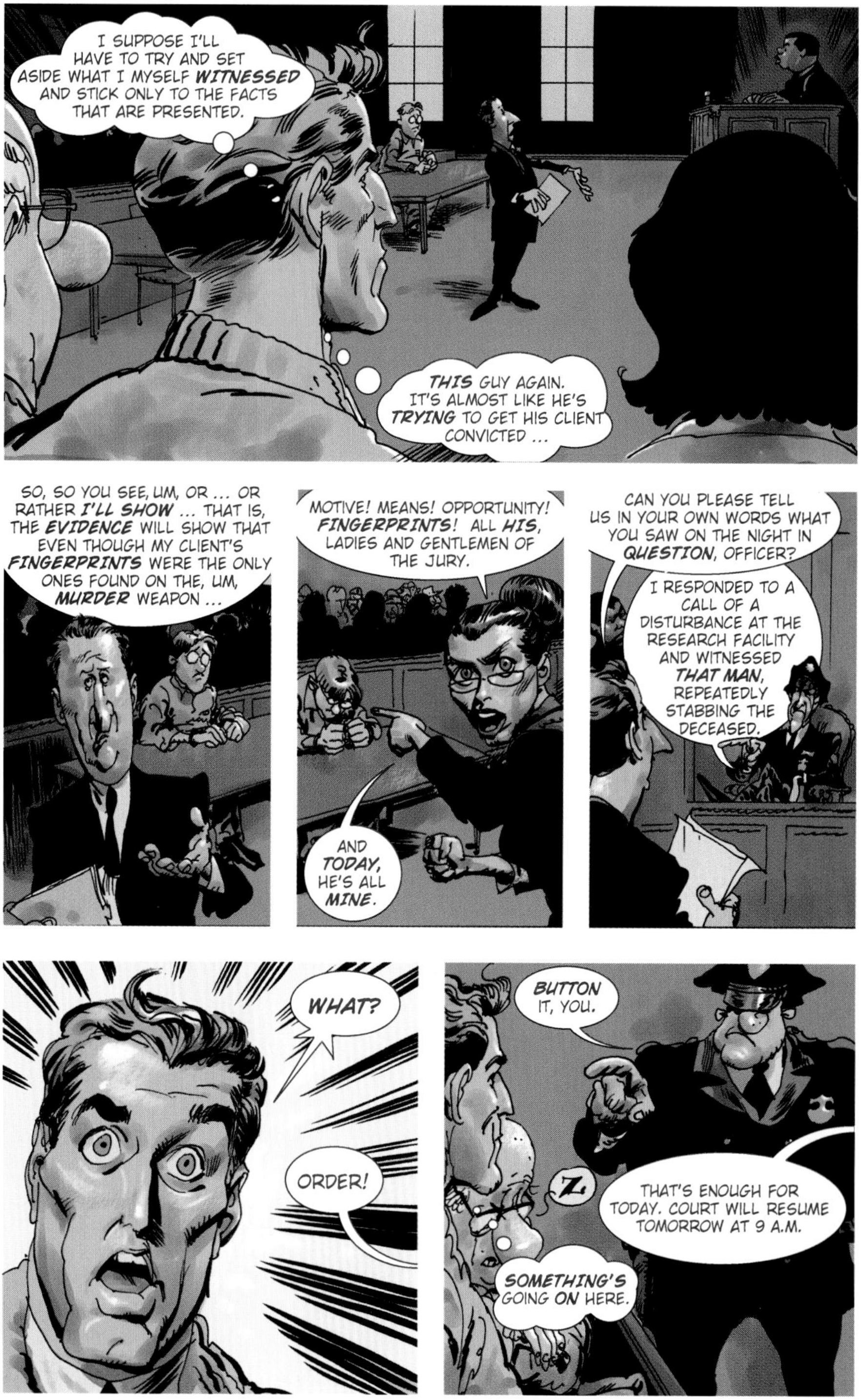
I SUPPOSE I'LL HAVE TO TRY AND SET ASIDE WHAT I MYSELF WITNESSED AND STICK ONLY TO THE FACTS THAT ARE PRESENTED.
THIS GUY AGAIN. IT'S ALMOST LIKE HE'S TRYING TO GET HIS CLIENT CONVICTED ...
SO, SO YOU SEE, UM, OR ... OR RATHER I'LL SHOW ... THAT IS, THE EVIDENCE WILL SHOW THAT EVEN THOUGH MY CLIENT'S FINGERPRINTS WERE THE ONLY ONES FOUND ON THE, UM, MURDER WEAPON ...
MOTIVE! MEANS! OPPORTUNITY! FINGERPRINTS! ALL HIS, LADIES AND GENTLEMEN OF THE JURY.
AND TODAY, HE'S ALL MINE.
CAN YOU PLEASE TELL US IN YOUR OWN WORDS WHAT YOU SAW ON THE NIGHT IN QUESTION, OFFICER?
I RESPONDED TO A CALL OF A DISTURBANCE AT THE RESEARCH FACILITY AND WITNESSED THAT MAN, REPEATEDLY STABBING THE DECEASED.
WHAT?
ORDER!
BUTTON IT, YOU.
Z
THAT'S ENOUGH FOR TODAY. COURT WILL RESUME TOMORROW AT 9 A.M.
SOMETHING'S GOING ON HERE.

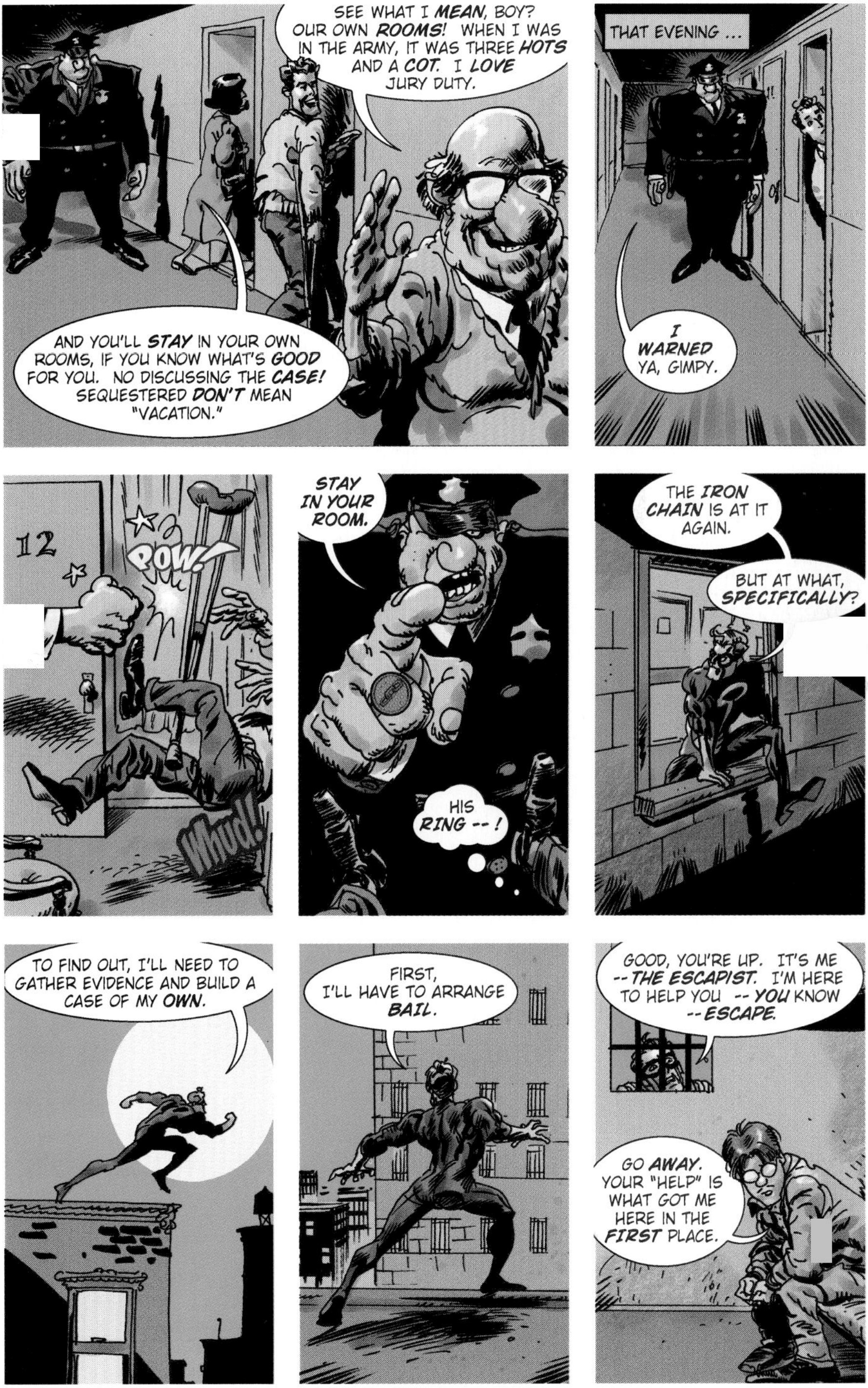
SEE WHAT I MEAN, BOY? OUR OWN ROOMS! WHEN I WAS IN THE ARMY, IT WAS THREE HOTS AND A COT. I LOVE JURY DUTY.
AND YOU'LL STAY IN YOUR OWN ROOMS, IF YOU KNOW WHAT'S GOOD FOR YOU. NO DISCUSSING THE CASE! SEQUESTERED DON'T MEAN "VACATION."
THAT EVENING ...
I WARNED YA, GIMPY.
12
POW!
WHUD!
STAY IN YOUR ROOM.
HIS RING -- !
THE IRON CHAIN IS AT IT AGAIN.
BUT AT WHAT, SPECIFICALLY?
TO FIND OUT, I'LL NEED TO GATHER EVIDENCE AND BUILD A CASE OF MY OWN.
FIRST, I'LL HAVE TO ARRANGE BAIL.
GOOD, YOU'RE UP. IT'S ME -- THE ESCAPIST. I'M HERE TO HELP YOU -- YOU KNOW -- ESCAPE.
GO AWAY. YOUR "HELP" IS WHAT GOT ME HERE IN THE FIRST PLACE.

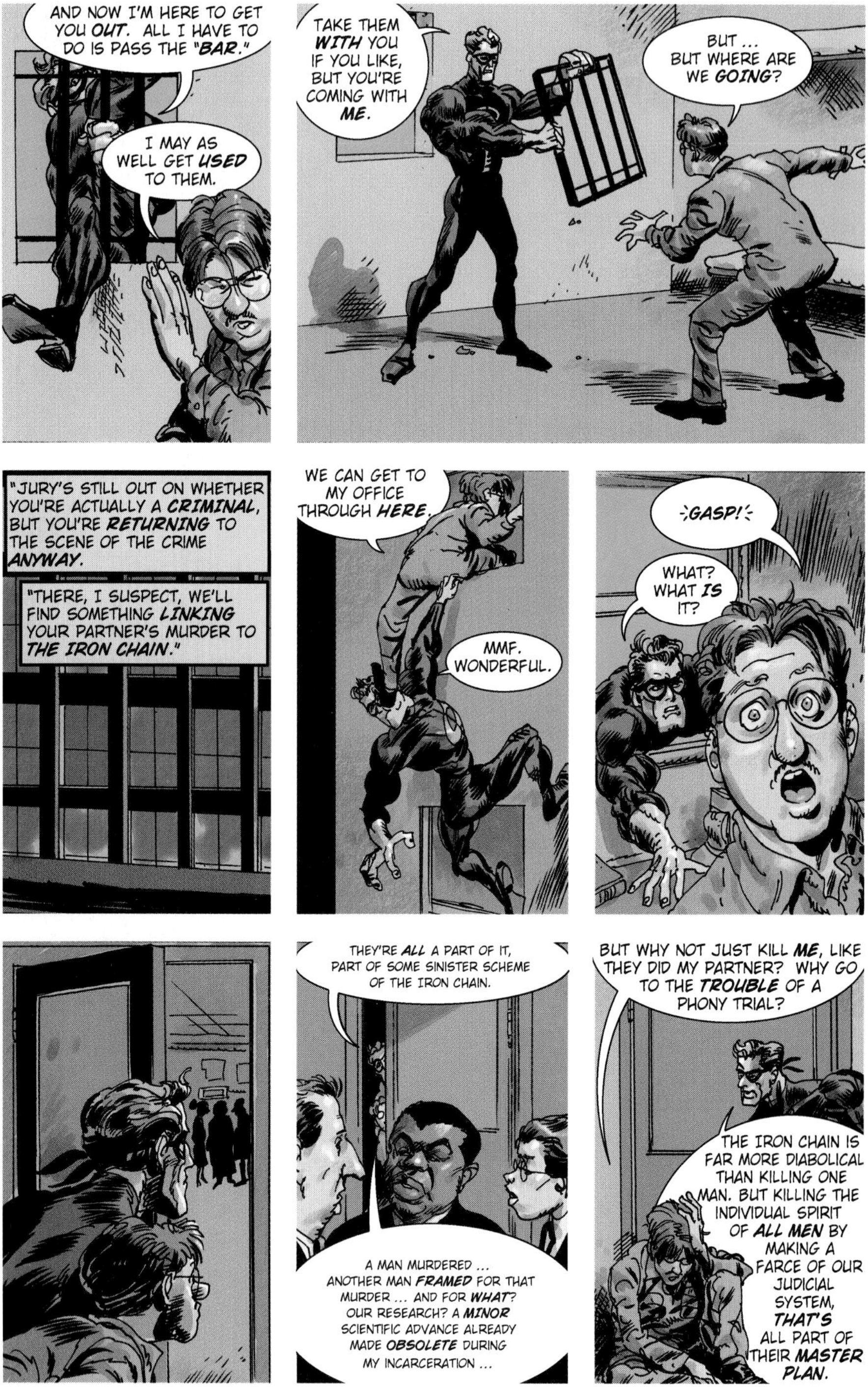
AND NOW I'M HERE TO GET YOU OUT. ALL I HAVE TO DO IS PASS THE "BAR."
I MAY AS WELL GET USED TO THEM.
TAKE THEM WITH YOU IF YOU LIKE, BUT YOU'RE COMING WITH ME.
BUT ... BUT WHERE ARE WE GOING?
"JURY'S STILL OUT ON WHETHER YOU'RE ACTUALLY A CRIMINAL, BUT YOU'RE RETURNING TO THE SCENE OF THE CRIME ANYWAY.
"THERE, I SUSPECT, WE'LL FIND SOMETHING LINKING YOUR PARTNER'S MURDER TO THE IRON CHAIN."
WE CAN GET TO MY OFFICE THROUGH HERE.
MMF. WONDERFUL.
GASP!
WHAT? WHAT IS IT?
THEY'RE ALL A PART OF IT, PART OF SOME SINISTER SCHEME OF THE IRON CHAIN.
A MAN MURDERED ... ANOTHER MAN FRAMED FOR THAT MURDER ... AND FOR WHAT? OUR RESEARCH? A MINOR SCIENTIFIC ADVANCE ALREADY MADE OBSOLETE DURING MY INCARCERATION ...
BUT WHY NOT JUST KILL ME, LIKE THEY DID MY PARTNER? WHY GO TO THE TROUBLE OF A PHONY TRIAL?
THE IRON CHAIN IS FAR MORE DIABOLICAL THAN KILLING ONE MAN. BUT KILLING THE INDIVIDUAL SPIRIT OF ALL MEN BY MAKING A FARCE OF OUR JUDICIAL SYSTEM, THAT'S ALL PART OF THEIR MASTER PLAN.

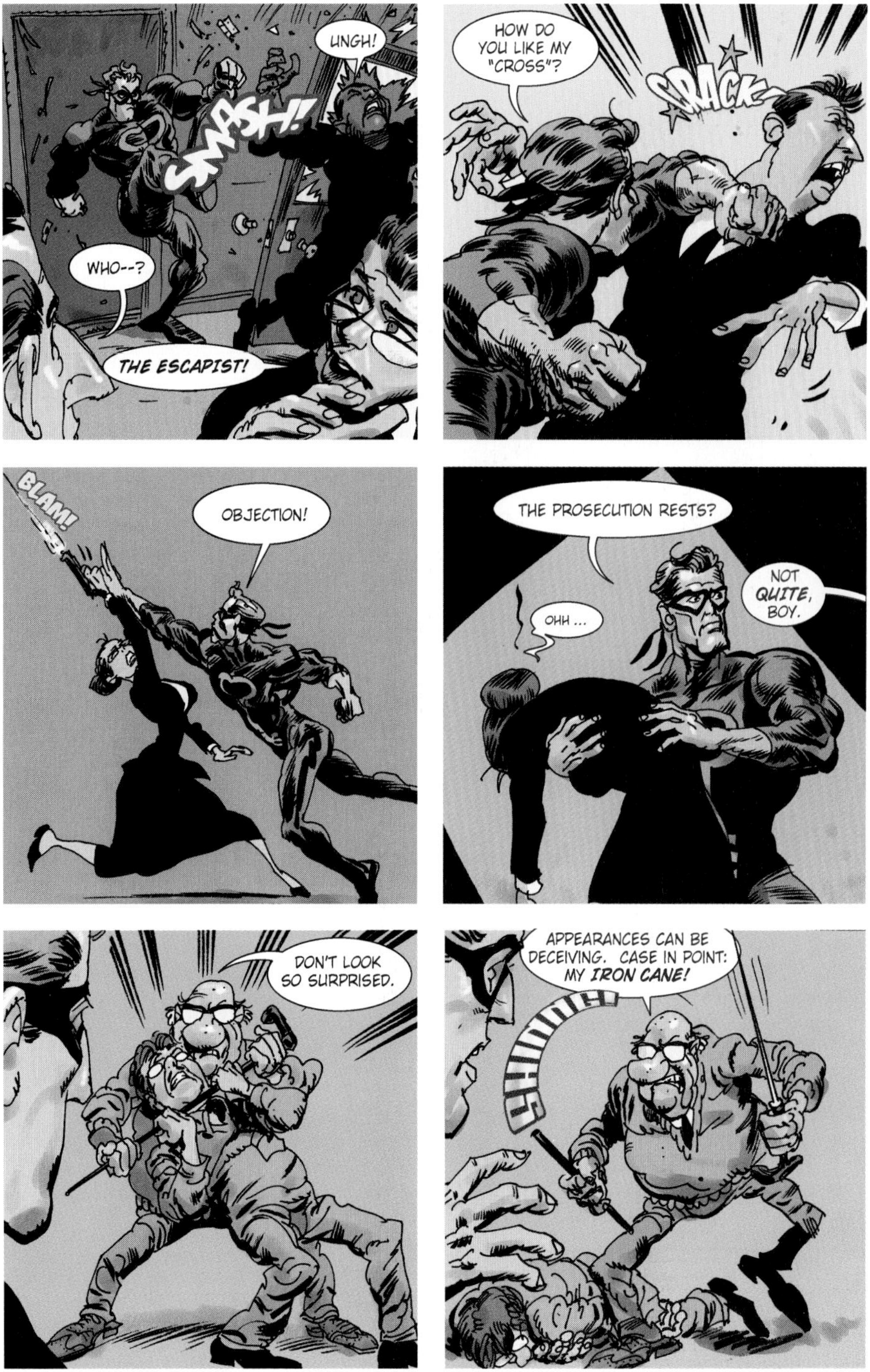
SMASH!
UNGH!
WHO--?
THE ESCAPIST!
HOW DO YOU LIKE MY "CROSS"?
CRACK
BLAM!
OBJECTION!
THE PROSECUTION RESTS?
NOT QUITE, BOY.
OHH ...
DON'T LOOK SO SURPRISED.
APPEARANCES CAN BE DECEIVING. CASE IN POINT: MY IRON CANE!

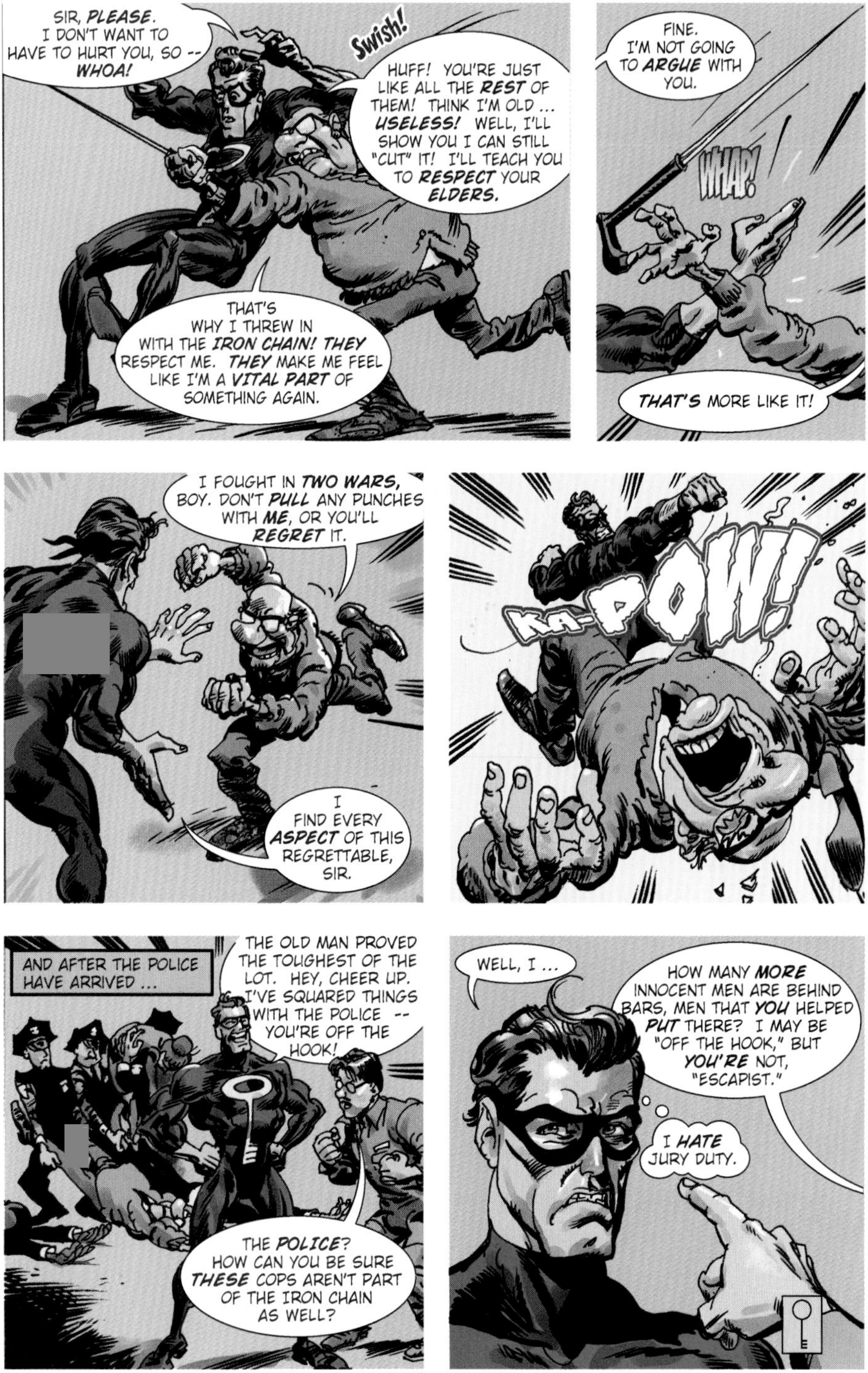
SIR, PLEASE. I DON'T WANT TO HAVE TO HURT YOU, SO -- WHOA!
Swish!
HUFF! YOU'RE JUST LIKE ALL THE REST OF THEM! THINK I'M OLD ... USELESS! WELL, I'LL SHOW YOU I CAN STILL "CUT" IT! I'LL TEACH YOU TO RESPECT YOUR ELDERS.
THAT'S WHY I THREW IN WITH THE IRON CHAIN! THEY RESPECT ME. THEY MAKE ME FEEL LIKE I'M A VITAL PART OF SOMETHING AGAIN.
FINE. I'M NOT GOING TO ARGUE WITH YOU.
WHAP!
THAT'S MORE LIKE IT!
I FOUGHT IN TWO WARS, BOY. DON'T PULL ANY PUNCHES WITH ME, OR YOU'LL REGRET IT.
I FIND EVERY ASPECT OF THIS REGRETTABLE, SIR.
KA-POW!
AND AFTER THE POLICE HAVE ARRIVED ...
THE OLD MAN PROVED THE TOUGHEST OF THE LOT. HEY, CHEER UP. I'VE SQUARED THINGS WITH THE POLICE -- YOU'RE OFF THE HOOK!
THE POLICE? HOW CAN YOU BE SURE THESE COPS AREN'T PART OF THE IRON CHAIN AS WELL?
WELL, I ...
HOW MANY MORE INNOCENT MEN ARE BEHIND BARS, MEN THAT YOU HELPED PUT THERE? I MAY BE "OFF THE HOOK," BUT YOU'RE NOT, "ESCAPIST."
I HATE JURY DUTY.

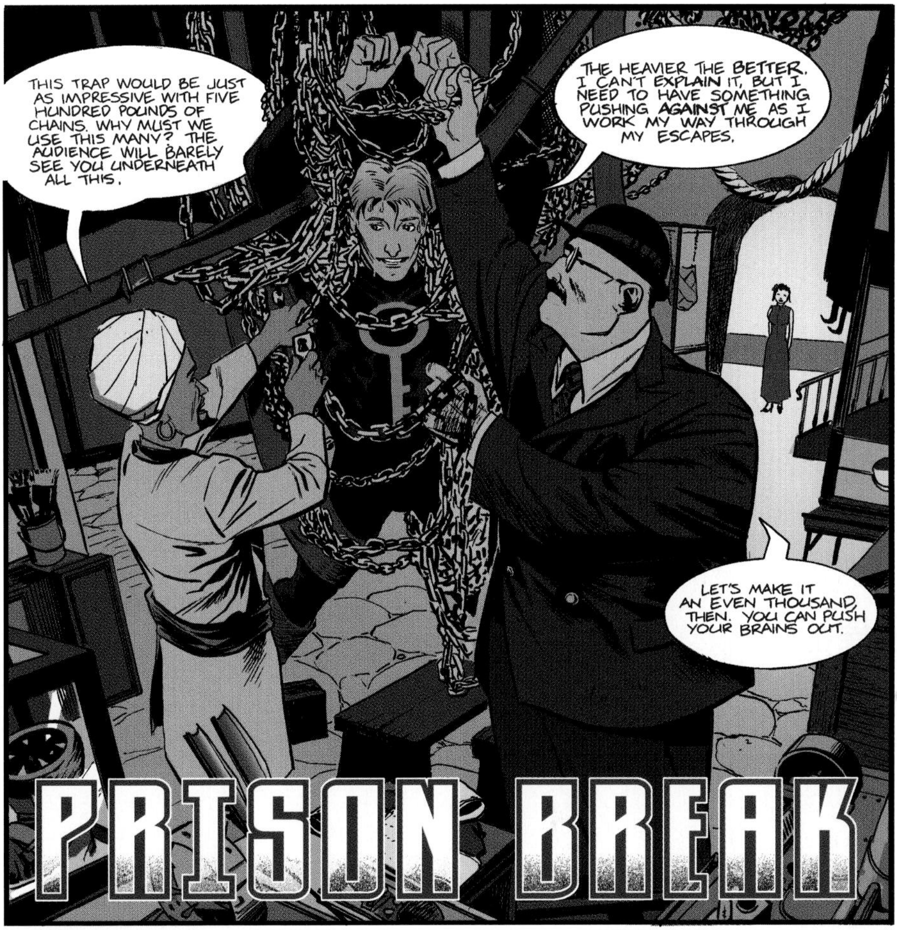
THIS TRAP WOULD BE JUST AS IMPRESSIVE WITH FIVE HUNDRED POUNDS OF CHAINS. WHY MUST WE USE THIS MANY? THE AUDIENCE WILL BARELY SEE YOU UNDERNEATH ALL THIS.
THE HEAVIER THE BETTER. I CAN'T EXPLAIN IT, BUT I NEED TO HAVE SOMETHING PUSHING AGAINST ME AS I WORK MY WAY THROUGH MY ESCAPES.
LET'S MAKE IT AN EVEN THOUSAND, THEN. YOU CAN PUSH YOUR BRAINS OUT.
PRISON BREAK

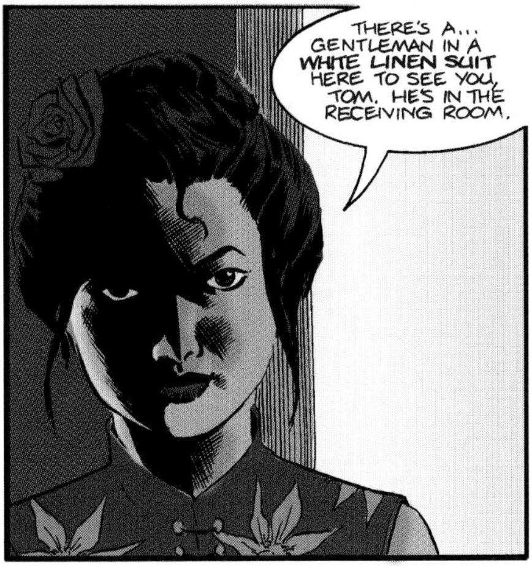
THERE'S A... GENTLEMAN IN A WHITE LINEN SUIT HERE TO SEE YOU, TOM. HE'S IN THE RECEIVING ROOM.

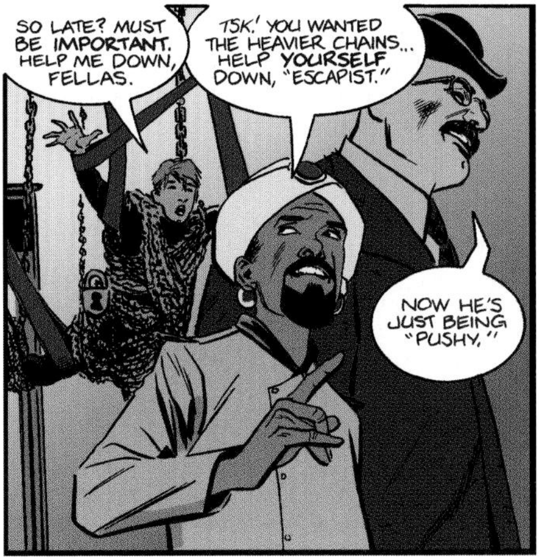
SO LATE? MUST BE IMPORTANT. HELP ME DOWN, FELLAS.
TSK! YOU WANTED THE HEAVIER CHAINS... HELP YOURSELF DOWN, "ESCAPIST."
NOW HE'S JUST BEING "PUSHY."

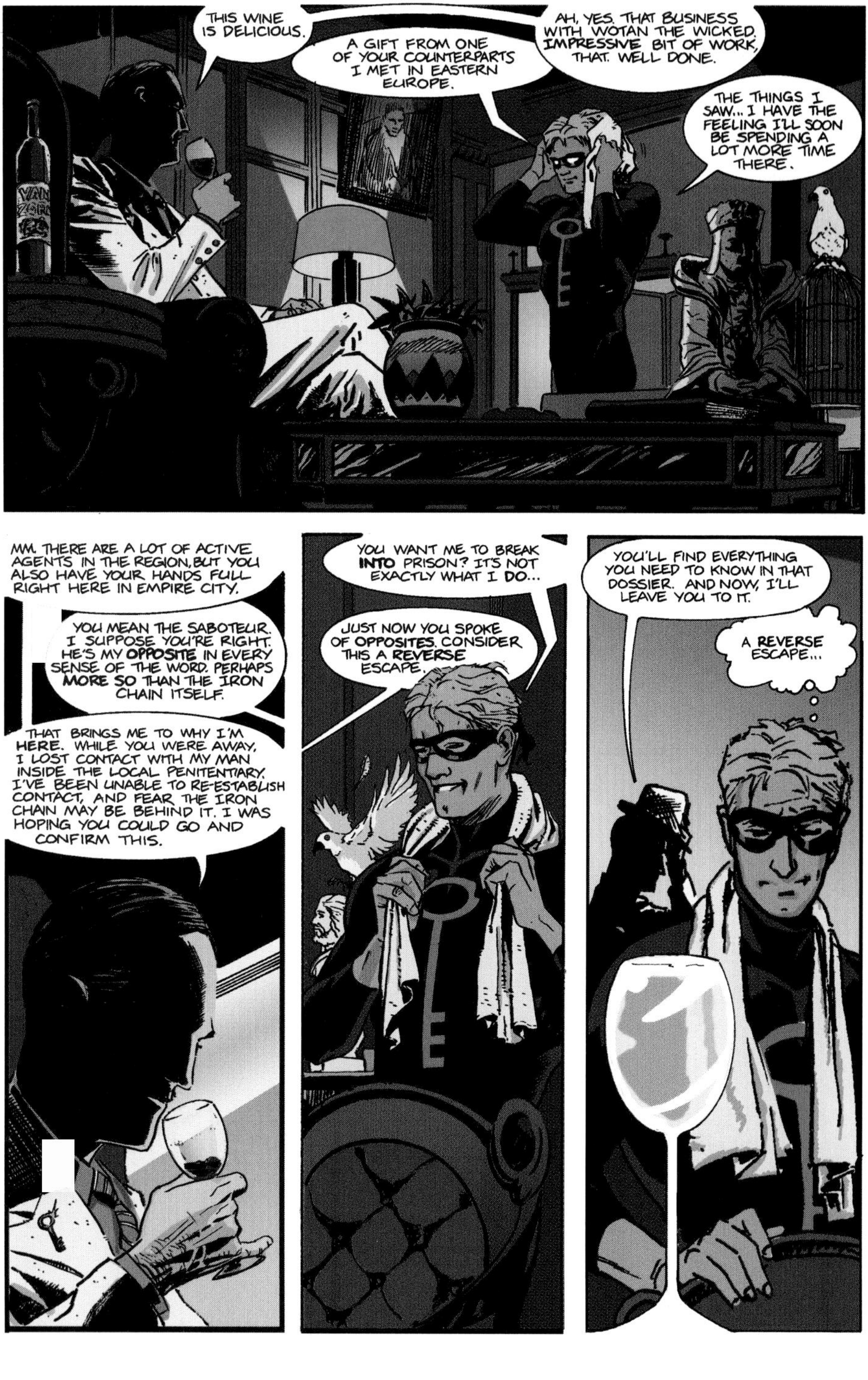
THIS WINE IS DELICIOUS.
A GIFT FROM ONE OF YOUR COUNTERPARTS I MET IN EASTERN EUROPE.
AH, YES. THAT BUSINESS WITH WOTAN THE WICKED. IMPRESSIVE BIT OF WORK, THAT. WELL DONE.
THE THINGS I SAW... I HAVE THE FEELING I'LL SOON BE SPENDING A LOT MORE TIME THERE.
MM. THERE ARE A LOT OF ACTIVE AGENTS IN THE REGION, BUT YOU ALSO HAVE YOUR HANDS FULL RIGHT HERE IN EMPIRE CITY.
YOU MEAN THE SABOTEUR. I SUPPOSE YOU'RE RIGHT. HE'S MY OPPOSITE IN EVERY SENSE OF THE WORD. PERHAPS MORE SO THAN THE IRON CHAIN ITSELF.
THAT BRINGS ME TO WHY I'M HERE. WHILE YOU WERE AWAY, I LOST CONTACT WITH MY MAN INSIDE THE LOCAL PENITENTIARY. I'VE BEEN UNABLE TO RE-ESTABLISH CONTACT, AND FEAR THE IRON CHAIN MAY BE BEHIND IT. I WAS HOPING YOU COULD GO AND CONFIRM THIS.
YOU WANT ME TO BREAK INTO PRISON? IT'S NOT EXACTLY WHAT I DO...
JUST NOW YOU SPOKE OF OPPOSITES. CONSIDER THIS A REVERSE ESCAPE.
YOU'LL FIND EVERYTHING YOU NEED TO KNOW IN THAT DOSSIER. AND NOW, I'LL LEAVE YOU TO IT.
A REVERSE ESCAPE...

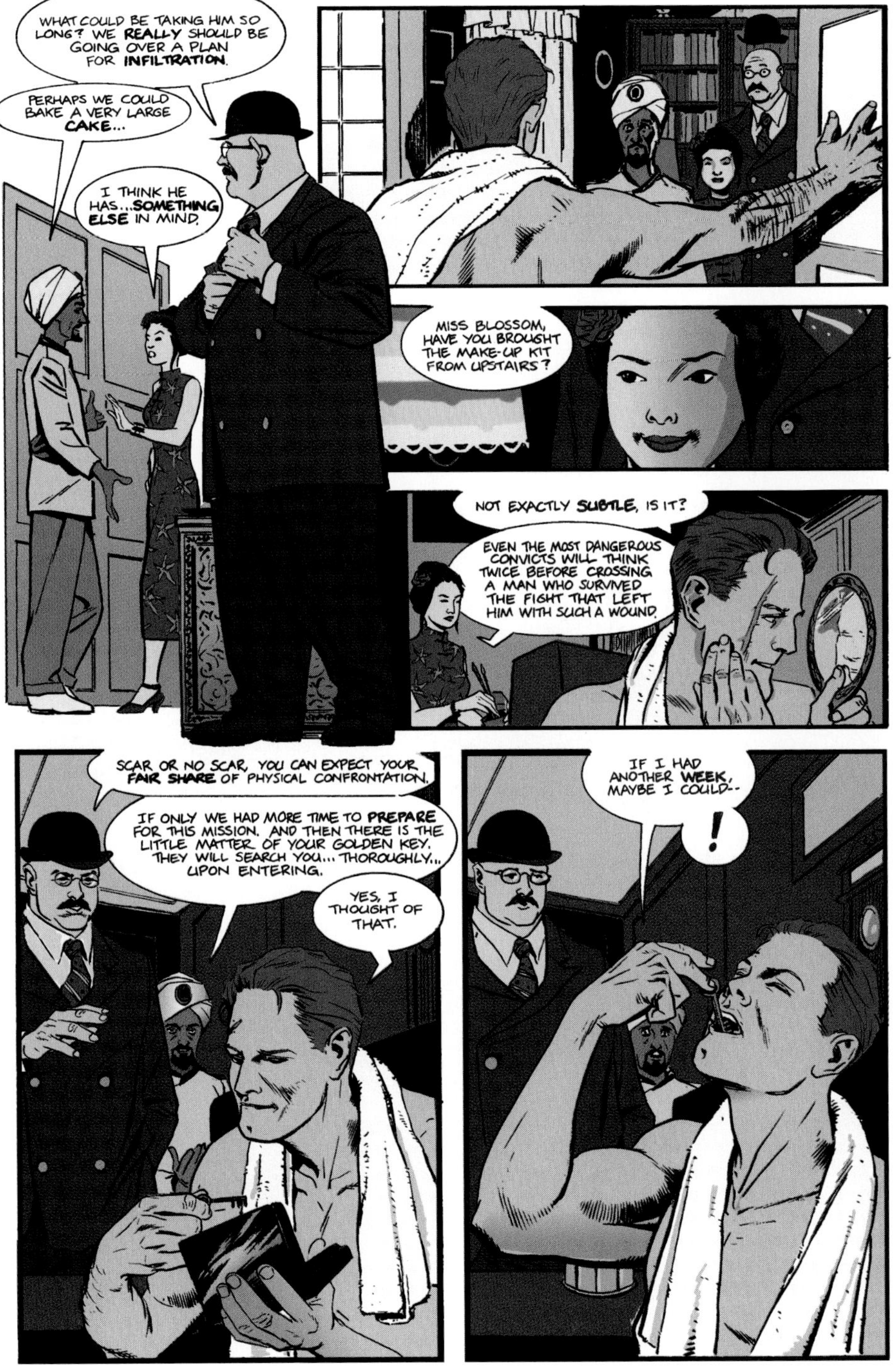
WHAT COULD BE TAKING HIM SO LONG? WE REALLY SHOULD BE GOING OVER A PLAN FOR INFILTRATION.
PERHAPS WE COULD BAKE A VERY LARGE CAKE...
I THINK HE HAS...SOMETHING ELSE IN MIND.
MISS BLOSSOM, HAVE YOU BROUGHT THE MAKE-UP KIT FROM UPSTAIRS?
NOT EXACTLY SUBTLE, IS IT?
EVEN THE MOST DANGEROUS CONVICTS WILL THINK TWICE BEFORE CROSSING A MAN WHO SURVIVED THE FIGHT THAT LEFT HIM WITH SUCH A WOUND.
SCAR OR NO SCAR, YOU CAN EXPECT YOUR FAIR SHARE OF PHYSICAL CONFRONTATION.
IF ONLY WE HAD MORE TIME TO PREPARE FOR THIS MISSION. AND THEN THERE IS THE LITTLE MATTER OF YOUR GOLDEN KEY. THEY WILL SEARCH YOU... THOROUGHLY... UPON ENTERING.
YES, I THOUGHT OF THAT.
IF I HAD ANOTHER WEEK, MAYBE I COULD--
!

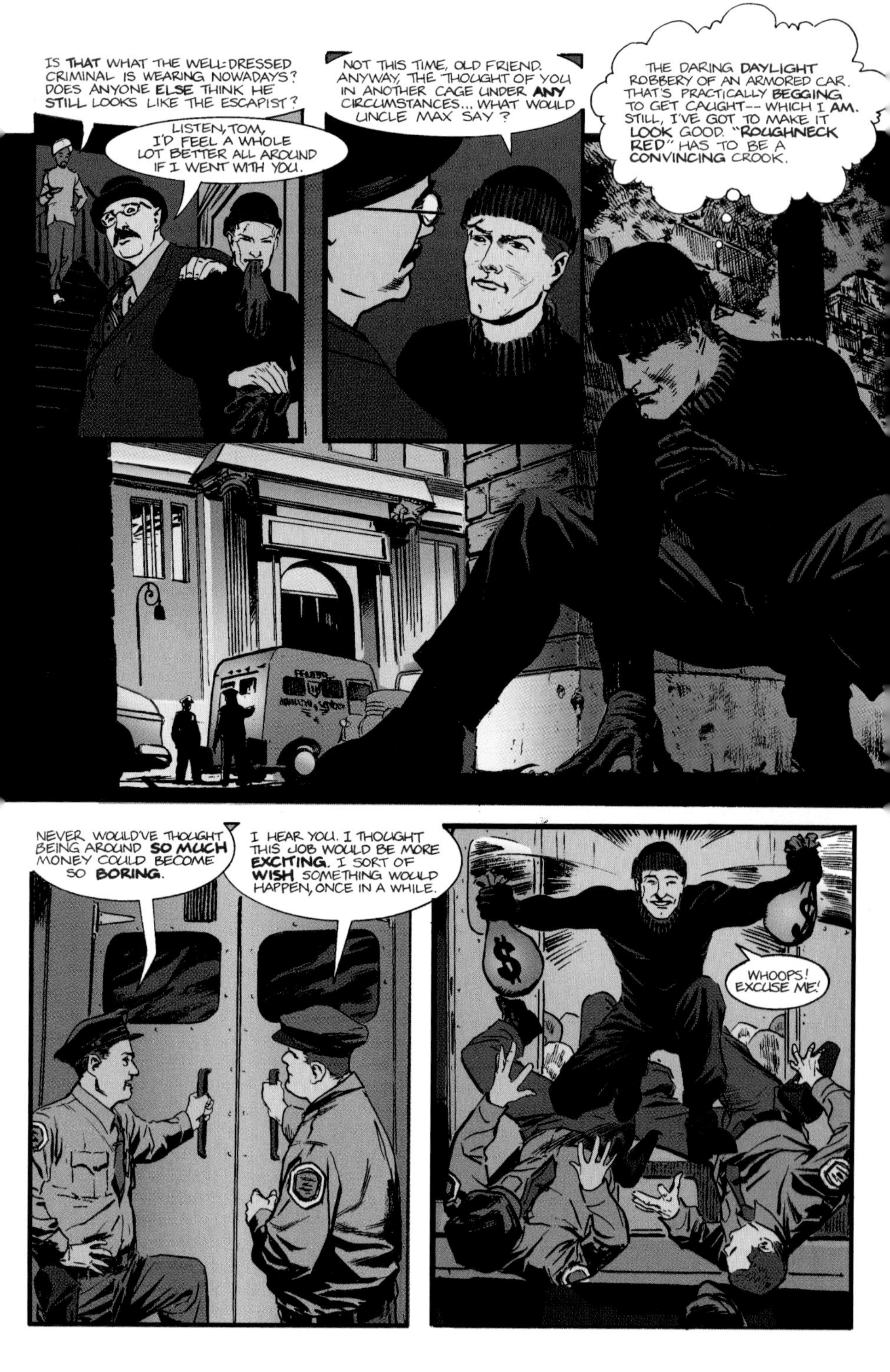
IS THAT WHAT THE WELL-DRESSED CRIMINAL IS WEARING NOWADAYS? DOES ANYONE ELSE THINK HE STILL LOOKS LIKE THE ESCAPIST?
LISTEN, TOM, I'D FEEL A WHOLE LOT BETTER ALL AROUND IF I WENT WITH YOU.
NOT THIS TIME, OLD FRIEND. ANYWAY, THE THOUGHT OF YOU IN ANOTHER CAGE UNDER ANY CIRCUMSTANCES... WHAT WOULD UNCLE MAX SAY?
THE DARING DAYLIGHT ROBBERY OF AN ARMORED CAR. THAT'S PRACTICALLY BEGGING TO GET CAUGHT-- WHICH I AM. STILL, I'VE GOT TO MAKE IT LOOK GOOD. "ROUGHNECK RED" HAS TO BE A CONVINCING CROOK.
NEVER WOULD'VE THOUGHT BEING AROUND SO MUCH MONEY COULD BECOME SO BORING.
I HEAR YOU. I THOUGHT THIS JOB WOULD BE MORE EXCITING. I SORT OF WISH SOMETHING WOULD HAPPEN, ONCE IN A WHILE.
WHOOPS! EXCUSE ME!

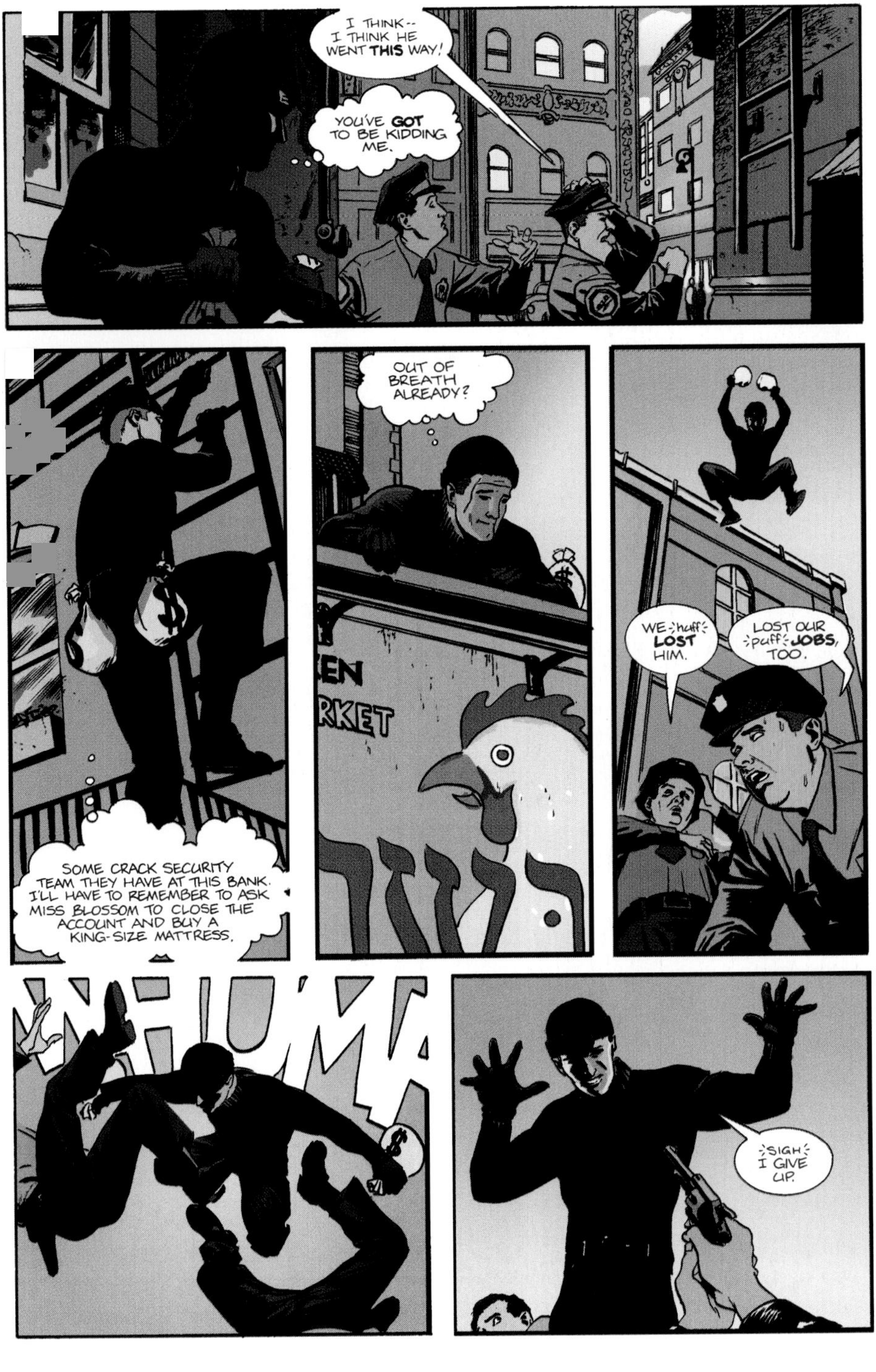
I THINK-- I THINK HE WENT THIS WAY!
YOU'VE GOT TO BE KIDDING ME.
SOME CRACK SECURITY TEAM THEY HAVE AT THIS BANK. I'LL HAVE TO REMEMBER TO ASK MISS BLOSSOM TO CLOSE THE ACCOUNT AND BUY A KING-SIZE MATTRESS.
OUT OF BREATH ALREADY?
WE huff LOST HIM.
LOST OUR puff JOBS, TOO.
SIGH I GIVE UP.

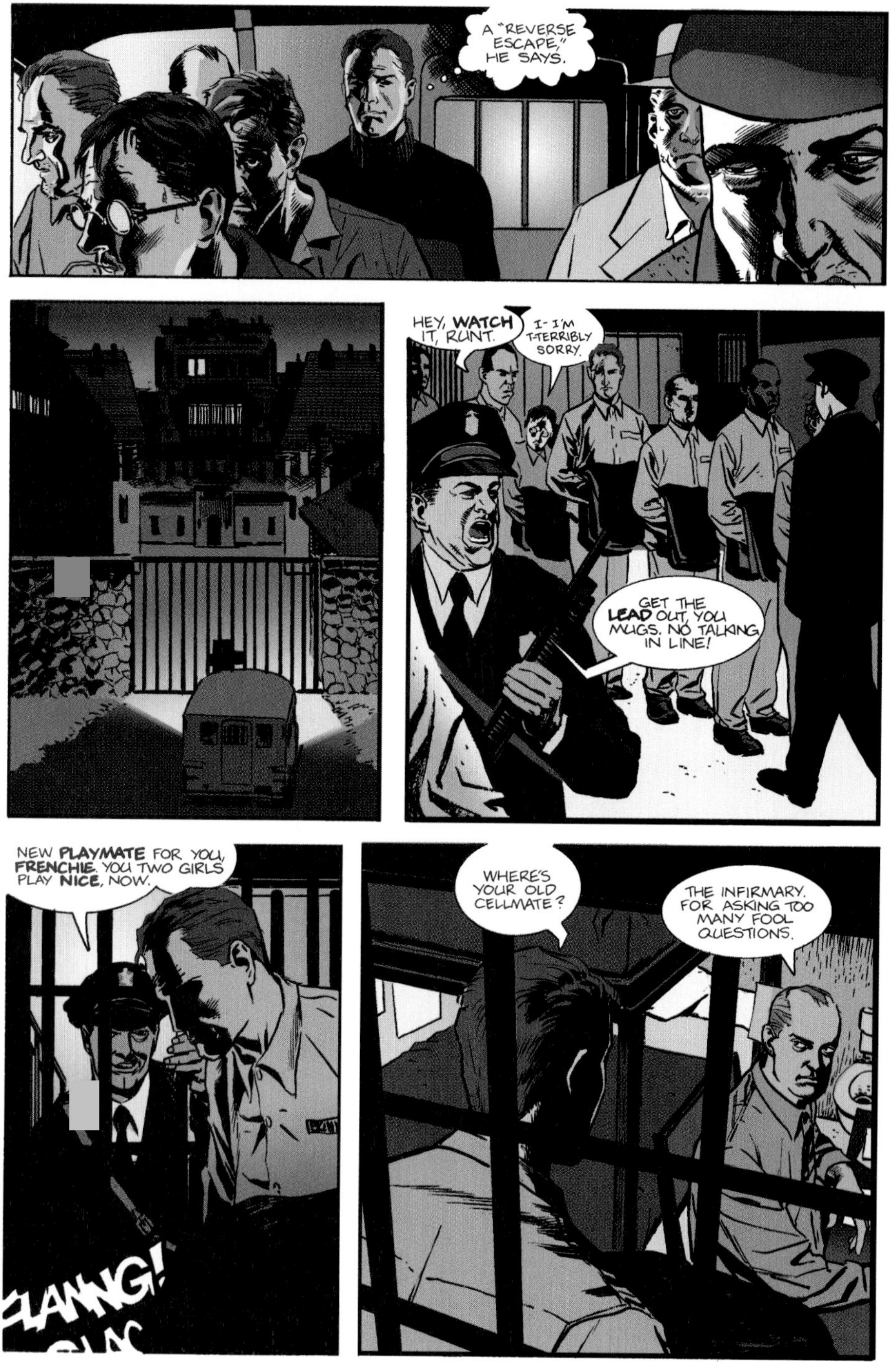
A "REVERSE ESCAPE," HE SAYS.
HEY, WATCH IT, RUNT.
I- I'M T-TERRIBLY SORRY.
GET THE LEAD OUT, YOU MUGS. NO TALKING IN LINE!
NEW PLAYMATE FOR YOU, FRENCHIE. YOU TWO GIRLS PLAY NICE, NOW.
CLANNG!
WHERE'S YOUR OLD CELLMATE?
THE INFIRMARY. FOR ASKING TOO MANY FOOL QUESTIONS.

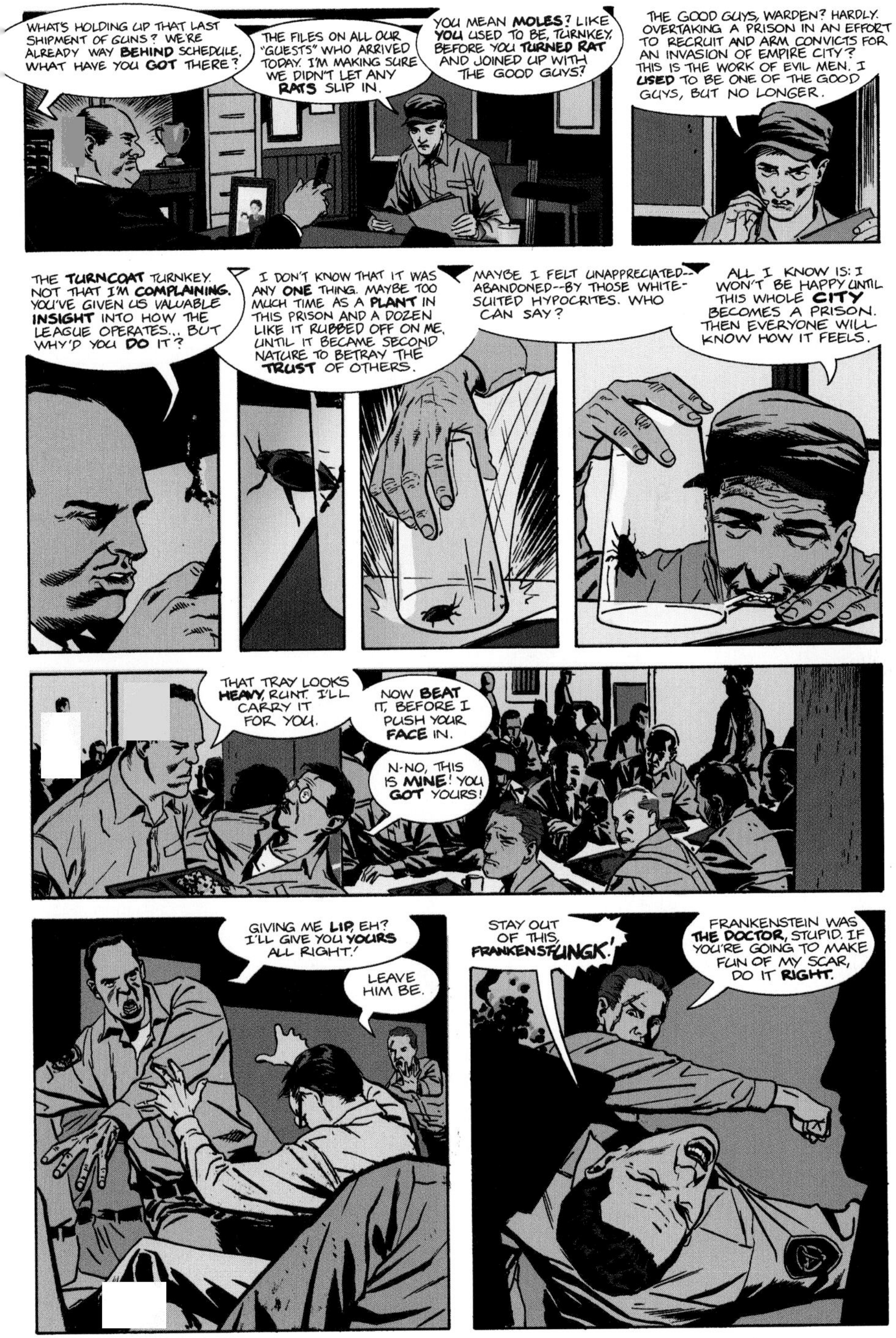
WHAT'S HOLDING UP THAT LAST SHIPMENT OF GUNS? WE'RE ALREADY WAY BEHIND SCHEDULE. WHAT HAVE YOU GOT THERE?
THE FILES ON ALL OUR "GUESTS" WHO ARRIVED TODAY. I'M MAKING SURE WE DIDN'T LET ANY RATS SLIP IN.
YOU MEAN MOLES? LIKE YOU USED TO BE, TURNKEY, BEFORE YOU TURNED RAT AND JOINED UP WITH THE GOOD GUYS?
THE GOOD GUYS, WARDEN? HARDLY. OVERTAKING A PRISON IN AN EFFORT TO RECRUIT AND ARM CONVICTS FOR AN INVASION OF EMPIRE CITY? THIS IS THE WORK OF EVIL MEN. I USED TO BE ONE OF THE GOOD GUYS, BUT NO LONGER.
THE TURNCOAT TURNKEY. NOT THAT I'M COMPLAINING. YOU'VE GIVEN US VALUABLE INSIGHT INTO HOW THE LEAGUE OPERATES... BUT WHY'D YOU DO IT?
I DON'T KNOW THAT IT WAS ANY ONE THING. MAYBE TOO MUCH TIME AS A PLANT IN THIS PRISON AND A DOZEN LIKE IT RUBBED OFF ON ME, UNTIL IT BECAME SECOND NATURE TO BETRAY THE TRUST OF OTHERS.
MAYBE I FELT UNAPPRECIATED-- ABANDONED--BY THOSE WHITE-SUITED HYPOCRITES. WHO CAN SAY?
ALL I KNOW IS: I WON'T BE HAPPY UNTIL THIS WHOLE CITY BECOMES A PRISON. THEN EVERYONE WILL KNOW HOW IT FEELS.
THAT TRAY LOOKS HEAVY, RUNT. I'LL CARRY IT FOR YOU.
NOW BEAT IT, BEFORE I PUSH YOUR FACE IN.
N-NO, THIS IS MINE! YOU GOT YOURS!
GIVING ME LIP, EH? I'LL GIVE YOU YOURS ALL RIGHT!
LEAVE HIM BE.
STAY OUT OF THIS, FRANKENSTUNGK!
FRANKENSTEIN WAS THE DOCTOR, STUPID. IF YOU'RE GOING TO MAKE FUN OF MY SCAR, DO IT RIGHT.

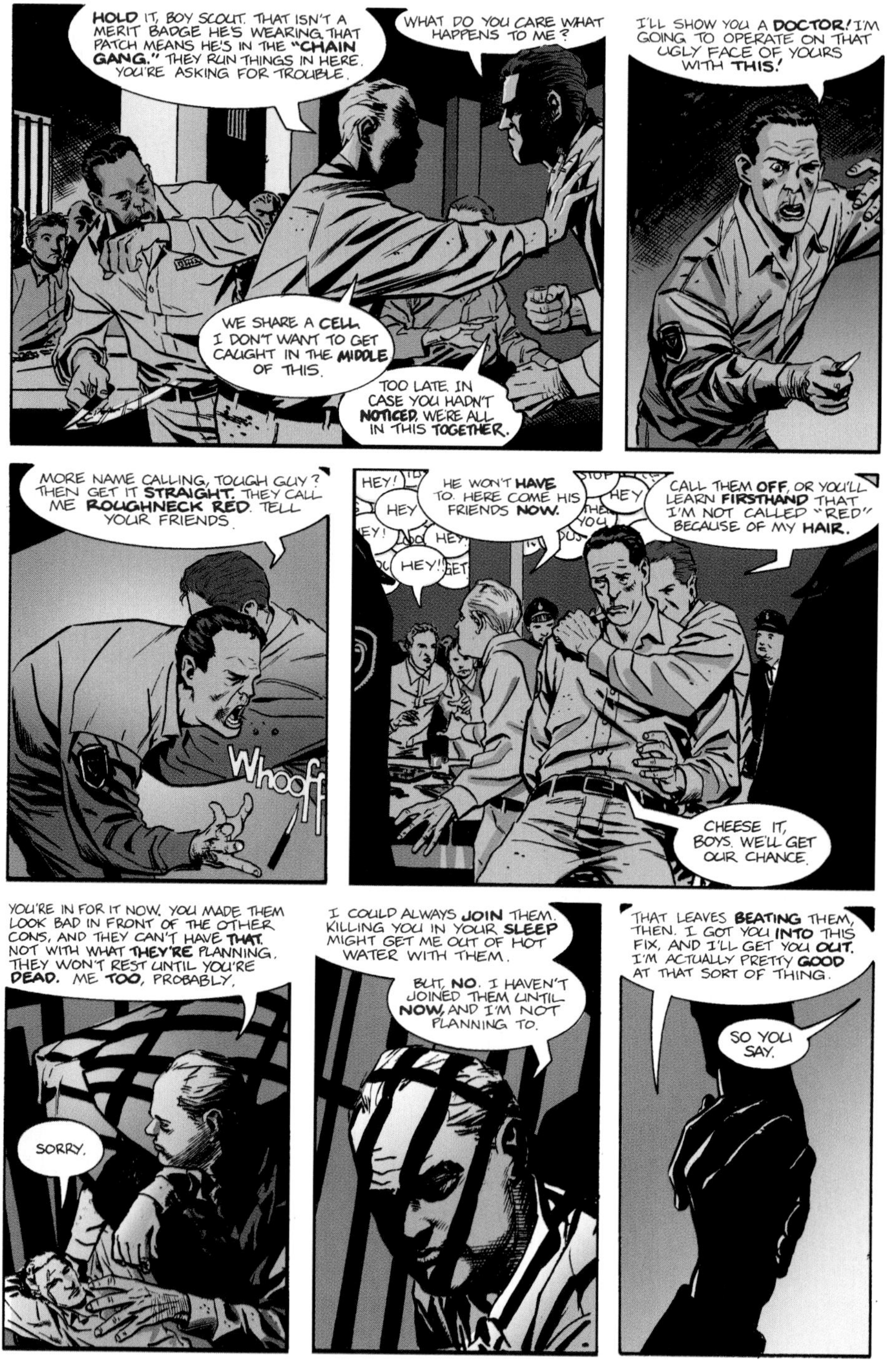
HOLD IT, BOY SCOUT. THAT ISN'T A MERIT BADGE HE'S WEARING. THAT PATCH MEANS HE'S IN THE "CHAIN GANG." THEY RUN THINGS IN HERE. YOU'RE ASKING FOR TROUBLE.
WHAT DO YOU CARE WHAT HAPPENS TO ME?
WE SHARE A CELL. I DON'T WANT TO GET CAUGHT IN THE MIDDLE OF THIS.
TOO LATE. IN CASE YOU HADN'T NOTICED, WE'RE ALL IN THIS TOGETHER.
I'LL SHOW YOU A DOCTOR! I'M GOING TO OPERATE ON THAT UGLY FACE OF YOURS WITH THIS!
MORE NAME CALLING, TOUGH GUY? THEN GET IT STRAIGHT. THEY CALL ME ROUGHNECK RED. TELL YOUR FRIENDS.
Whoof!
HEY!
HEY
HEY!!
HE WON'T HAVE TO. HERE COME HIS FRIENDS NOW.
HEY
CALL THEM OFF, OR YOU'LL LEARN FIRSTHAND THAT I'M NOT CALLED "RED" BECAUSE OF MY HAIR.
CHEESE IT, BOYS. WE'LL GET OUR CHANCE.
YOU'RE IN FOR IT NOW. YOU MADE THEM LOOK BAD IN FRONT OF THE OTHER CONS, AND THEY CAN'T HAVE THAT. NOT WITH WHAT THEY'RE PLANNING. THEY WON'T REST UNTIL YOU'RE DEAD. ME TOO, PROBABLY.
SORRY.
I COULD ALWAYS JOIN THEM. KILLING YOU IN YOUR SLEEP MIGHT GET ME OUT OF HOT WATER WITH THEM.
BUT, NO. I HAVEN'T JOINED THEM UNTIL NOW, AND I'M NOT PLANNING TO.
THAT LEAVES BEATING THEM, THEN. I GOT YOU INTO THIS FIX, AND I'LL GET YOU OUT. I'M ACTUALLY PRETTY GOOD AT THAT SORT OF THING.
SO YOU SAY.

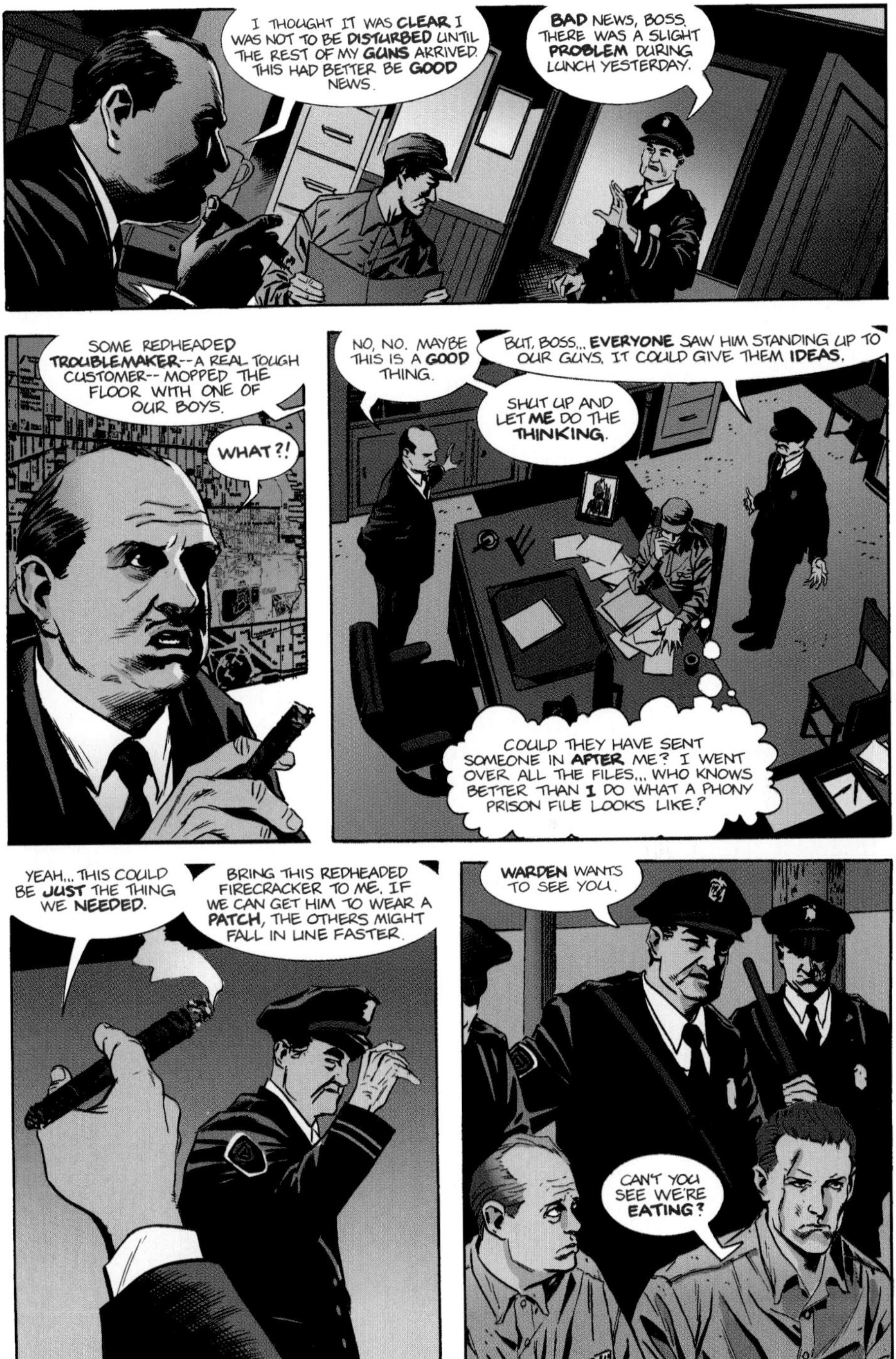
I THOUGHT IT WAS CLEAR I WAS NOT TO BE DISTURBED UNTIL THE REST OF MY GUNS ARRIVED. THIS HAD BETTER BE GOOD NEWS.
BAD NEWS, BOSS. THERE WAS A SLIGHT PROBLEM DURING LUNCH YESTERDAY.
SOME REDHEADED TROUBLEMAKER--A REAL TOUGH CUSTOMER-- MOPPED THE FLOOR WITH ONE OF OUR BOYS.
WHAT?!
NO, NO. MAYBE THIS IS A GOOD THING.
BUT, BOSS... EVERYONE SAW HIM STANDING UP TO OUR GUYS. IT COULD GIVE THEM IDEAS.
SHUT UP AND LET ME DO THE THINKING.
COULD THEY HAVE SENT SOMEONE IN AFTER ME? I WENT OVER ALL THE FILES... WHO KNOWS BETTER THAN I DO WHAT A PHONY PRISON FILE LOOKS LIKE?
YEAH... THIS COULD BE JUST THE THING WE NEEDED.
BRING THIS REDHEADED FIRECRACKER TO ME. IF WE CAN GET HIM TO WEAR A PATCH, THE OTHERS MIGHT FALL IN LINE FASTER.
WARDEN WANTS TO SEE YOU.
CAN'T YOU SEE WE'RE EATING?

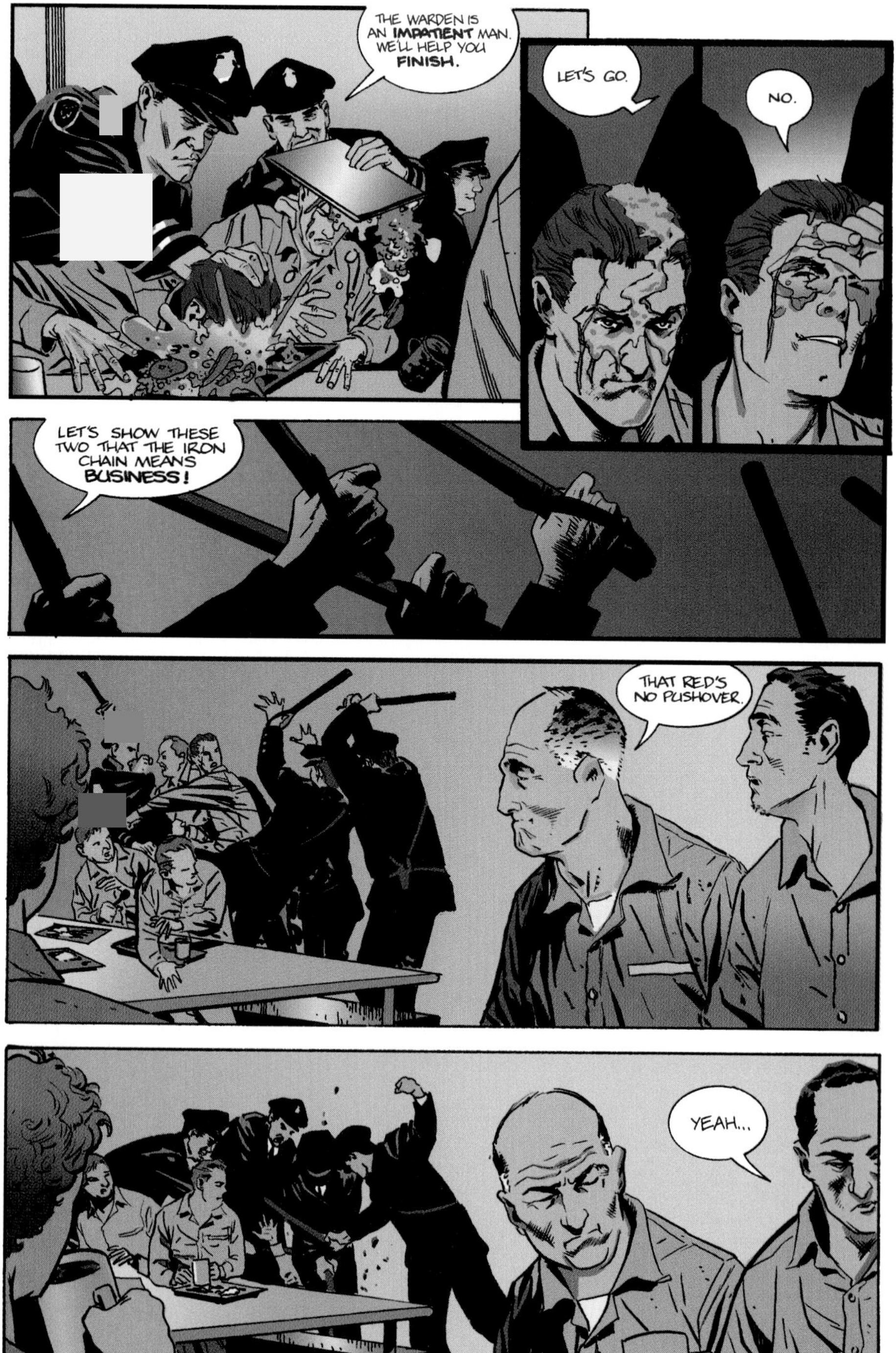
THE WARDEN IS AN IMPATIENT MAN. WE'LL HELP YOU FINISH.
LET'S GO.
NO.
LET'S SHOW THESE TWO THAT THE IRON CHAIN MEANS BUSINESS!
THAT RED'S NO PUSHOVER.
YEAH...

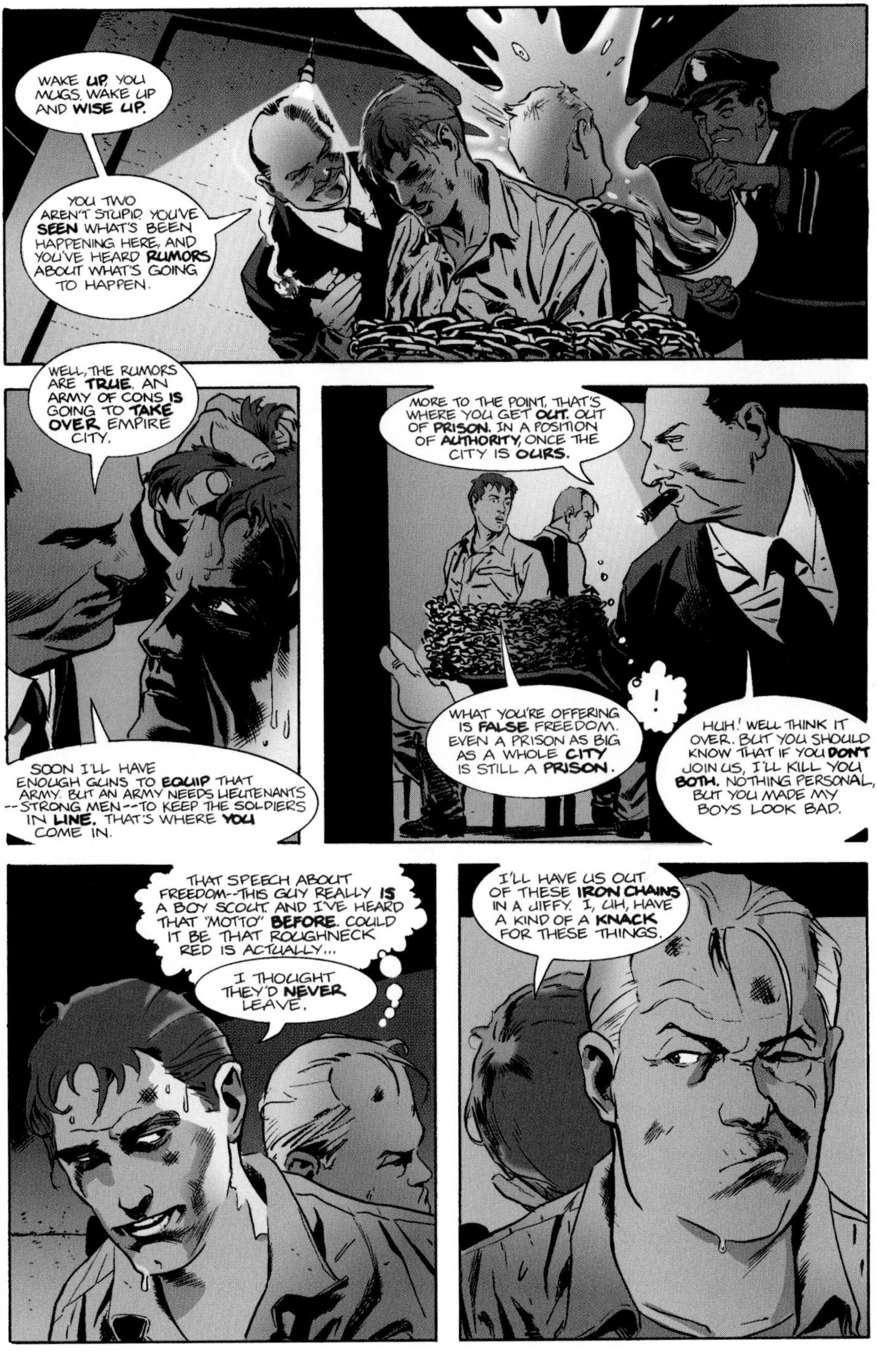
WAKE UP, YOU MUGS. WAKE UP AND WISE UP.
YOU TWO AREN'T STUPID. YOU'VE SEEN WHAT'S BEEN HAPPENING HERE, AND YOU'VE HEARD RUMORS ABOUT WHAT'S GOING TO HAPPEN.
WELL, THE RUMORS ARE TRUE. AN ARMY OF CONS IS GOING TO TAKE OVER EMPIRE CITY.
SOON I'LL HAVE ENOUGH GUNS TO EQUIP THAT ARMY. BUT AN ARMY NEEDS LIEUTENANTS --STRONG MEN--TO KEEP THE SOLDIERS IN LINE. THAT'S WHERE YOU COME IN.
MORE TO THE POINT, THAT'S WHERE YOU GET OUT. OUT OF PRISON. IN A POSITION OF AUTHORITY, ONCE THE CITY IS OURS.
WHAT YOU'RE OFFERING IS FALSE FREEDOM. EVEN A PRISON AS BIG AS A WHOLE CITY IS STILL A PRISON.
!
HUH! WELL THINK IT OVER. BUT YOU SHOULD KNOW THAT IF YOU DON'T JOIN US, I'LL KILL YOU BOTH. NOTHING PERSONAL, BUT YOU MADE MY BOYS LOOK BAD.
THAT SPEECH ABOUT FREEDOM--THIS GUY REALLY IS A BOY SCOUT. AND I'VE HEARD THAT "MOTTO" BEFORE. COULD IT BE THAT ROUGHNECK RED IS ACTUALLY...
I THOUGHT THEY'D NEVER LEAVE.
I'LL HAVE US OUT OF THESE IRON CHAINS IN A JIFFY. I, UH, HAVE A KIND OF A KNACK FOR THESE THINGS.

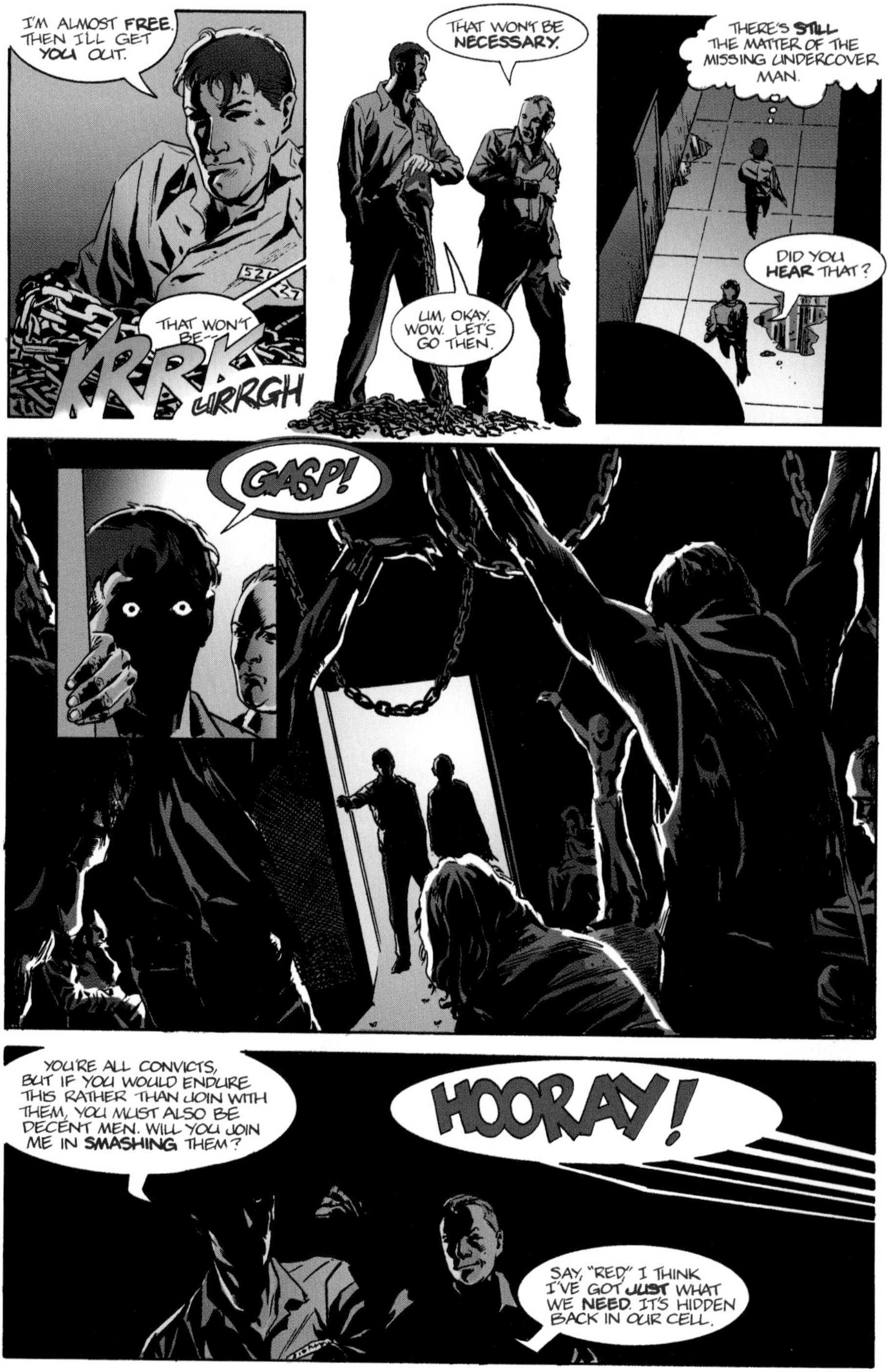
I'M ALMOST **FREE**. THEN I'LL GET **YOU** OUT.
THAT WON'T BE--
KRRK URRGH
THAT WON'T BE **NECESSARY**.
UM, OKAY. WOW. LET'S GO THEN.
THERE'S **STILL** THE MATTER OF THE MISSING UNDERCOVER MAN.
DID YOU **HEAR** THAT?
GASP!
YOU'RE ALL CONVICTS, BUT IF YOU WOULD ENDURE THIS RATHER THAN JOIN WITH THEM, YOU MUST ALSO BE DECENT MEN. WILL YOU JOIN ME IN **SMASHING** THEM?
HOORAY!
SAY, "RED," I THINK I'VE GOT **JUST** WHAT WE **NEED**. IT'S HIDDEN BACK IN OUR CELL.

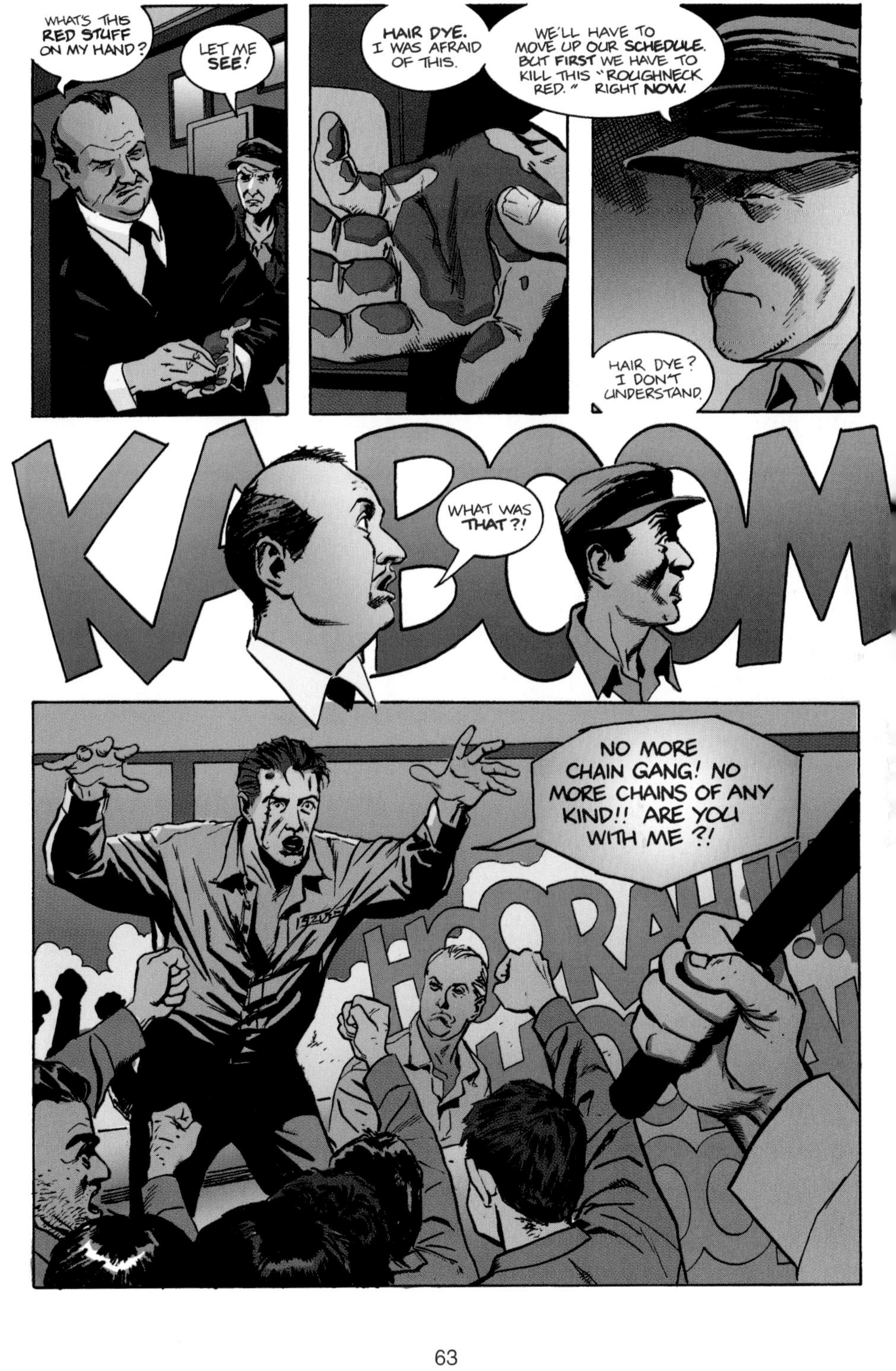
WHAT'S THIS RED STUFF ON MY HAND?
LET ME SEE!
HAIR DYE. I WAS AFRAID OF THIS.
WE'LL HAVE TO MOVE UP OUR SCHEDULE. BUT FIRST WE HAVE TO KILL THIS "ROUGHNECK RED." RIGHT NOW.
HAIR DYE? I DON'T UNDERSTAND.
KABOOM
WHAT WAS THAT?!
NO MORE CHAIN GANG! NO MORE CHAINS OF ANY KIND!! ARE YOU WITH ME?!

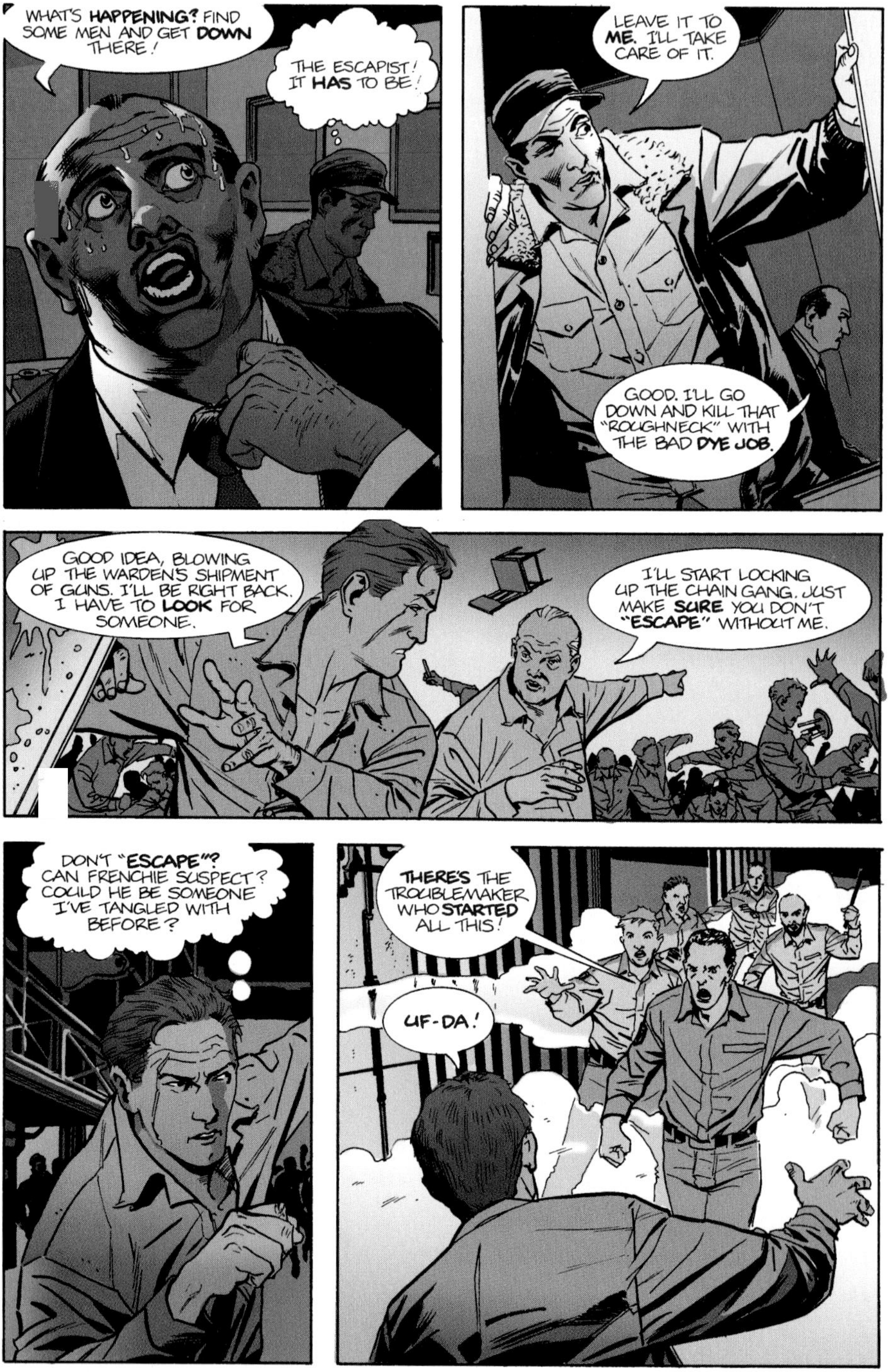
WHAT'S HAPPENING? FIND SOME MEN AND GET DOWN THERE!
THE ESCAPIST! IT HAS TO BE!
LEAVE IT TO ME. I'LL TAKE CARE OF IT.
GOOD. I'LL GO DOWN AND KILL THAT "ROUGHNECK" WITH THE BAD DYE JOB.
GOOD IDEA, BLOWING UP THE WARDEN'S SHIPMENT OF GUNS. I'LL BE RIGHT BACK. I HAVE TO LOOK FOR SOMEONE.
I'LL START LOCKING UP THE CHAIN GANG. JUST MAKE SURE YOU DON'T "ESCAPE" WITHOUT ME.
DON'T "ESCAPE"? CAN FRENCHIE SUSPECT? COULD HE BE SOMEONE I'VE TANGLED WITH BEFORE?
THERE'S THE TROUBLEMAKER WHO STARTED ALL THIS!
UF-DA!

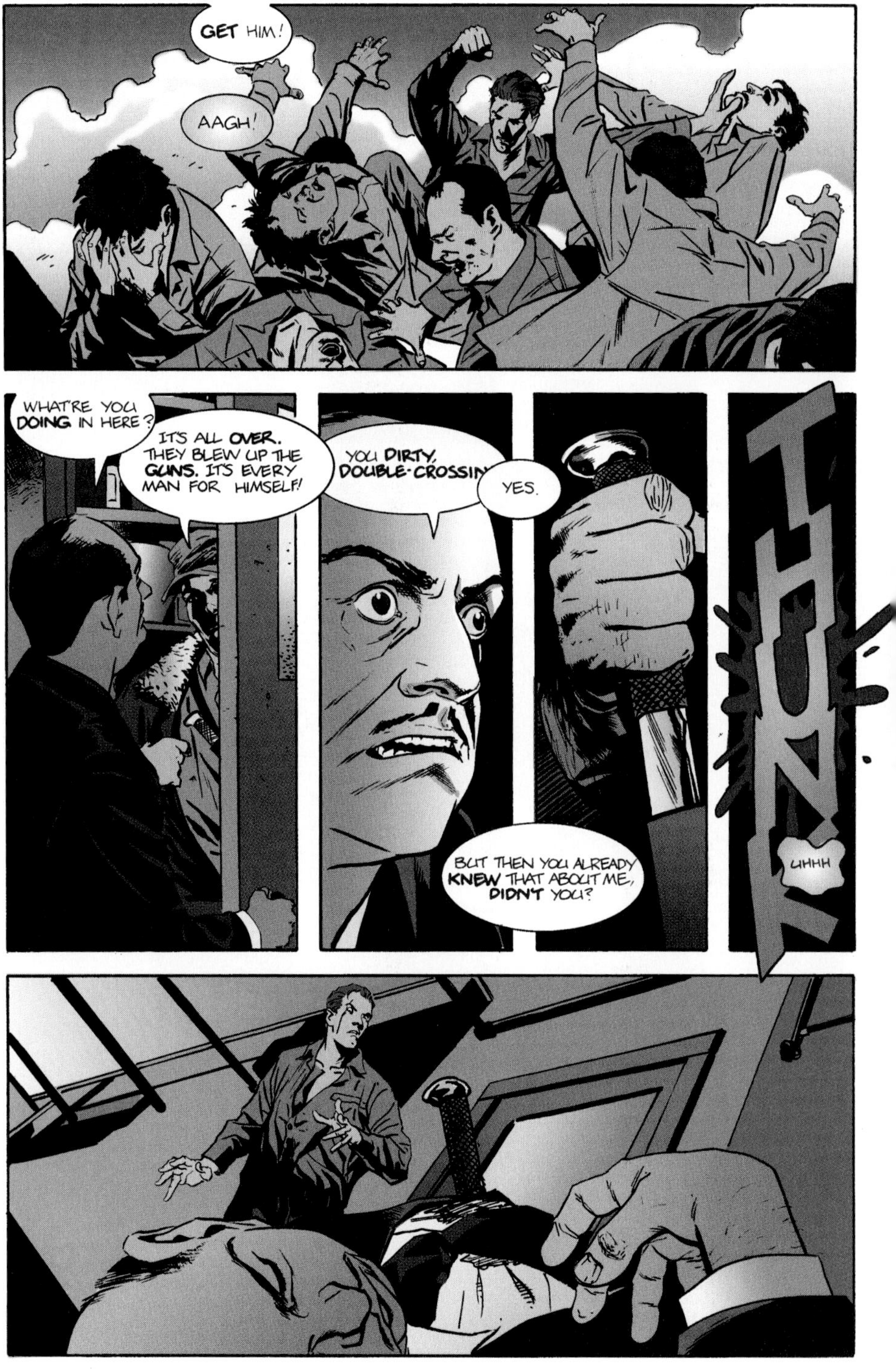

GET HIM!
AAGH!
WHAT'RE YOU DOING IN HERE?
IT'S ALL OVER. THEY BLEW UP THE GUNS. IT'S EVERY MAN FOR HIMSELF!
YOU DIRTY, DOUBLE-CROSSIN
YES.
BUT THEN YOU ALREADY KNEW THAT ABOUT ME, DIDN'T YOU?
THUNK
UHHH

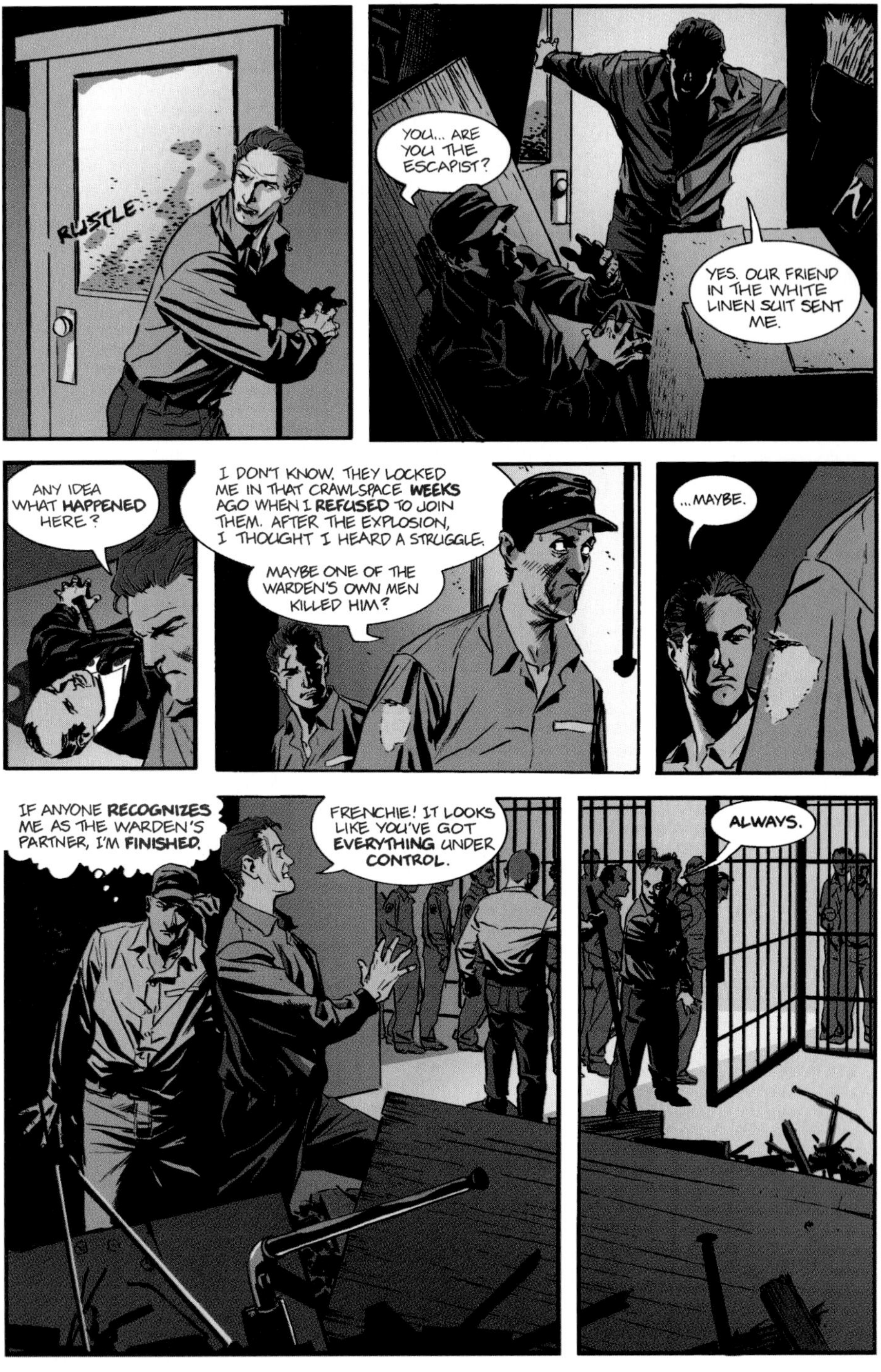
RUSTLE
YOU... ARE YOU THE ESCAPIST?
YES. OUR FRIEND IN THE WHITE LINEN SUIT SENT ME.
ANY IDEA WHAT HAPPENED HERE?
I DON'T KNOW. THEY LOCKED ME IN THAT CRAWLSPACE WEEKS AGO WHEN I REFUSED TO JOIN THEM. AFTER THE EXPLOSION, I THOUGHT I HEARD A STRUGGLE.
MAYBE ONE OF THE WARDEN'S OWN MEN KILLED HIM?
...MAYBE.
IF ANYONE RECOGNIZES ME AS THE WARDEN'S PARTNER, I'M FINISHED.
FRENCHIE! IT LOOKS LIKE YOU'VE GOT EVERYTHING UNDER CONTROL.
ALWAYS.

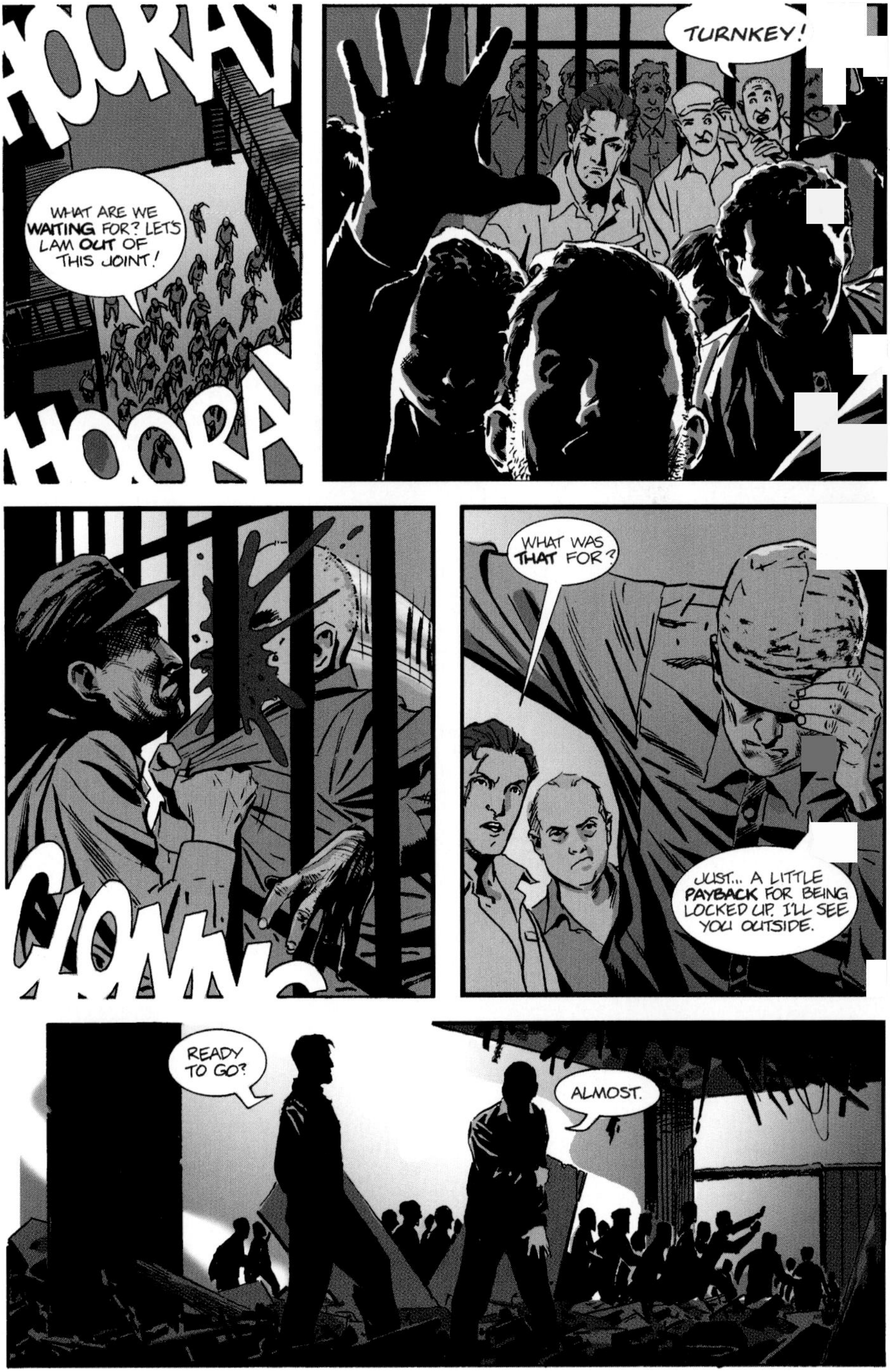
HOORAY
WHAT ARE WE WAITING FOR? LET'S LAM OUT OF THIS JOINT!
HOORA
TURNKEY!
CLOMMG
WHAT WAS THAT FOR?
JUST... A LITTLE PAYBACK FOR BEING LOCKED UP. I'LL SEE YOU OUTSIDE.
READY TO GO?
ALMOST.

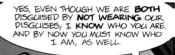

THIS IS FOR YOU.

A LITTLE SOUVENIR FROM OUR **LAST** ENCOUNTER. I'VE KEPT IT EVER SINCE.

YES, EVEN THOUGH WE ARE **BOTH** DISGUISED BY **NOT WEARING** OUR DISGUISES, I **KNOW** WHO YOU ARE. AND BY NOW YOU MUST KNOW WHO I AM, AS WELL.

THE SABOTEUR. THAT BOMB YOU MADE SHOULD HAVE BEEN MY FIRST CLUE.

YOU **WERE** CLUELESS. THIS WOULD HAVE BEEN OUR **FINAL SHOWDOWN** IF I HADN'T **BROKEN** MY ARM IN **THREE PLACES** WRIGGLING OUT OF THOSE **ACCURSED** CHAINS. HOW **DO** YOU DO IT?

BUT WHY ARE YOU EVEN **HERE**? WHY DID YOU HELP ME STOP THE IRON CHAIN?

BECAUSE THIS IS **MY** CITY. NOT **THEIRS**! NOT EVEN **YOURS**! EMPIRE CITY **BELONGS TO ME**!

YOU'RE THE **MAN** OF THE **HOUR**, RED!

WAIT!

HOORAY HOORAY

68

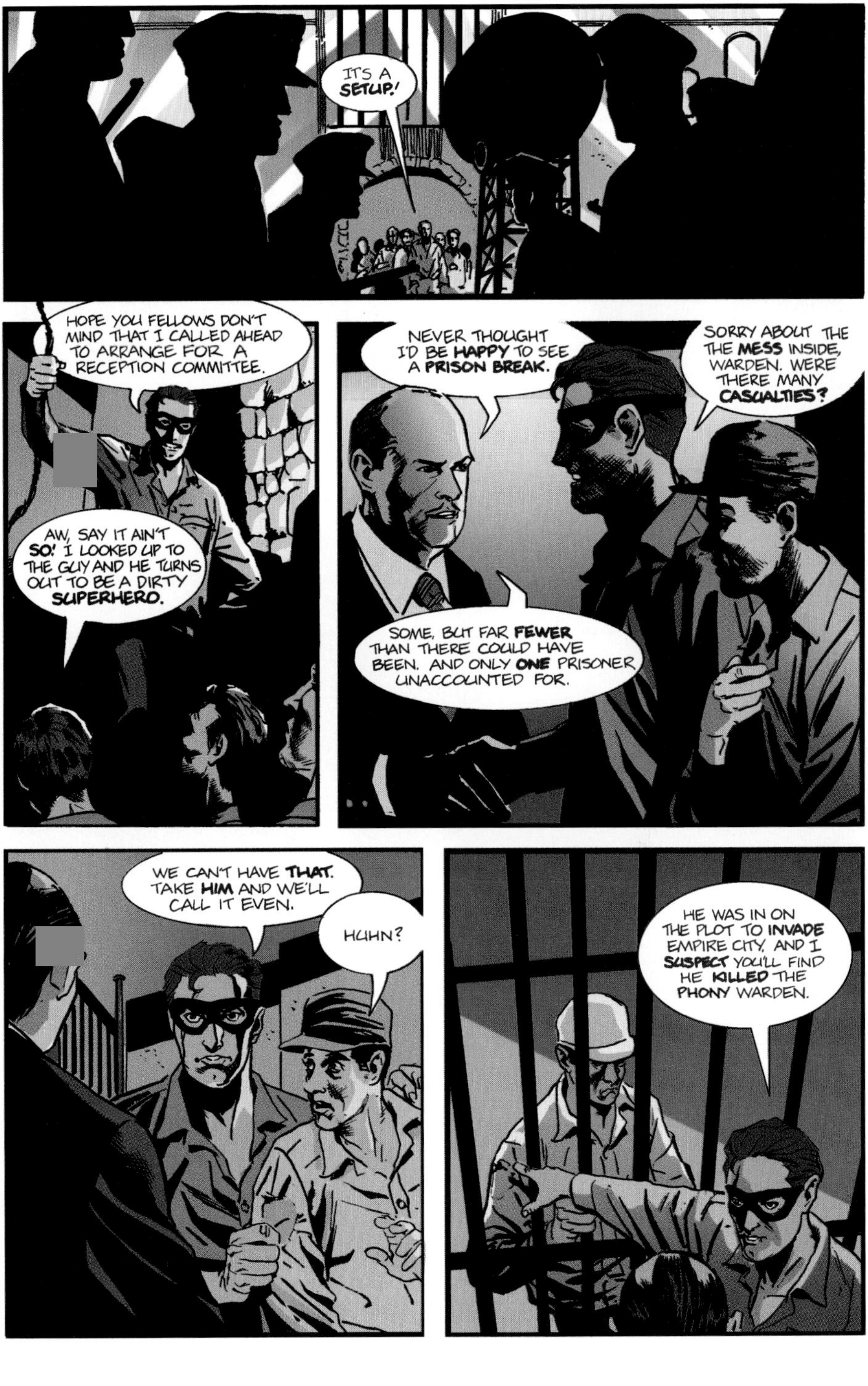

IT'S A SETUP!
HOPE YOU FELLOWS DON'T MIND THAT I CALLED AHEAD TO ARRANGE FOR A RECEPTION COMMITTEE.
AW, SAY IT AIN'T SO! I LOOKED UP TO THE GUY AND HE TURNS OUT TO BE A DIRTY SUPERHERO.
NEVER THOUGHT I'D BE HAPPY TO SEE A PRISON BREAK.
SORRY ABOUT THE THE MESS INSIDE, WARDEN. WERE THERE MANY CASUALTIES?
SOME, BUT FAR FEWER THAN THERE COULD HAVE BEEN. AND ONLY ONE PRISONER UNACCOUNTED FOR.
WE CAN'T HAVE THAT. TAKE HIM AND WE'LL CALL IT EVEN.
HUHN?
HE WAS IN ON THE PLOT TO INVADE EMPIRE CITY, AND I SUSPECT YOU'LL FIND HE KILLED THE PHONY WARDEN.

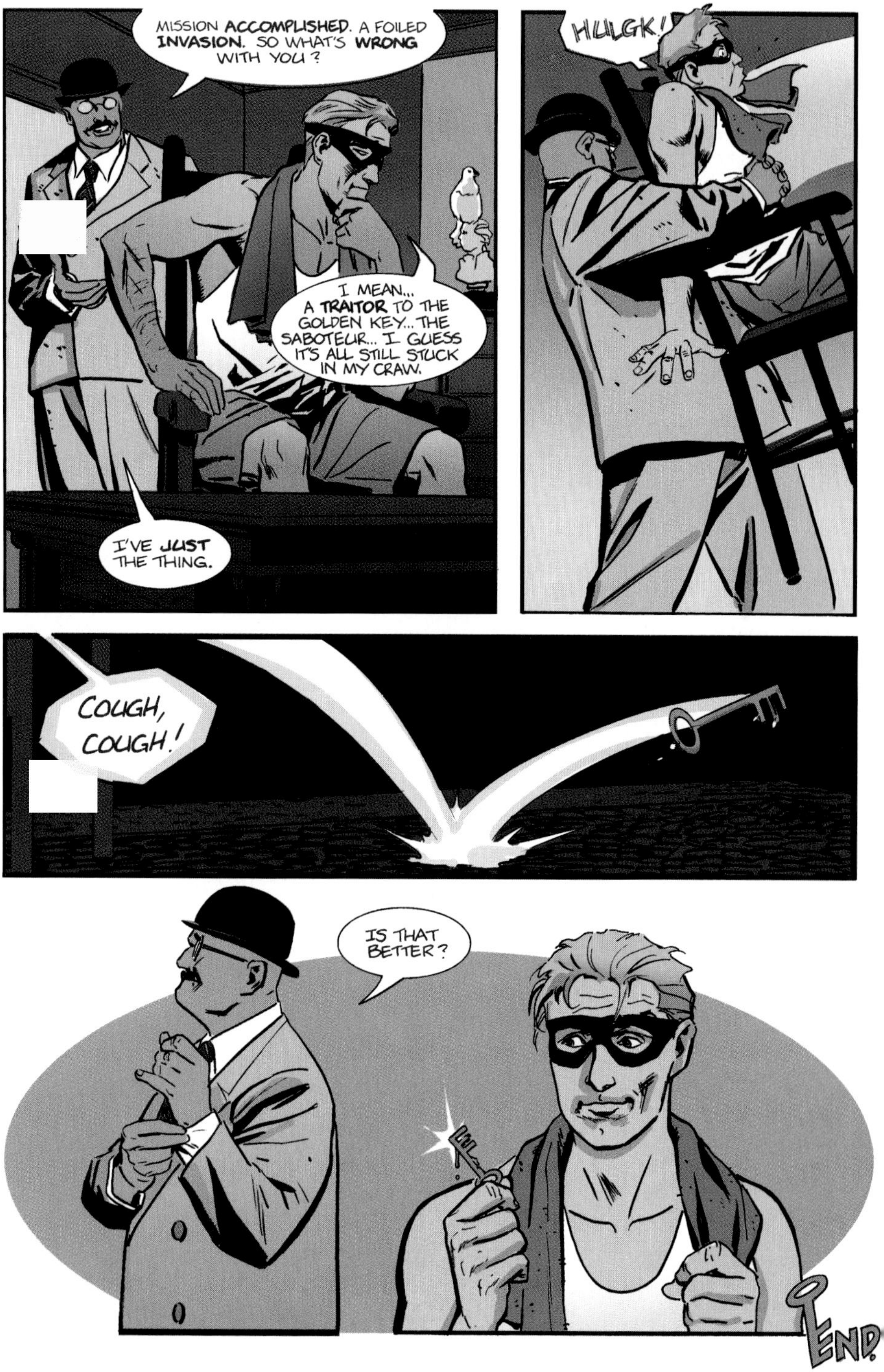
MISSION ACCOMPLISHED. A FOILED INVASION. SO WHAT'S WRONG WITH YOU?
I MEAN... A TRAITOR TO THE GOLDEN KEY... THE SABOTEUR... I GUESS IT'S ALL STILL STUCK IN MY CRAW.
I'VE JUST THE THING.
HULGK!
COUGH, COUGH!
IS THAT BETTER?
END.

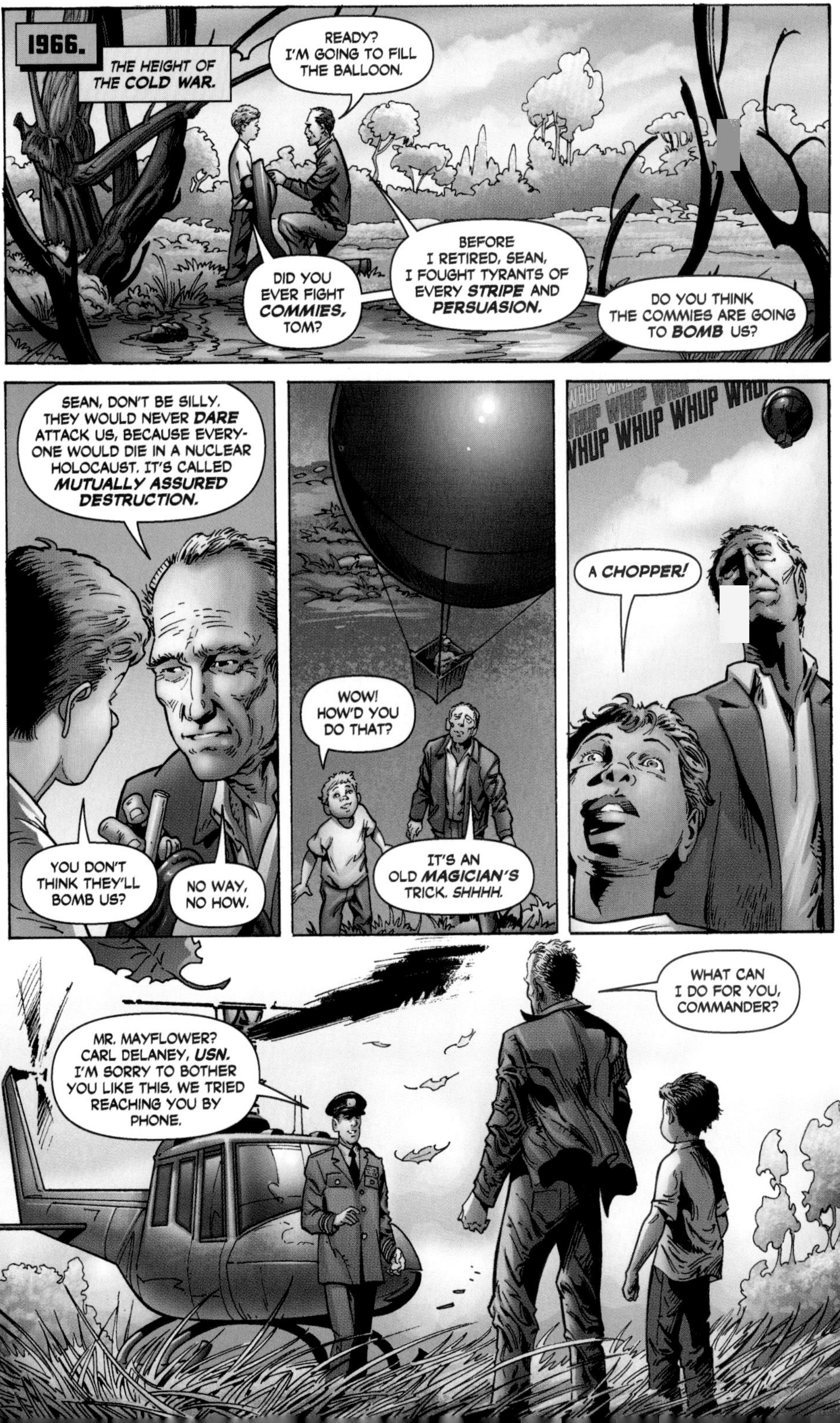
1966.
THE HEIGHT OF THE COLD WAR.
READY? I'M GOING TO FILL THE BALLOON.
DID YOU EVER FIGHT COMMIES, TOM?
BEFORE I RETIRED, SEAN, I FOUGHT TYRANTS OF EVERY STRIPE AND PERSUASION.
DO YOU THINK THE COMMIES ARE GOING TO BOMB US?
SEAN, DON'T BE SILLY. THEY WOULD NEVER DARE ATTACK US, BECAUSE EVERY-ONE WOULD DIE IN A NUCLEAR HOLOCAUST. IT'S CALLED MUTUALLY ASSURED DESTRUCTION.
YOU DON'T THINK THEY'LL BOMB US?
NO WAY, NO HOW.
WOW! HOW'D YOU DO THAT?
IT'S AN OLD MAGICIAN'S TRICK. SHHHH.
WHUP WHUP WHUP WHUP
A CHOPPER!
WHAT CAN I DO FOR YOU, COMMANDER?
MR. MAYFLOWER? CARL DELANEY, USN. I'M SORRY TO BOTHER YOU LIKE THIS. WE TRIED REACHING YOU BY PHONE.

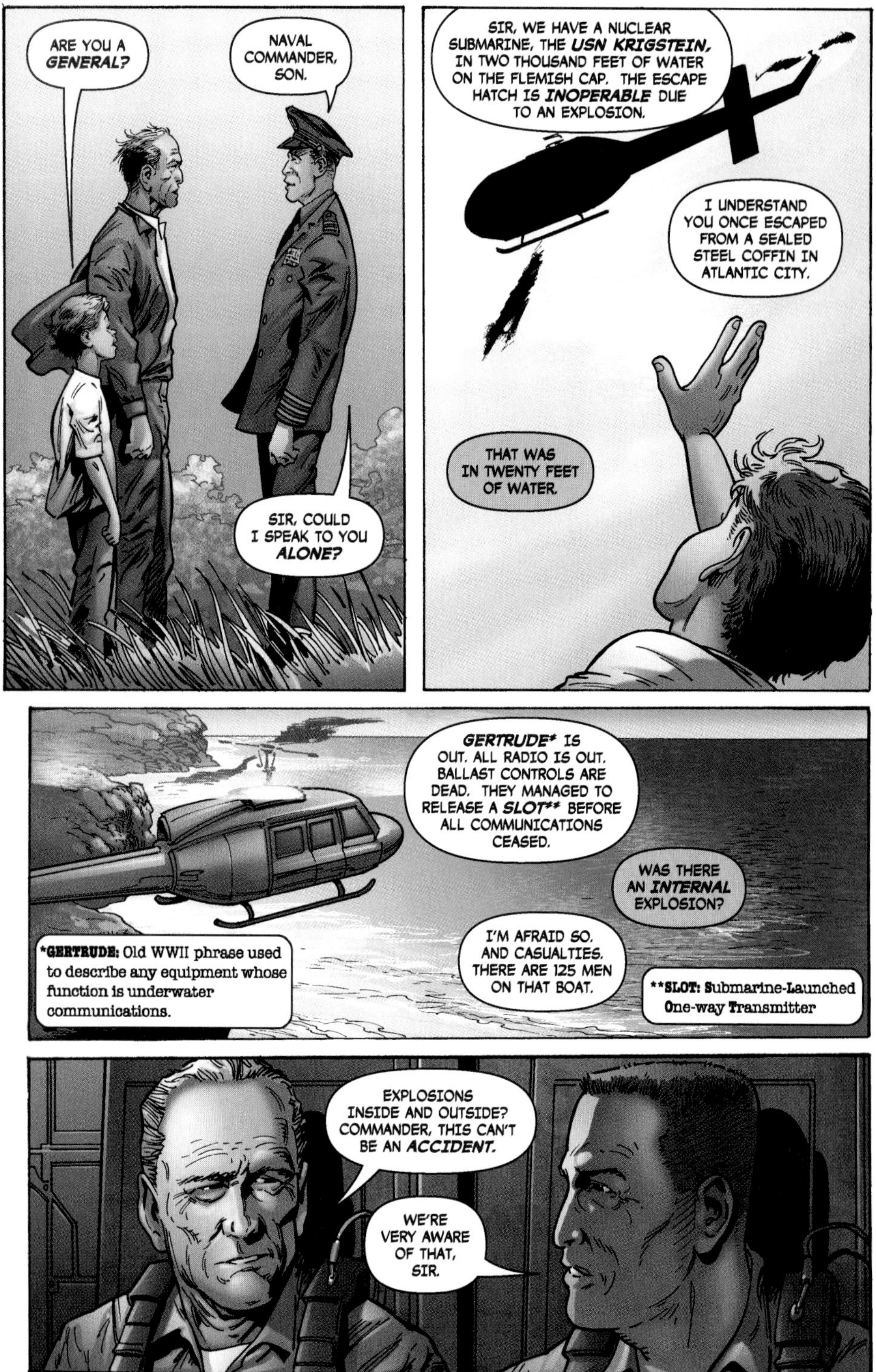
ARE YOU A GENERAL?
NAVAL COMMANDER, SON.
SIR, COULD I SPEAK TO YOU ALONE?
SIR, WE HAVE A NUCLEAR SUBMARINE, THE USN KRIGSTEIN, IN TWO THOUSAND FEET OF WATER ON THE FLEMISH CAP. THE ESCAPE HATCH IS INOPERABLE DUE TO AN EXPLOSION.
I UNDERSTAND YOU ONCE ESCAPED FROM A SEALED STEEL COFFIN IN ATLANTIC CITY.
THAT WAS IN TWENTY FEET OF WATER.
GERTRUDE* IS OUT. ALL RADIO IS OUT. BALLAST CONTROLS ARE DEAD. THEY MANAGED TO RELEASE A SLOT** BEFORE ALL COMMUNICATIONS CEASED.
WAS THERE AN INTERNAL EXPLOSION?
I'M AFRAID SO. AND CASUALTIES. THERE ARE 125 MEN ON THAT BOAT.
*GERTRUDE: Old WWII phrase used to describe any equipment whose function is underwater communications.
**SLOT: Submarine-Launched One-way Transmitter
EXPLOSIONS INSIDE AND OUTSIDE? COMMANDER, THIS CAN'T BE AN ACCIDENT.
WE'RE VERY AWARE OF THAT, SIR.

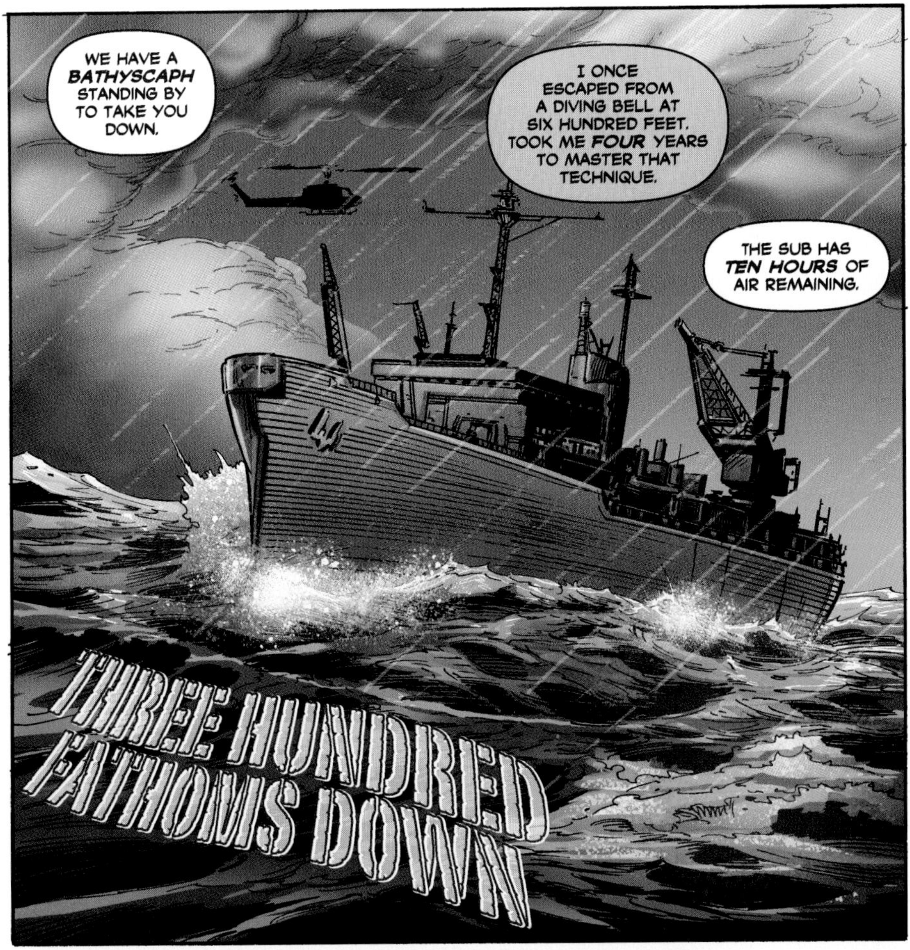
WE HAVE A BATHYSCAPH STANDING BY TO TAKE YOU DOWN.
I ONCE ESCAPED FROM A DIVING BELL AT SIX HUNDRED FEET. TOOK ME FOUR YEARS TO MASTER THAT TECHNIQUE.
THE SUB HAS TEN HOURS OF AIR REMAINING.
THREE HUNDRED FATHOMS DOWN

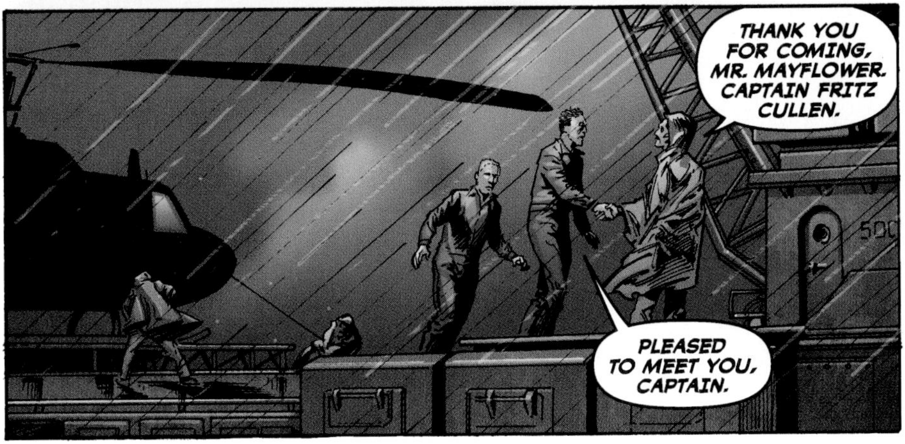
THANK YOU FOR COMING, MR. MAYFLOWER. CAPTAIN FRITZ CULLEN.
PLEASED TO MEET YOU, CAPTAIN.

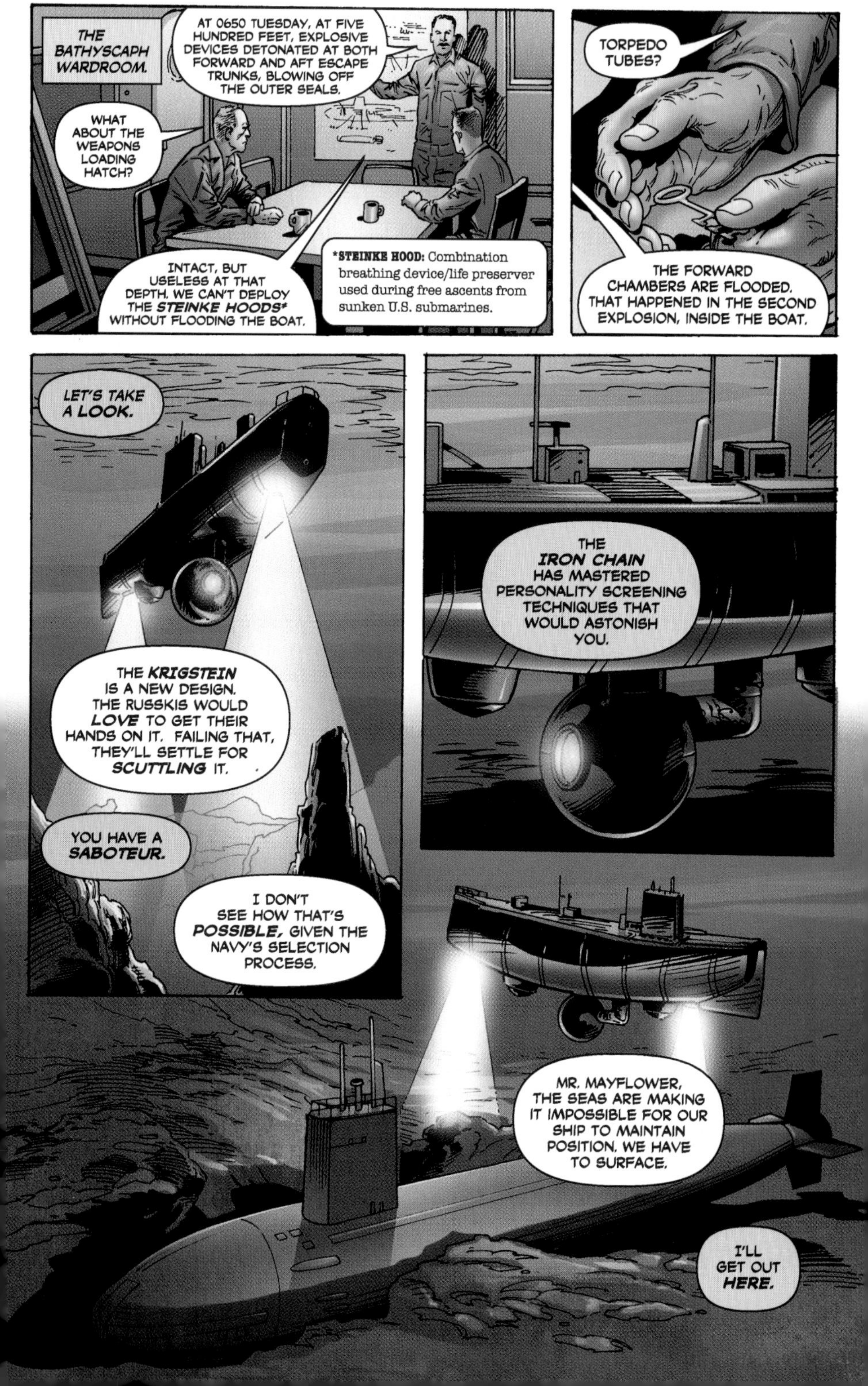
THE BATHYSCAPH WARDROOM.
AT 0650 TUESDAY, AT FIVE HUNDRED FEET, EXPLOSIVE DEVICES DETONATED AT BOTH FORWARD AND AFT ESCAPE TRUNKS, BLOWING OFF THE OUTER SEALS.
WHAT ABOUT THE WEAPONS LOADING HATCH?
INTACT, BUT USELESS AT THAT DEPTH. WE CAN'T DEPLOY THE STEINKE HOODS* WITHOUT FLOODING THE BOAT.
*STEINKE HOOD: Combination breathing device/life preserver used during free ascents from sunken U.S. submarines.
TORPEDO TUBES?
THE FORWARD CHAMBERS ARE FLOODED. THAT HAPPENED IN THE SECOND EXPLOSION, INSIDE THE BOAT.
LET'S TAKE A LOOK.
THE KRIGSTEIN IS A NEW DESIGN. THE RUSSKIS WOULD LOVE TO GET THEIR HANDS ON IT. FAILING THAT, THEY'LL SETTLE FOR SCUTTLING IT.
YOU HAVE A SABOTEUR.
I DON'T SEE HOW THAT'S POSSIBLE, GIVEN THE NAVY'S SELECTION PROCESS.
THE IRON CHAIN HAS MASTERED PERSONALITY SCREENING TECHNIQUES THAT WOULD ASTONISH YOU.
MR. MAYFLOWER, THE SEAS ARE MAKING IT IMPOSSIBLE FOR OUR SHIP TO MAINTAIN POSITION. WE HAVE TO SURFACE.
I'LL GET OUT HERE.

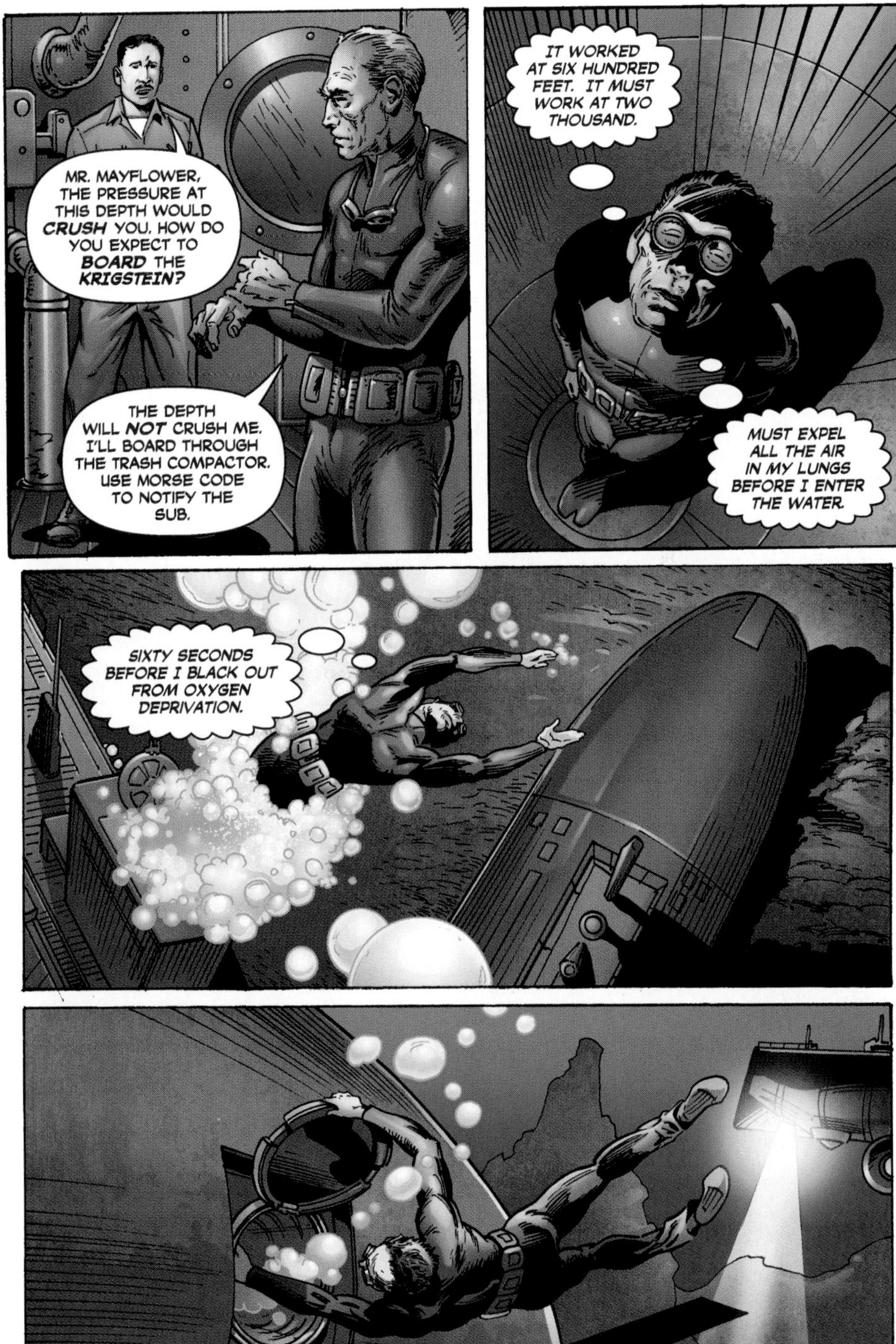
MR. MAYFLOWER, THE PRESSURE AT THIS DEPTH WOULD **CRUSH** YOU. HOW DO YOU EXPECT TO **BOARD** THE **KRIGSTEIN?**
THE DEPTH WILL **NOT** CRUSH ME. I'LL BOARD THROUGH THE TRASH COMPACTOR. USE MORSE CODE TO NOTIFY THE SUB.
IT WORKED AT SIX HUNDRED FEET. IT MUST WORK AT TWO THOUSAND.
MUST EXPEL ALL THE AIR IN MY LUNGS BEFORE I ENTER THE WATER.
SIXTY SECONDS BEFORE I BLACK OUT FROM OXYGEN DEPRIVATION.

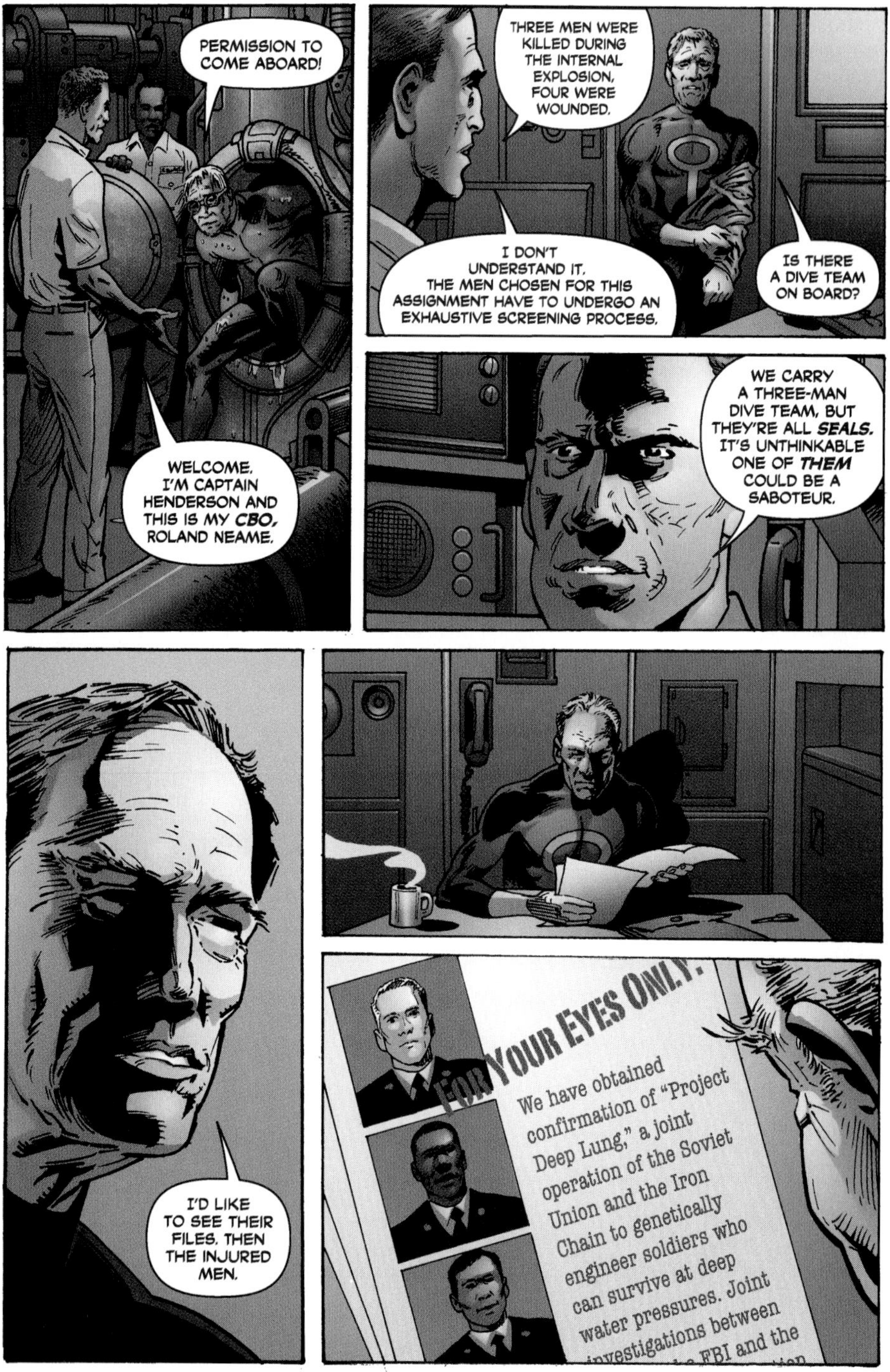
PERMISSION TO COME ABOARD!
WELCOME. I'M CAPTAIN HENDERSON AND THIS IS MY *CBO,* ROLAND NEAME.
THREE MEN WERE KILLED DURING THE INTERNAL EXPLOSION, FOUR WERE WOUNDED.
I DON'T UNDERSTAND IT. THE MEN CHOSEN FOR THIS ASSIGNMENT HAVE TO UNDERGO AN EXHAUSTIVE SCREENING PROCESS.
IS THERE A DIVE TEAM ON BOARD?
WE CARRY A THREE-MAN DIVE TEAM, BUT THEY'RE ALL *SEALS.* IT'S UNTHINKABLE ONE OF *THEM* COULD BE A SABOTEUR.
I'D LIKE TO SEE THEIR FILES. THEN THE INJURED MEN.
FOR YOUR EYES ONLY.
We have obtained confirmation of "Project Deep Lung," a joint operation of the Soviet Union and the Iron Chain to genetically engineer soldiers who can survive at deep water pressures. Joint investigations between

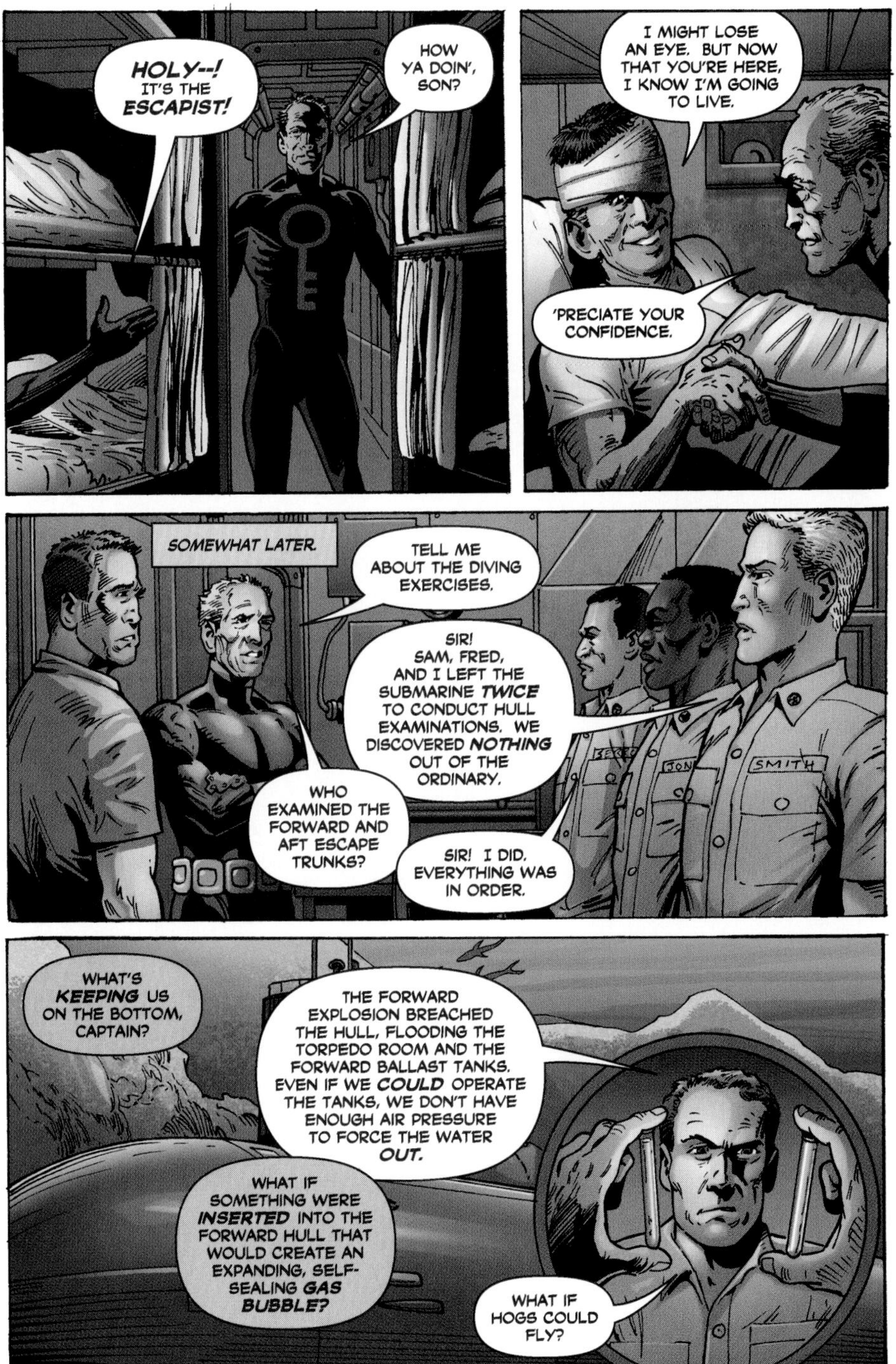
HOLY--! IT'S THE ESCAPIST!
HOW YA DOIN', SON?
I MIGHT LOSE AN EYE. BUT NOW THAT YOU'RE HERE, I KNOW I'M GOING TO LIVE.
'PRECIATE YOUR CONFIDENCE.
SOMEWHAT LATER.
TELL ME ABOUT THE DIVING EXERCISES.
SIR! SAM, FRED, AND I LEFT THE SUBMARINE TWICE TO CONDUCT HULL EXAMINATIONS. WE DISCOVERED NOTHING OUT OF THE ORDINARY.
SMITH
WHO EXAMINED THE FORWARD AND AFT ESCAPE TRUNKS?
SIR! I DID. EVERYTHING WAS IN ORDER.
WHAT'S KEEPING US ON THE BOTTOM, CAPTAIN?
THE FORWARD EXPLOSION BREACHED THE HULL, FLOODING THE TORPEDO ROOM AND THE FORWARD BALLAST TANKS. EVEN IF WE COULD OPERATE THE TANKS, WE DON'T HAVE ENOUGH AIR PRESSURE TO FORCE THE WATER OUT.
WHAT IF SOMETHING WERE INSERTED INTO THE FORWARD HULL THAT WOULD CREATE AN EXPANDING, SELF-SEALING GAS BUBBLE?
WHAT IF HOGS COULD FLY?

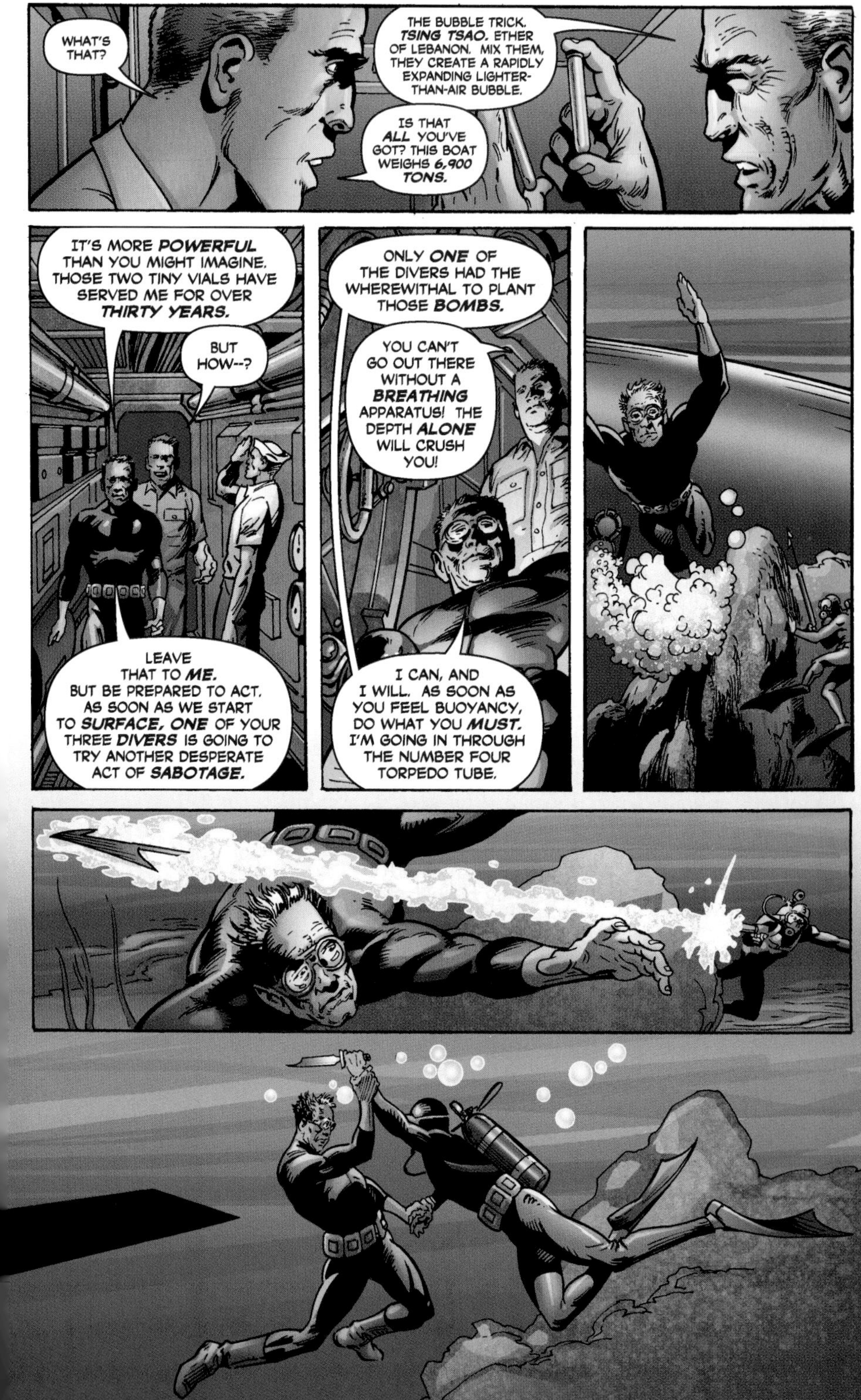
WHAT'S THAT?
THE BUBBLE TRICK. TSING TSAO. ETHER OF LEBANON. MIX THEM, THEY CREATE A RAPIDLY EXPANDING LIGHTER-THAN-AIR BUBBLE.
IS THAT ALL YOU'VE GOT? THIS BOAT WEIGHS 6,900 TONS.
IT'S MORE POWERFUL THAN YOU MIGHT IMAGINE. THOSE TWO TINY VIALS HAVE SERVED ME FOR OVER THIRTY YEARS.
BUT HOW--?
LEAVE THAT TO ME. BUT BE PREPARED TO ACT. AS SOON AS WE START TO SURFACE, ONE OF YOUR THREE DIVERS IS GOING TO TRY ANOTHER DESPERATE ACT OF SABOTAGE.
ONLY ONE OF THE DIVERS HAD THE WHEREWITHAL TO PLANT THOSE BOMBS.
YOU CAN'T GO OUT THERE WITHOUT A BREATHING APPARATUS! THE DEPTH ALONE WILL CRUSH YOU!
I CAN, AND I WILL. AS SOON AS YOU FEEL BUOYANCY, DO WHAT YOU MUST. I'M GOING IN THROUGH THE NUMBER FOUR TORPEDO TUBE.

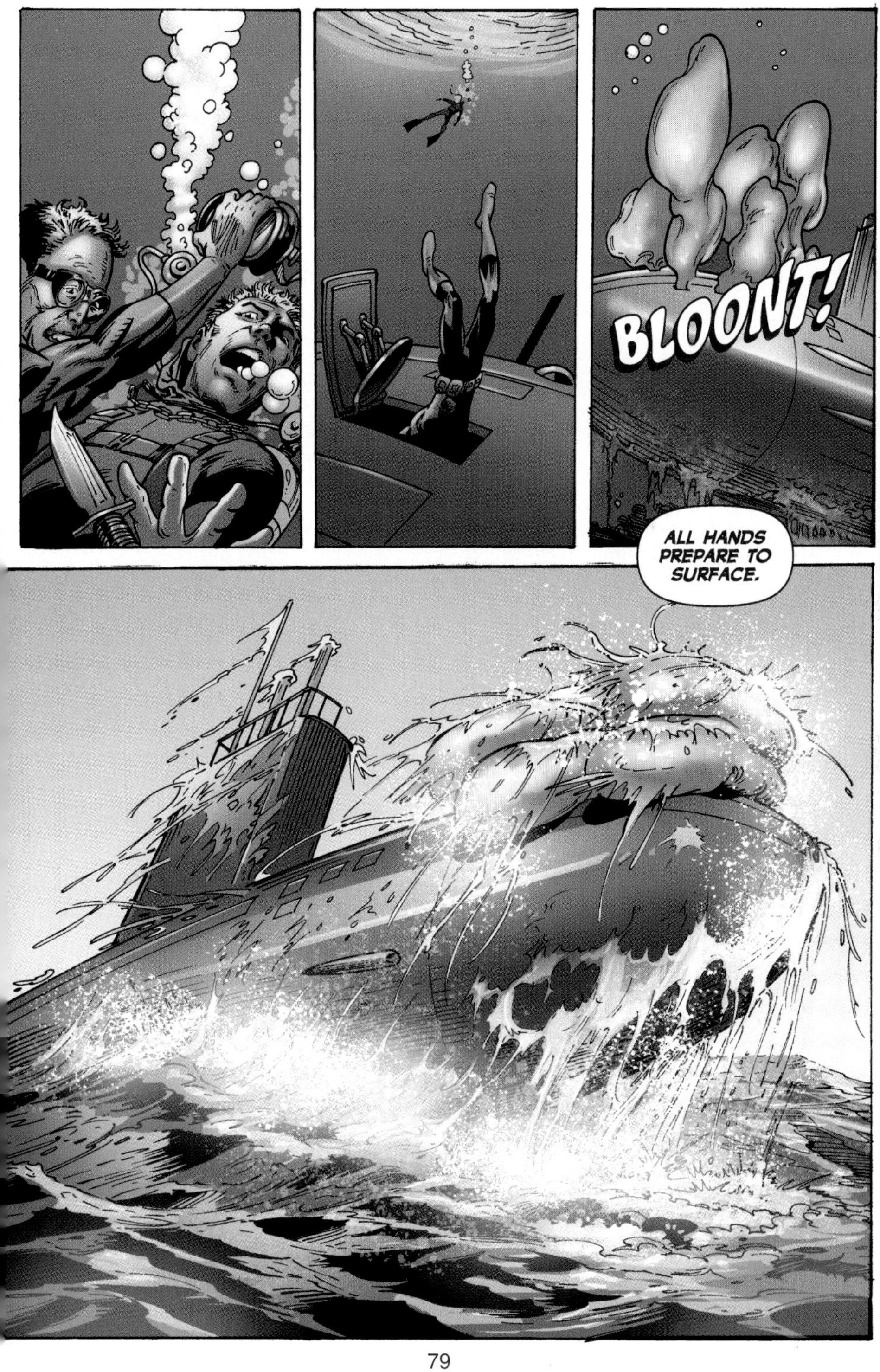
BLOONT!
ALL HANDS PREPARE TO SURFACE.

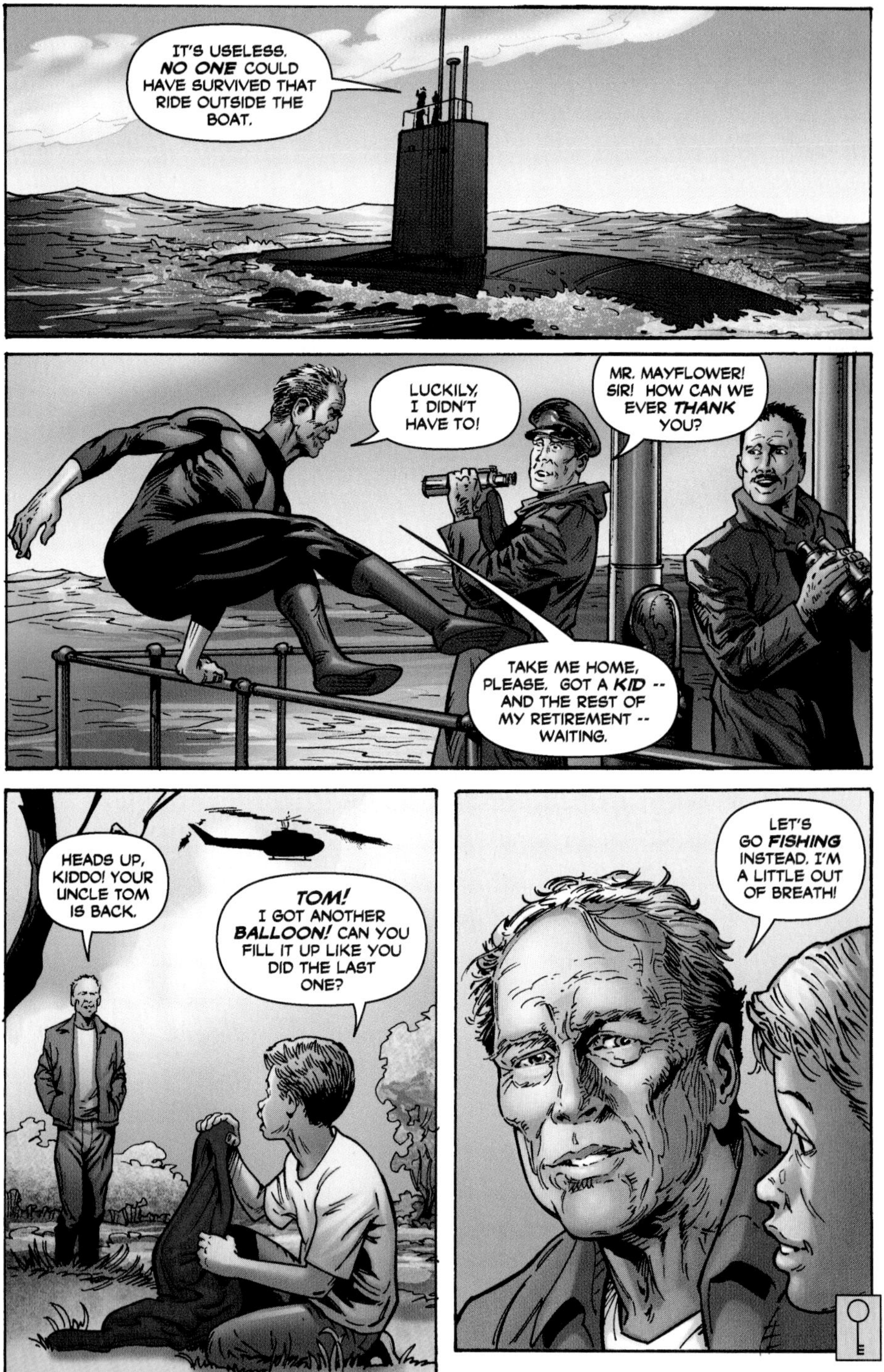
IT'S USELESS. NO ONE COULD HAVE SURVIVED THAT RIDE OUTSIDE THE BOAT.
LUCKILY, I DIDN'T HAVE TO!
MR. MAYFLOWER! SIR! HOW CAN WE EVER THANK YOU?
TAKE ME HOME, PLEASE. GOT A KID -- AND THE REST OF MY RETIREMENT -- WAITING.
HEADS UP, KIDDO! YOUR UNCLE TOM IS BACK.
TOM! I GOT ANOTHER BALLOON! CAN YOU FILL IT UP LIKE YOU DID THE LAST ONE?
LET'S GO FISHING INSTEAD. I'M A LITTLE OUT OF BREATH!

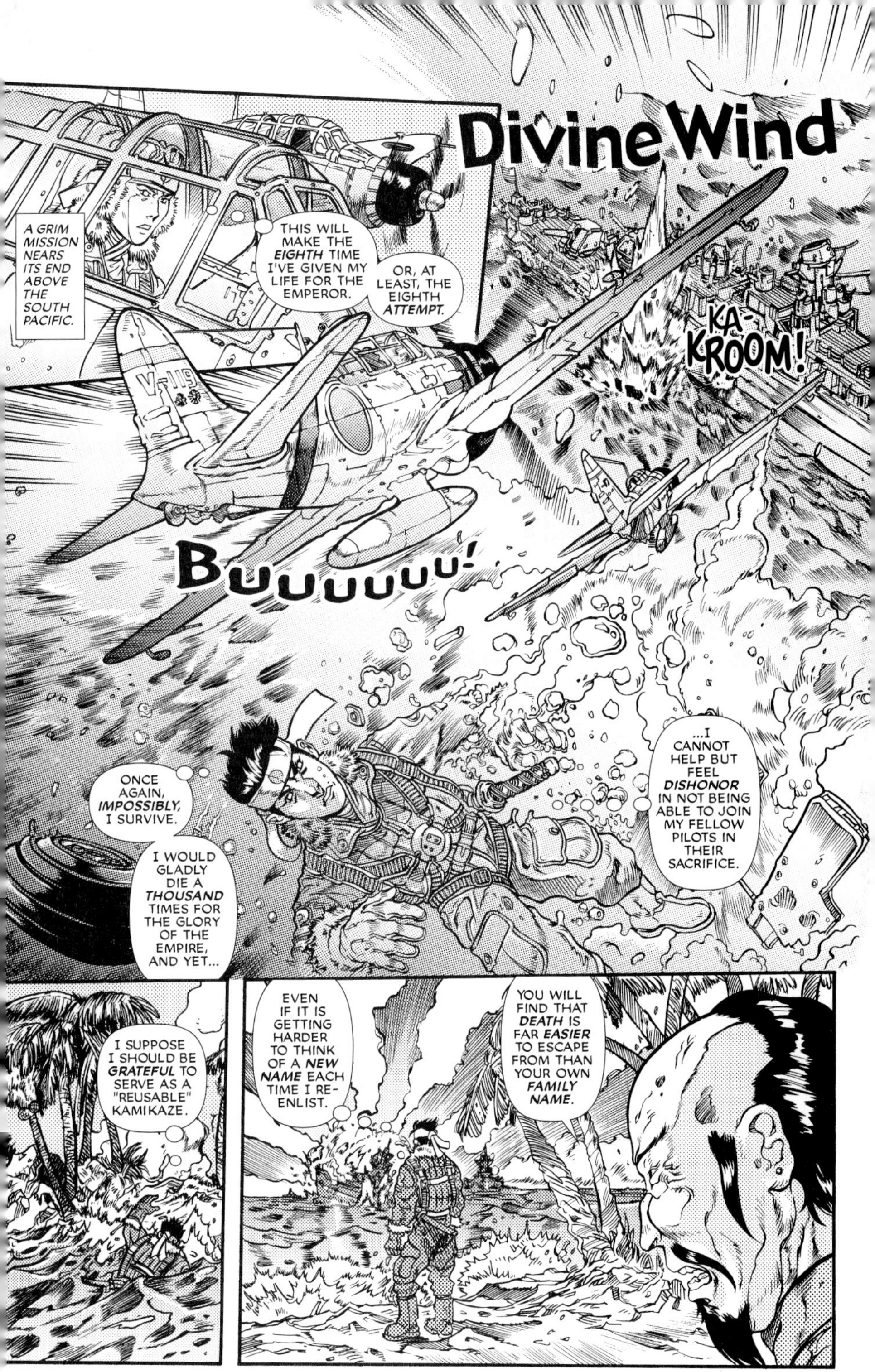

Divine Wind
A GRIM MISSION NEARS ITS END ABOVE THE SOUTH PACIFIC.
THIS WILL MAKE THE *EIGHTH* TIME I'VE GIVEN MY LIFE FOR THE EMPEROR.
OR, AT LEAST, THE EIGHTH *ATTEMPT.*
KA-KROOM!
BUUUUUUU!
ONCE AGAIN, *IMPOSSIBLY,* I SURVIVE.
I WOULD GLADLY DIE A *THOUSAND* TIMES FOR THE GLORY OF THE EMPIRE, AND YET...
...I CANNOT HELP BUT FEEL *DISHONOR* IN NOT BEING ABLE TO JOIN MY FELLOW PILOTS IN THEIR SACRIFICE.
I SUPPOSE I SHOULD BE *GRATEFUL* TO SERVE AS A "REUSABLE" KAMIKAZE.
EVEN IF IT IS GETTING HARDER TO THINK OF A *NEW NAME* EACH TIME I RE-ENLIST.
YOU WILL FIND THAT *DEATH* IS FAR *EASIER* TO ESCAPE FROM THAN YOUR OWN *FAMILY NAME.*

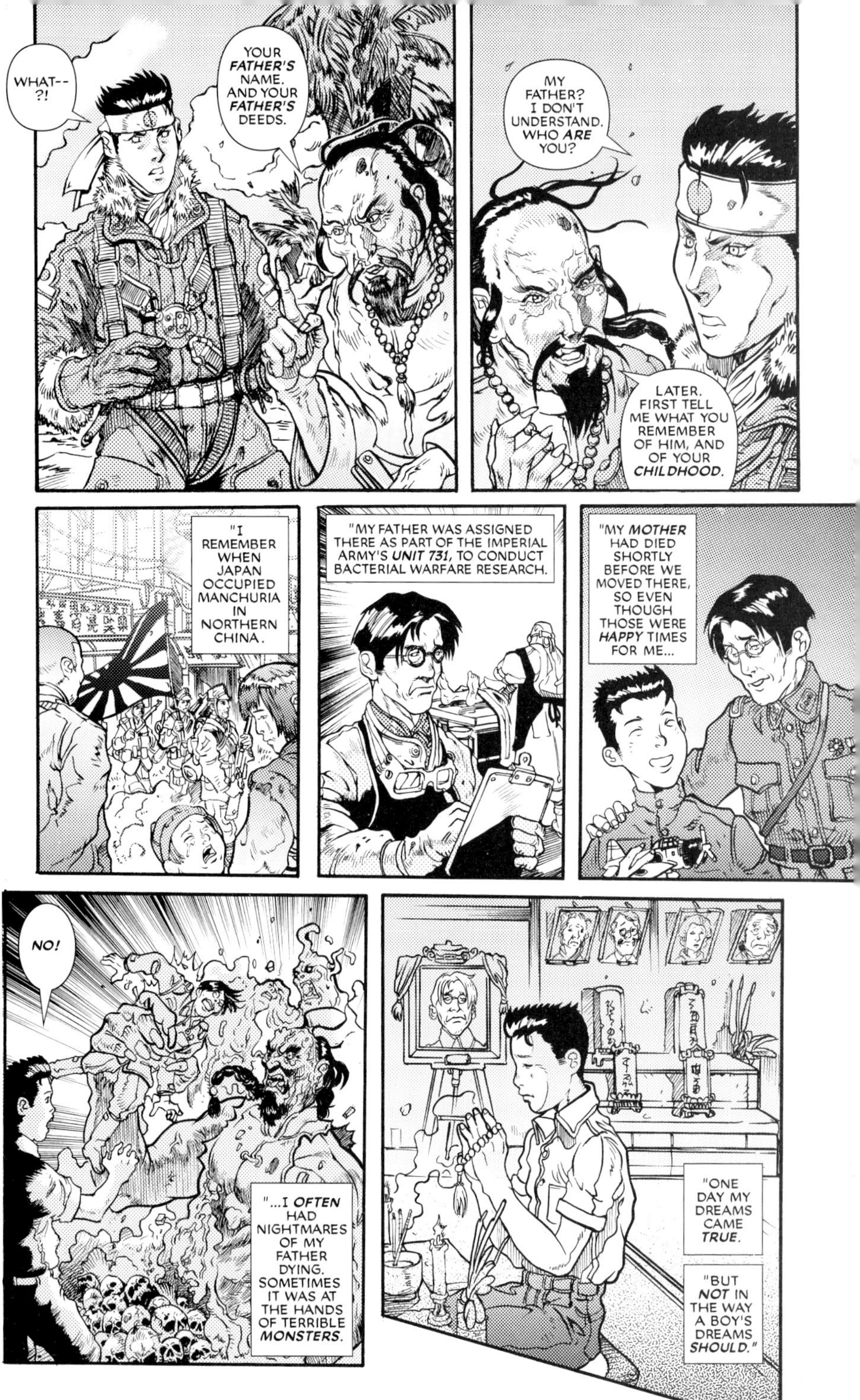
WHAT-- ?!
YOUR FATHER'S NAME. AND YOUR FATHER'S DEEDS.
MY FATHER? I DON'T UNDERSTAND. WHO ARE YOU?
LATER. FIRST TELL ME WHAT YOU REMEMBER OF HIM, AND OF YOUR CHILDHOOD.
"I REMEMBER WHEN JAPAN OCCUPIED MANCHURIA IN NORTHERN CHINA.
"MY FATHER WAS ASSIGNED THERE AS PART OF THE IMPERIAL ARMY'S UNIT 731, TO CONDUCT BACTERIAL WARFARE RESEARCH.
"MY MOTHER HAD DIED SHORTLY BEFORE WE MOVED THERE, SO EVEN THOUGH THOSE WERE HAPPY TIMES FOR ME...
NO!
"...I OFTEN HAD NIGHTMARES OF MY FATHER DYING. SOMETIMES IT WAS AT THE HANDS OF TERRIBLE MONSTERS.
"ONE DAY MY DREAMS CAME TRUE.
"BUT NOT IN THE WAY A BOY'S DREAMS SHOULD."

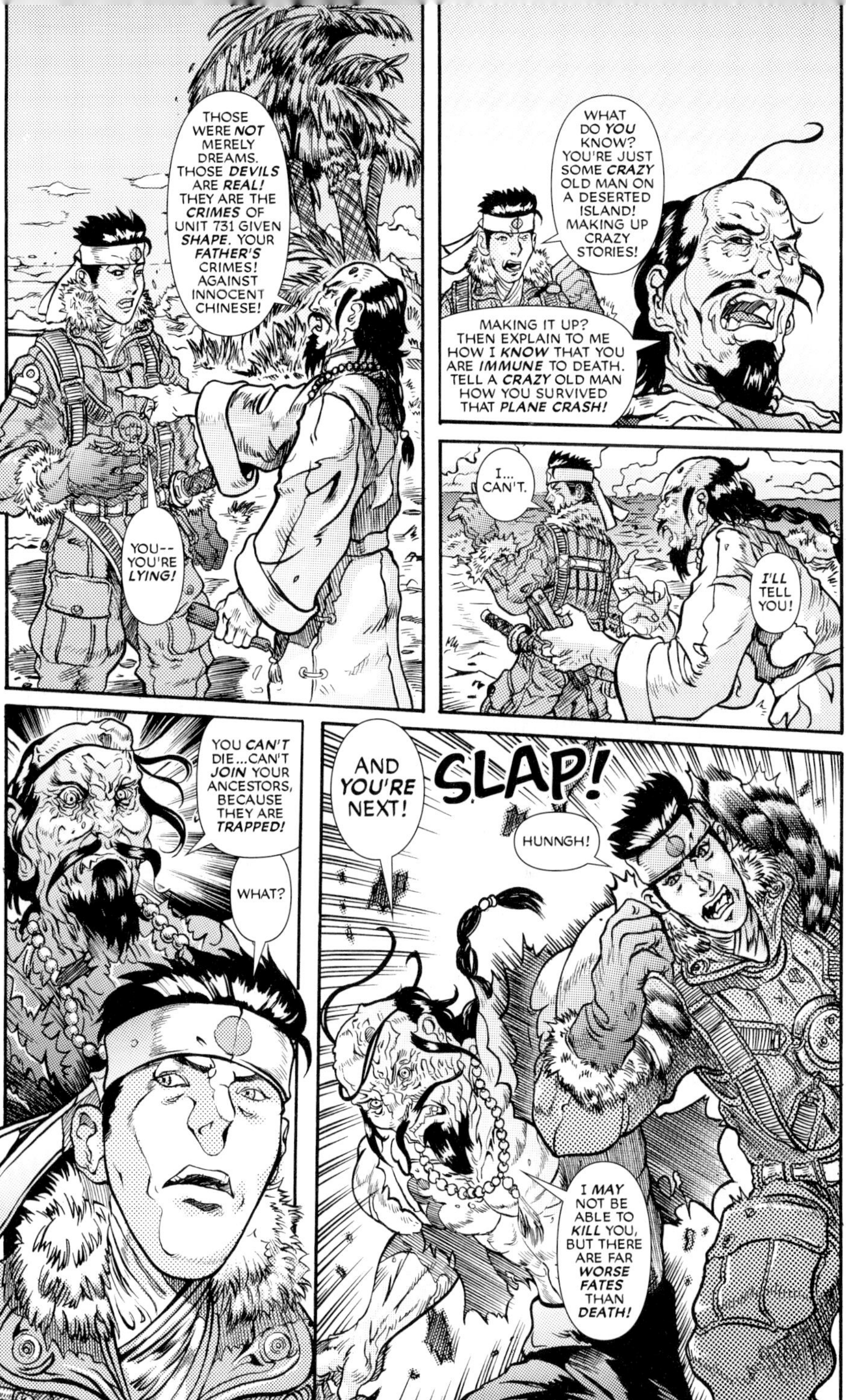
THOSE WERE NOT MERELY DREAMS. THOSE DEVILS ARE REAL! THEY ARE THE CRIMES OF UNIT 731 GIVEN SHAPE. YOUR FATHER'S CRIMES! AGAINST INNOCENT CHINESE!
YOU-- YOU'RE LYING!
WHAT DO YOU KNOW? YOU'RE JUST SOME CRAZY OLD MAN ON A DESERTED ISLAND! MAKING UP CRAZY STORIES!
MAKING IT UP? THEN EXPLAIN TO ME HOW I KNOW THAT YOU ARE IMMUNE TO DEATH. TELL A CRAZY OLD MAN HOW YOU SURVIVED THAT PLANE CRASH!
I... CAN'T.
I'LL TELL YOU!
YOU CAN'T DIE...CAN'T JOIN YOUR ANCESTORS, BECAUSE THEY ARE TRAPPED!
WHAT?
AND YOU'RE NEXT!
SLAP!
HUNNGH!
I MAY NOT BE ABLE TO KILL YOU, BUT THERE ARE FAR WORSE FATES THAN DEATH!

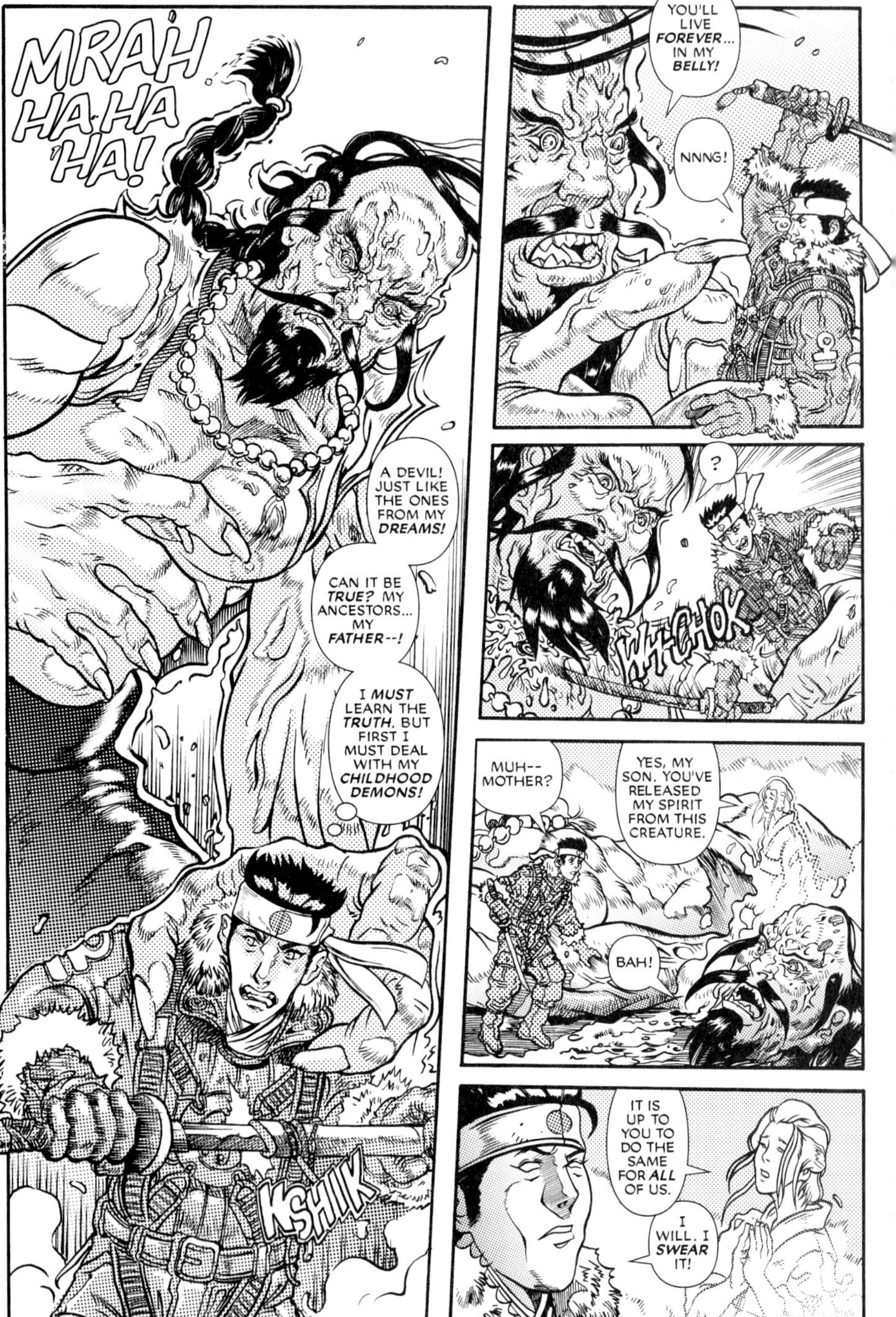
MRAH HA-HA HA!
A DEVIL! JUST LIKE THE ONES FROM MY DREAMS!
CAN IT BE TRUE? MY ANCESTORS... MY FATHER--!
I MUST LEARN THE TRUTH. BUT FIRST I MUST DEAL WITH MY CHILDHOOD DEMONS!
KSHIK
YOU'LL LIVE FOREVER... IN MY BELLY!
NNNG!
?
WHCHOK
MUH-- MOTHER?
YES, MY SON. YOU'VE RELEASED MY SPIRIT FROM THIS CREATURE.
BAH!
IT IS UP TO YOU TO DO THE SAME FOR ALL OF US.
I WILL. I SWEAR IT!

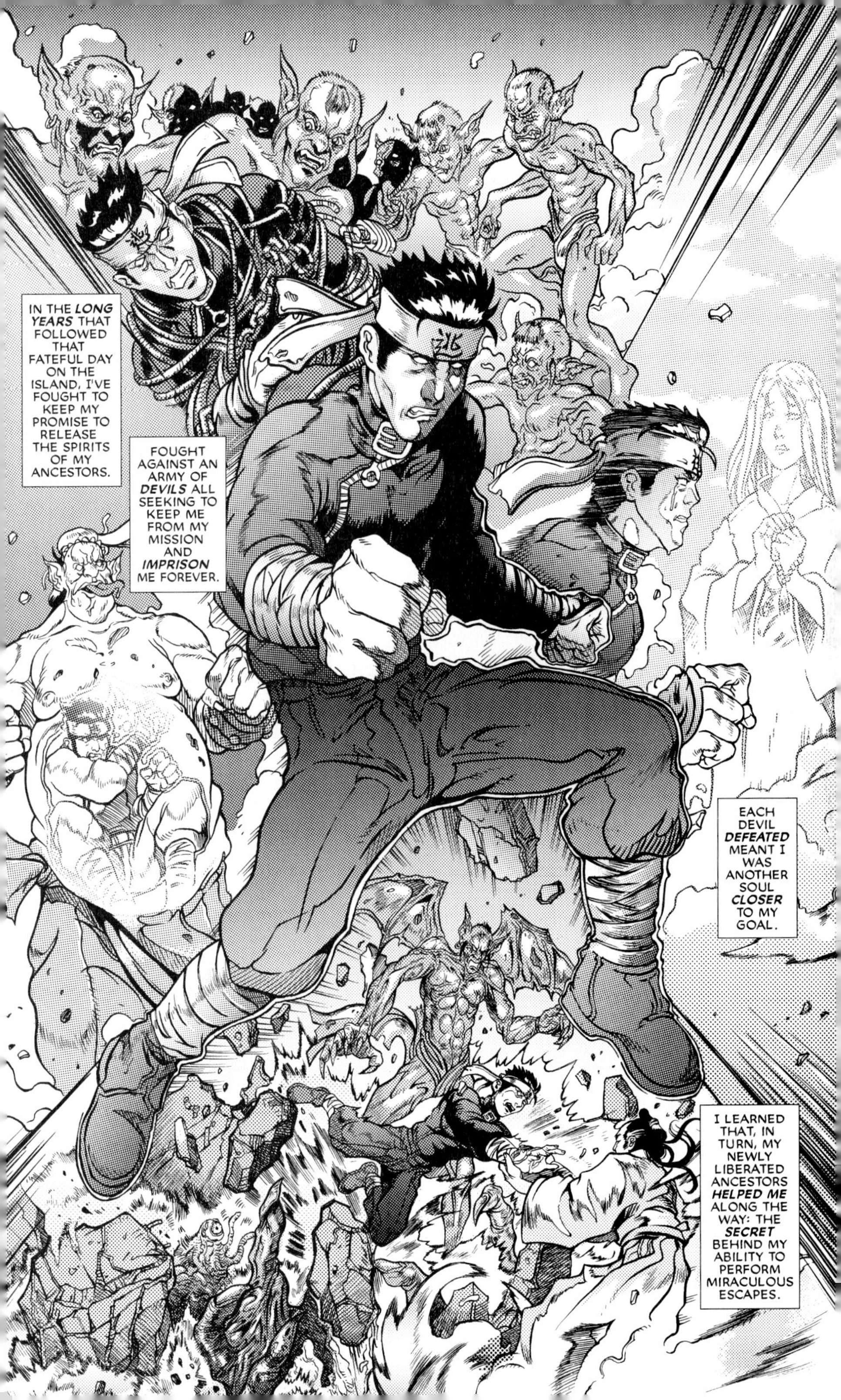
IN THE LONG YEARS THAT FOLLOWED THAT FATEFUL DAY ON THE ISLAND, I'VE FOUGHT TO KEEP MY PROMISE TO RELEASE THE SPIRITS OF MY ANCESTORS.
FOUGHT AGAINST AN ARMY OF DEVILS ALL SEEKING TO KEEP ME FROM MY MISSION AND IMPRISON ME FOREVER.
EACH DEVIL DEFEATED MEANT I WAS ANOTHER SOUL CLOSER TO MY GOAL.
I LEARNED THAT, IN TURN, MY NEWLY LIBERATED ANCESTORS HELPED ME ALONG THE WAY: THE SECRET BEHIND MY ABILITY TO PERFORM MIRACULOUS ESCAPES.

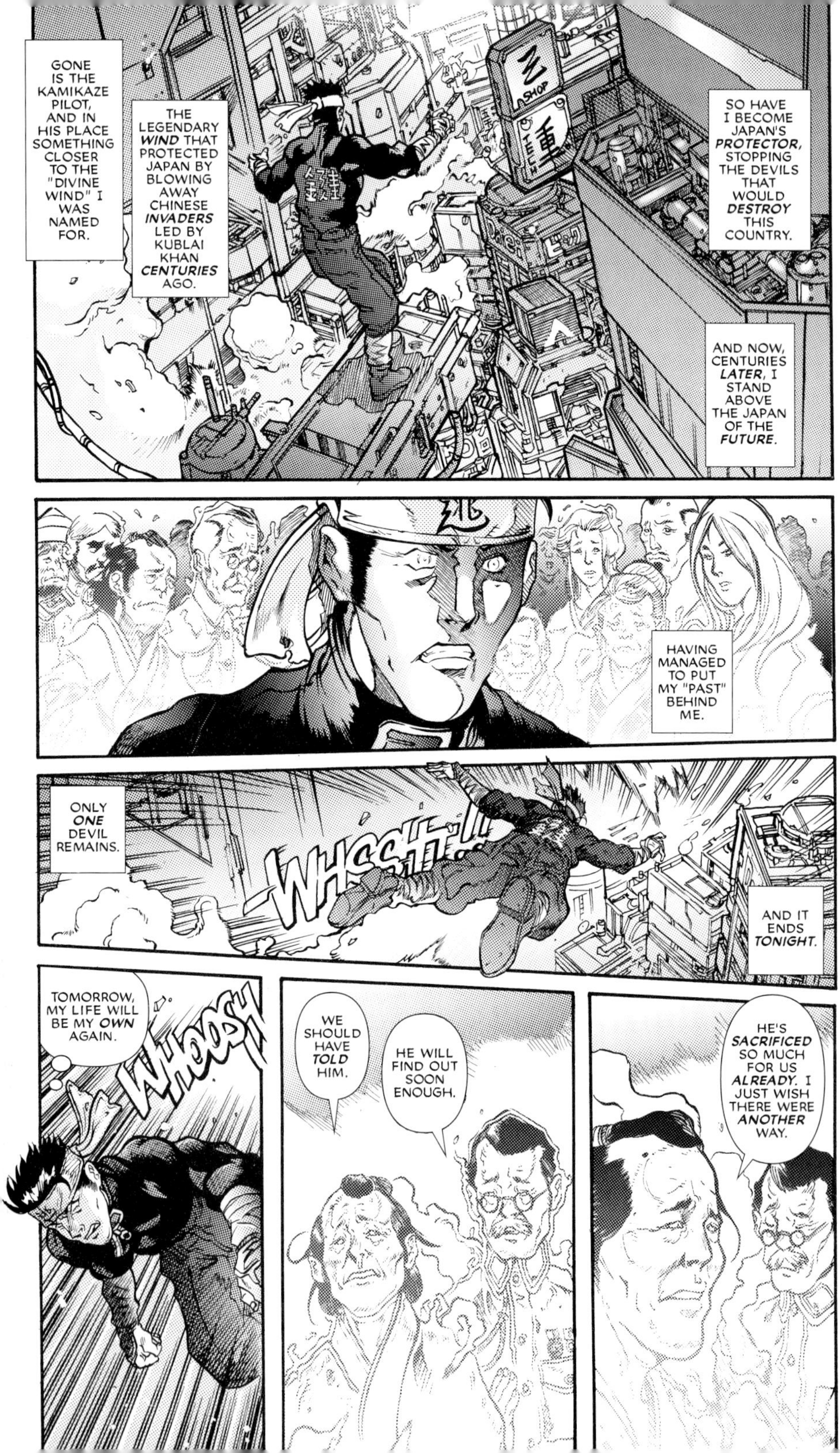
GONE IS THE KAMIKAZE PILOT, AND IN HIS PLACE SOMETHING CLOSER TO THE "DIVINE WIND" I WAS NAMED FOR.
THE LEGENDARY WIND THAT PROTECTED JAPAN BY BLOWING AWAY CHINESE INVADERS LED BY KUBLAI KHAN CENTURIES AGO.
SHOP
TECH
SO HAVE I BECOME JAPAN'S PROTECTOR, STOPPING THE DEVILS THAT WOULD DESTROY THIS COUNTRY.
AND NOW, CENTURIES LATER, I STAND ABOVE THE JAPAN OF THE FUTURE.
HAVING MANAGED TO PUT MY "PAST" BEHIND ME.
ONLY ONE DEVIL REMAINS.
WHSSH!!
AND IT ENDS TONIGHT.
TOMORROW, MY LIFE WILL BE MY OWN AGAIN.
WHOOSH
WE SHOULD HAVE TOLD HIM.
HE WILL FIND OUT SOON ENOUGH.
HE'S SACRIFICED SO MUCH FOR US ALREADY. I JUST WISH THERE WERE ANOTHER WAY.

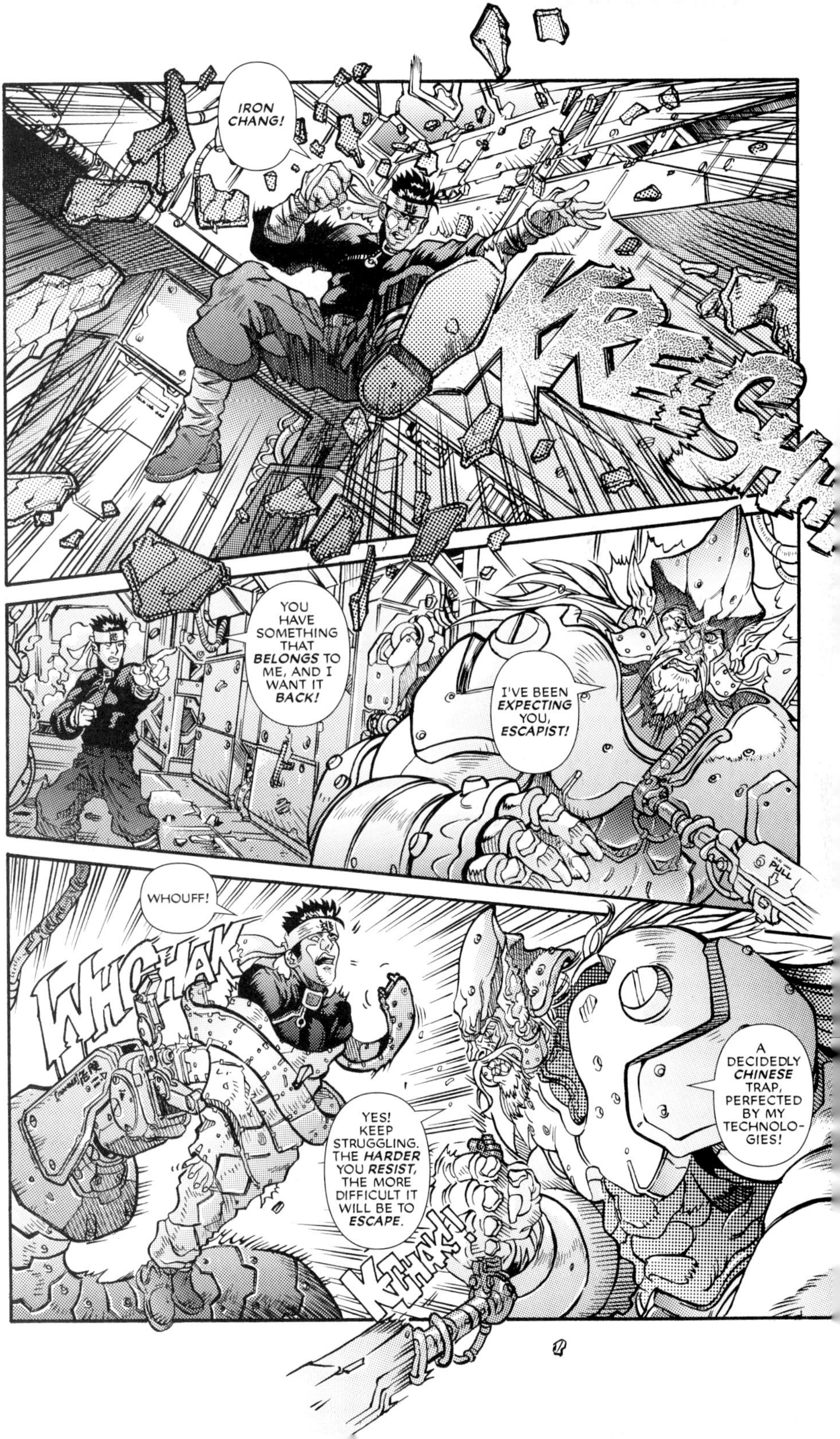
IRON CHANG!
YOU HAVE SOMETHING THAT *BELONGS* TO ME, AND I WANT IT *BACK!*
I'VE BEEN *EXPECTING* YOU, *ESCAPIST!*
PULL
WHOUFF!
WHCHAK
A DECIDEDLY *CHINESE* TRAP, PERFECTED BY MY TECHNOLO-GIES!
YES! KEEP STRUGGLING. THE *HARDER* YOU *RESIST,* THE MORE DIFFICULT IT WILL BE TO *ESCAPE.*
KCHAK!

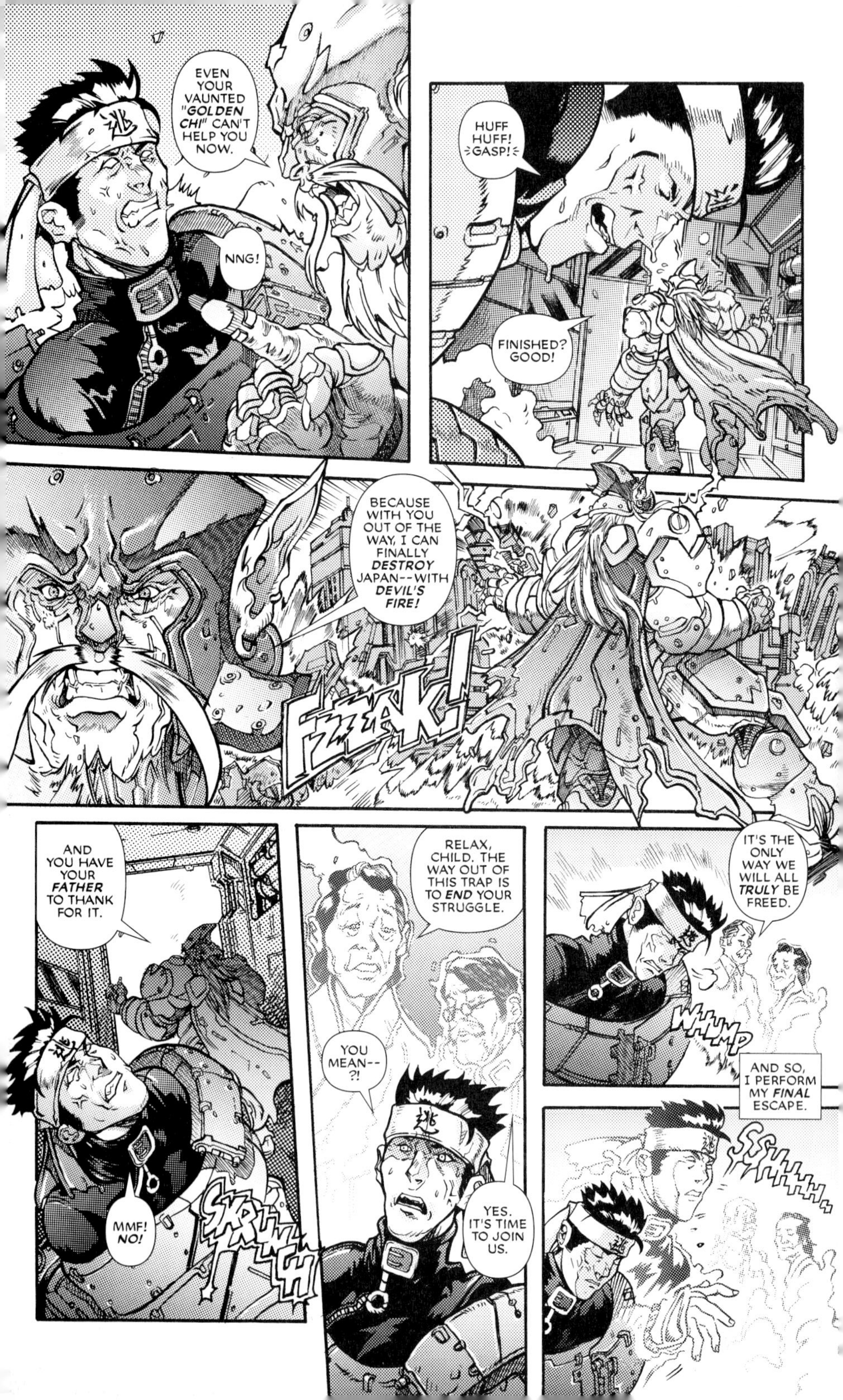

EVEN YOUR VAUNTED "GOLDEN CHI" CAN'T HELP YOU NOW.
NNG!
HUFF HUFF! GASP!
FINISHED? GOOD!
BECAUSE WITH YOU OUT OF THE WAY, I CAN FINALLY DESTROY JAPAN--WITH DEVIL'S FIRE!
FZZAK!
AND YOU HAVE YOUR FATHER TO THANK FOR IT.
MMF! NO!
SKRUNCH
RELAX, CHILD. THE WAY OUT OF THIS TRAP IS TO END YOUR STRUGGLE.
YOU MEAN-- ?!
YES. IT'S TIME TO JOIN US.
IT'S THE ONLY WAY WE WILL ALL TRULY BE FREED.
WHUMP
AND SO, I PERFORM MY FINAL ESCAPE.
SSHHHHH

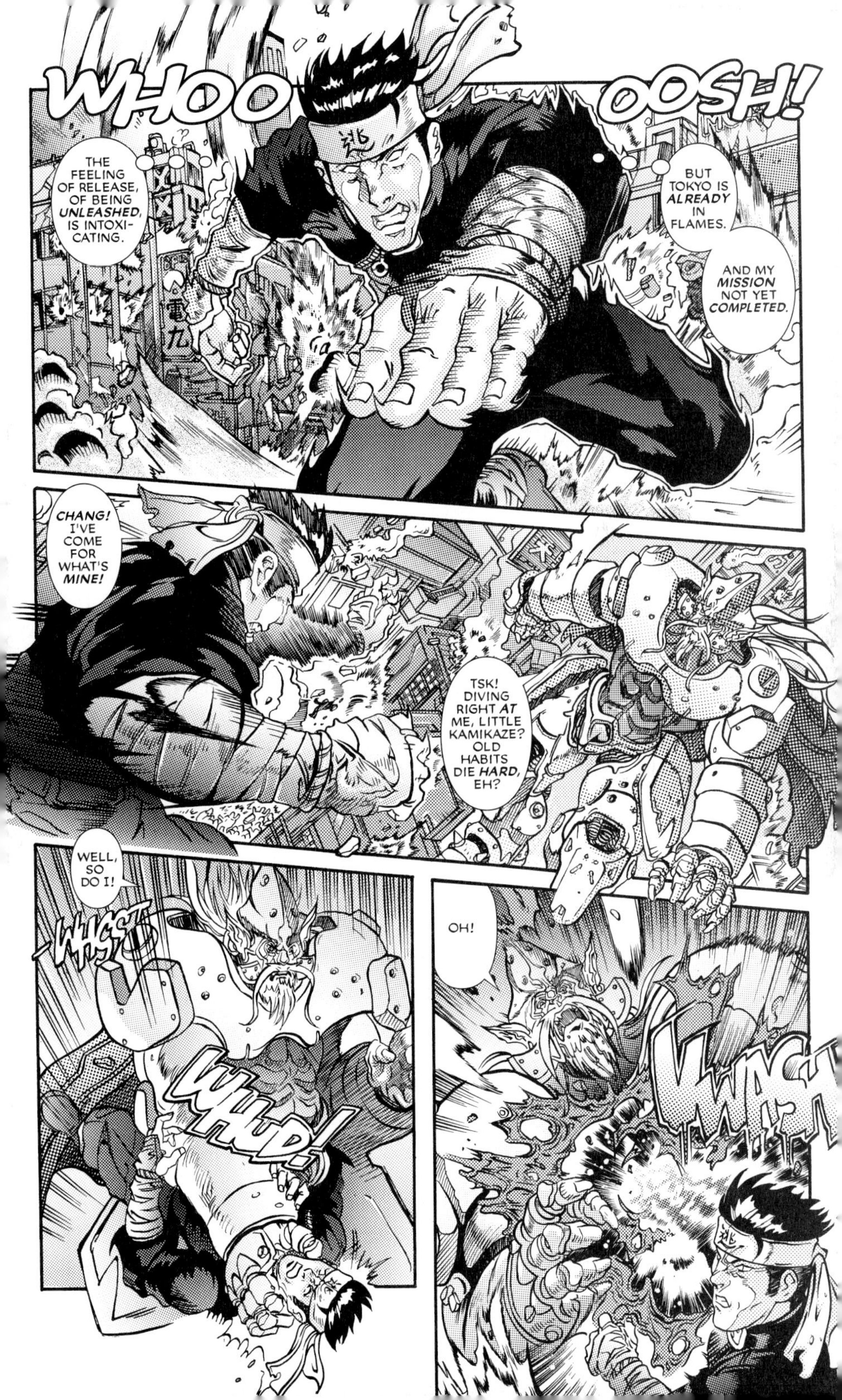
WHOO
OOSH!
THE FEELING OF RELEASE, OF BEING UNLEASHED, IS INTOXI-CATING.
BUT TOKYO IS ALREADY IN FLAMES.
AND MY MISSION NOT YET COMPLETED.
CHANG! I'VE COME FOR WHAT'S MINE!
TSK! DIVING RIGHT AT ME, LITTLE KAMIKAZE? OLD HABITS DIE HARD, EH?
WELL, SO DO I!
WHSST
WHUD!
OH!

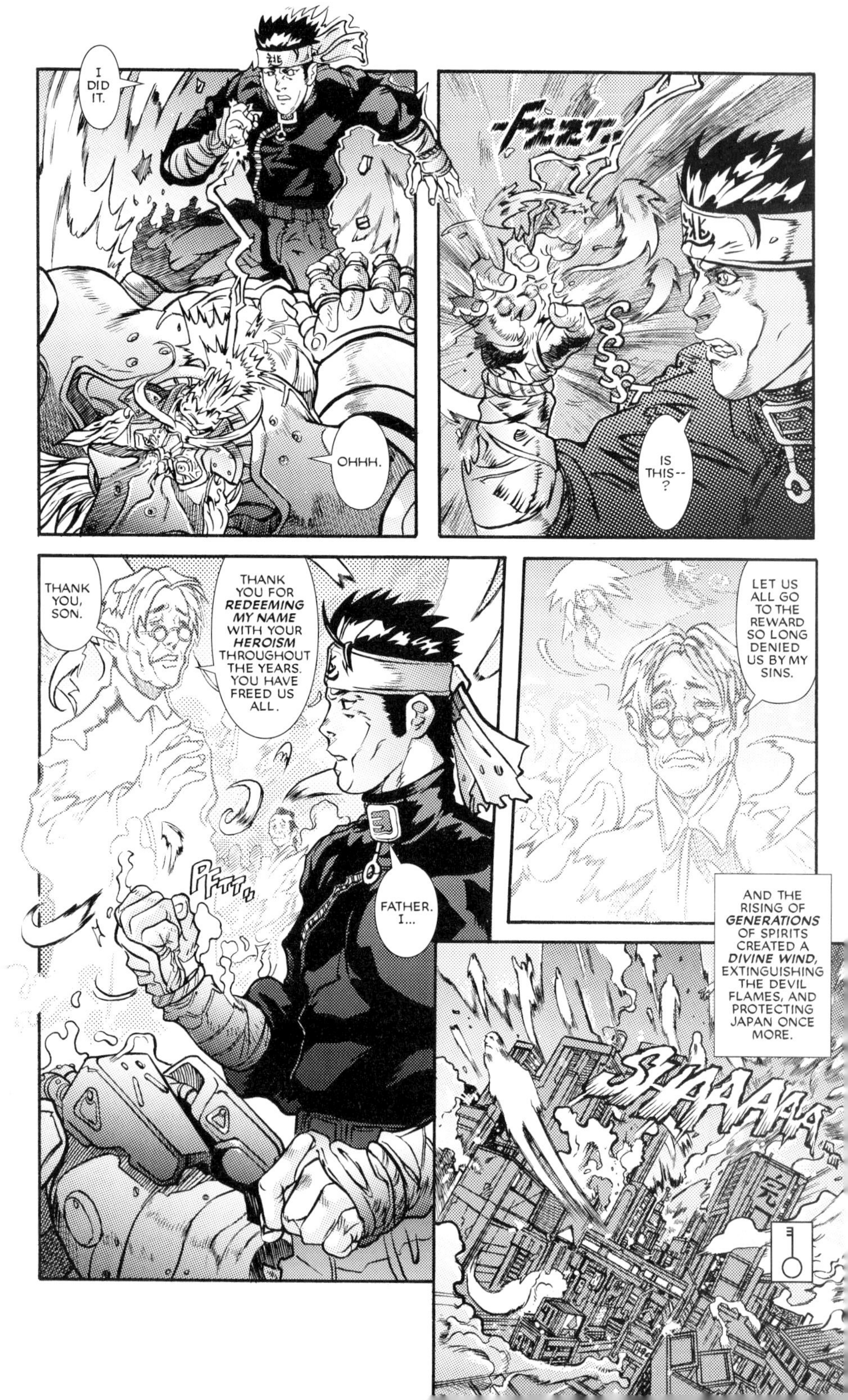

I DID IT.
OHHH.
FZZT
SSSST
IS THIS--?
THANK YOU, SON.
THANK YOU FOR ***REDEEMING MY NAME*** WITH YOUR ***HEROISM*** THROUGHOUT THE YEARS. YOU HAVE FREED US ALL.
PFTTT
FATHER. I...
LET US ALL GO TO THE REWARD SO LONG DENIED US BY MY SINS.
AND THE RISING OF ***GENERATIONS*** OF SPIRITS CREATED A ***DIVINE WIND,*** EXTINGUISHING THE DEVIL FLAMES, AND PROTECTING JAPAN ONCE MORE.
SHAAAAA
完

"DIVINE WIND"

POST SCRIPT

by Kevin McCarthy

THE DESIRE TO EXPLOIT THE INCREASING POPULARITY OF JAPANESE comic books — or *manga* — in the U.S. led to the rediscovery, some twenty years later, of one of the better-kept secrets in the long and checkered history of Kavalier & Clay's Escapist.

In 1983, the Omnigrip Corporation had licensed to Kodansha, on a one-year trial basis, the rights to publish original *Escapist* material in Japan, where the renowned master *manga* artist known only as "Tonikoro" produced an astounding twenty pages of artwork per week, depicting all-new and decidedly different adventures of a Japanese Escapist for Kodansha's *Shukan Shonen Magazine* (Weekly Boys' Magazine).

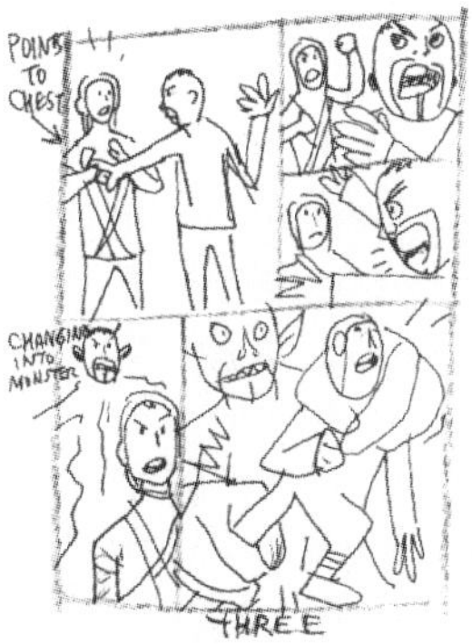
POINTS TO CHEST
CHANGING INTO MONSTER
THREE

An original *manga* Escapist layout page, with English-language notes, lends some credence to the supposition that Sam Clay wrote these stories for the Japanese market. *From the McCarthy collection.*

The writer — or writers — for the 1000-plus pages was never credited, but one persistent rumor has it that it was none other than Sammy Clay himself who penned (with the aid of a translator) the adventures of a young kamikaze pilot who became "The God of Escapes," thereby giving Japan one of its most controversial *manga* of all time.

Supporting the Clay-as-author rumor is the inclusion of "politically sensitive" material such as an anti-imperialist subtext and at least one direct reference to a shameful event in Japan's history — the biological warfare research conducted by the Japanese Army in Manchuria in the 1930s and 1940s — as evidenced in the preceding story. Some experts submit than only a "barbarian" like Clay would even have *considered* the use of such touchy subject matter.

It is felt that this controversy is what kept the Escapist *manga* from selling as well as it could have … but the limited scope of the Omnigrip license (which prohibited the production of toys or animation) is what really prevented the Escapist serial from becoming the "break-out" success it should have been. Kodansha's *Escapist* license expired in 1984 and was not renewed. Two years later, when Katsuhiro Otomo's *Akira* exploded on the scene, Otomo would cite Tonikoro's version of the Escapist as an influence.

Truly, it is the draftsmanship of Tonikoro that makes the *manga* Escapist — and the encapsulation of that epic story reprinted herein — such a treasure. Among other things, the artist was especially notorious for his attention to detail (witness the inverted Escapist key logo created by the zipper and collar of the hero's costume).

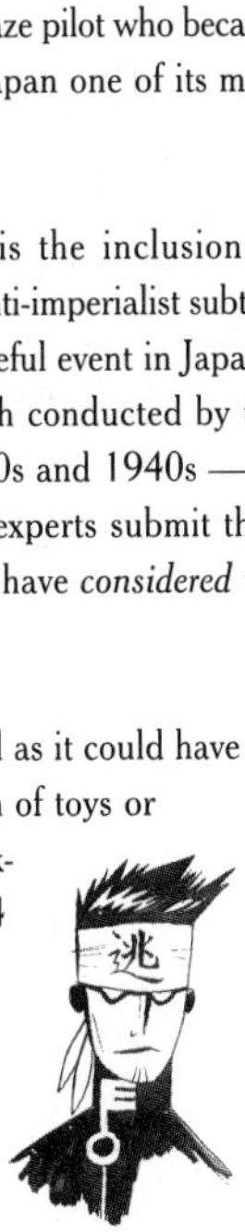
逃

Tonikoro's inverted Escapist key logo, from an early character design sheet.

THE ESCAPEGOAT by Kavalier and Clay

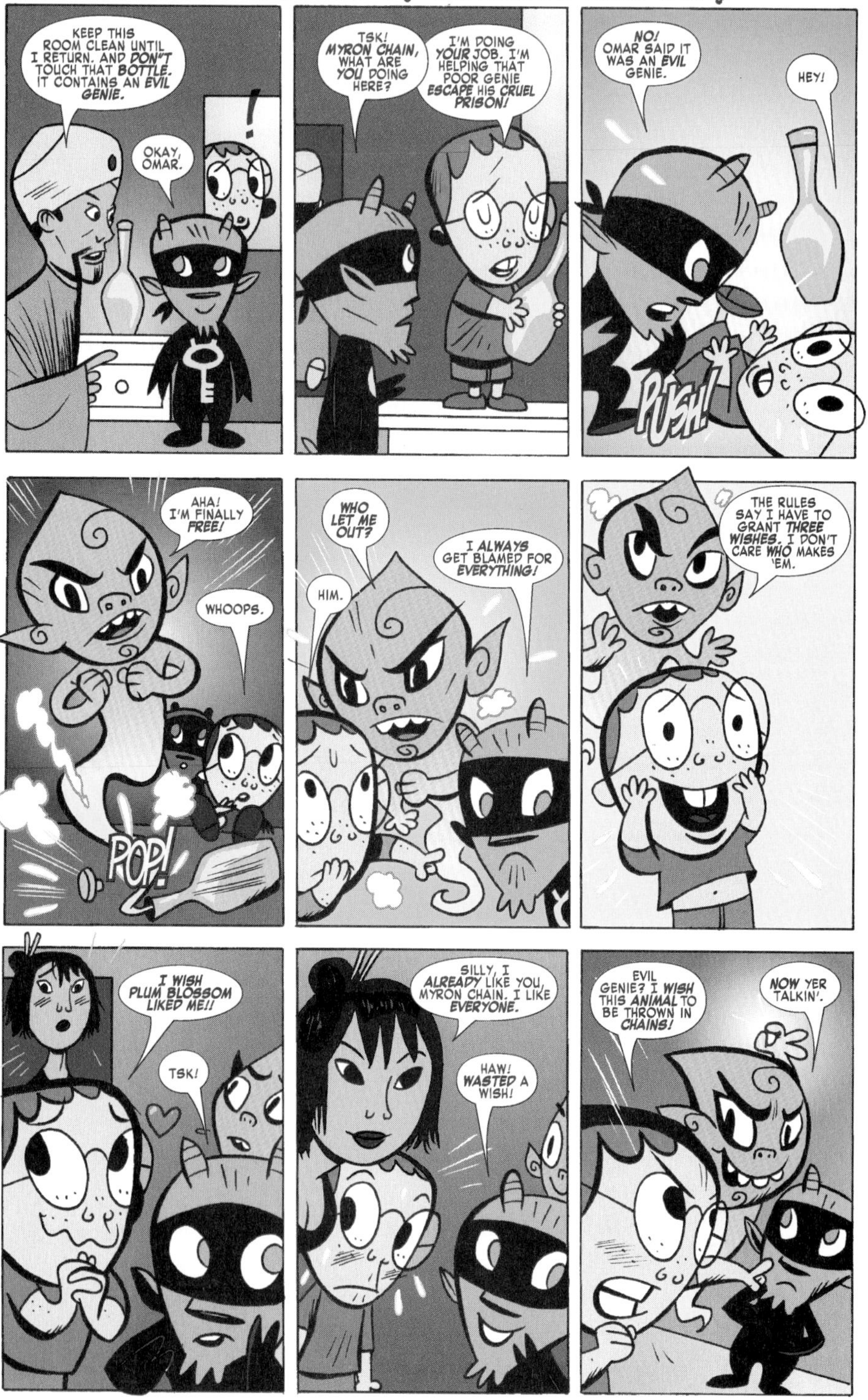

KEEP THIS ROOM CLEAN UNTIL I RETURN. AND DON'T TOUCH THAT BOTTLE. IT CONTAINS AN EVIL GENIE.
OKAY, OMAR.
!
TSK! MYRON CHAIN, WHAT ARE YOU DOING HERE?
I'M DOING YOUR JOB. I'M HELPING THAT POOR GENIE ESCAPE HIS CRUEL PRISON!
NO! OMAR SAID IT WAS AN EVIL GENIE.
HEY!
PUSH!
AHA! I'M FINALLY FREE!
WHOOPS.
POP!
WHO LET ME OUT?
HIM.
I ALWAYS GET BLAMED FOR EVERYTHING!
THE RULES SAY I HAVE TO GRANT THREE WISHES. I DON'T CARE WHO MAKES 'EM.
I WISH PLUM BLOSSOM LIKED ME!!
TSK!
SILLY, I ALREADY LIKE YOU, MYRON CHAIN. I LIKE EVERYONE.
HAW! WASTED A WISH!
EVIL GENIE? I WISH THIS ANIMAL TO BE THROWN IN CHAINS!
NOW YER TALKIN'.

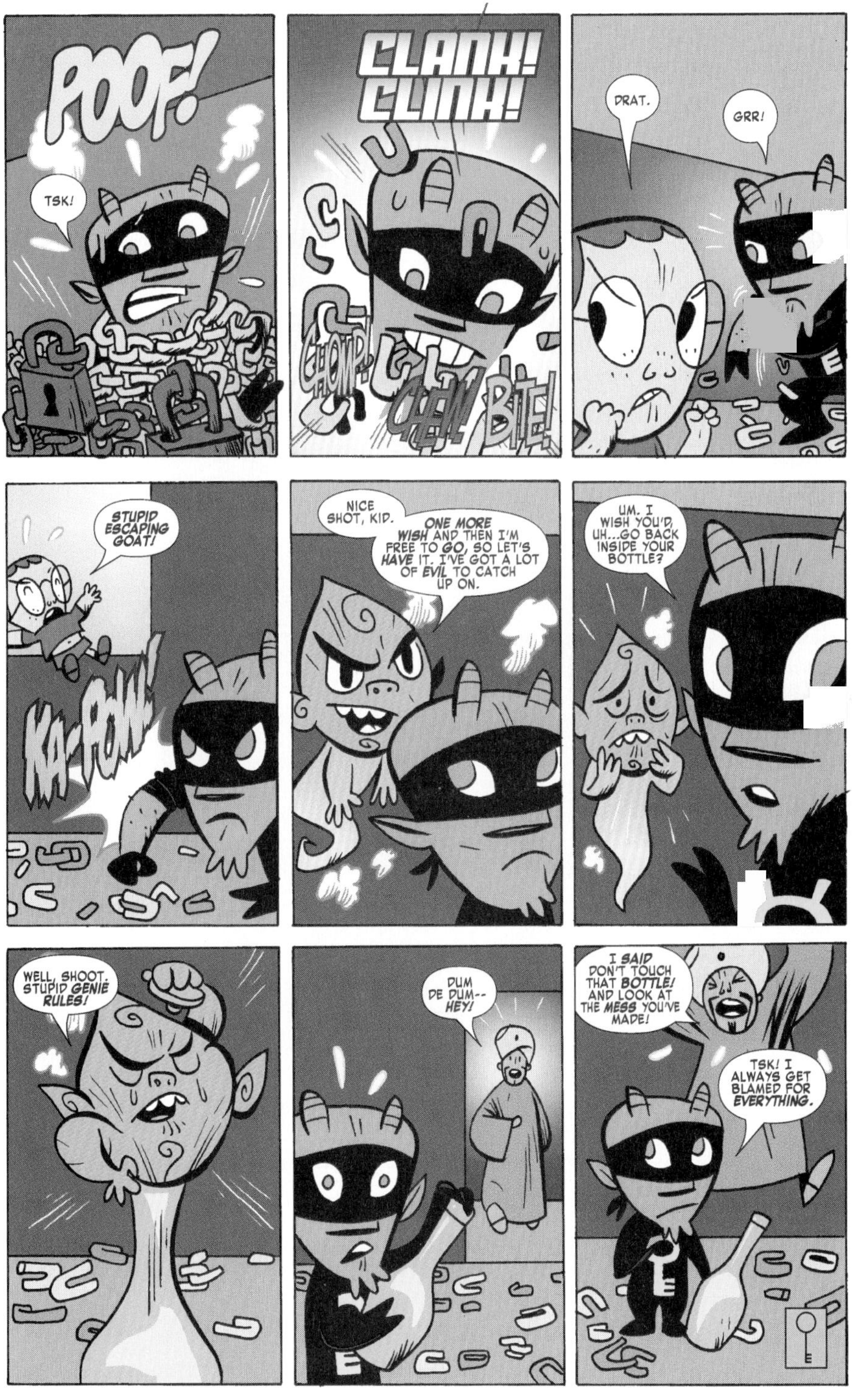
POOF!
TSK!
CLANK! CLINK!
CHOMP!
CHEW!
BITE!
DRAT.
GRR!
STUPID ESCAPING GOAT!
KA-POW!
NICE SHOT, KID.
ONE MORE WISH AND THEN I'M FREE TO GO, SO LET'S HAVE IT. I'VE GOT A LOT OF EVIL TO CATCH UP ON.
UM. I WISH YOU'D, UH...GO BACK INSIDE YOUR BOTTLE?
WELL, SHOOT. STUPID GENIE RULES!
DUM DE DUM-- HEY!
I SAID DON'T TOUCH THAT BOTTLE! AND LOOK AT THE MESS YOU'VE MADE!
TSK! I ALWAYS GET BLAMED FOR EVERYTHING.

LUNA MOTH

WHILE THE ESCAPIST WAS SURELY THE MOST SUCCESSFUL OF ALL Kavalier & Clay comic book characters, no serious scholar of the medium can deny the impact that Luna Moth had on the readership at large. Legend has it that the mysterious Mistress of the Night was based, in fact, on Rosa Luxemburg Saks, who, as Rose Saxon, wound up chronicling many of the winged woman's adventures herself. [It is also interesting to note that Miss Saks was married to Sam Clay for several years, after having first dated Joe Kavalier prior to his enlistment in the armed forces during World War II.]

The first issue of the (mostly) quarterly *All Doll* series introduced Luna Moth in early 1941. At that time, as Michael Chabon notes in *The Amazing Adventures of Kavalier and Clay*, "the addition of sex to the costumed-hero concept was a natural and, apart from a few minor efforts at other companies — the Sorceress of Zoom, the Woman in Red — yet to be attempted." Bear in mind that National Periodical Publications' Wonder Woman did not debut until *All-Star* #8, cover-dated December 1941-January 1942.

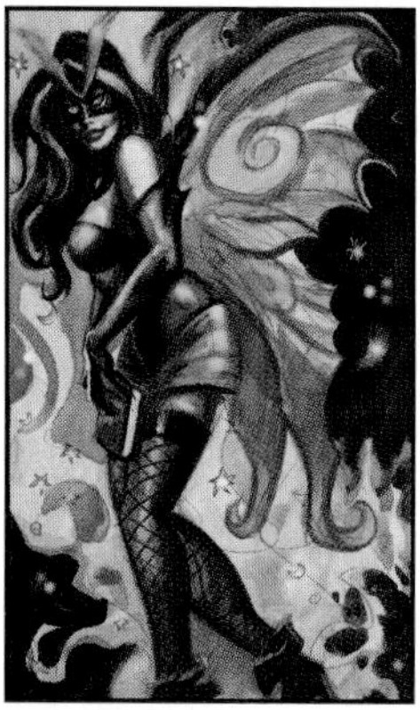

A painterly approach to Luna Moth. Courtesy of the Dan Brereton collection.

Though initially resistant to the moth-like attributes of the character, Empire Comics publishers Sheldon Anapol and Jack Ashkenazy were won over by her sales potential — specifically by Kavalier's pulchritudinous pinup design: again, according to Chabon, "a woman with the legs of Dolores Del Rio, black witchy hair, and breasts each the size of her head."

Like the Escapist, Luna Moth would undergo a variety of costume and other changes through the years, reflecting the evolving tastes of the comic book industry. One of the more dramatic transformations occurred in 1974, at the height of the Sunshine Comics years, when comics luminary Jim Starlin took a short break from *Captain Marvel* to write and draw a Luna Moth story, re-presented herein with newly remastered digital color effects by Christie Scheele and Krista Ward.

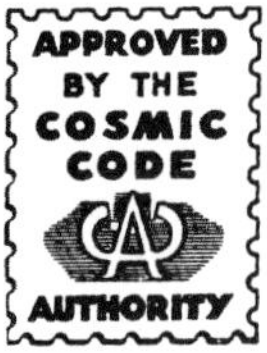
APPROVED
BY THE
COSMIC
CODE
CA
AUTHORITY

["Reckonings" was completed during Starlin's "cosmic" period, and in fact, letterer Tom Orzechowski altered the Comics Code Authority sticker on the cover of that particular issue of *All Doll* (#123) to read "approved by the Cosmic Code Authority"! The joke caught publisher Danny Sonnenschein's eye, however, and he immediately had it corrected. It's worth noting, as do Steve Duin and Mike Richardson in their massive tome, *Comics: Between the Panels*, that Orzechowski was eventually able to slip the anagram past a not-so-eagle-eyed editor at Marvel Comics, on issue #179 of *Strange Tales*.]

In the character's formative years, however, Rose Saxon eschewed the pen-and-ink medium prevalent in comics of the time in favor of rather lush (and one might even argue wanton) watercolors — no doubt a direct result of the many romance comics covers Miss Saxon was also painting during the late '40s and early '50s. Both "The Mechanist" and "Old Flame" reflect the more painterly approach to Luna Moth pioneered by the character's lady chronicler.

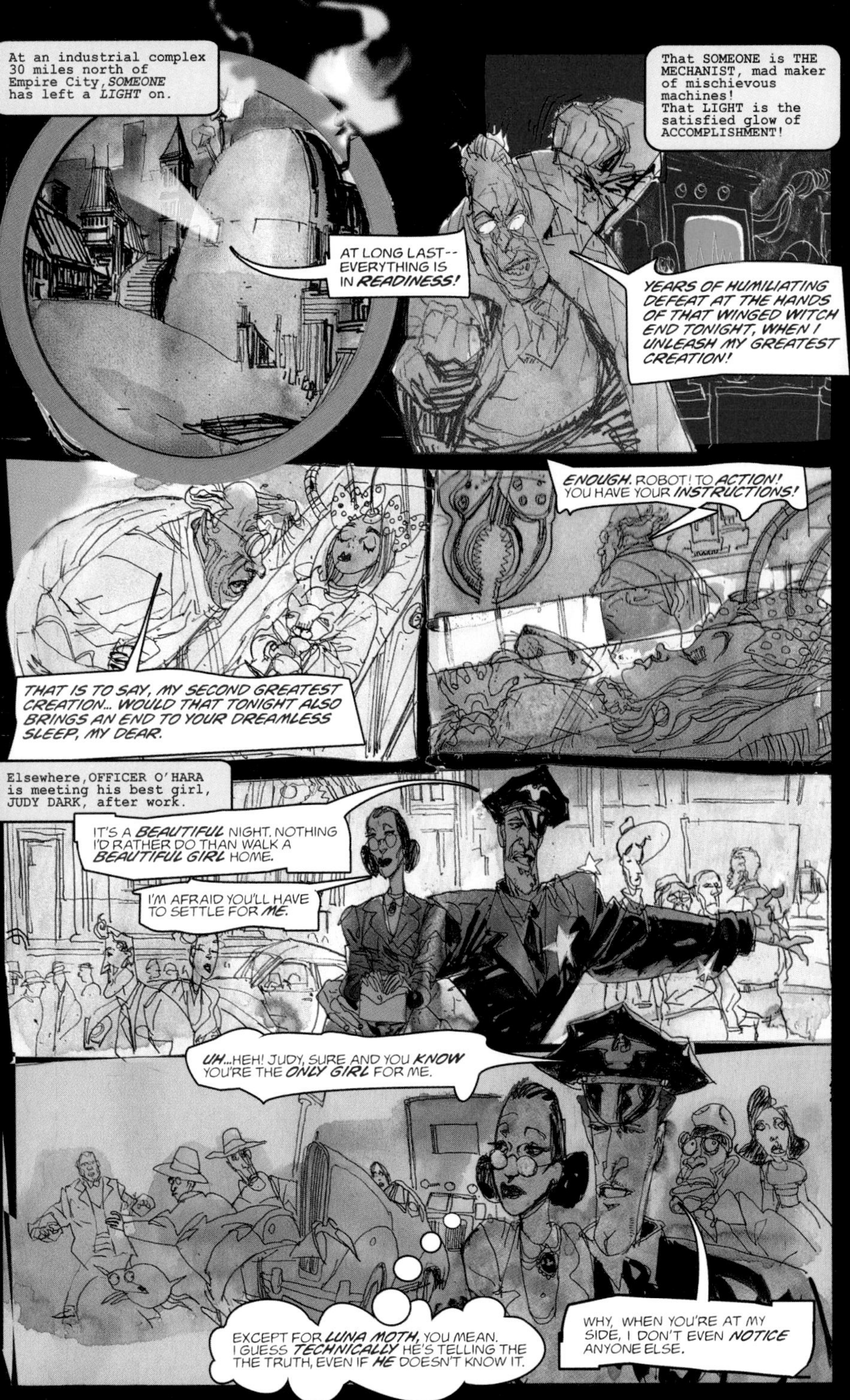

At an industrial complex 30 miles north of Empire City, SOMEONE has left a LIGHT on.
That SOMEONE is THE MECHANIST, mad maker of mischievous machines! That LIGHT is the satisfied glow of ACCOMPLISHMENT!
AT LONG LAST-- EVERYTHING IS IN READINESS!
YEARS OF HUMILIATING DEFEAT AT THE HANDS OF THAT WINGED WITCH END TONIGHT, WHEN I UNLEASH MY GREATEST CREATION!
THAT IS TO SAY, MY SECOND GREATEST CREATION... WOULD THAT TONIGHT ALSO BRINGS AN END TO YOUR DREAMLESS SLEEP, MY DEAR.
ENOUGH. ROBOT! TO ACTION! YOU HAVE YOUR INSTRUCTIONS!
Elsewhere, OFFICER O'HARA is meeting his best girl, JUDY DARK, after work.
IT'S A BEAUTIFUL NIGHT. NOTHING I'D RATHER DO THAN WALK A BEAUTIFUL GIRL HOME.
I'M AFRAID YOU'LL HAVE TO SETTLE FOR ME.
UH...HEH! JUDY, SURE AND YOU KNOW YOU'RE THE ONLY GIRL FOR ME.
EXCEPT FOR LUNA MOTH, YOU MEAN. I GUESS TECHNICALLY HE'S TELLING THE THE TRUTH, EVEN IF HE DOESN'T KNOW IT.
WHY, WHEN YOU'RE AT MY SIDE, I DON'T EVEN NOTICE ANYONE ELSE.

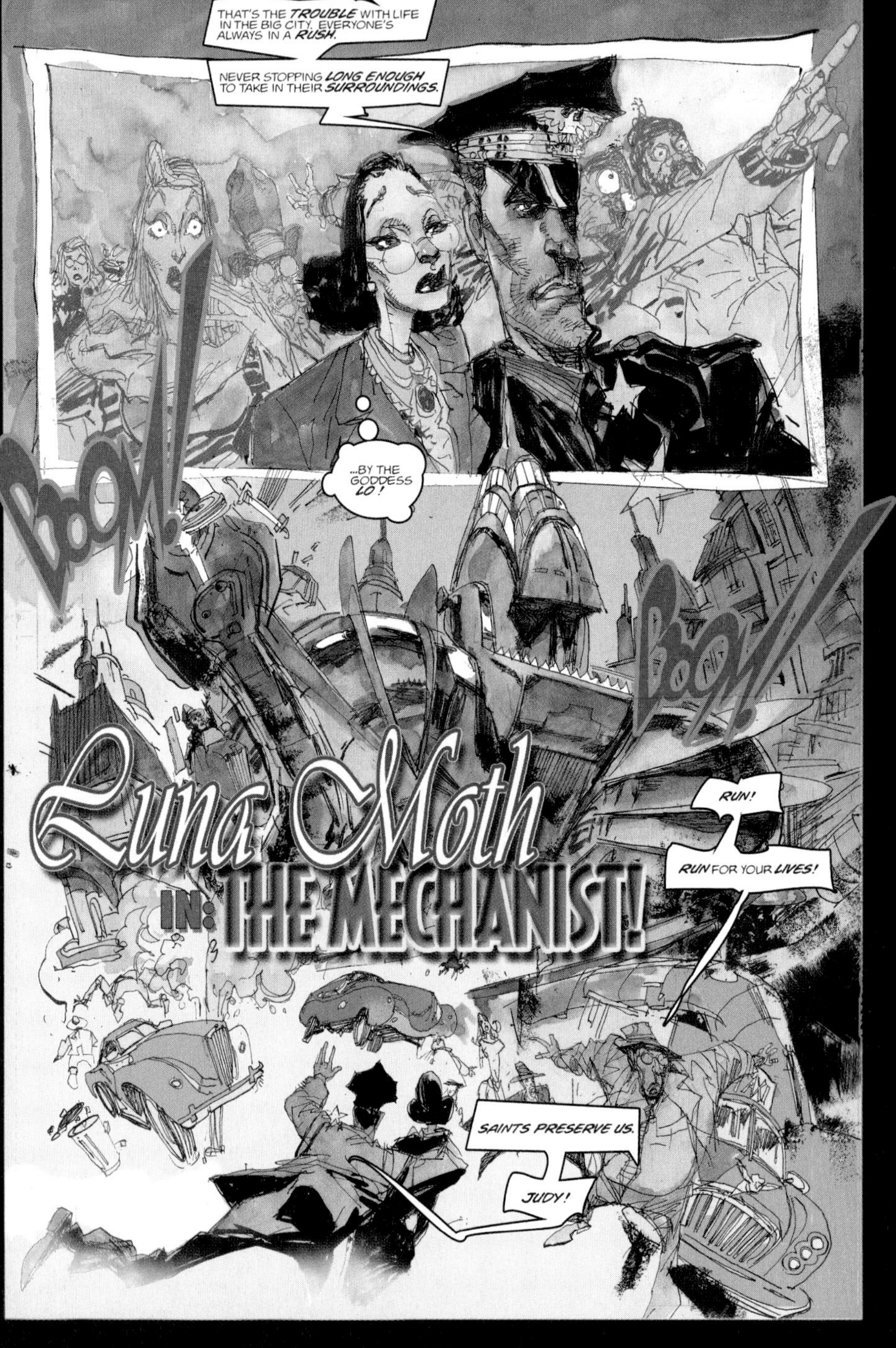
THAT'S THE TROUBLE WITH LIFE IN THE BIG CITY. EVERYONE'S ALWAYS IN A RUSH.
NEVER STOPPING LONG ENOUGH TO TAKE IN THEIR SURROUNDINGS.
...BY THE GODDESS LO!
BOOM!
BOOM!
Luna Moth
IN: THE MECHANIST!
RUN!
RUN FOR YOUR LIVES!
SAINTS PRESERVE US.
JUDY!

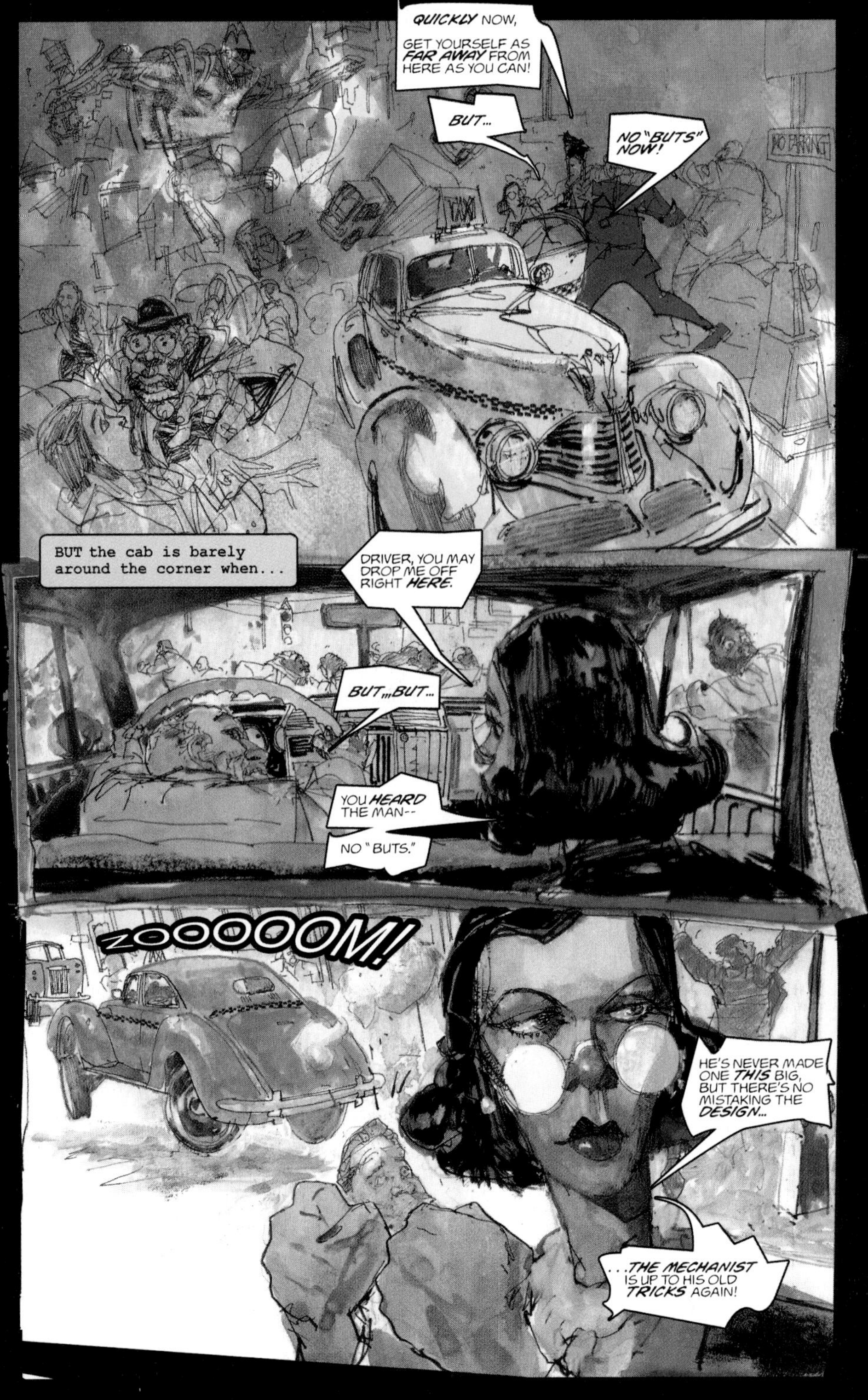
QUICKLY NOW,
GET YOURSELF AS FAR AWAY FROM HERE AS YOU CAN!
BUT...
NO "BUTS" NOW!
NO PARKING
TAXI
BUT the cab is barely around the corner when...
DRIVER, YOU MAY DROP ME OFF RIGHT HERE.
BUT...BUT...
YOU HEARD THE MAN--
NO "BUTS."
ZOOOOOOM!
HE'S NEVER MADE ONE THIS BIG, BUT THERE'S NO MISTAKING THE DESIGN...
...THE MECHANIST IS UP TO HIS OLD TRICKS AGAIN!

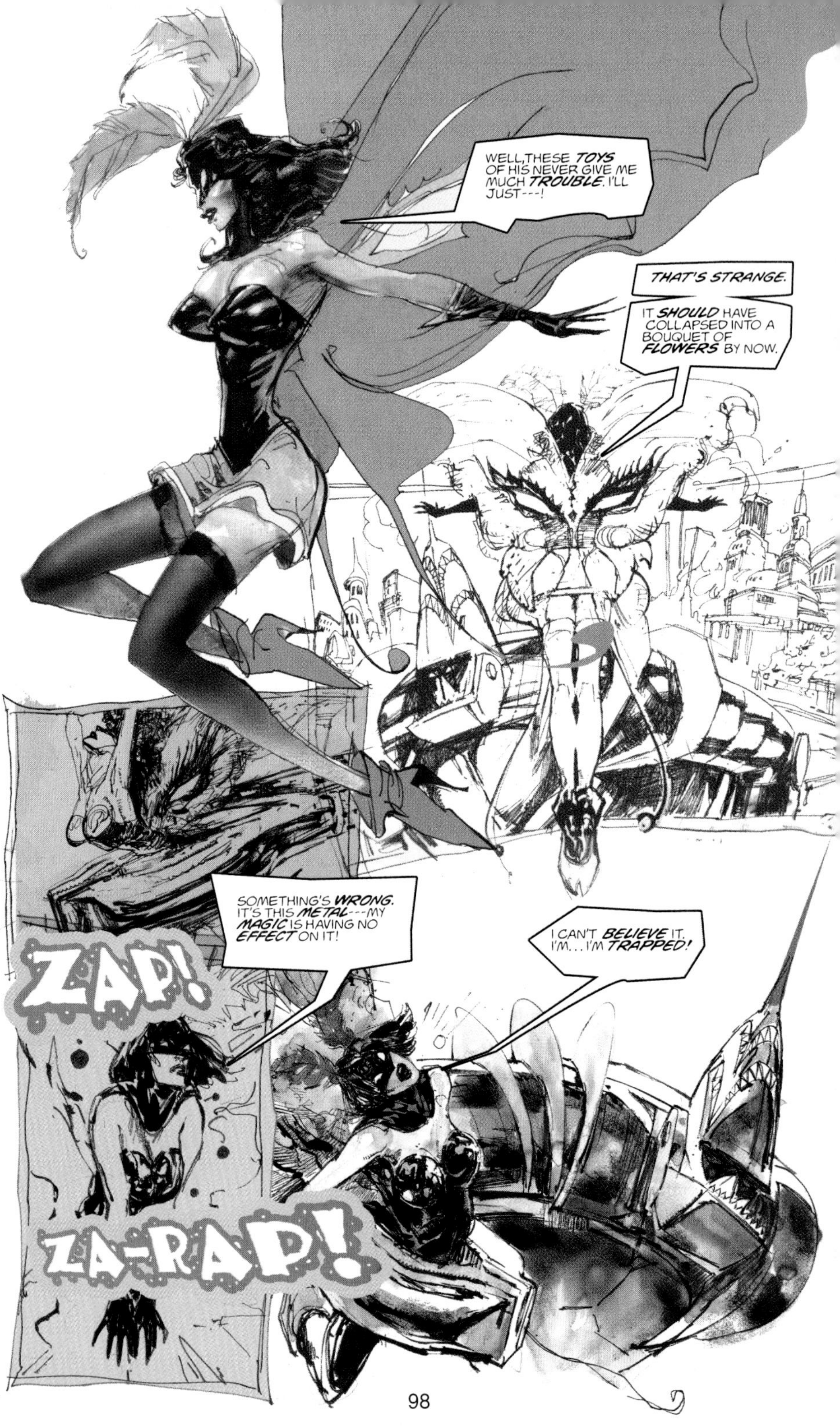
WELL, THESE TOYS OF HIS NEVER GIVE ME MUCH TROUBLE. I'LL JUST---!
THAT'S STRANGE.
IT SHOULD HAVE COLLAPSED INTO A BOUQUET OF FLOWERS BY NOW.
SOMETHING'S WRONG. IT'S THIS METAL---MY MAGIC IS HAVING NO EFFECT ON IT!
ZAP!
ZA-RAP!
I CAN'T BELIEVE IT. I'M... I'M TRAPPED!

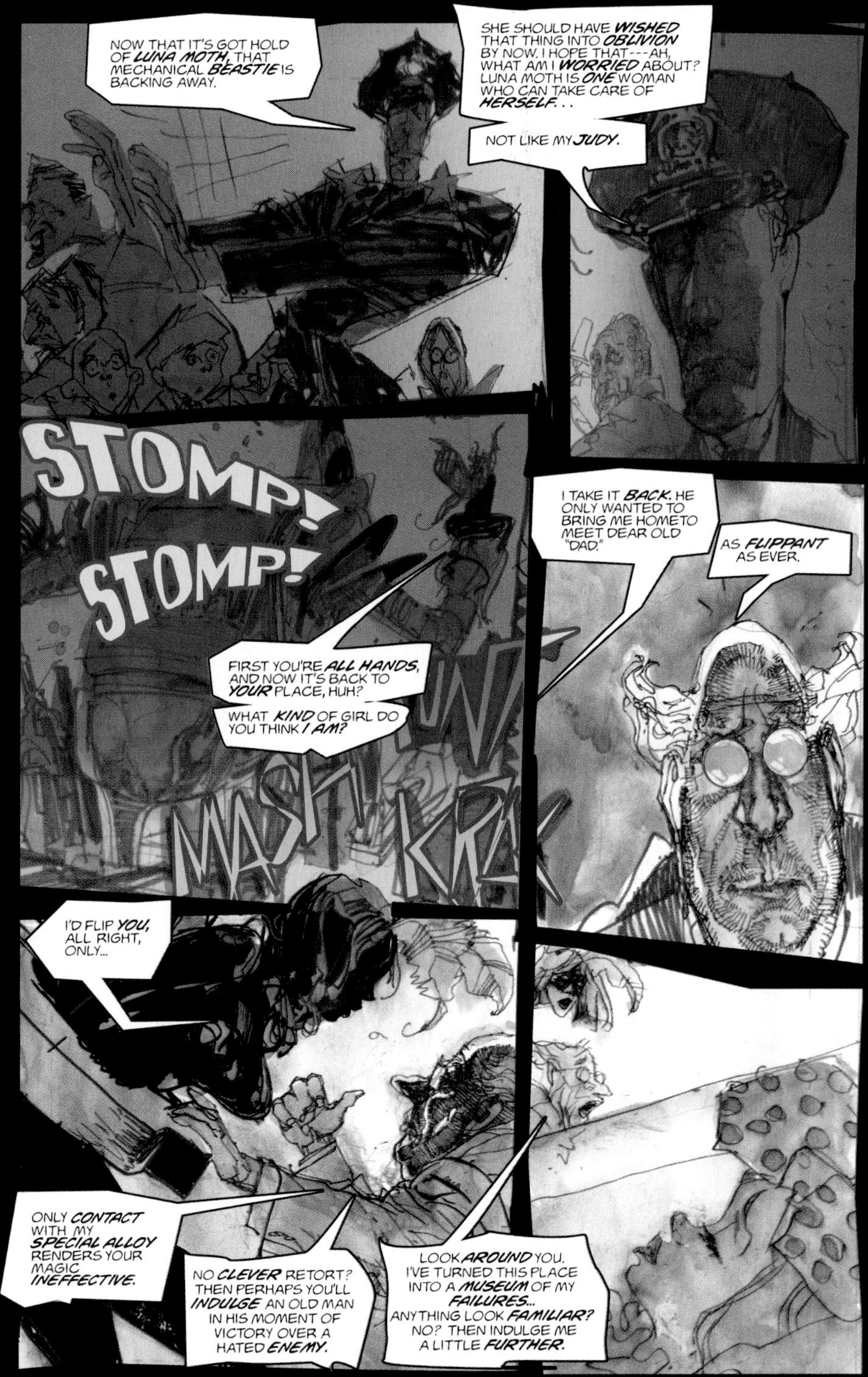
NOW THAT IT'S GOT HOLD OF *LUNA MOTH*, THAT MECHANICAL *BEASTIE* IS BACKING AWAY.
SHE SHOULD HAVE *WISHED* THAT THING INTO *OBLIVION* BY NOW. I HOPE THAT---AH, WHAT AM I *WORRIED* ABOUT? LUNA MOTH IS *ONE* WOMAN WHO CAN TAKE CARE OF *HERSELF*. . .
NOT LIKE MY *JUDY*.
STOMP!
STOMP!
FIRST YOU'RE *ALL HANDS*, AND NOW IT'S BACK TO *YOUR* PLACE, HUH?
WHAT *KIND* OF GIRL DO YOU THINK *I AM*?
I TAKE IT *BACK*. HE ONLY WANTED TO BRING ME HOMETO MEET DEAR OLD "DAD."
AS *FLIPPANT* AS EVER.
I'D FLIP *YOU*, ALL RIGHT, ONLY...
ONLY *CONTACT* WITH MY *SPECIAL ALLOY* RENDERS YOUR MAGIC *INEFFECTIVE*.
NO *CLEVER* RETORT? THEN PERHAPS YOU'LL *INDULGE* AN OLD MAN IN HIS MOMENT OF VICTORY OVER A HATED *ENEMY*.
LOOK *AROUND* YOU. I'VE TURNED THIS PLACE INTO A *MUSEUM* OF MY *FAILURES*... ANYTHING LOOK *FAMILIAR*? NO? THEN INDULGE ME A LITTLE *FURTHER*.

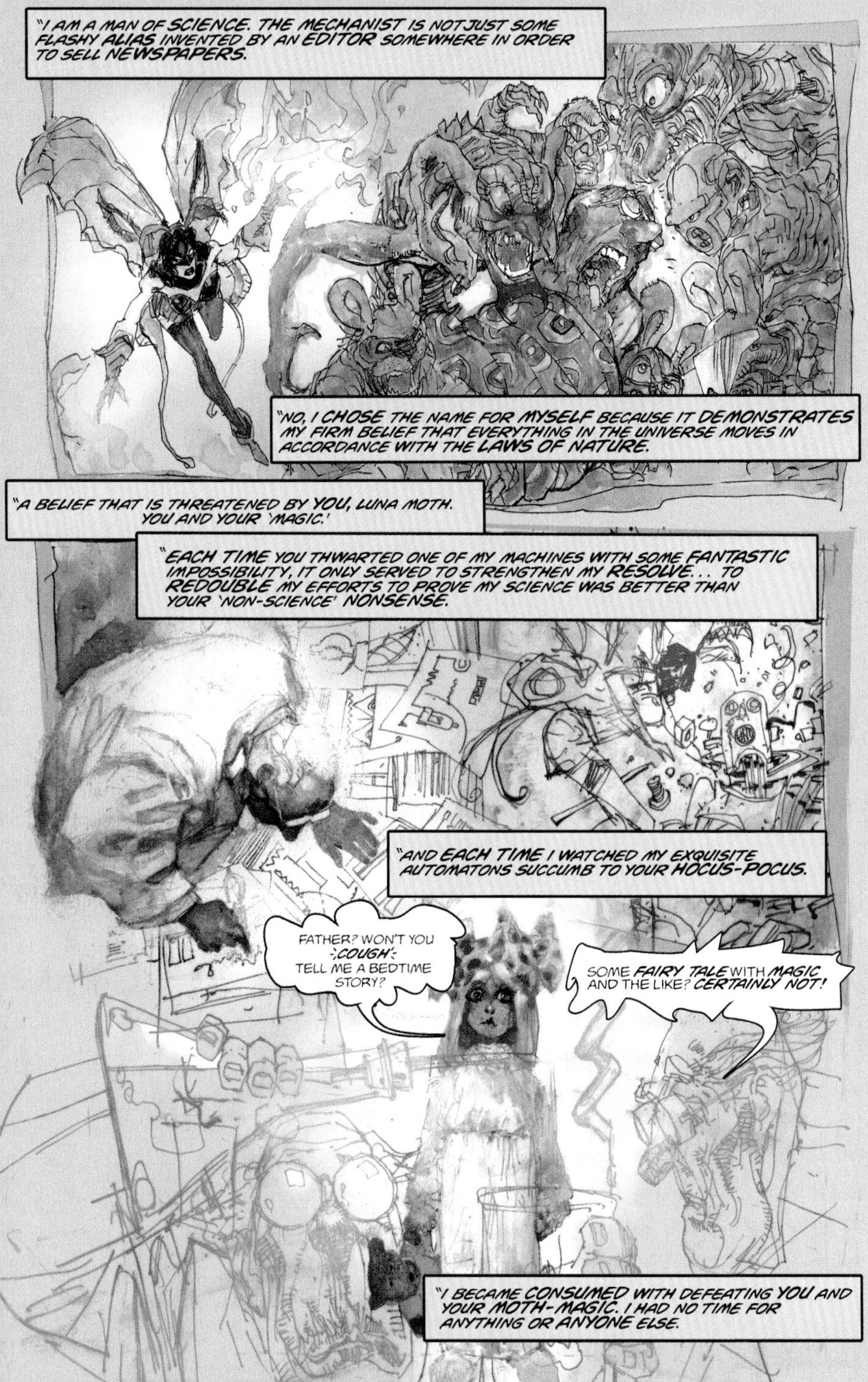
"I AM A MAN OF SCIENCE. THE MECHANIST IS NOT JUST SOME FLASHY ALIAS INVENTED BY AN EDITOR SOMEWHERE IN ORDER TO SELL NEWSPAPERS.
"NO, I CHOSE THE NAME FOR MYSELF BECAUSE IT DEMONSTRATES MY FIRM BELIEF THAT EVERYTHING IN THE UNIVERSE MOVES IN ACCORDANCE WITH THE LAWS OF NATURE.
"A BELIEF THAT IS THREATENED BY YOU, LUNA MOTH. YOU AND YOUR 'MAGIC.'
"EACH TIME YOU THWARTED ONE OF MY MACHINES WITH SOME FANTASTIC IMPOSSIBILITY, IT ONLY SERVED TO STRENGTHEN MY RESOLVE... TO REDOUBLE MY EFFORTS TO PROVE MY SCIENCE WAS BETTER THAN YOUR 'NON-SCIENCE' NONSENSE.
"AND EACH TIME I WATCHED MY EXQUISITE AUTOMATONS SUCCUMB TO YOUR HOCUS-POCUS.
FATHER? WON'T YOU -COUGH- TELL ME A BEDTIME STORY?
SOME FAIRY TALE WITH MAGIC AND THE LIKE? CERTAINLY NOT!
"I BECAME CONSUMED WITH DEFEATING YOU AND YOUR MOTH-MAGIC. I HAD NO TIME FOR ANYTHING OR ANYONE ELSE.

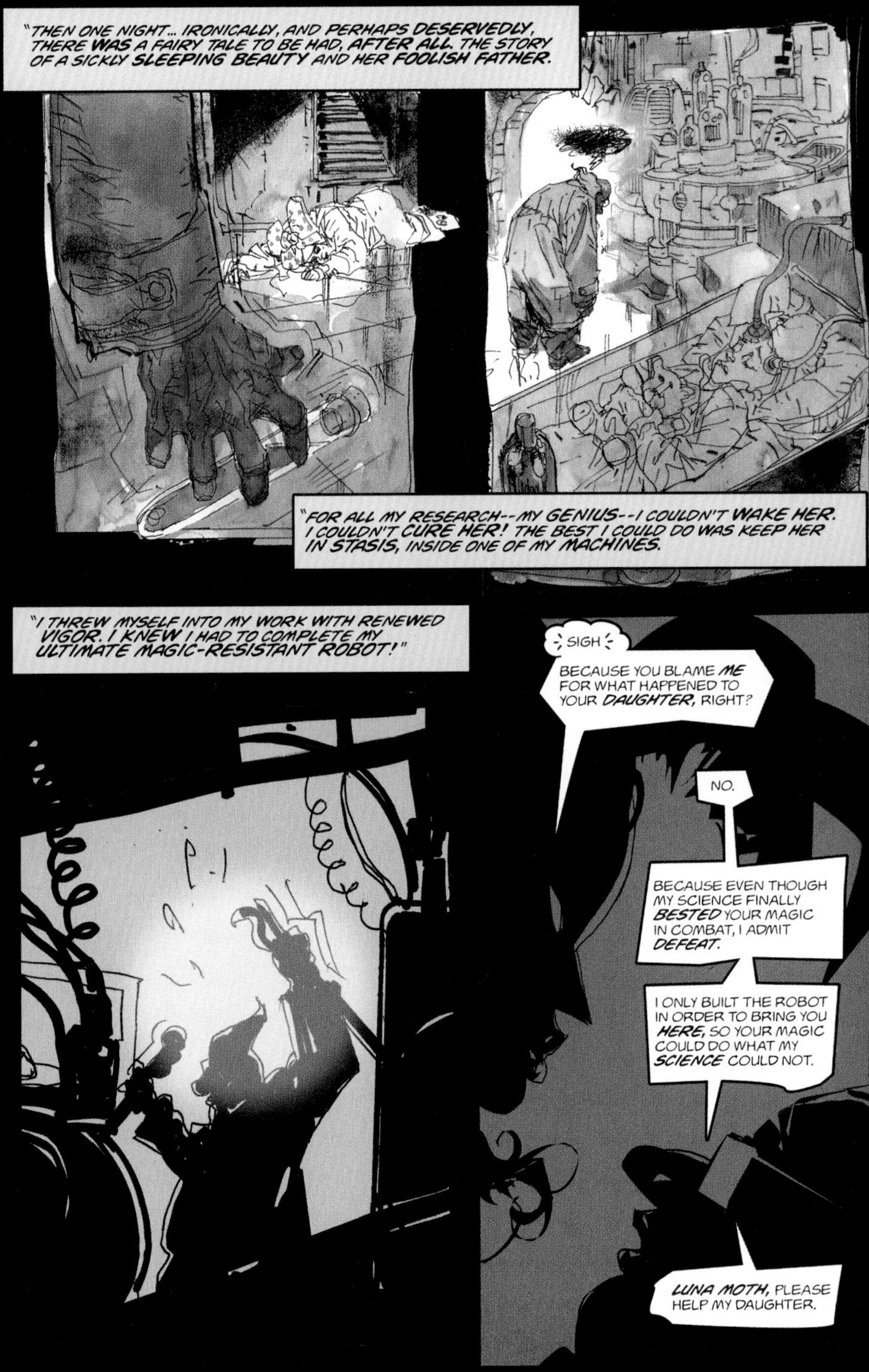
"THEN ONE NIGHT... IRONICALLY, AND PERHAPS DESERVEDLY, THERE WAS A FAIRY TALE TO BE HAD, AFTER ALL. THE STORY OF A SICKLY SLEEPING BEAUTY AND HER FOOLISH FATHER.
"FOR ALL MY RESEARCH--MY GENIUS--I COULDN'T WAKE HER. I COULDN'T CURE HER! THE BEST I COULD DO WAS KEEP HER IN STASIS, INSIDE ONE OF MY MACHINES.
"I THREW MYSELF INTO MY WORK WITH RENEWED VIGOR. I KNEW I HAD TO COMPLETE MY ULTIMATE MAGIC-RESISTANT ROBOT!"
SIGH
BECAUSE YOU BLAME ME FOR WHAT HAPPENED TO YOUR DAUGHTER, RIGHT?
NO.
BECAUSE EVEN THOUGH MY SCIENCE FINALLY BESTED YOUR MAGIC IN COMBAT, I ADMIT DEFEAT.
I ONLY BUILT THE ROBOT IN ORDER TO BRING YOU HERE, SO YOUR MAGIC COULD DO WHAT MY SCIENCE COULD NOT.
LUNA MOTH, PLEASE HELP MY DAUGHTER.

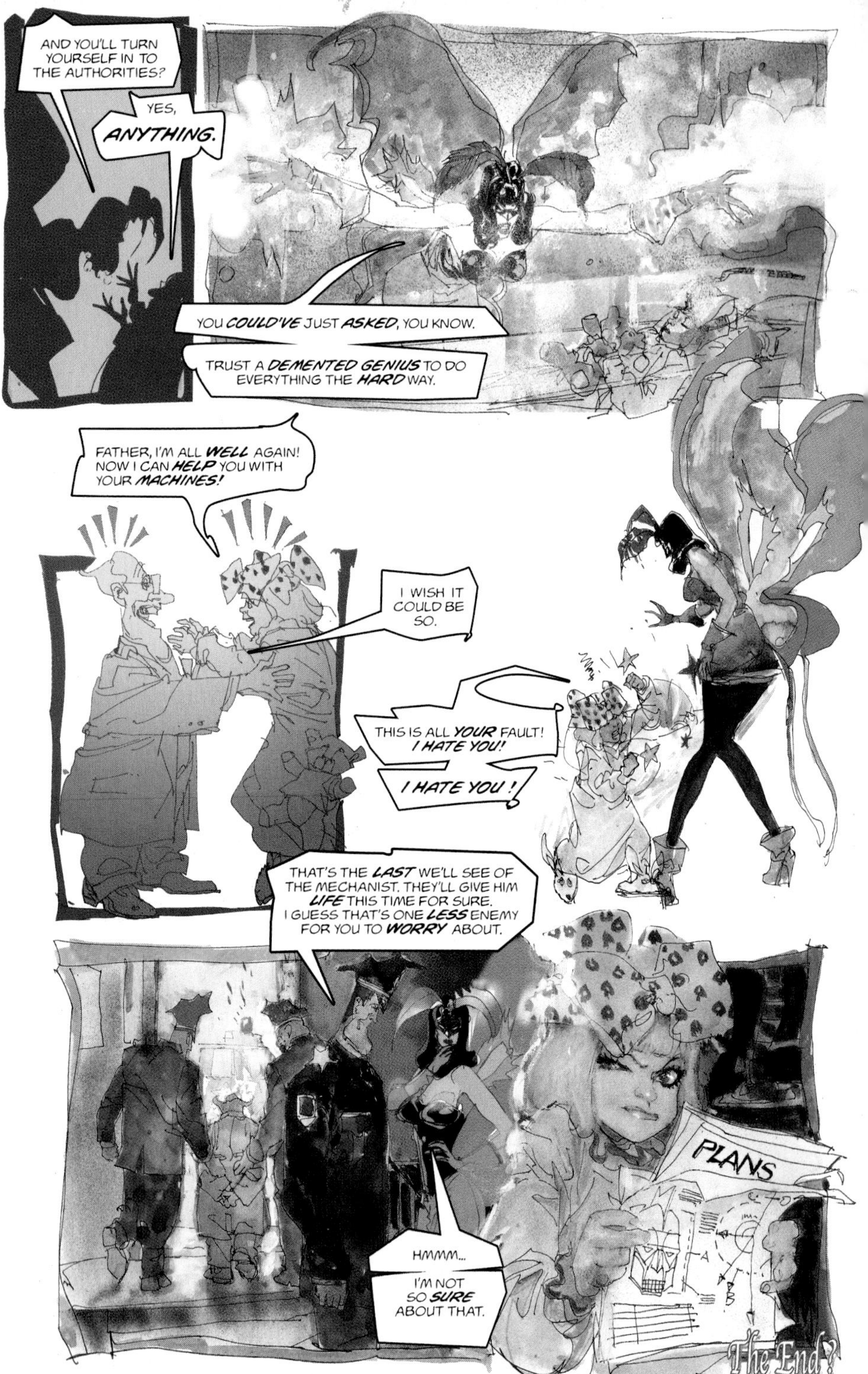
AND YOU'LL TURN YOURSELF IN TO THE AUTHORITIES?
YES, ANYTHING.
YOU COULD'VE JUST ASKED, YOU KNOW.
TRUST A DEMENTED GENIUS TO DO EVERYTHING THE HARD WAY.
FATHER, I'M ALL WELL AGAIN! NOW I CAN HELP YOU WITH YOUR MACHINES!
I WISH IT COULD BE SO.
THIS IS ALL YOUR FAULT! I HATE YOU!
I HATE YOU!
THAT'S THE LAST WE'LL SEE OF THE MECHANIST. THEY'LL GIVE HIM LIFE THIS TIME FOR SURE. I GUESS THAT'S ONE LESS ENEMY FOR YOU TO WORRY ABOUT.
HMMM...
I'M NOT SO SURE ABOUT THAT.
PLANS
The End?

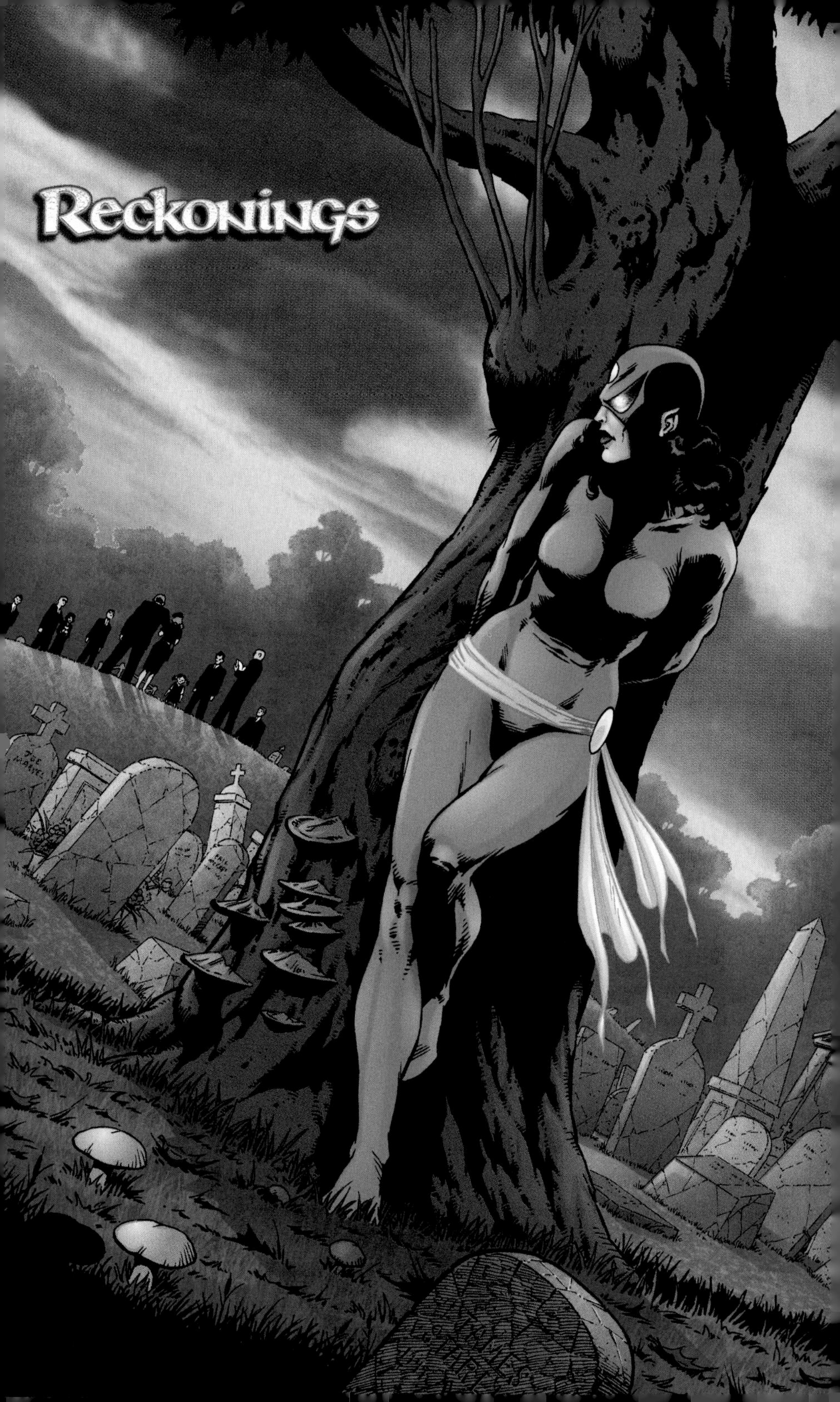
Reckonings

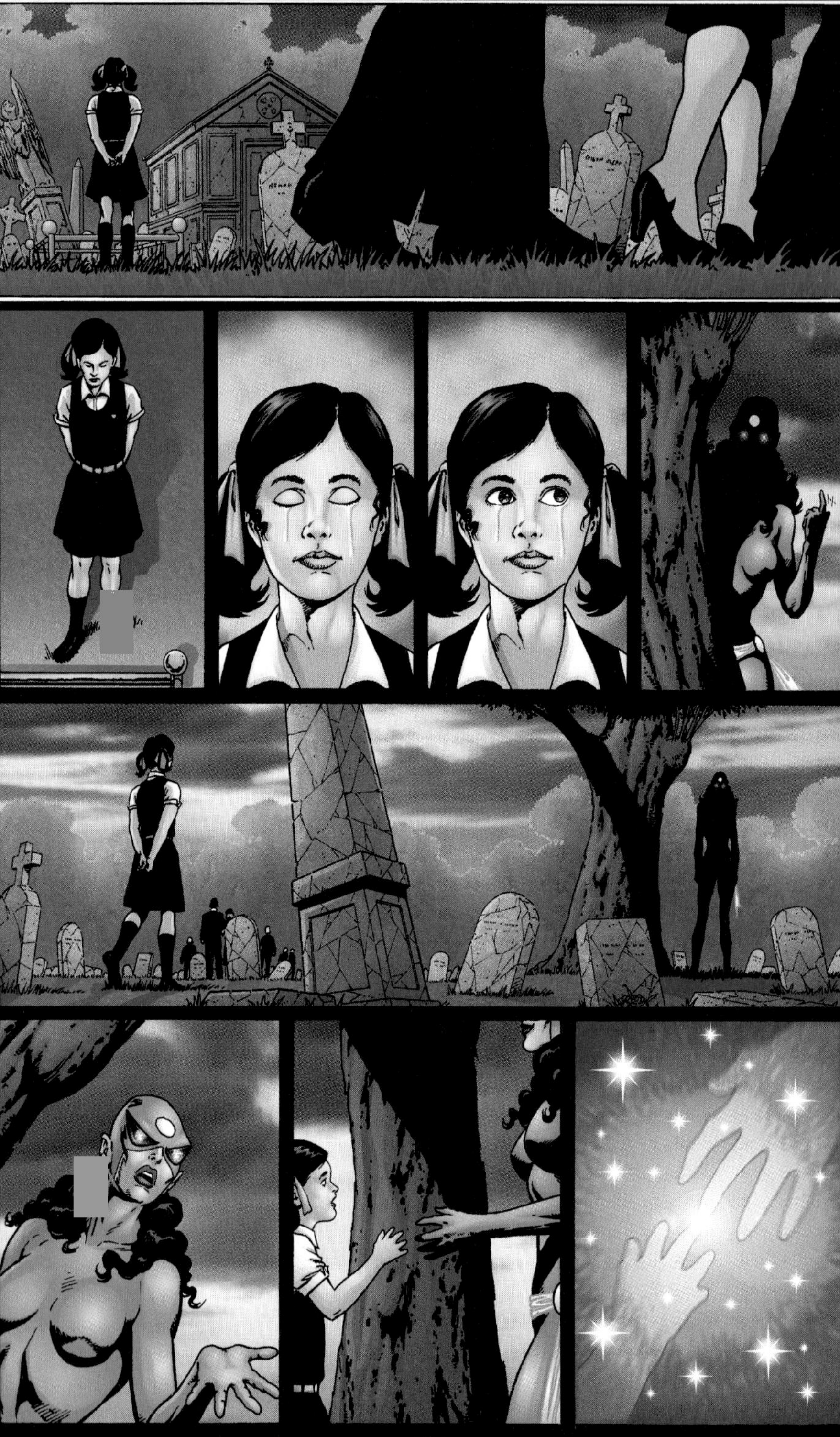

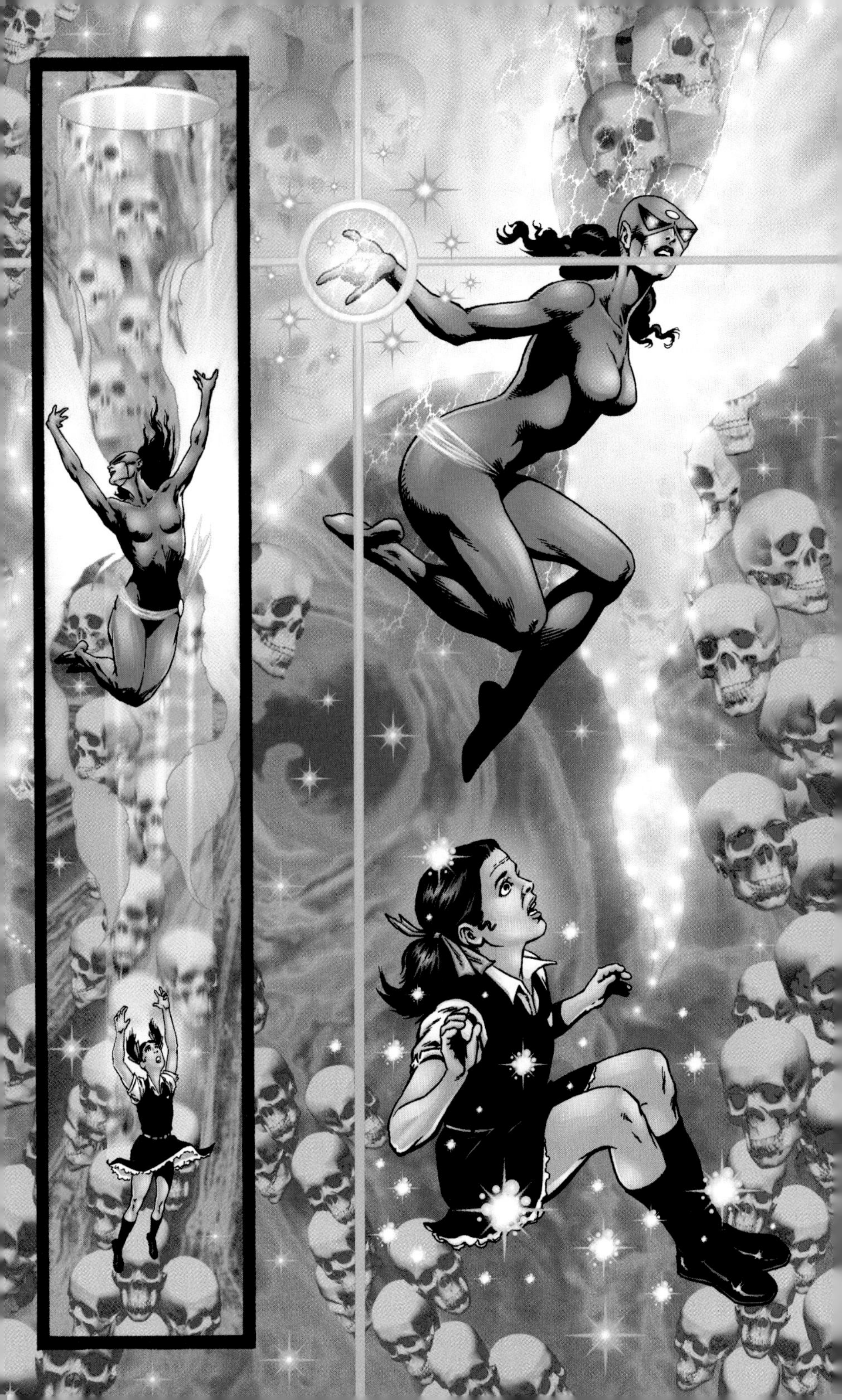

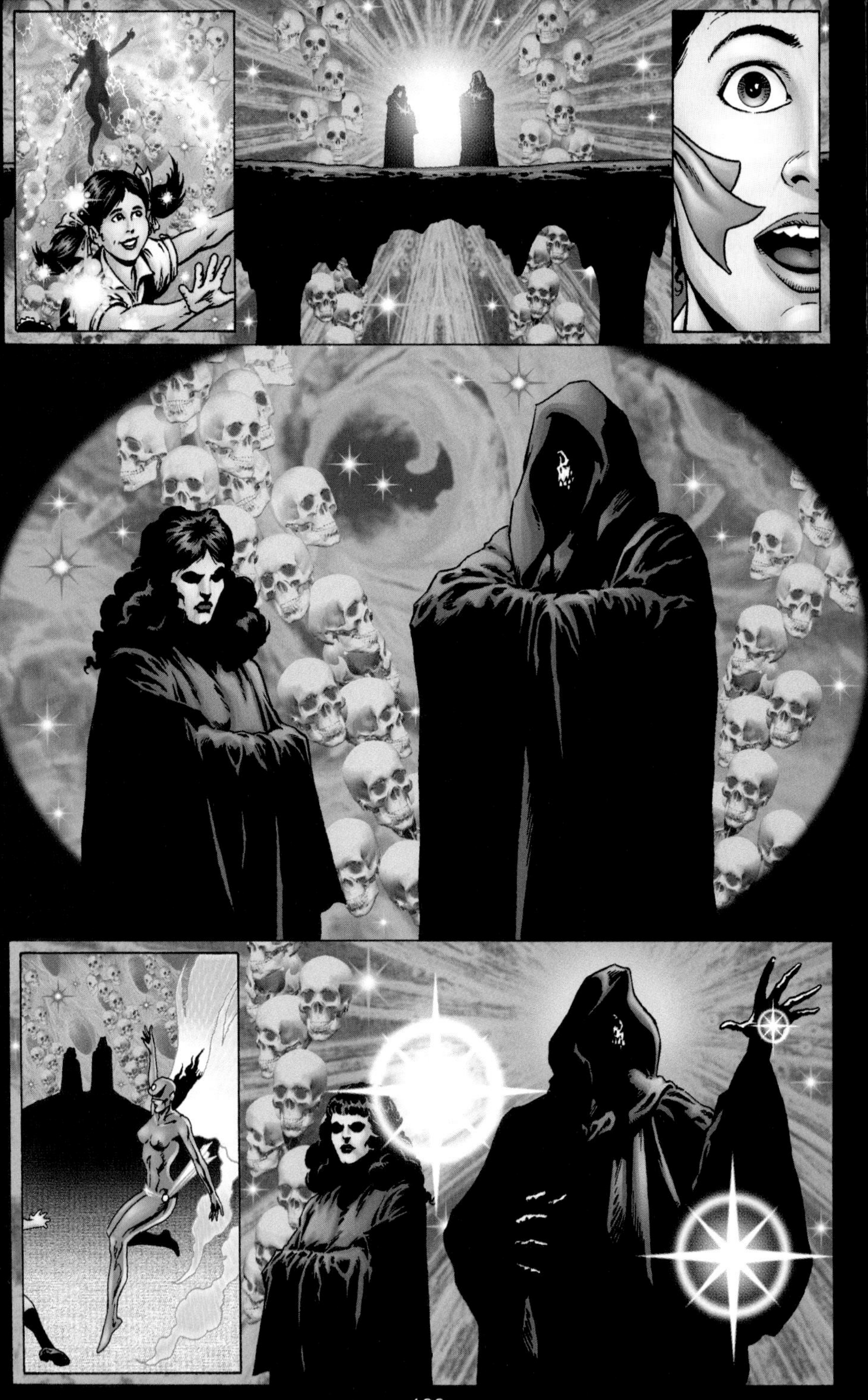

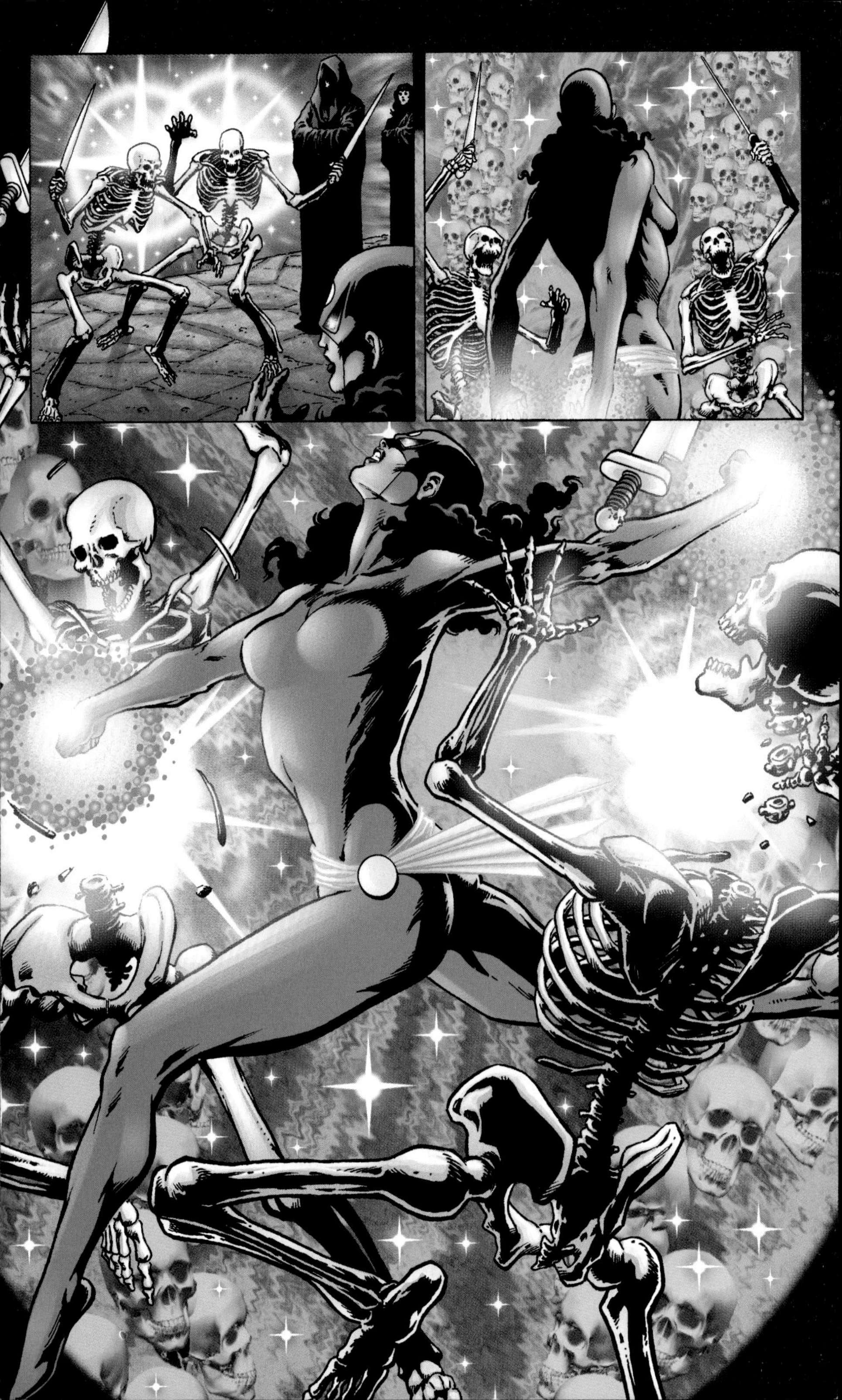

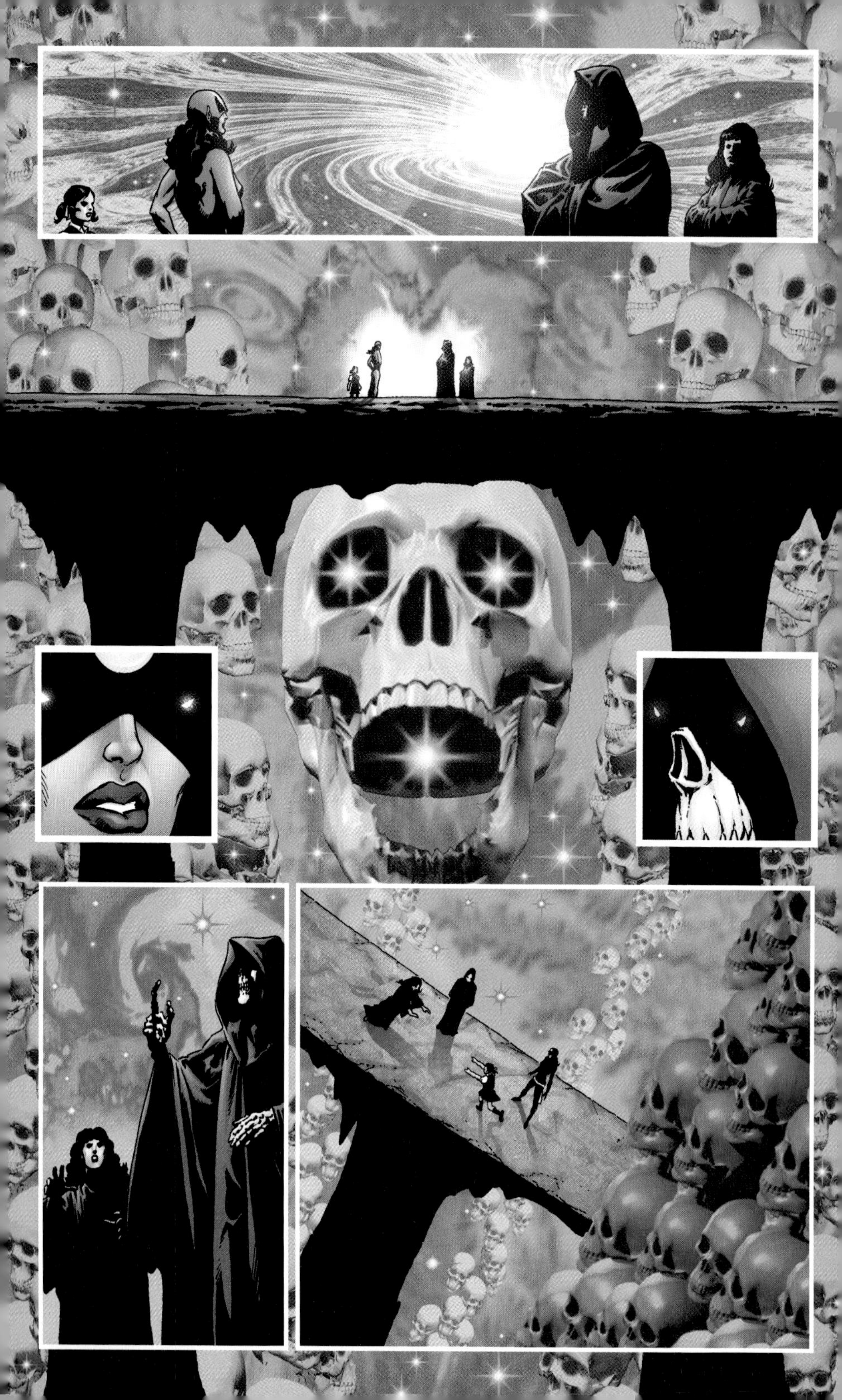

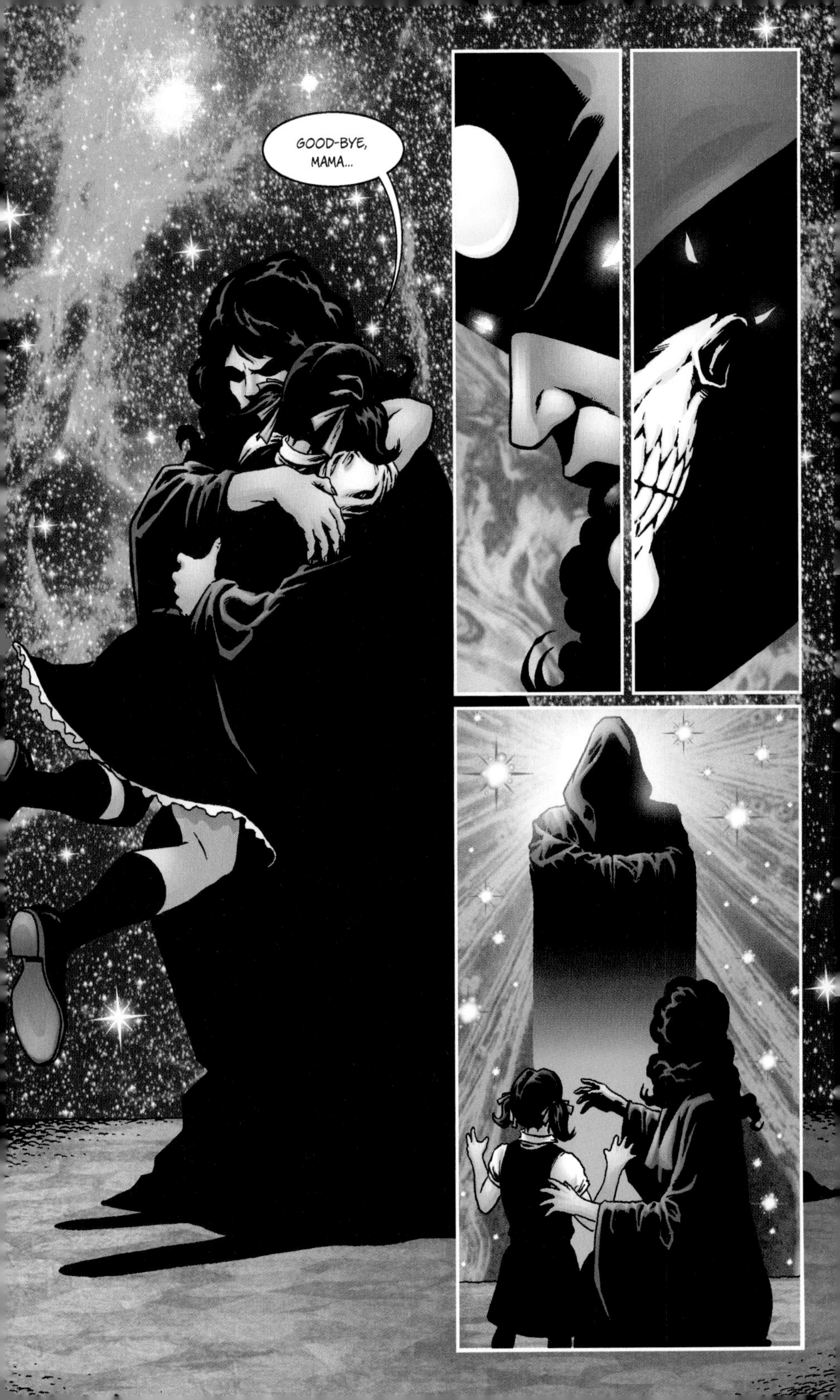
GOOD-BYE, MAMA...

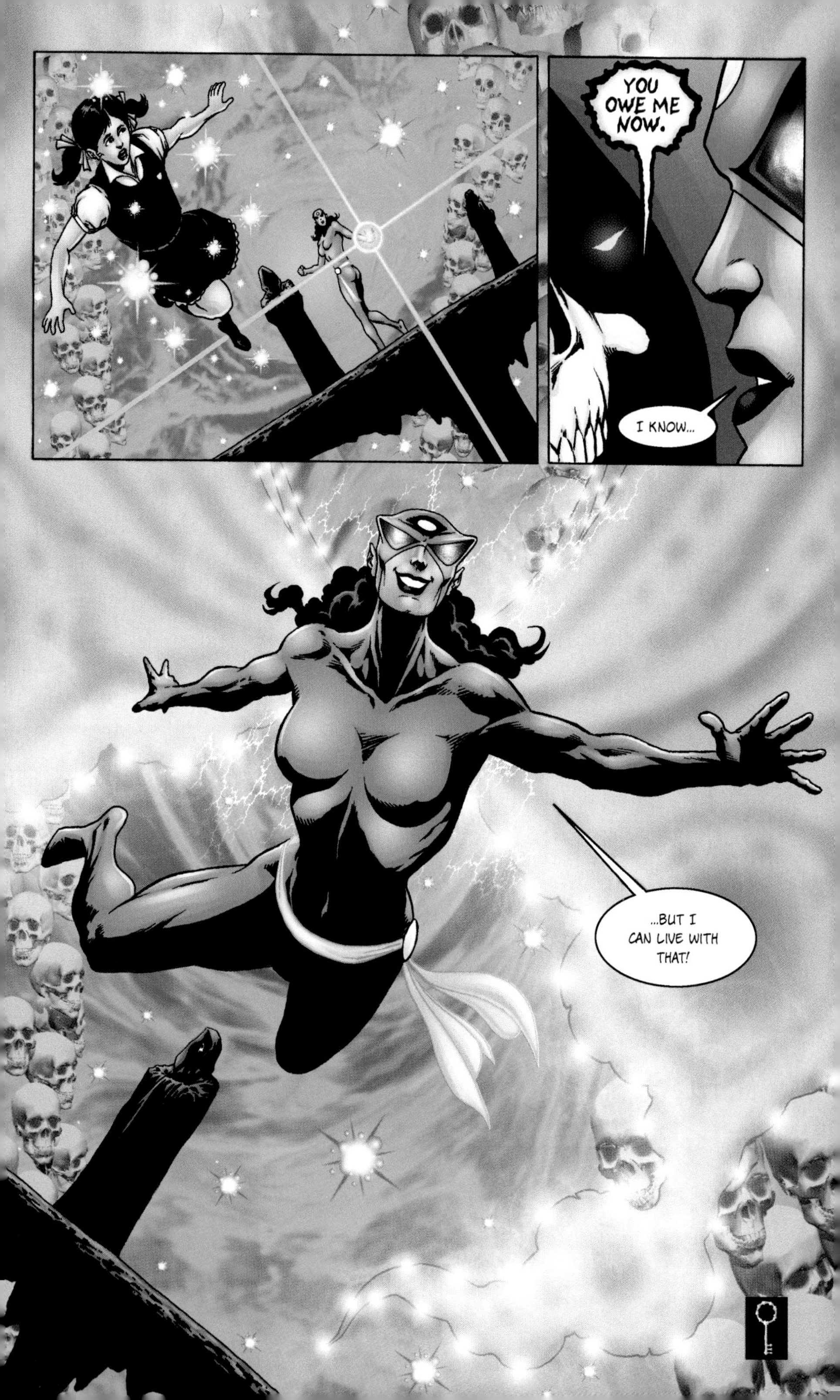
YOU OWE ME NOW.
I KNOW...
...BUT I CAN LIVE WITH THAT!

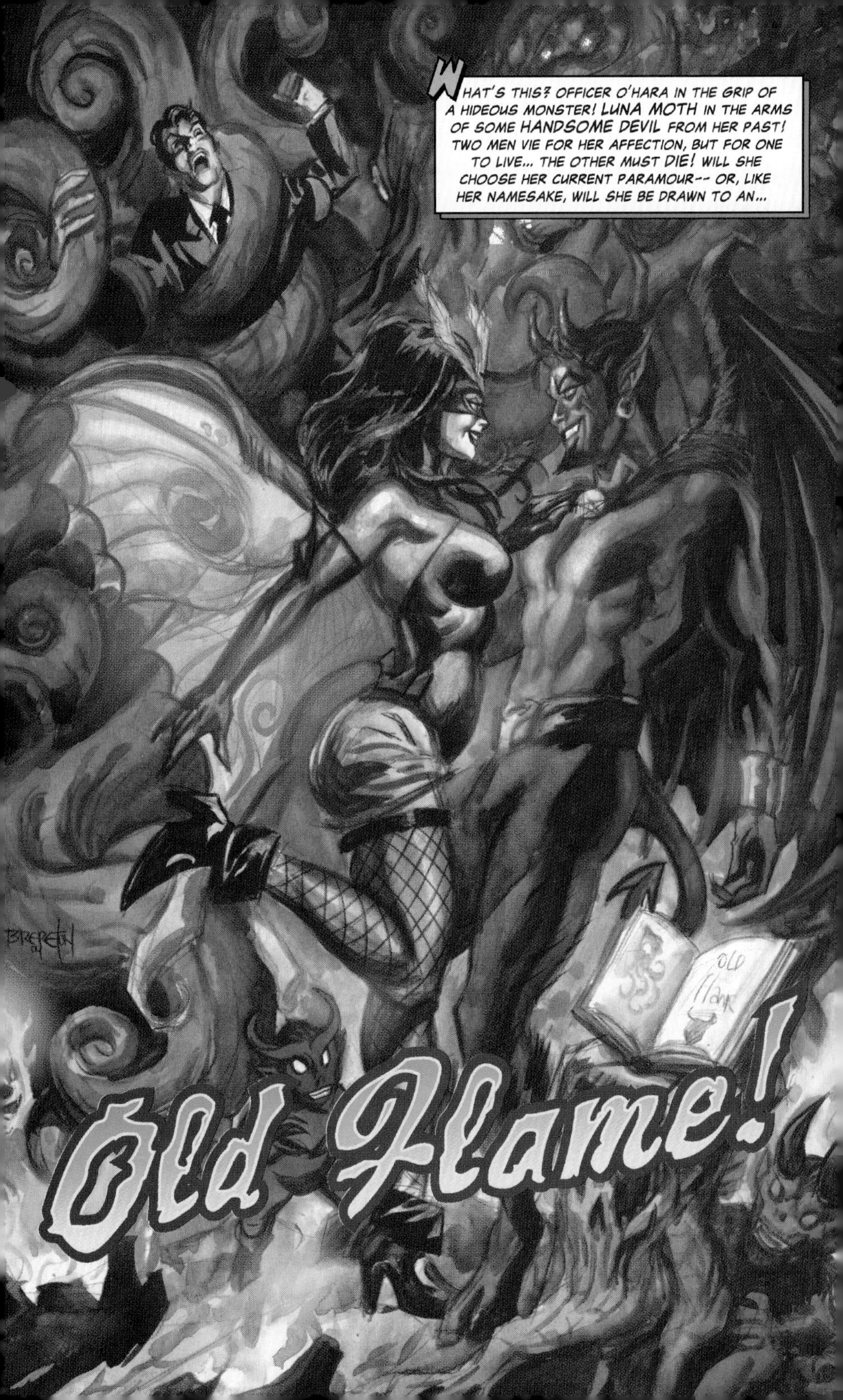
WHAT'S THIS? OFFICER O'HARA IN THE GRIP OF A HIDEOUS MONSTER! LUNA MOTH IN THE ARMS OF SOME HANDSOME DEVIL FROM HER PAST! TWO MEN VIE FOR HER AFFECTION, BUT FOR ONE TO LIVE... THE OTHER MUST DIE! WILL SHE CHOOSE HER CURRENT PARAMOUR-- OR, LIKE HER NAMESAKE, WILL SHE BE DRAWN TO AN...
Old Flame!

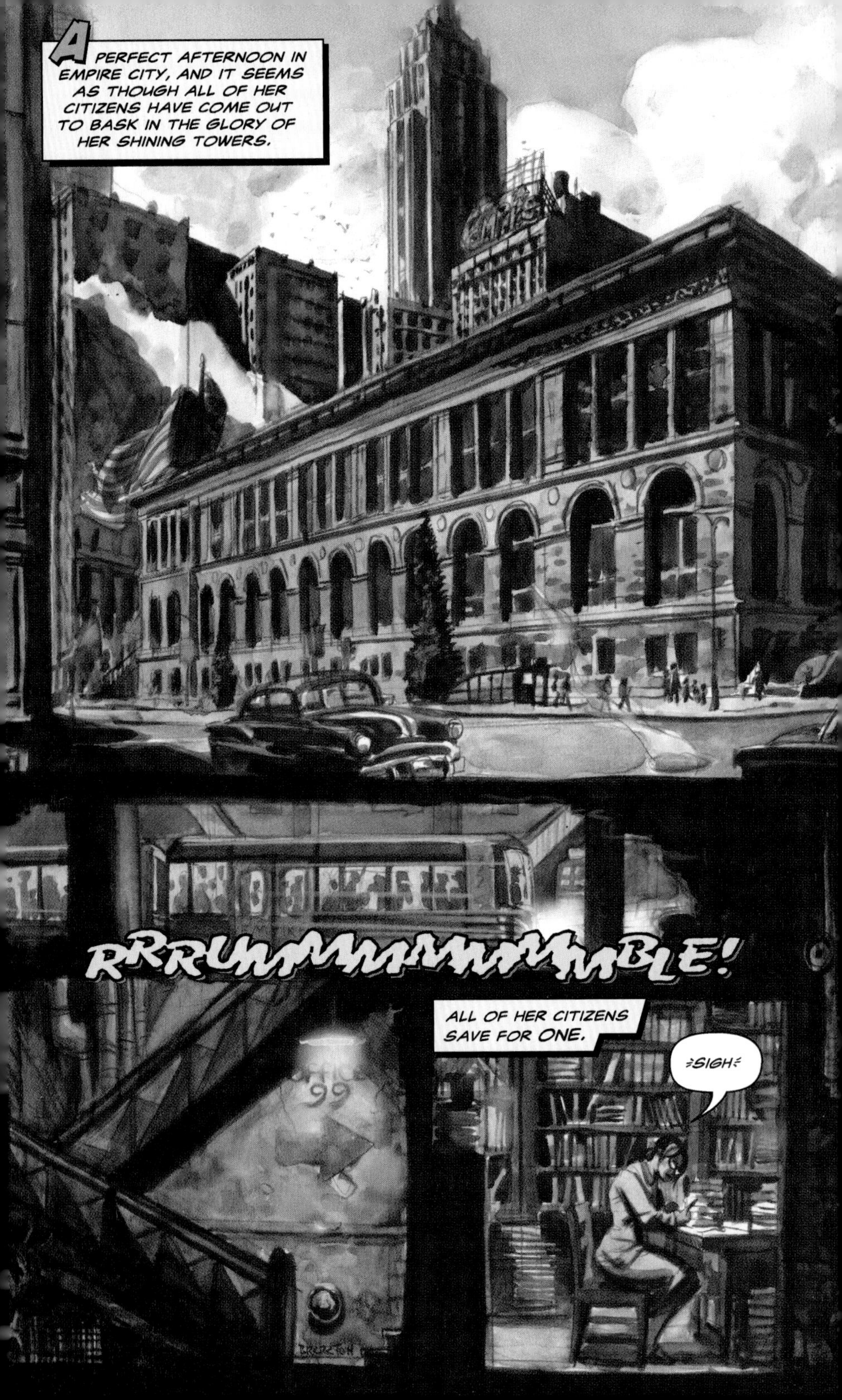
A PERFECT AFTERNOON IN EMPIRE CITY, AND IT SEEMS AS THOUGH ALL OF HER CITIZENS HAVE COME OUT TO BASK IN THE GLORY OF HER SHINING TOWERS.
RRRUMMMMMMMMBLE!
ALL OF HER CITIZENS SAVE FOR ONE.
SIGH

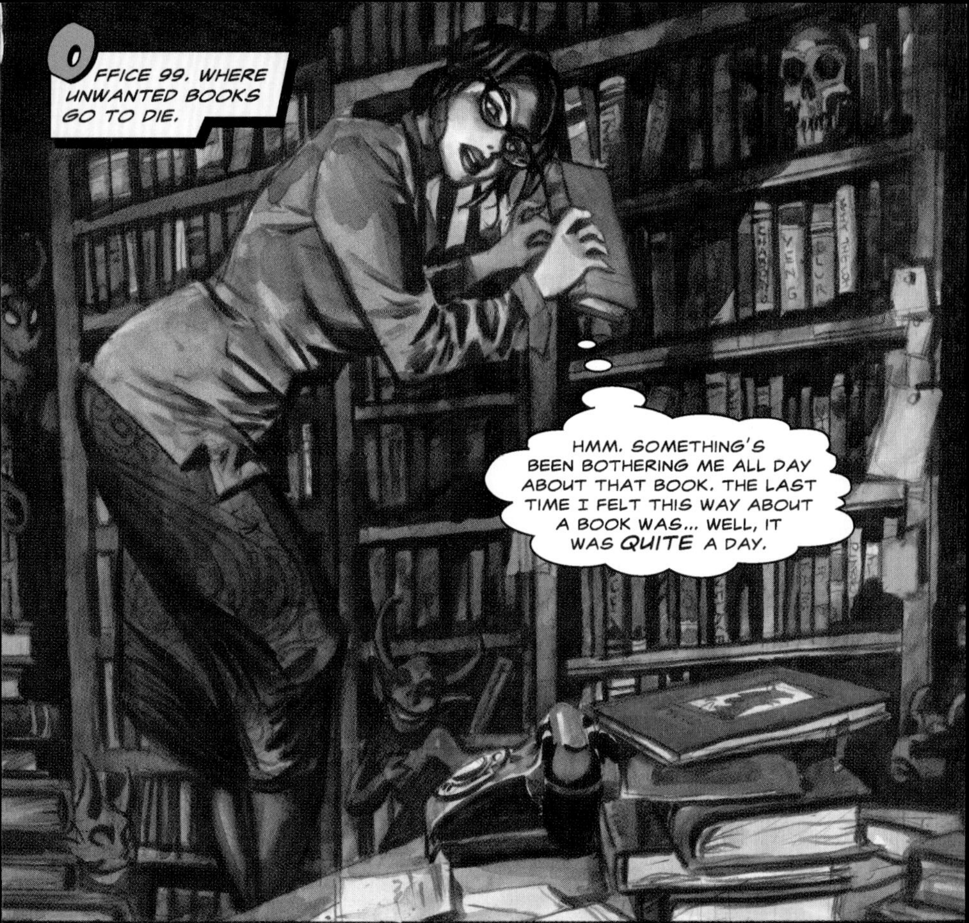
OFFICE 99. WHERE UNWANTED BOOKS GO TO DIE.
HMM. SOMETHING'S BEEN BOTHERING ME ALL DAY ABOUT THAT BOOK. THE LAST TIME I FELT THIS WAY ABOUT A BOOK WAS... WELL, IT WAS QUITE A DAY.

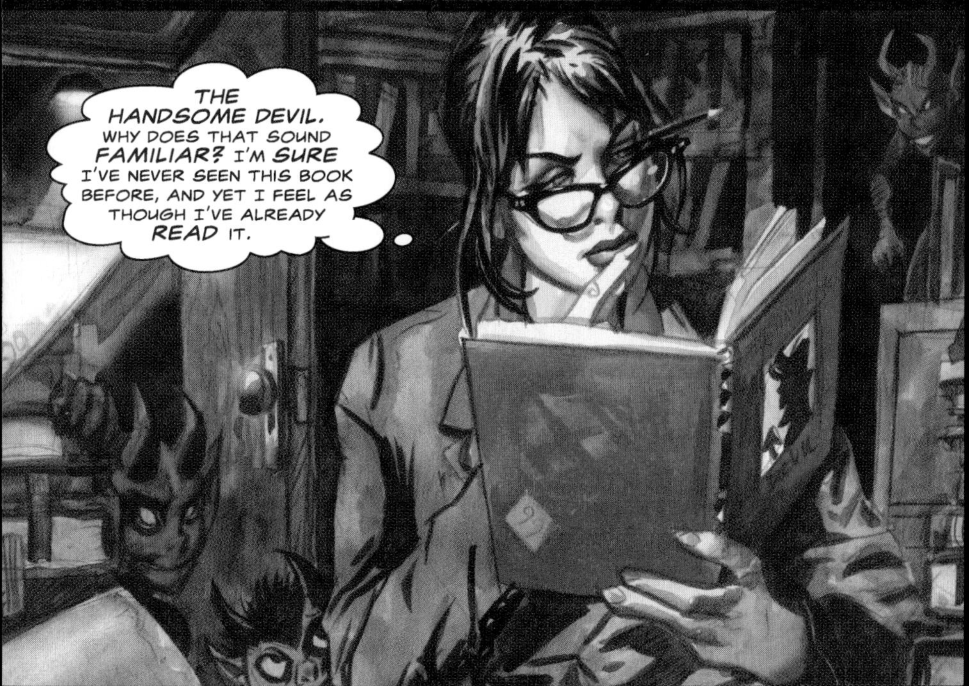
THE HANDSOME DEVIL. WHY DOES THAT SOUND FAMILIAR? I'M SURE I'VE NEVER SEEN THIS BOOK BEFORE, AND YET I FEEL AS THOUGH I'VE ALREADY READ IT.

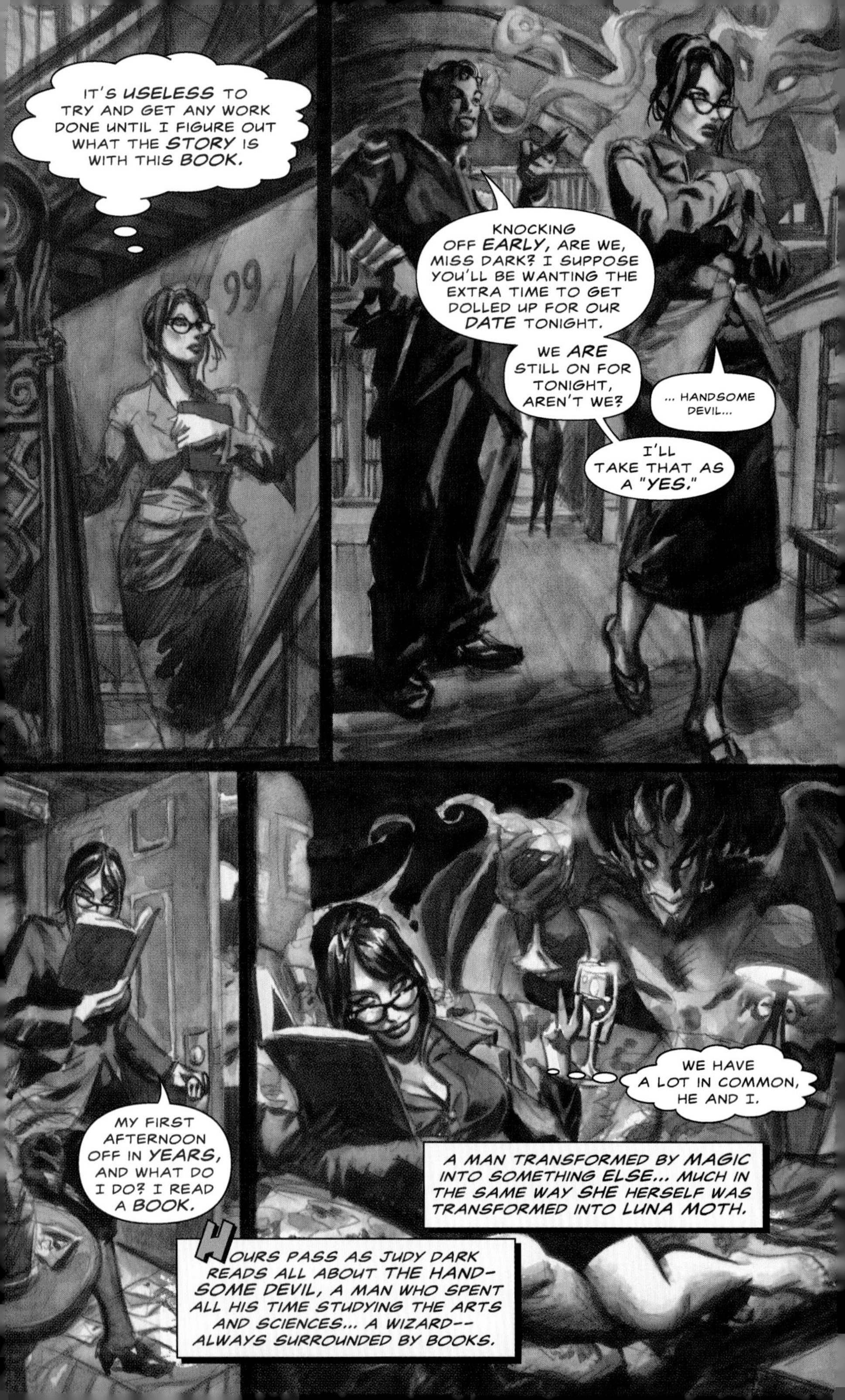
IT'S USELESS TO TRY AND GET ANY WORK DONE UNTIL I FIGURE OUT WHAT THE STORY IS WITH THIS BOOK.
KNOCKING OFF EARLY, ARE WE, MISS DARK? I SUPPOSE YOU'LL BE WANTING THE EXTRA TIME TO GET DOLLED UP FOR OUR DATE TONIGHT.
WE ARE STILL ON FOR TONIGHT, AREN'T WE?
... HANDSOME DEVIL...
I'LL TAKE THAT AS A "YES."
MY FIRST AFTERNOON OFF IN YEARS, AND WHAT DO I DO? I READ A BOOK.
WE HAVE A LOT IN COMMON, HE AND I.
A MAN TRANSFORMED BY MAGIC INTO SOMETHING ELSE... MUCH IN THE SAME WAY SHE HERSELF WAS TRANSFORMED INTO LUNA MOTH.
HOURS PASS AS JUDY DARK READS ALL ABOUT THE HANDSOME DEVIL, A MAN WHO SPENT ALL HIS TIME STUDYING THE ARTS AND SCIENCES... A WIZARD--ALWAYS SURROUNDED BY BOOKS.

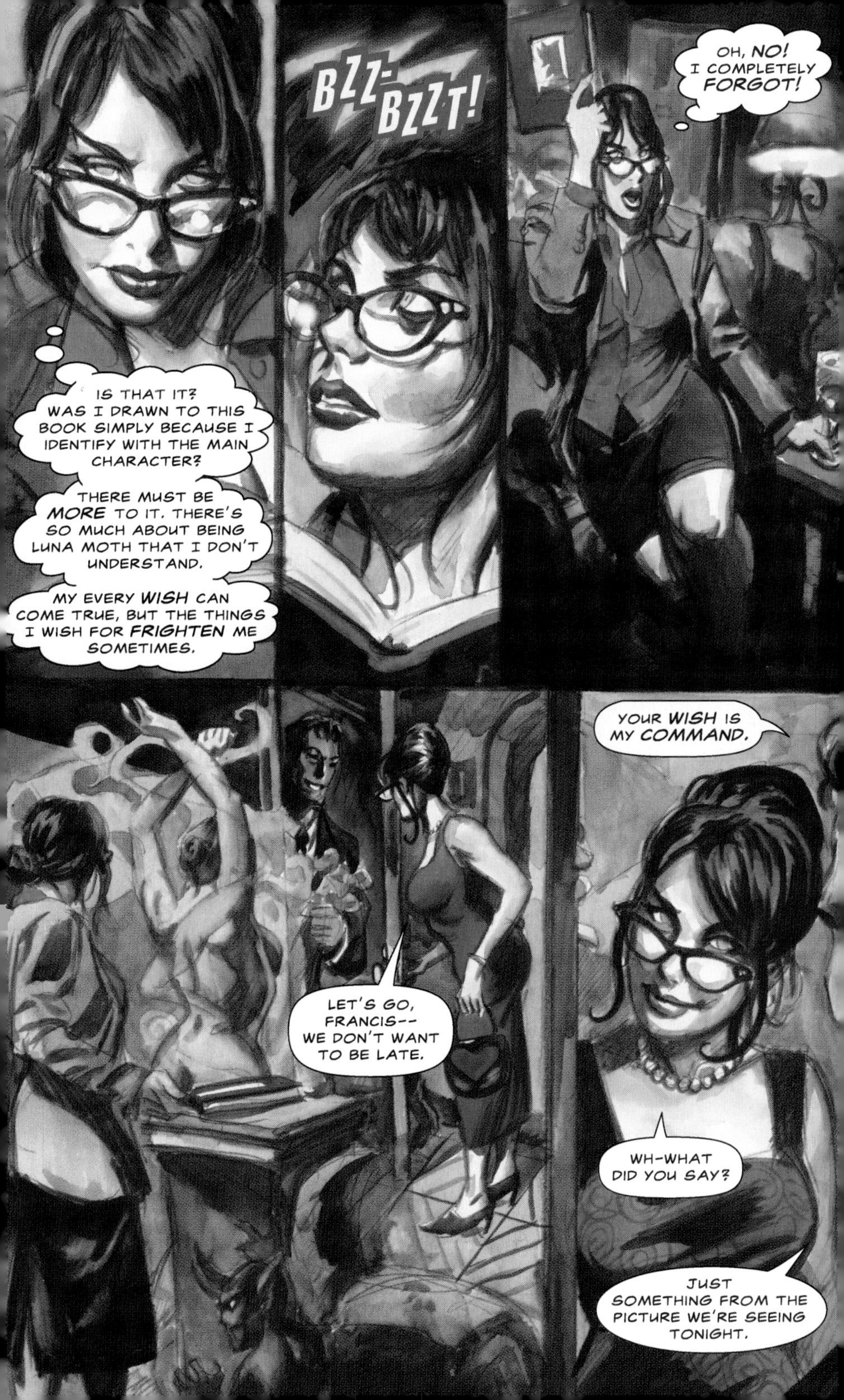
IS THAT IT? WAS I DRAWN TO THIS BOOK SIMPLY BECAUSE I IDENTIFY WITH THE MAIN CHARACTER?
THERE MUST BE MORE TO IT. THERE'S SO MUCH ABOUT BEING LUNA MOTH THAT I DON'T UNDERSTAND.
MY EVERY WISH CAN COME TRUE, BUT THE THINGS I WISH FOR FRIGHTEN ME SOMETIMES.
BZZ-BZZT!
OH, NO! I COMPLETELY FORGOT!
LET'S GO, FRANCIS-- WE DON'T WANT TO BE LATE.
YOUR WISH IS MY COMMAND.
WH-WHAT DID YOU SAY?
JUST SOMETHING FROM THE PICTURE WE'RE SEEING TONIGHT.

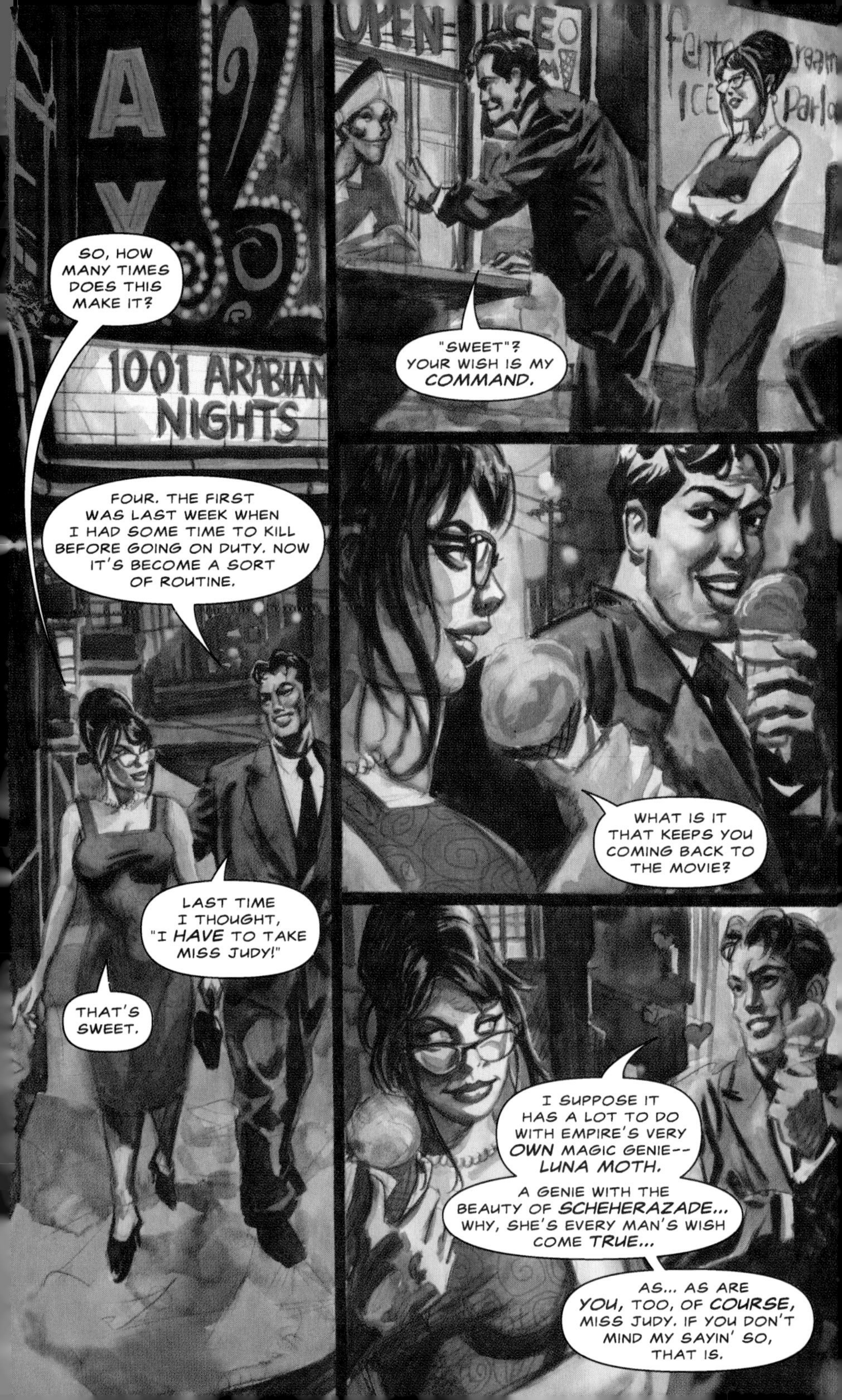
SO, HOW MANY TIMES DOES THIS MAKE IT?
1001 ARABIAN NIGHTS
FOUR. THE FIRST WAS LAST WEEK WHEN I HAD SOME TIME TO KILL BEFORE GOING ON DUTY. NOW IT'S BECOME A SORT OF ROUTINE.
LAST TIME I THOUGHT, "I *HAVE* TO TAKE MISS JUDY!"
THAT'S SWEET.
OPEN
"SWEET"? YOUR WISH IS MY *COMMAND.*
WHAT IS IT THAT KEEPS YOU COMING BACK TO THE MOVIE?
I SUPPOSE IT HAS A LOT TO DO WITH EMPIRE'S VERY *OWN* MAGIC GENIE-- *LUNA MOTH.*
A GENIE WITH THE BEAUTY OF *SCHEHERAZADE...* WHY, SHE'S EVERY MAN'S WISH COME *TRUE...*
AS... AS ARE *YOU,* TOO, OF *COURSE,* MISS JUDY. IF YOU DON'T MIND MY SAYIN' SO, THAT IS.

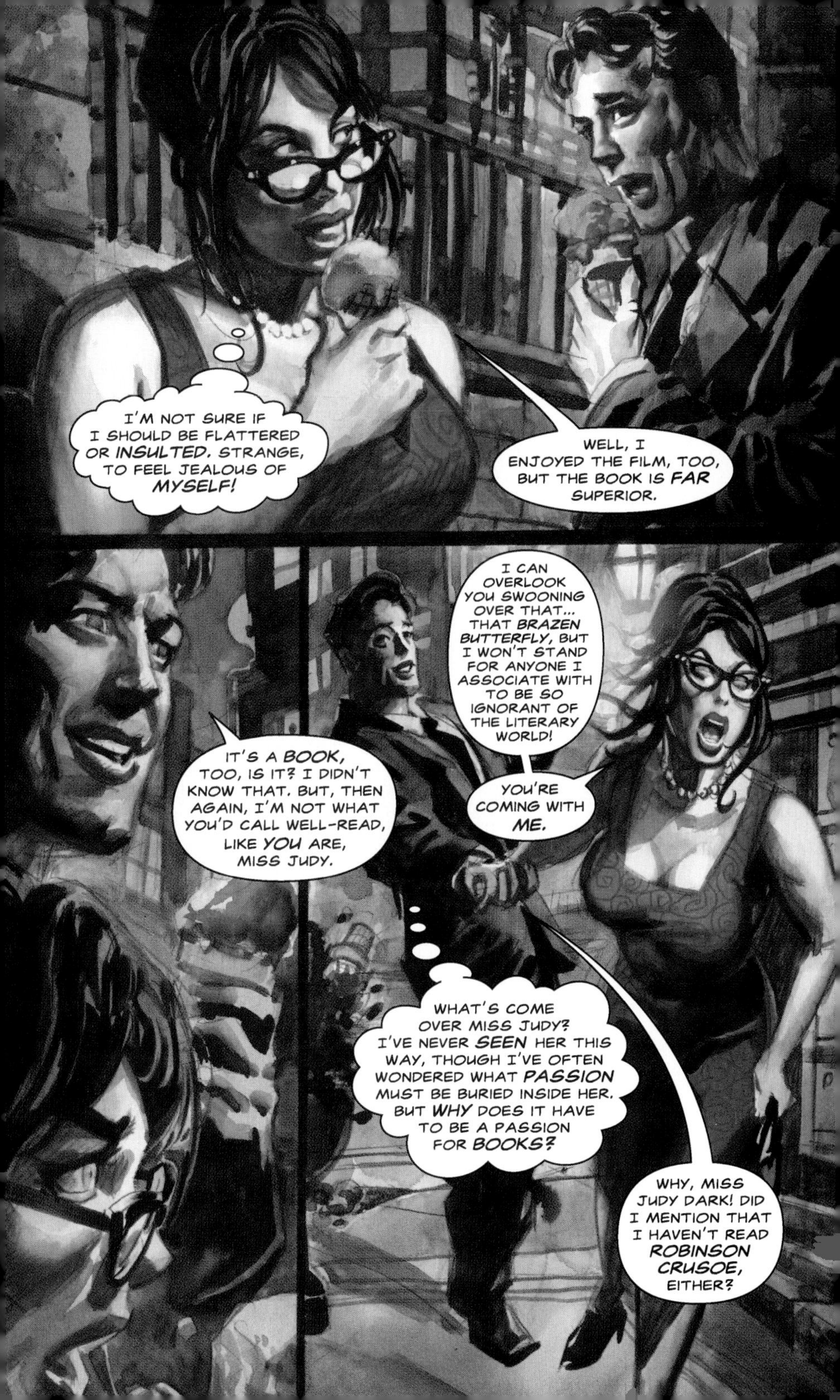
I'M NOT SURE IF I SHOULD BE FLATTERED OR INSULTED. STRANGE, TO FEEL JEALOUS OF MYSELF!
WELL, I ENJOYED THE FILM, TOO, BUT THE BOOK IS FAR SUPERIOR.
IT'S A BOOK, TOO, IS IT? I DIDN'T KNOW THAT. BUT, THEN AGAIN, I'M NOT WHAT YOU'D CALL WELL-READ, LIKE YOU ARE, MISS JUDY.
I CAN OVERLOOK YOU SWOONING OVER THAT... THAT BRAZEN BUTTERFLY, BUT I WON'T STAND FOR ANYONE I ASSOCIATE WITH TO BE SO IGNORANT OF THE LITERARY WORLD!
YOU'RE COMING WITH ME.
WHAT'S COME OVER MISS JUDY? I'VE NEVER SEEN HER THIS WAY, THOUGH I'VE OFTEN WONDERED WHAT PASSION MUST BE BURIED INSIDE HER. BUT WHY DOES IT HAVE TO BE A PASSION FOR BOOKS?
WHY, MISS JUDY DARK! DID I MENTION THAT I HAVEN'T READ ROBINSON CRUSOE, EITHER?

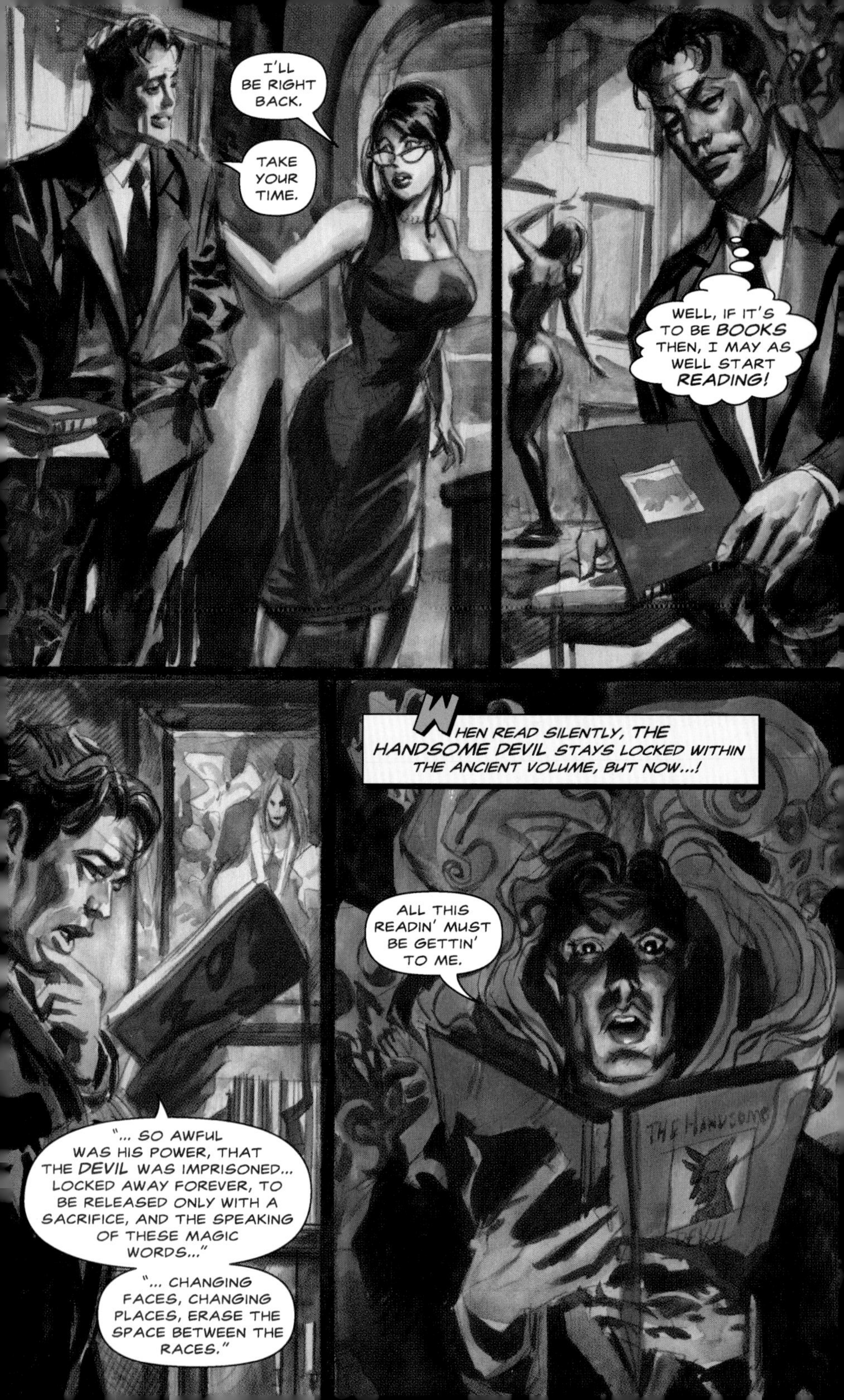
I'LL BE RIGHT BACK.
TAKE YOUR TIME.
WELL, IF IT'S TO BE BOOKS THEN, I MAY AS WELL START READING!
"... SO AWFUL WAS HIS POWER, THAT THE DEVIL WAS IMPRISONED... LOCKED AWAY FOREVER, TO BE RELEASED ONLY WITH A SACRIFICE, AND THE SPEAKING OF THESE MAGIC WORDS..."
"... CHANGING FACES, CHANGING PLACES, ERASE THE SPACE BETWEEN THE RACES."
WHEN READ SILENTLY, THE HANDSOME DEVIL STAYS LOCKED WITHIN THE ANCIENT VOLUME, BUT NOW...!
ALL THIS READIN' MUST BE GETTIN' TO ME.
THE HANDSOME

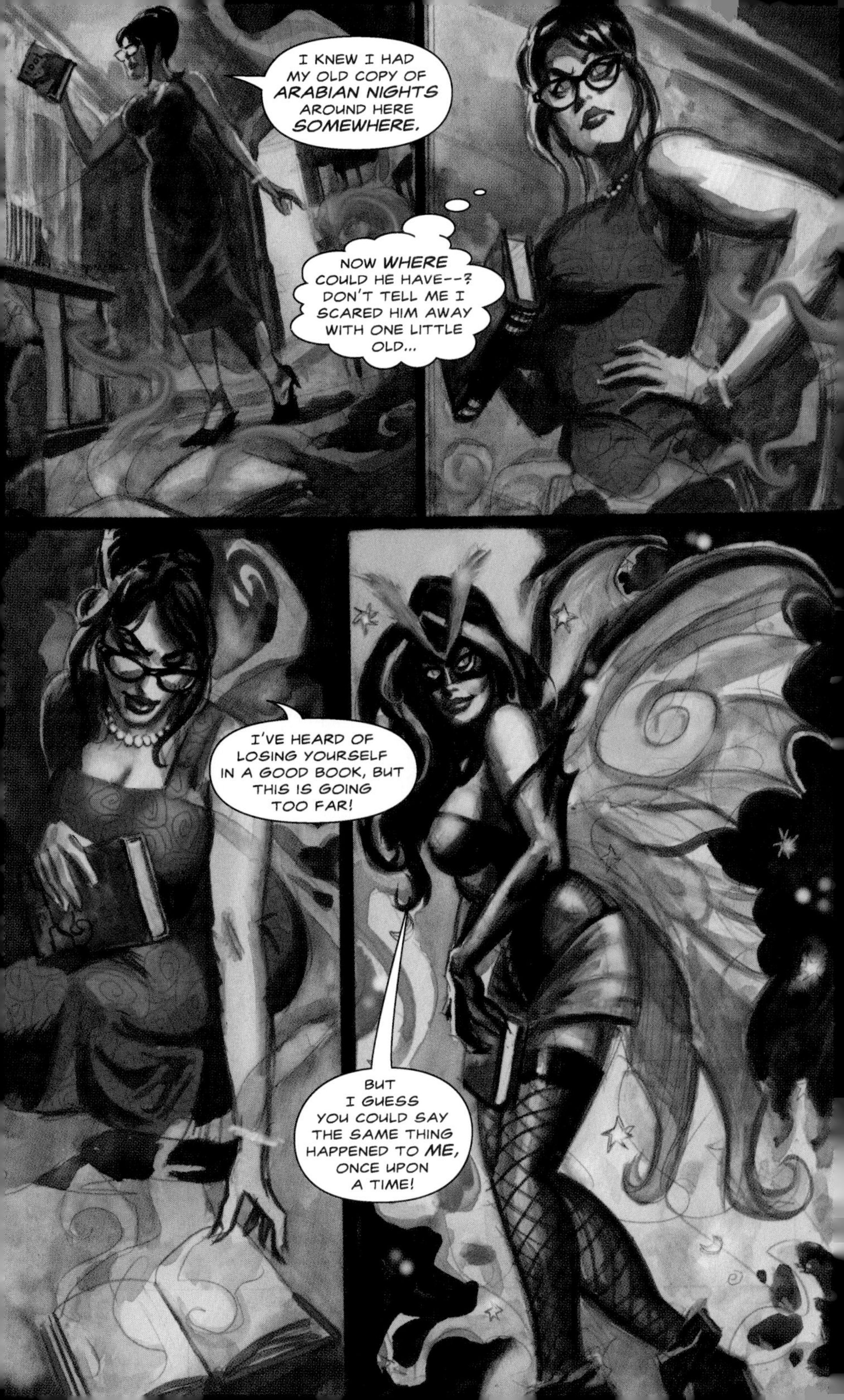
I KNEW I HAD MY OLD COPY OF ARABIAN NIGHTS AROUND HERE SOMEWHERE.
NOW WHERE COULD HE HAVE--? DON'T TELL ME I SCARED HIM AWAY WITH ONE LITTLE OLD...
I'VE HEARD OF LOSING YOURSELF IN A GOOD BOOK, BUT THIS IS GOING TOO FAR!
BUT I GUESS YOU COULD SAY THE SAME THING HAPPENED TO ME, ONCE UPON A TIME!

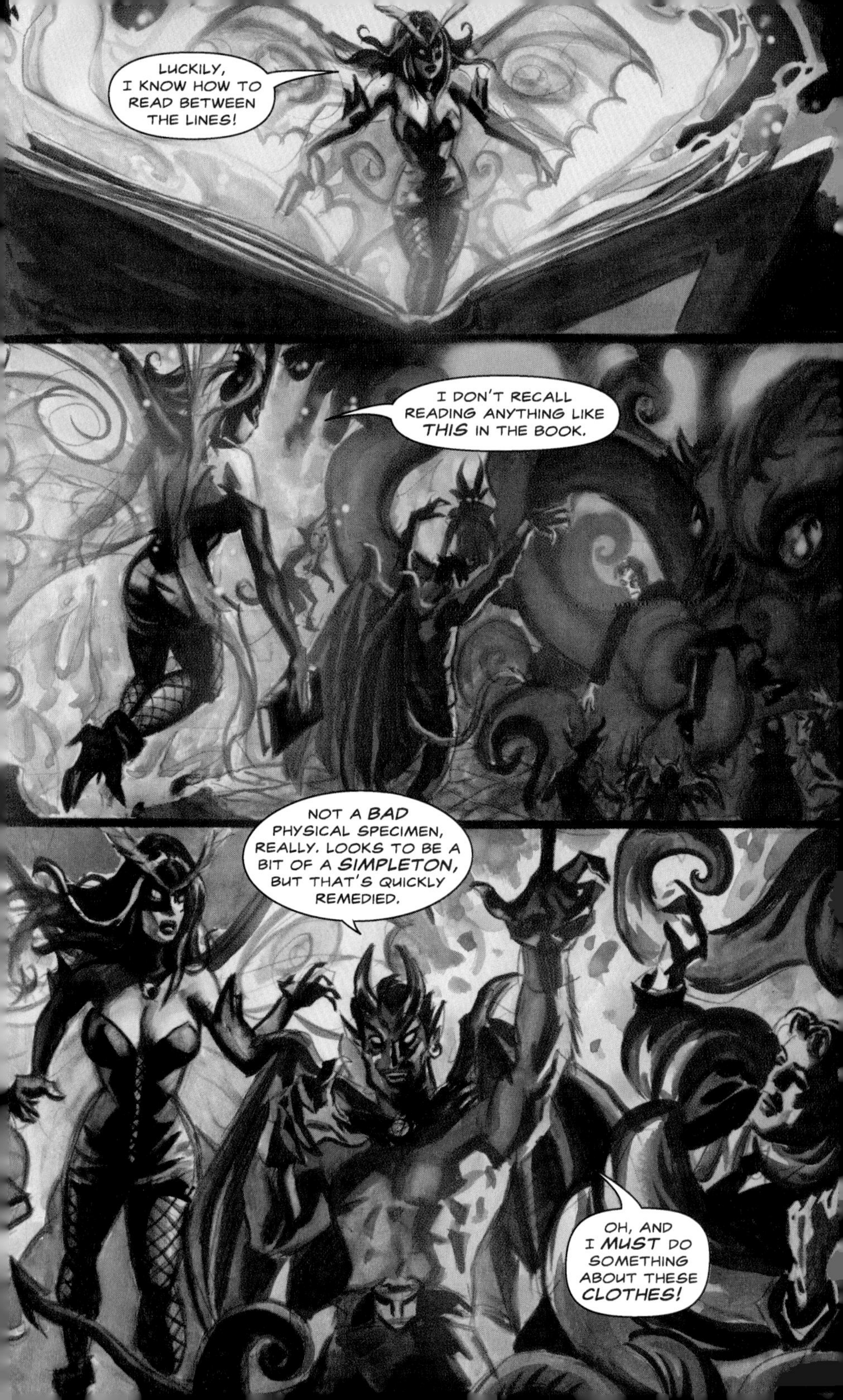
LUCKILY, I KNOW HOW TO READ BETWEEN THE LINES!
I DON'T RECALL READING ANYTHING LIKE *THIS* IN THE BOOK.
NOT A *BAD* PHYSICAL SPECIMEN, REALLY. LOOKS TO BE A BIT OF A *SIMPLETON*, BUT THAT'S QUICKLY REMEDIED.
OH, AND I *MUST* DO SOMETHING ABOUT THESE *CLOTHES!*

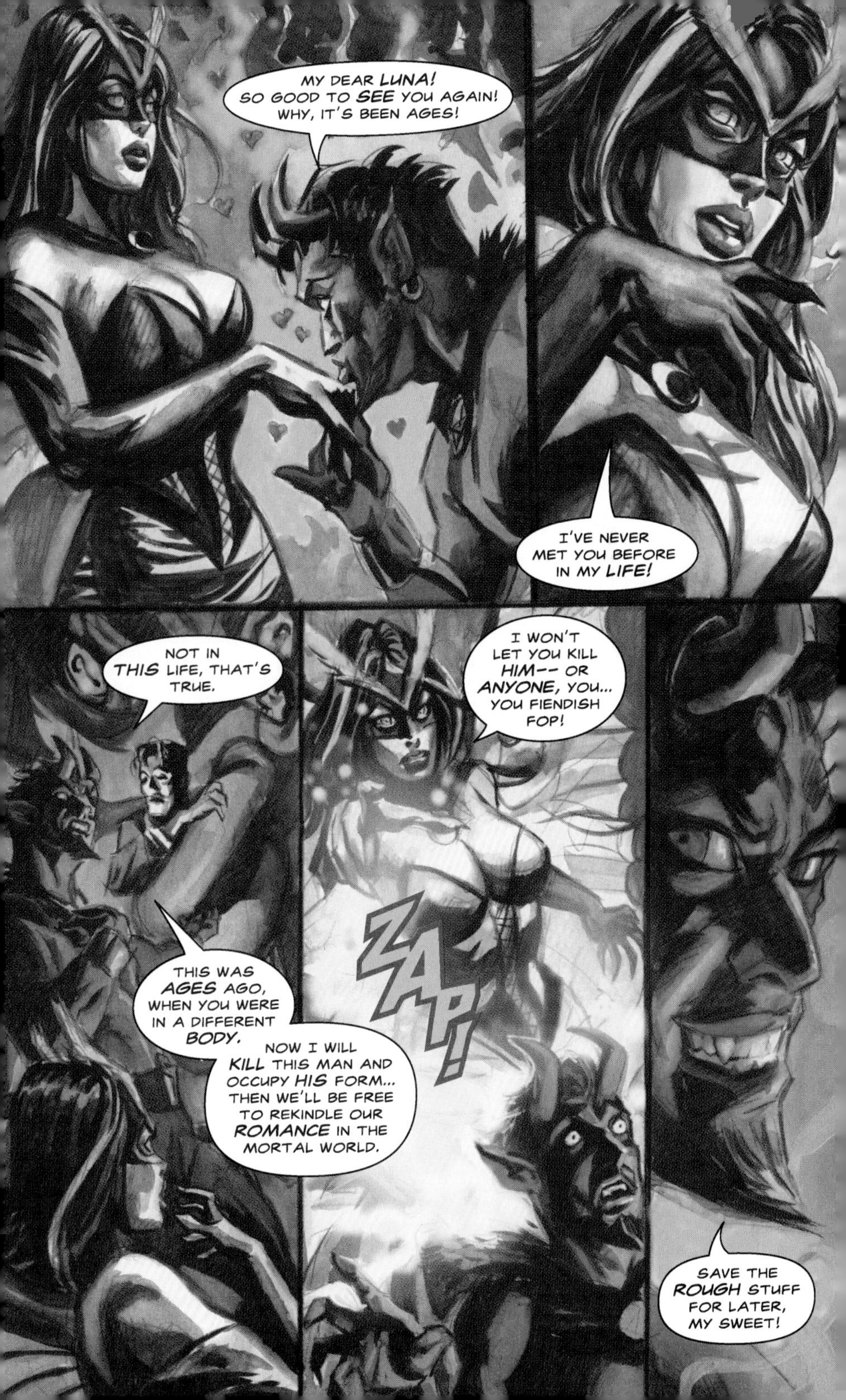
MY DEAR LUNA! SO GOOD TO SEE YOU AGAIN! WHY, IT'S BEEN AGES!
I'VE NEVER MET YOU BEFORE IN MY LIFE!
NOT IN THIS LIFE, THAT'S TRUE.
THIS WAS AGES AGO, WHEN YOU WERE IN A DIFFERENT BODY.
NOW I WILL KILL THIS MAN AND OCCUPY HIS FORM... THEN WE'LL BE FREE TO REKINDLE OUR ROMANCE IN THE MORTAL WORLD.
I WON'T LET YOU KILL HIM-- OR ANYONE, YOU... YOU FIENDISH FOP!
ZAP!
SAVE THE ROUGH STUFF FOR LATER, MY SWEET!

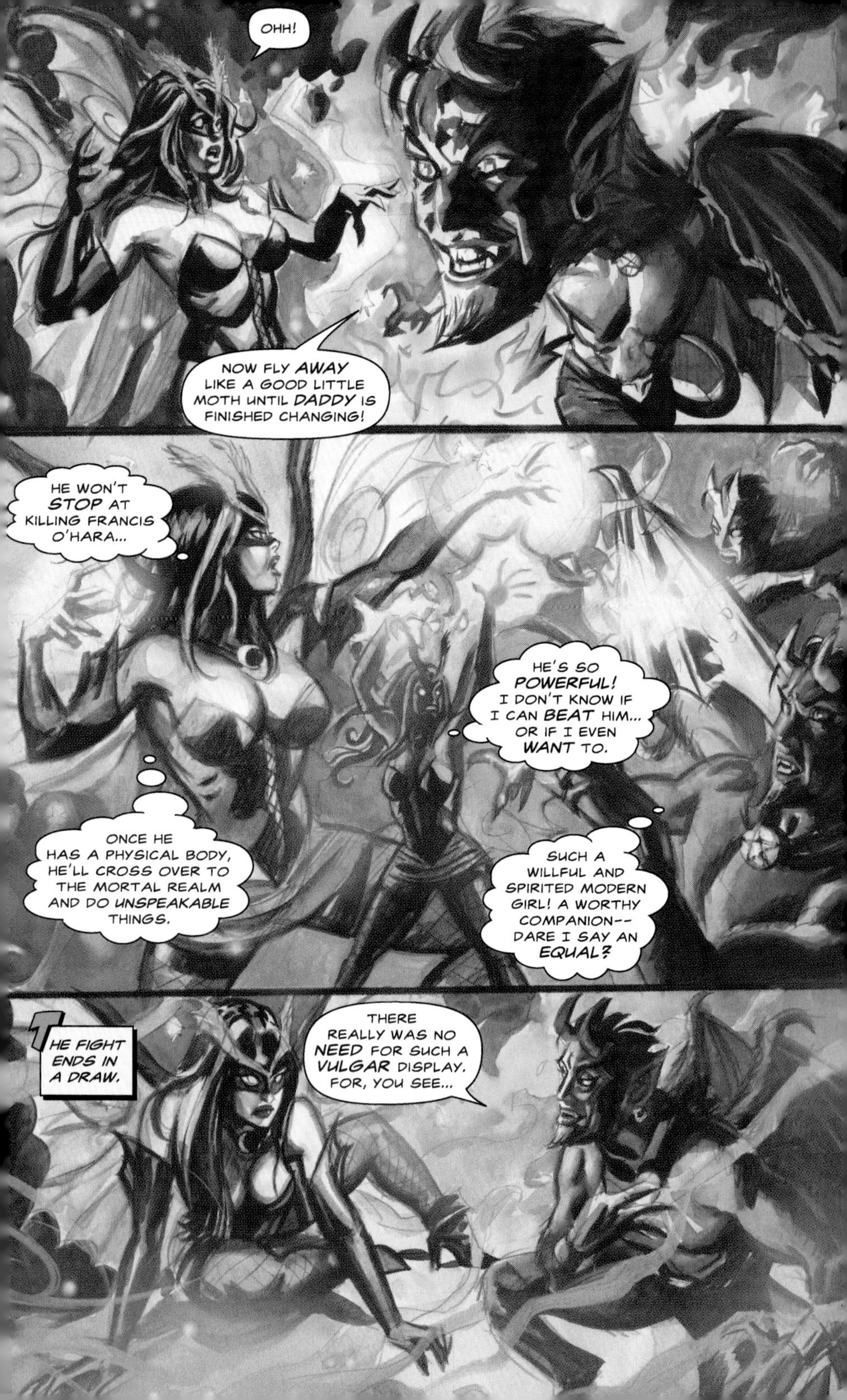
OHH!
NOW FLY AWAY LIKE A GOOD LITTLE MOTH UNTIL DADDY IS FINISHED CHANGING!
HE WON'T STOP AT KILLING FRANCIS O'HARA...
ONCE HE HAS A PHYSICAL BODY, HE'LL CROSS OVER TO THE MORTAL REALM AND DO UNSPEAKABLE THINGS.
HE'S SO POWERFUL! I DON'T KNOW IF I CAN BEAT HIM... OR IF I EVEN WANT TO.
SUCH A WILLFUL AND SPIRITED MODERN GIRL! A WORTHY COMPANION-- DARE I SAY AN EQUAL?
THE FIGHT ENDS IN A DRAW.
THERE REALLY WAS NO NEED FOR SUCH A VULGAR DISPLAY. FOR, YOU SEE...

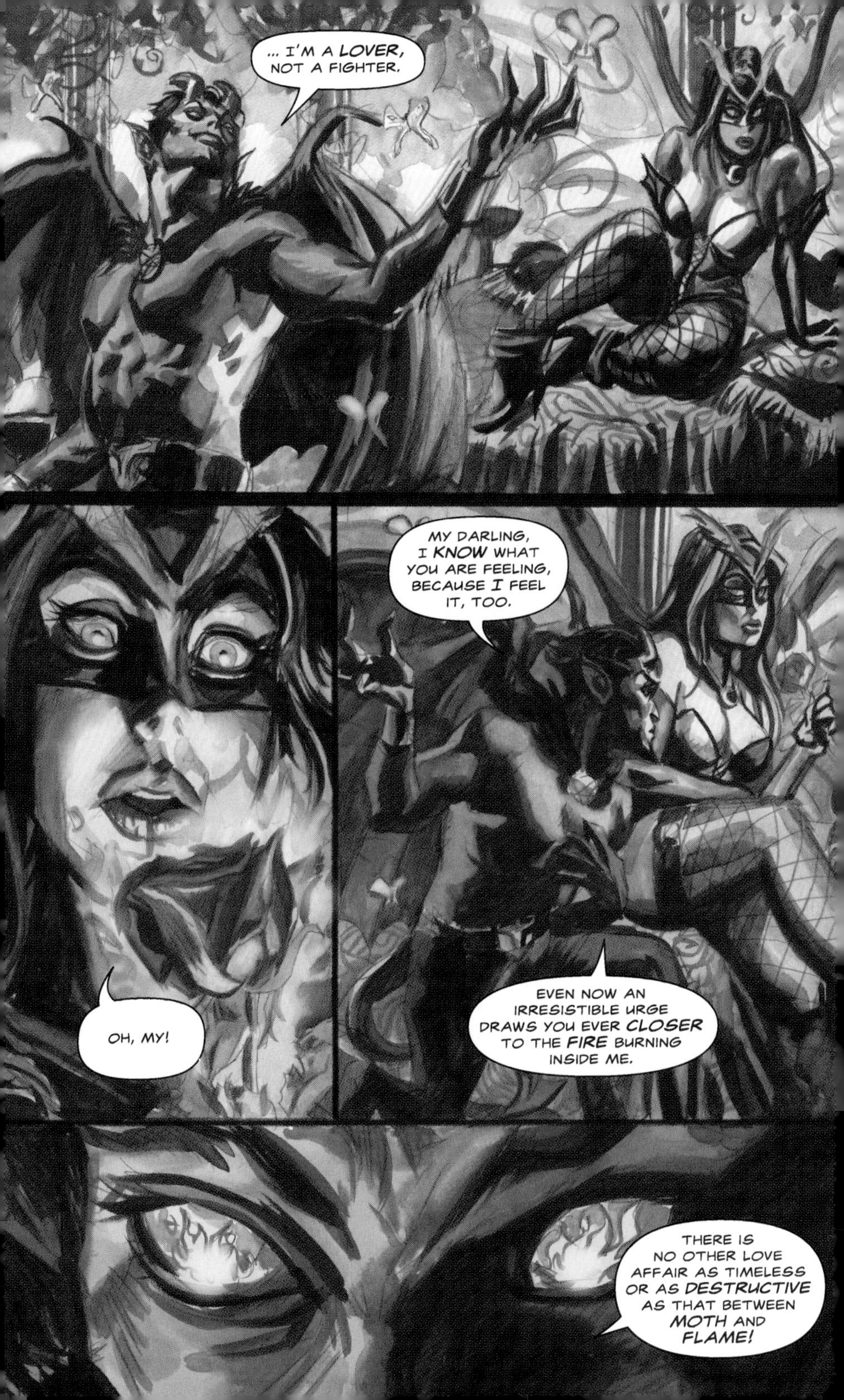
... I'M A LOVER, NOT A FIGHTER.
OH, MY!
MY DARLING, I KNOW WHAT YOU ARE FEELING, BECAUSE I FEEL IT, TOO.
EVEN NOW AN IRRESISTIBLE URGE DRAWS YOU EVER CLOSER TO THE FIRE BURNING INSIDE ME.
THERE IS NO OTHER LOVE AFFAIR AS TIMELESS OR AS DESTRUCTIVE AS THAT BETWEEN MOTH AND FLAME!

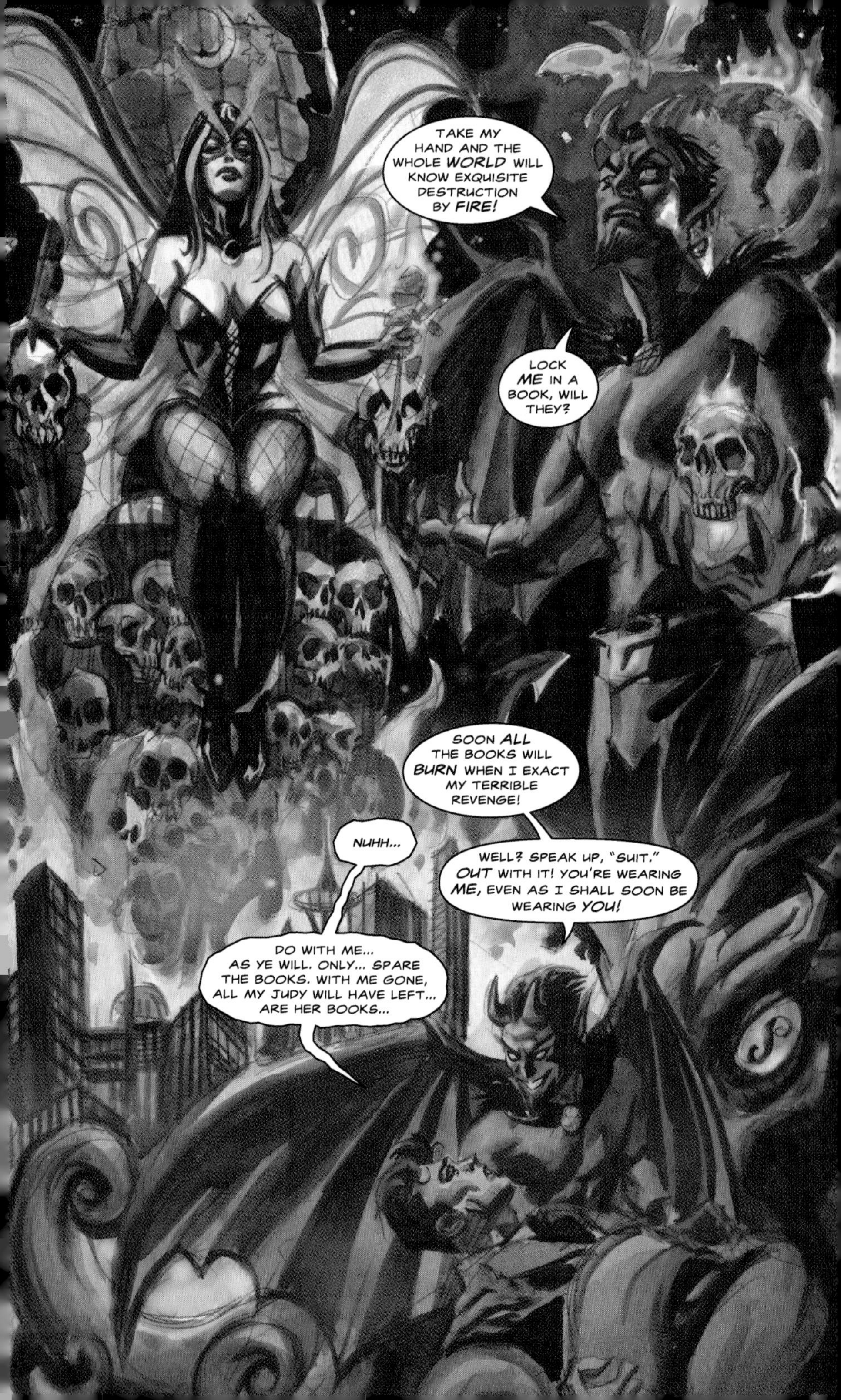
TAKE MY HAND AND THE WHOLE WORLD WILL KNOW EXQUISITE DESTRUCTION BY FIRE!
LOCK ME IN A BOOK, WILL THEY?
SOON ALL THE BOOKS WILL BURN WHEN I EXACT MY TERRIBLE REVENGE!
NUHH...
WELL? SPEAK UP, "SUIT." OUT WITH IT! YOU'RE WEARING ME, EVEN AS I SHALL SOON BE WEARING YOU!
DO WITH ME... AS YE WILL. ONLY... SPARE THE BOOKS. WITH ME GONE, ALL MY JUDY WILL HAVE LEFT... ARE HER BOOKS...

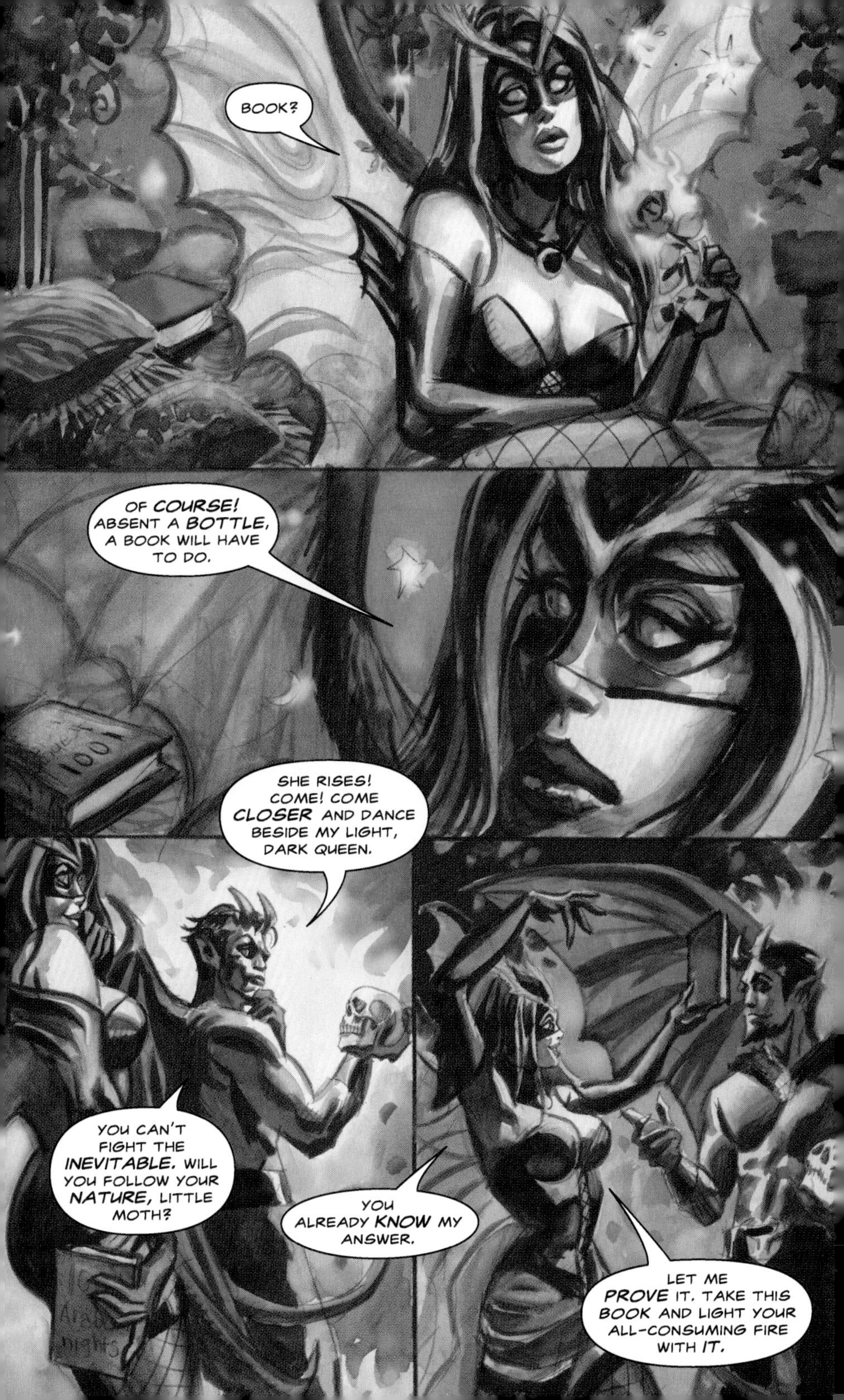
BOOK?
OF COURSE! ABSENT A BOTTLE, A BOOK WILL HAVE TO DO.
SHE RISES! COME! COME CLOSER AND DANCE BESIDE MY LIGHT, DARK QUEEN.
YOU CAN'T FIGHT THE INEVITABLE. WILL YOU FOLLOW YOUR NATURE, LITTLE MOTH?
YOU ALREADY KNOW MY ANSWER.
LET ME PROVE IT. TAKE THIS BOOK AND LIGHT YOUR ALL-CONSUMING FIRE WITH IT.

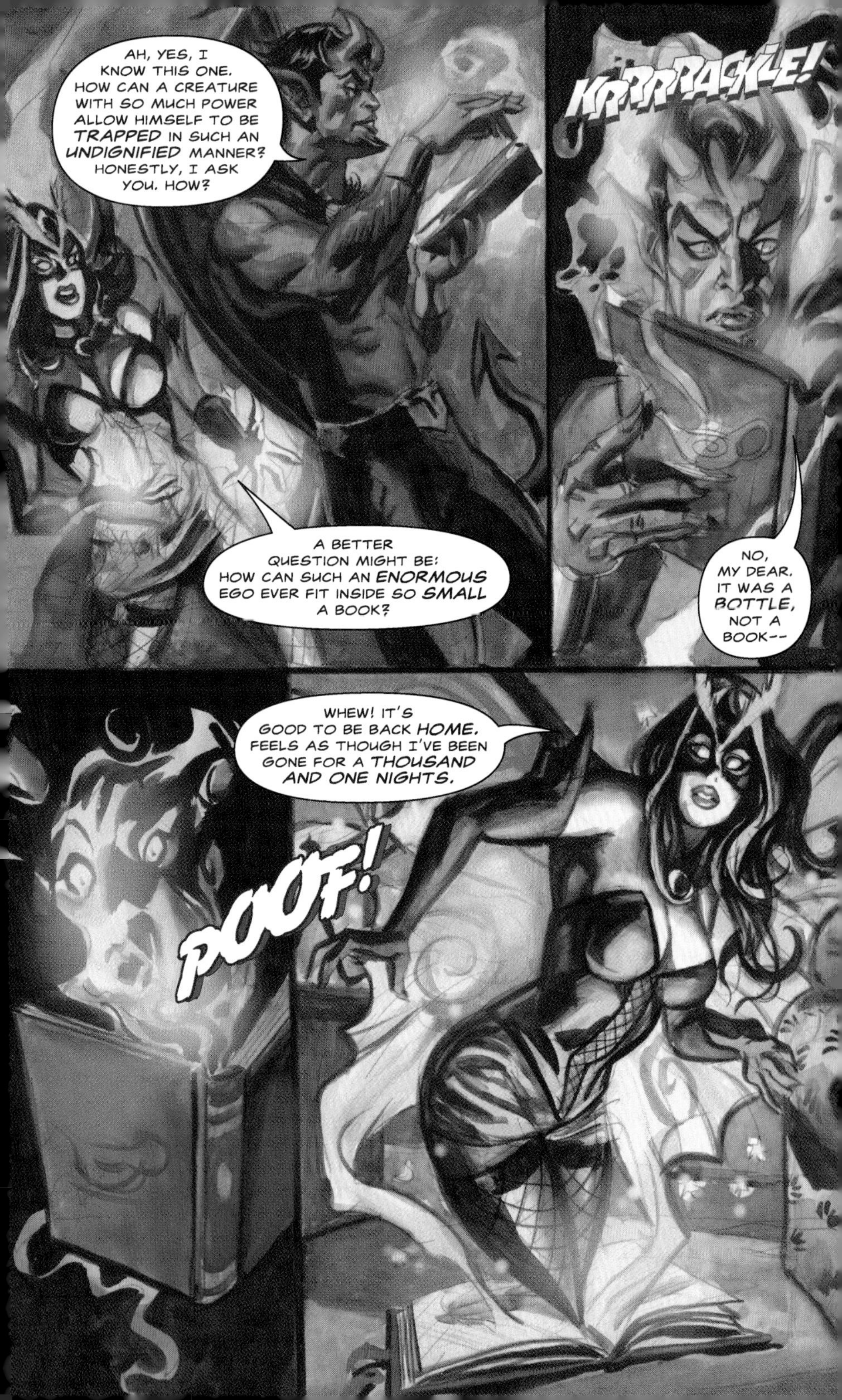
AH, YES, I KNOW THIS ONE. HOW CAN A CREATURE WITH SO MUCH POWER ALLOW HIMSELF TO BE TRAPPED IN SUCH AN UNDIGNIFIED MANNER? HONESTLY, I ASK YOU. HOW?
A BETTER QUESTION MIGHT BE: HOW CAN SUCH AN ENORMOUS EGO EVER FIT INSIDE SO SMALL A BOOK?
KRRRRACKLE!
NO, MY DEAR. IT WAS A BOTTLE, NOT A BOOK--
POOF!
WHEW! IT'S GOOD TO BE BACK HOME. FEELS AS THOUGH I'VE BEEN GONE FOR A THOUSAND AND ONE NIGHTS.

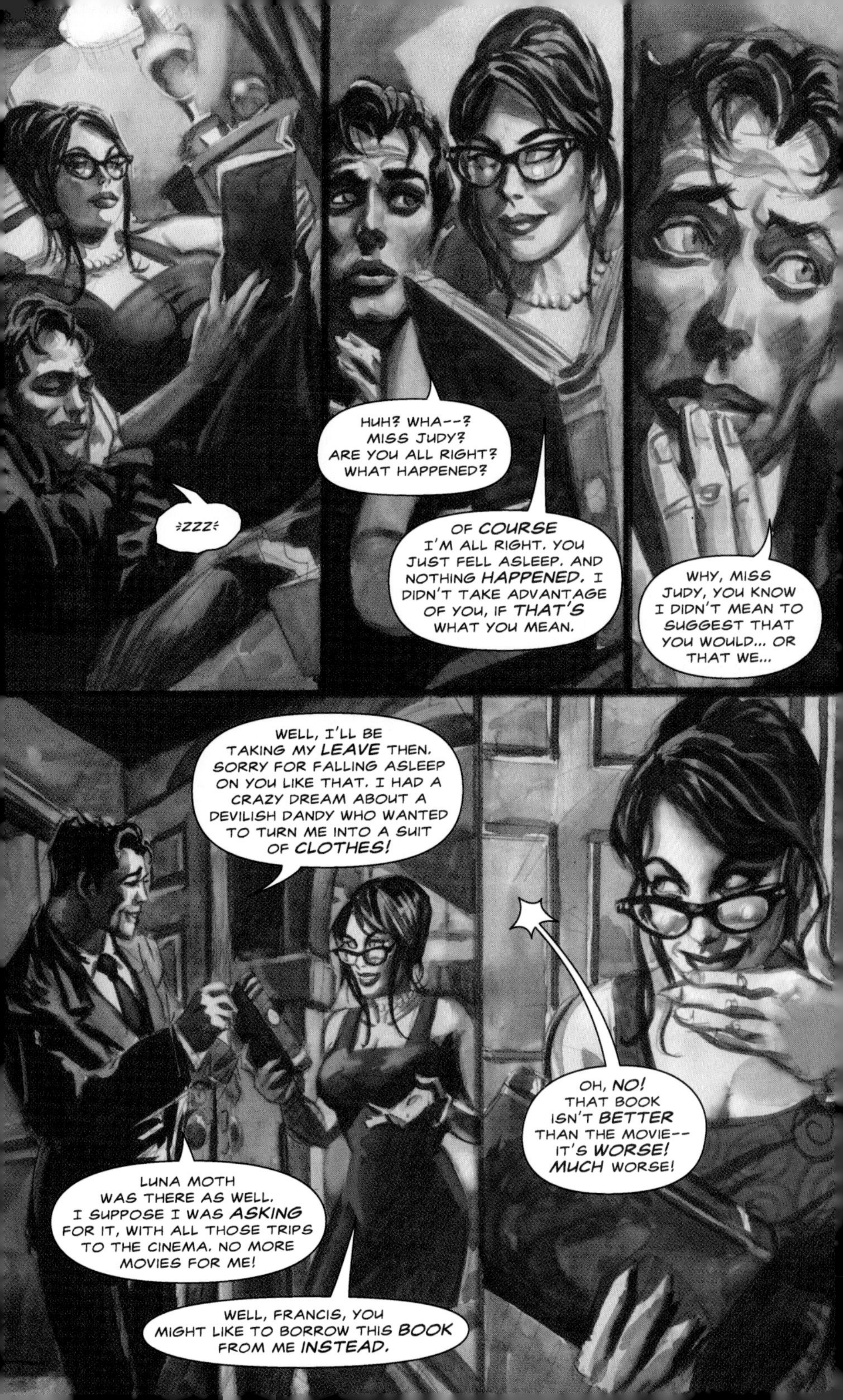
ZZZ
HUH? WHA--? MISS JUDY? ARE YOU ALL RIGHT? WHAT HAPPENED?
OF COURSE I'M ALL RIGHT. YOU JUST FELL ASLEEP. AND NOTHING HAPPENED. I DIDN'T TAKE ADVANTAGE OF YOU, IF THAT'S WHAT YOU MEAN.
WHY, MISS JUDY, YOU KNOW I DIDN'T MEAN TO SUGGEST THAT YOU WOULD... OR THAT WE...
WELL, I'LL BE TAKING MY LEAVE THEN. SORRY FOR FALLING ASLEEP ON YOU LIKE THAT. I HAD A CRAZY DREAM ABOUT A DEVILISH DANDY WHO WANTED TO TURN ME INTO A SUIT OF CLOTHES!
LUNA MOTH WAS THERE AS WELL. I SUPPOSE I WAS ASKING FOR IT, WITH ALL THOSE TRIPS TO THE CINEMA. NO MORE MOVIES FOR ME!
WELL, FRANCIS, YOU MIGHT LIKE TO BORROW THIS BOOK FROM ME INSTEAD.
OH, NO! THAT BOOK ISN'T BETTER THAN THE MOVIE-- IT'S WORSE! MUCH WORSE!

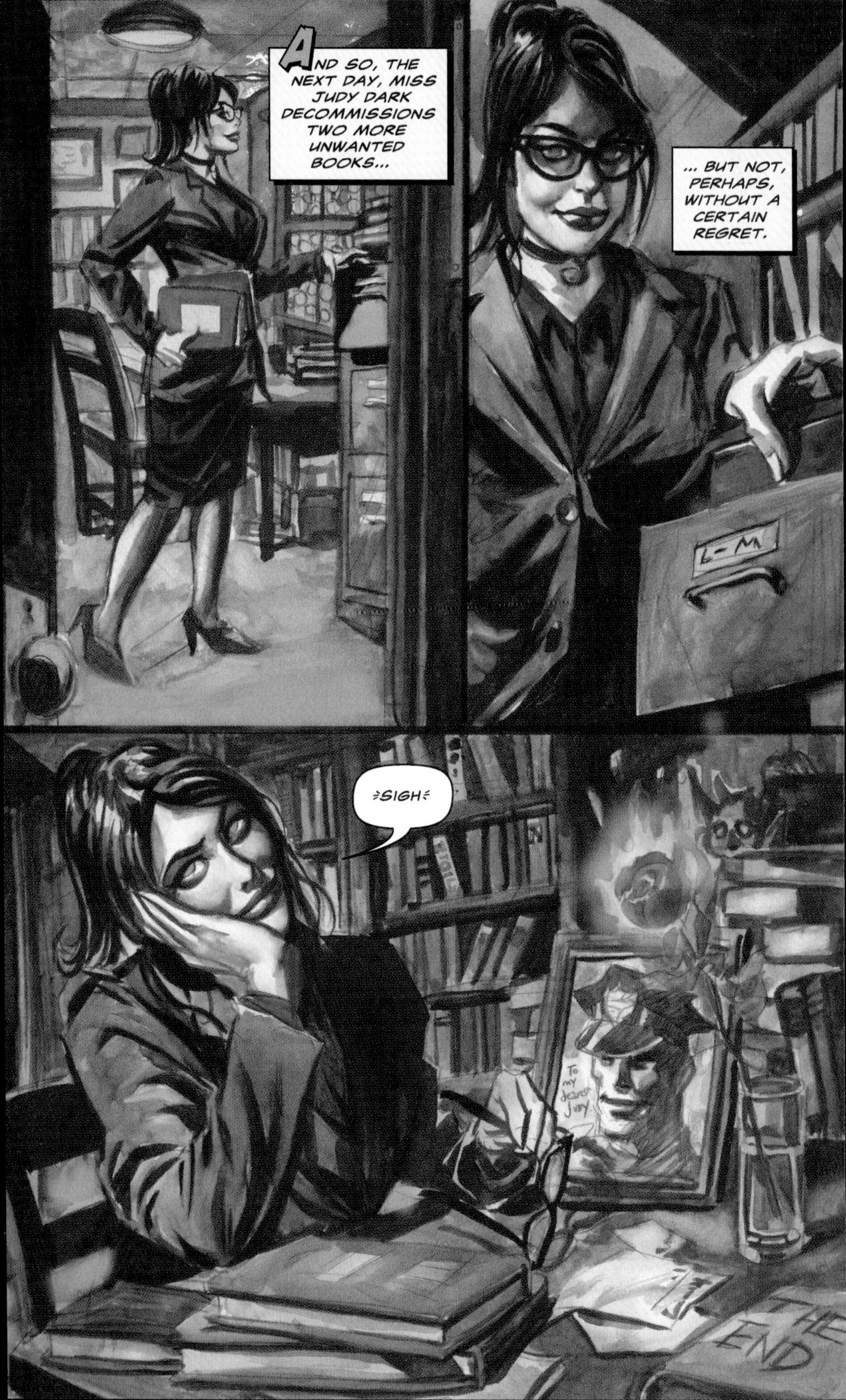
AND SO, THE NEXT DAY, MISS JUDY DARK DECOMMISSIONS TWO MORE UNWANTED BOOKS...
... BUT NOT, PERHAPS, WITHOUT A CERTAIN REGRET.
L-M
SIGH
To my dearest Judy
THE END

"THE LADY OR THE TIGER"

PREFACE

by Glen David Gold

COMICS ARE UNIQUE IN THE PRESENT DAY, IN THAT THE AUDIENCE HAS to wait for monthly installments, giving each episode weeks to steep in the memory before a new layer is added on. In this internet age, having to wait long enough to hit "refresh" on your browser toolbar strikes people as torture. To really find an antecedent for the lengthy comic book plot, one must look past even the intra-War era "Perils of Pauline"-type serials and back to serialized novels, such as those of Henry James.

The Portrait of a Lady, for instance, was the *Dark Knight Returns* of its day, taking up 13 months of *Macmillan's* in 1880-'81. In his prefaces to the New York edition (1907-'09), James refers to "the necessity, that is to say, of keeping the many narrative pots of slumgullion stew abubble" in explaining the art of how to end a chapter so that the reader won't just want to turn the page, but will want to buy another issue 30 days later.

Certain runs of 1970s to early '80s comic book epics carried a freight-train-like momentum. Consider the Kree-Skrull war, the Celestial Madonna, the Dark Phoenix story, the life and death (and life) of Elektra, and *The Escapist's* own "Dark Lady" storyline. All of them were built on rising tensions and were resolved in spectacular climaxes. All except for *The Escapist*.

We needn't retell the difficult creative history *The Escapist* endured in the 1970s. Constant turnover of creative teams, shifting political winds, and the brief promise of Hollywood-style attention sent the storylines into turmoil. Not since the disastrous 1968 pinup in which the Escapist urged readers to "Escape reality! Turn on!" (forever alienating artist Steve Ditko, whose own pro-free-market caption had been statted over) had our hero so rapidly changed directions.

And yet there came 1976, the Escapist's miracle year. Having found a brilliant artist in the form of Gene Colan, whose tenure on *Daredevil* and *Tomb of Dracula* made him a perfect delineator, Sunshine Comics editorial either relaxed — or rode roughshod (accounts differ) — on the writing team, who flourished. Quickly dropped were the child sidekicks (fandom had been loudly denouncing them in San Diego and in the *Reader* as coming from "Open Sesame Street") and the one-shot storylines. In their place was developed a fluid, multipart epic that showed a new seriousness and commitment to Tom Mayflower, the man and the hero.

By the sixth issue, a heady sort of rhythm had been established: each issue had a villain who was overcome with relative ease, but afterwards, each time, the Escapist paid some terrible price. First, wedges were placed between himself and the League, and then he grew grim and secretive around Omar, Plum Blossom, and Big Al himself. Alienated, lonely, he questioned how deeply the connection ran between himself and any of his allies.

Furthermore, he was tormented by dark dreams and waking visions of a woman whose face he couldn't quite see. During an otherwise easy tangle with Sagebrush, Tom Mayflower was so distracted by thoughts of this mysterious woman that he took a hard punch to the jaw that allowed the prickly supervillain to escape. Further, when Shiwan Khan, mystic of the Orient, attacked using the astral plane, Tom was led away by a vision of this woman — and directly into more danger. Was she good or evil? Everyone was dying to know.

The "Dark Lady" from *The Escapist* #53. © November 1976 Sunshine Media Group.

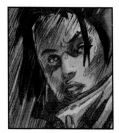

The November 1976 issue set up a tense situation: The Gotham Sniper had kidnapped six children from a school under the Escapist's protection, and Tom Mayflower, who seemed almost criminally unprepared, vowed to retrieve them. But, more thrillingly, it was promised in the final blurb: "NEXT ISSUE: THE DARK WOMAN REVEALED."

Any fan can tell you what happened next. The December 1976 issue was, shockingly, a fill-in, pencilled by George Tuska and inked by the prime indicator of a rush job, Vince Colletta. There was an editor's note on the splash indicating that the "Dreaded Deadline Doom" had caught them unawares and that all would be resolved in the first issue of the new year.

When that issue finally did appear, after an *eight-year* hiatus, it was clear that nothing had been resolved. It was revealed that the "Dark Woman" had been a figment of the Escapist's imagination, brought on by too much stress. He agreed that he and his partners needed to go on a well-needed vacation, during which they reapplied themselves to effecting escapes. And that was that.

Officially, nothing had happened, but, clearly, something *had* happened. It was said that in the unpublished story, the Escapist had finally met his match in the form of a woman who would both rescue him and destroy him. Beyond that, details were hard to come by.

In his preface to *The American*, Henry James recalls the creation of art on a serial's timeline with a kind of head-shaking wonder: what if he'd fallen ill? "Would that a character who so nobly entered my consciousness as easily as if he wore his own passkey might somehow join society with a similar *frisson*, in the richest sense, of mass, so that the audience might think of the weight of his consciousness with the same 'drop' as did my own; the repetition of dwelling upon his mark would seem to make him upright and 'real' in the same sense of an uncle who once visited but whose carriage has been long delayed. Would that a 'ghost' had finished his tale, might it seem as if 'Uncle' had been carried away and an incubus put in his place?"

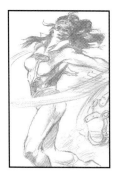

Original Colan pencil art for the woman of Tom Mayflower's dreams, before "remastered" coloring by Eisner Award nominee Paul Hornschemeier.

Which was exactly the complaint fandom had. After waiting eight years for resolution, they have had in fact to wait 20 more to find out what happened to "their" Escapist. Finally, the original artwork to this legendary story was recovered during Gene and Adrienne Colan's recent move from Vermont to Florida. It was still in its original pencil form, as the story had been suppressed before an inker had been assigned. So it is with great pleasure we bring you this missing puzzle piece, which isn't a "what if" so much as it is a "what was."

THE LADY OR THE TIGER

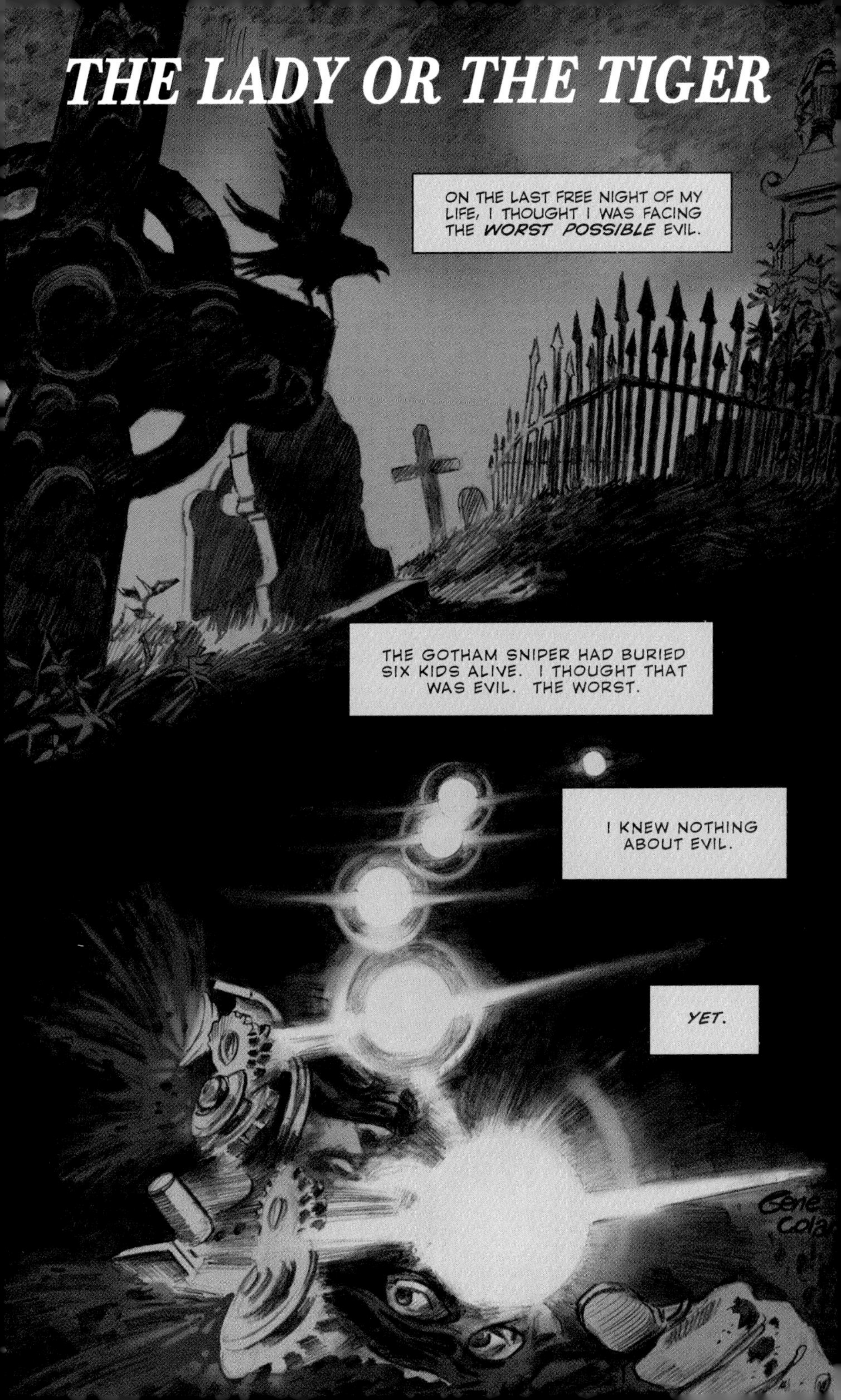
ON THE LAST FREE NIGHT OF MY LIFE, I THOUGHT I WAS FACING THE *WORST POSSIBLE* EVIL.
THE GOTHAM SNIPER HAD BURIED SIX KIDS ALIVE. I THOUGHT THAT WAS EVIL. THE WORST.
I KNEW NOTHING ABOUT EVIL.
YET.

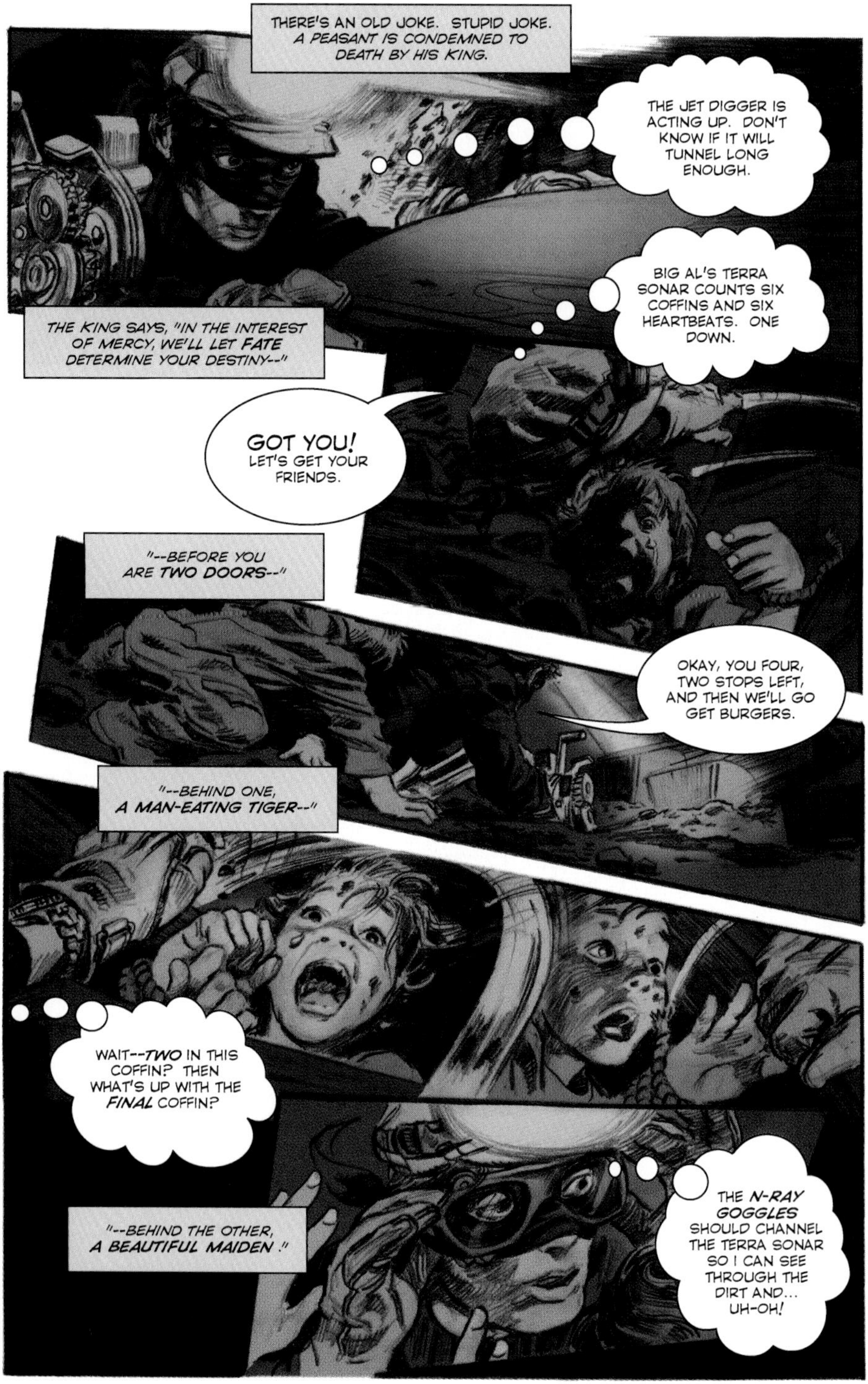
THERE'S AN OLD JOKE. STUPID JOKE. *A PEASANT IS CONDEMNED TO DEATH BY HIS KING.*
THE JET DIGGER IS ACTING UP. DON'T KNOW IF IT WILL TUNNEL LONG ENOUGH.
THE KING SAYS, "IN THE INTEREST OF MERCY, WE'LL LET FATE DETERMINE YOUR DESTINY--"
BIG AL'S TERRA SONAR COUNTS SIX COFFINS AND SIX HEARTBEATS. ONE DOWN.
GOT YOU! LET'S GET YOUR FRIENDS.
"--BEFORE YOU ARE TWO DOORS--"
OKAY, YOU FOUR, TWO STOPS LEFT, AND THEN WE'LL GO GET BURGERS.
"--BEHIND ONE, A MAN-EATING TIGER--"
WAIT--*TWO* IN THIS COFFIN? THEN WHAT'S UP WITH THE *FINAL* COFFIN?
"--BEHIND THE OTHER, A BEAUTIFUL MAIDEN."
THE *N-RAY GOGGLES* SHOULD CHANNEL THE TERRA SONAR SO I CAN SEE THROUGH THE DIRT AND... UH-OH!

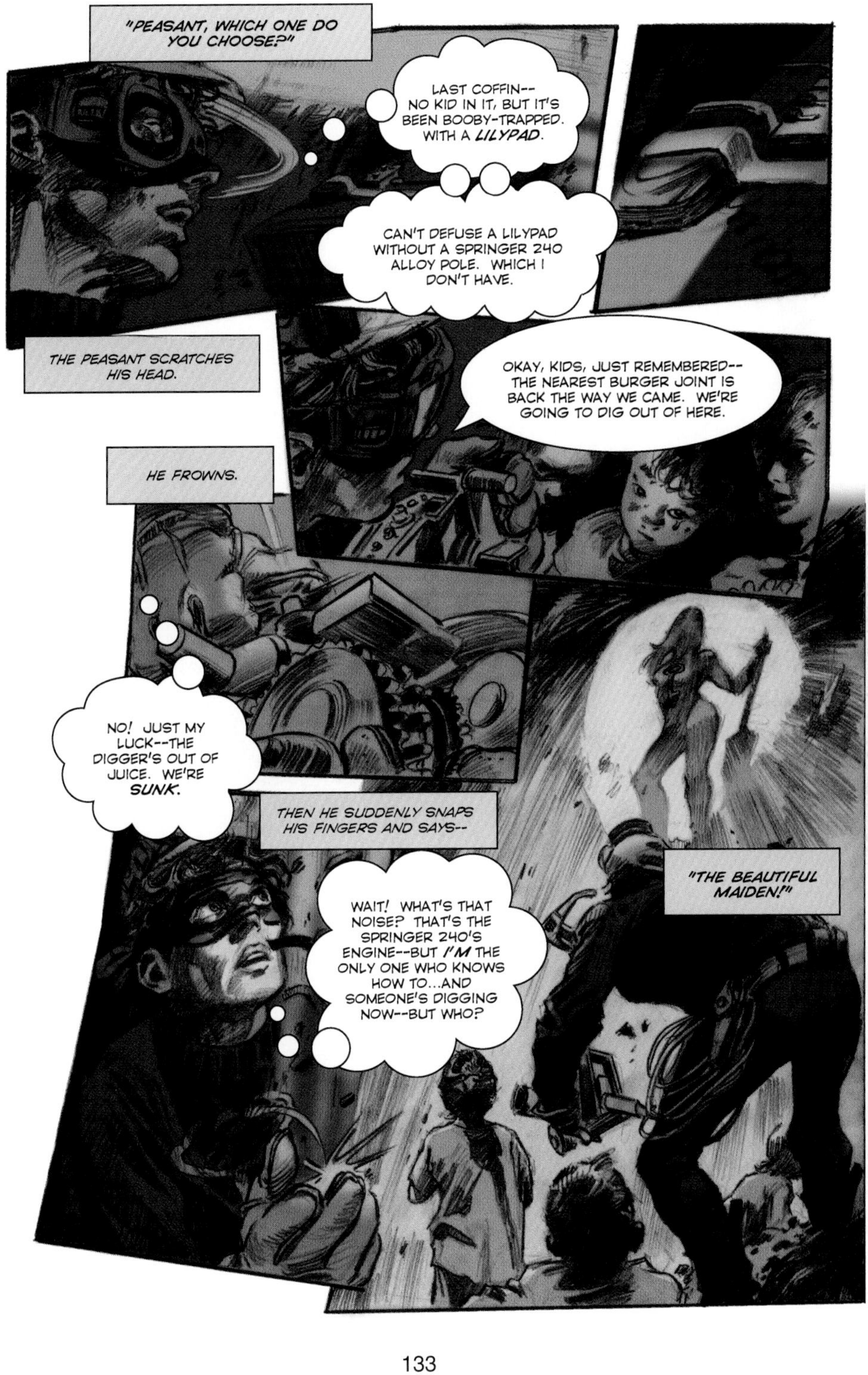
"PEASANT, WHICH ONE DO YOU CHOOSE?"
LAST COFFIN-- NO KID IN IT, BUT IT'S BEEN BOOBY-TRAPPED. WITH A *LILYPAD*.
CAN'T DEFUSE A LILYPAD WITHOUT A SPRINGER 240 ALLOY POLE. WHICH I DON'T HAVE.
THE PEASANT SCRATCHES HIS HEAD.
OKAY, KIDS, JUST REMEMBERED-- THE NEAREST BURGER JOINT IS BACK THE WAY WE CAME. WE'RE GOING TO DIG OUT OF HERE.
HE FROWNS.
NO! JUST MY LUCK--THE DIGGER'S OUT OF JUICE. WE'RE **SUNK**.
THEN HE SUDDENLY SNAPS HIS FINGERS AND SAYS--
"THE BEAUTIFUL MAIDEN!"
WAIT! WHAT'S THAT NOISE? THAT'S THE SPRINGER 240'S ENGINE--BUT *I'M* THE ONLY ONE WHO KNOWS HOW TO...AND SOMEONE'S DIGGING NOW--BUT WHO?

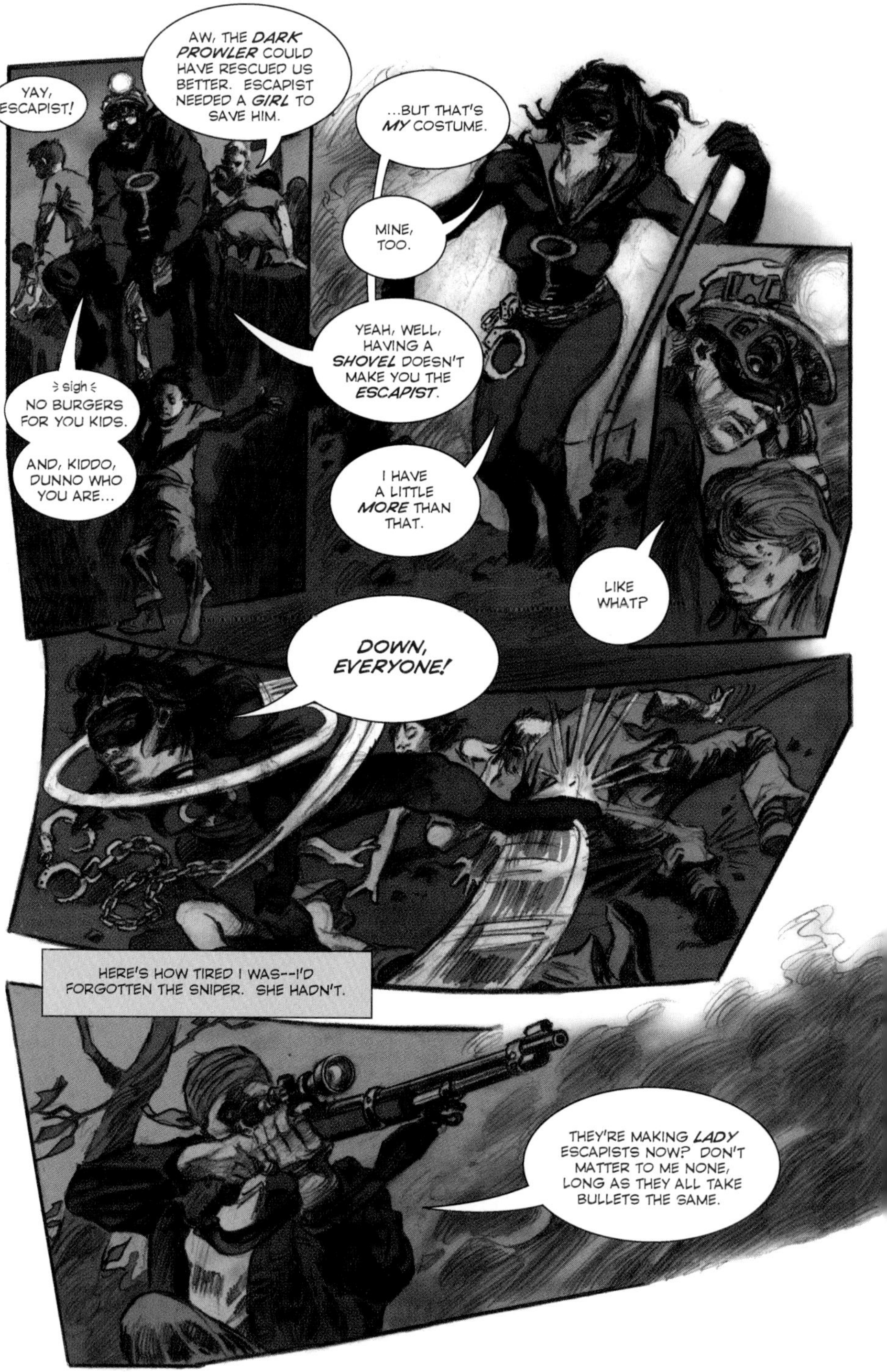
YAY, ESCAPIST!
AW, THE *DARK PROWLER* COULD HAVE RESCUED US BETTER. ESCAPIST NEEDED A *GIRL* TO SAVE HIM.
...BUT THAT'S *MY* COSTUME.
MINE, TOO.
YEAH, WELL, HAVING A *SHOVEL* DOESN'T MAKE YOU THE *ESCAPIST*.
sigh
NO BURGERS FOR YOU KIDS.
AND, KIDDO, DUNNO WHO YOU ARE...
I HAVE A LITTLE *MORE* THAN THAT.
LIKE WHAT?
DOWN, EVERYONE!
HERE'S HOW TIRED I WAS--I'D FORGOTTEN THE SNIPER. SHE HADN'T.
THEY'RE MAKING *LADY* ESCAPISTS NOW? DON'T MATTER TO ME NONE, LONG AS THEY ALL TAKE BULLETS THE SAME.

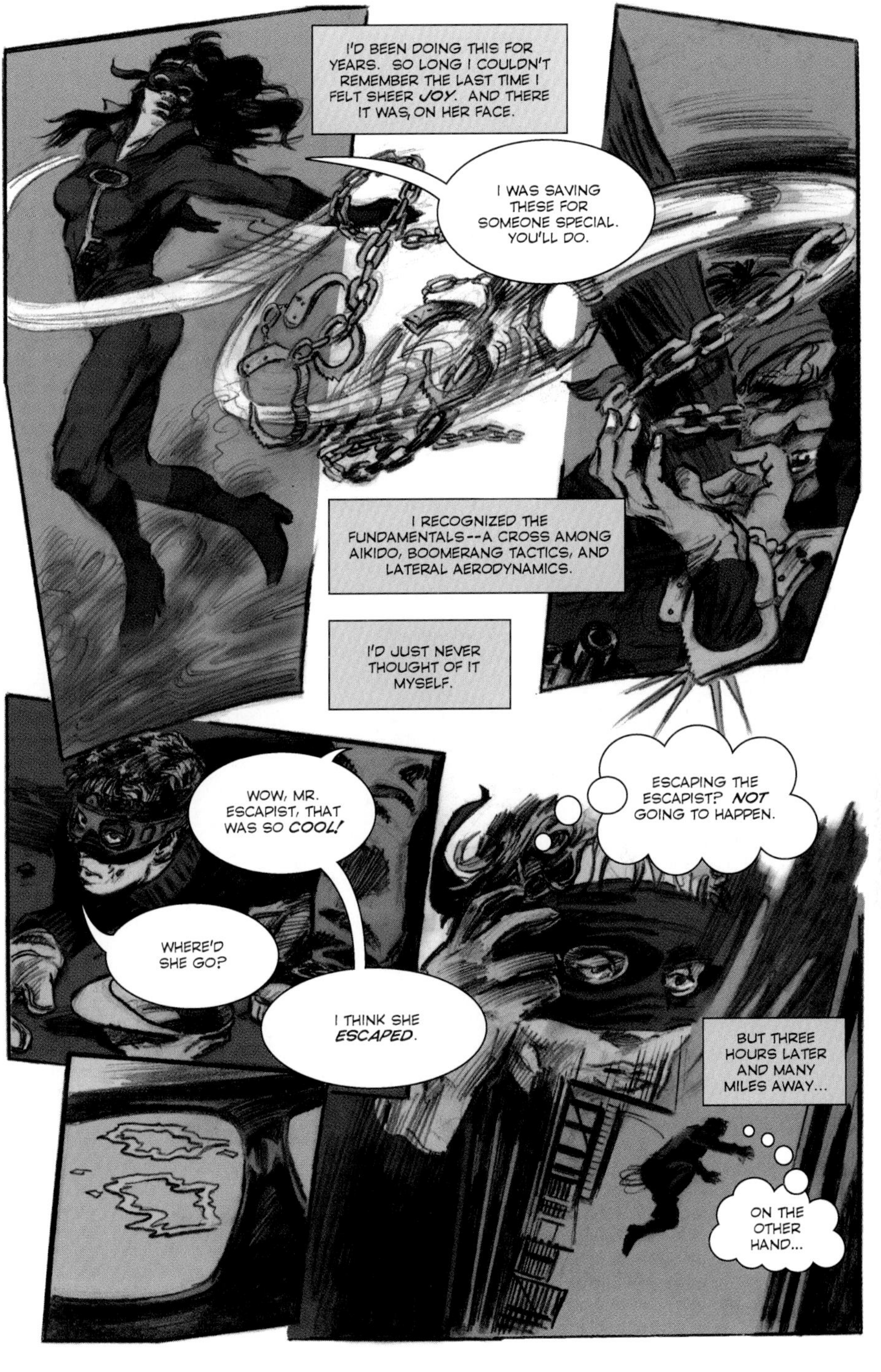

I'D BEEN DOING THIS FOR YEARS. SO LONG I COULDN'T REMEMBER THE LAST TIME I FELT SHEER *JOY*. AND THERE IT WAS, ON HER FACE.
I WAS SAVING THESE FOR SOMEONE SPECIAL. YOU'LL DO.
I RECOGNIZED THE FUNDAMENTALS--A CROSS AMONG AIKIDO, BOOMERANG TACTICS, AND LATERAL AERODYNAMICS.
I'D JUST NEVER THOUGHT OF IT MYSELF.
WOW, MR. ESCAPIST, THAT WAS SO ***COOL!***
WHERE'D SHE GO?
I THINK SHE ***ESCAPED***.
ESCAPING THE ESCAPIST? ***NOT*** GOING TO HAPPEN.
BUT THREE HOURS LATER AND MANY MILES AWAY...
ON THE OTHER HAND...

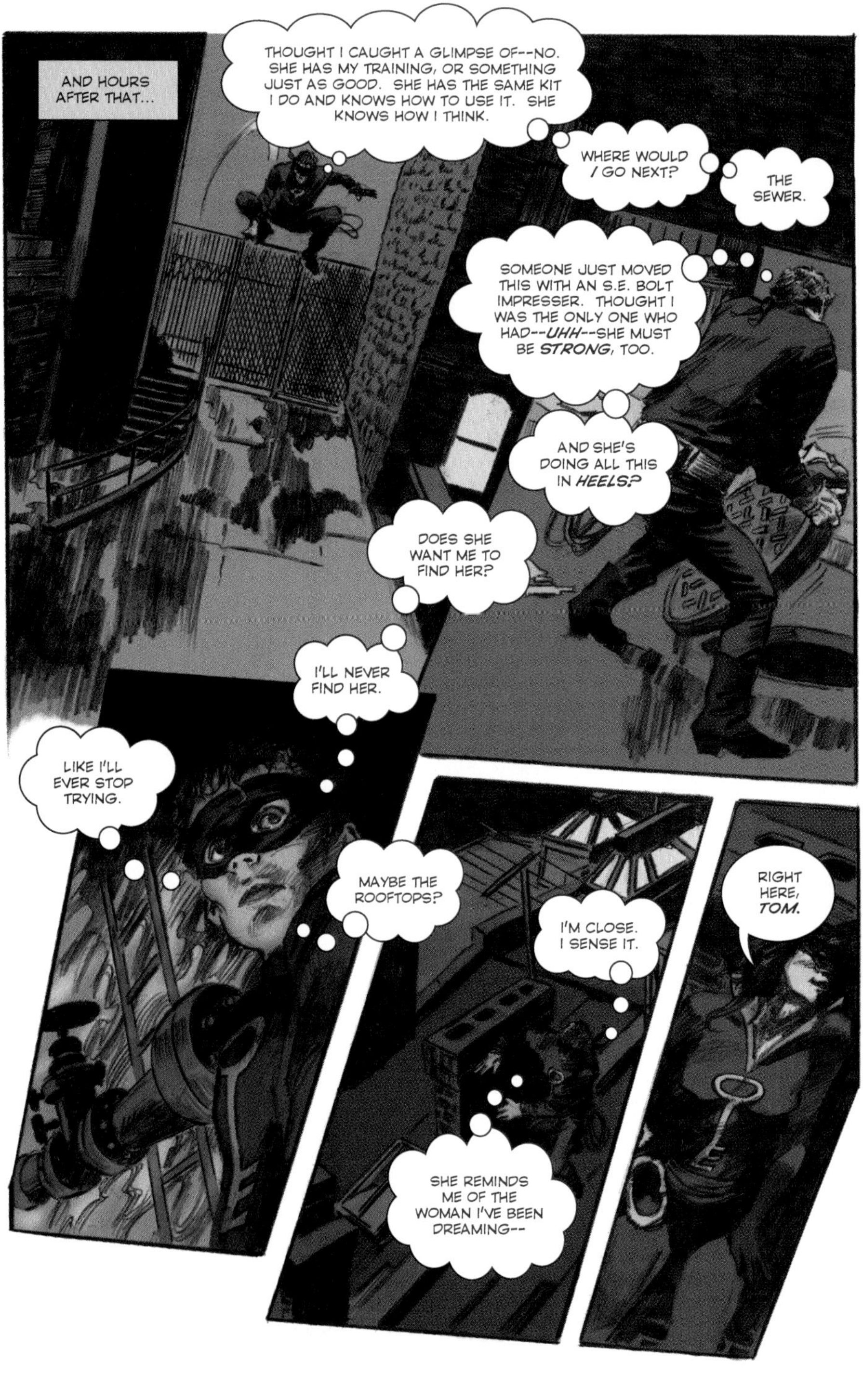
AND HOURS AFTER THAT...
THOUGHT I CAUGHT A GLIMPSE OF--NO. SHE HAS MY TRAINING, OR SOMETHING JUST AS GOOD. SHE HAS THE SAME KIT I DO AND KNOWS HOW TO USE IT. SHE KNOWS HOW I THINK.
WHERE WOULD *I* GO NEXT?
THE SEWER.
SOMEONE JUST MOVED THIS WITH AN S.E. BOLT IMPRESSER. THOUGHT I WAS THE ONLY ONE WHO HAD--*UHH*--SHE MUST BE *STRONG*, TOO.
AND SHE'S DOING ALL THIS IN *HEELS?*
DOES SHE WANT ME TO FIND HER?
I'LL NEVER FIND HER.
LIKE I'LL EVER STOP TRYING.
MAYBE THE ROOFTOPS?
I'M CLOSE. I SENSE IT.
SHE REMINDS ME OF THE WOMAN I'VE BEEN DREAMING--
RIGHT HERE, *TOM.*

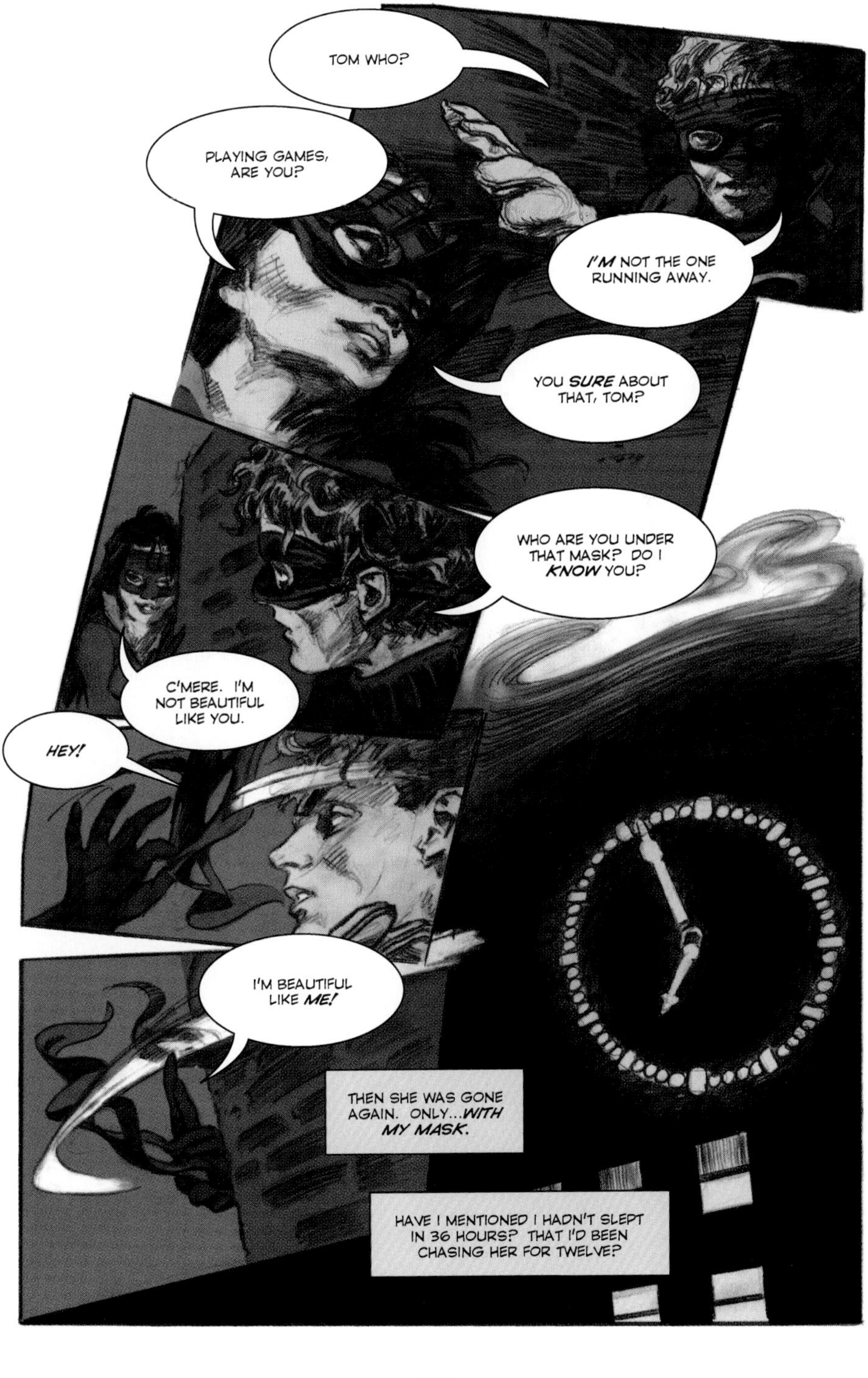
TOM WHO?
PLAYING GAMES, ARE YOU?
I'M NOT THE ONE RUNNING AWAY.
YOU SURE ABOUT THAT, TOM?
WHO ARE YOU UNDER THAT MASK? DO I KNOW YOU?
C'MERE. I'M NOT BEAUTIFUL LIKE YOU.
HEY!
I'M BEAUTIFUL LIKE ME!
THEN SHE WAS GONE AGAIN. ONLY...WITH MY MASK.
HAVE I MENTIONED I HADN'T SLEPT IN 36 HOURS? THAT I'D BEEN CHASING HER FOR TWELVE?

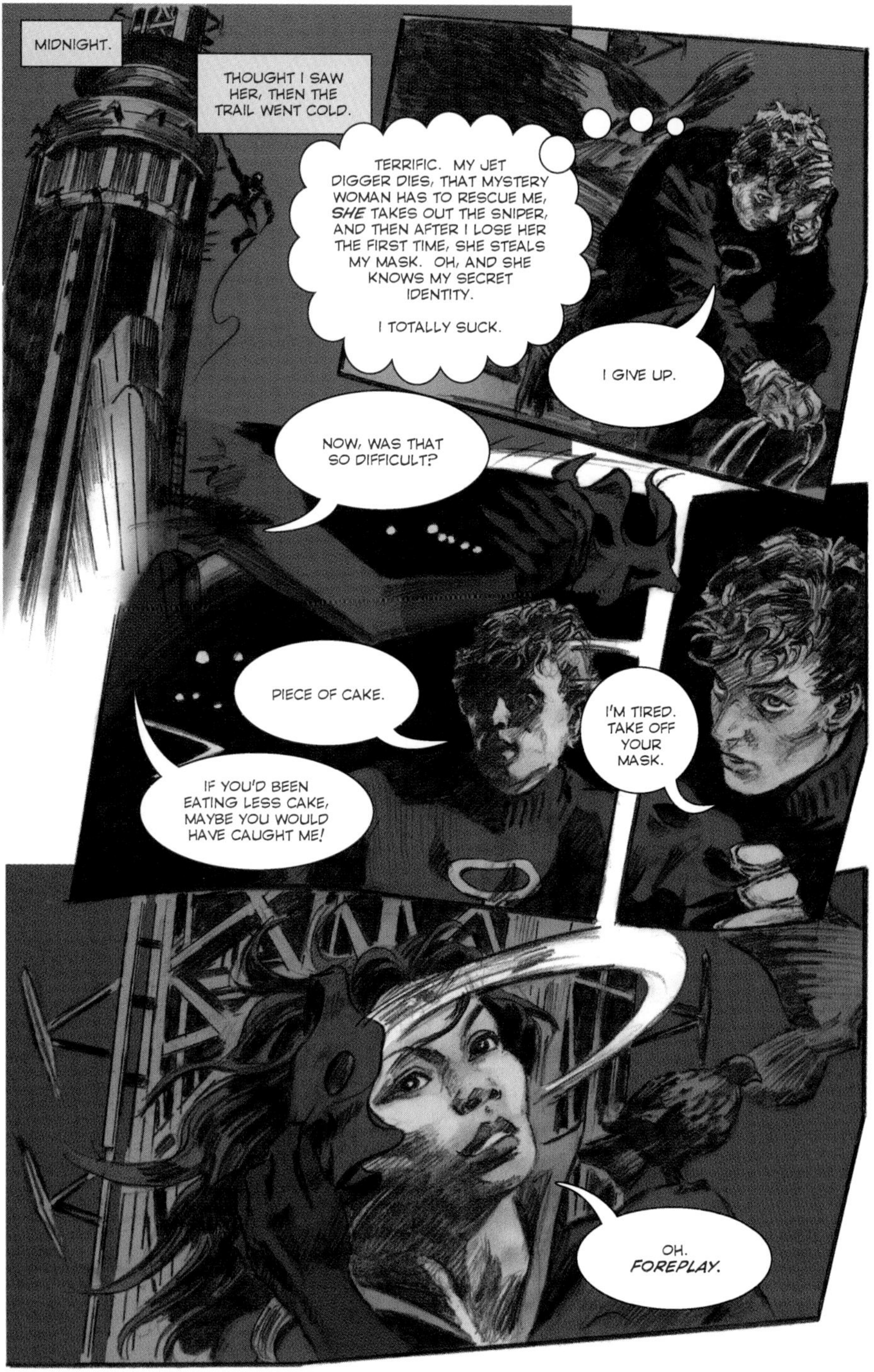
MIDNIGHT.
THOUGHT I SAW HER, THEN THE TRAIL WENT COLD.
TERRIFIC. MY JET DIGGER DIES, THAT MYSTERY WOMAN HAS TO RESCUE ME, *SHE* TAKES OUT THE SNIPER, AND THEN AFTER I LOSE HER THE FIRST TIME, SHE STEALS MY MASK. OH, AND SHE KNOWS MY SECRET IDENTITY.
I TOTALLY SUCK.
I GIVE UP.
NOW, WAS THAT SO DIFFICULT?
PIECE OF CAKE.
IF YOU'D BEEN EATING LESS CAKE, MAYBE YOU WOULD HAVE CAUGHT ME!
I'M TIRED. TAKE OFF YOUR MASK.
OH. ***FOREPLAY.***

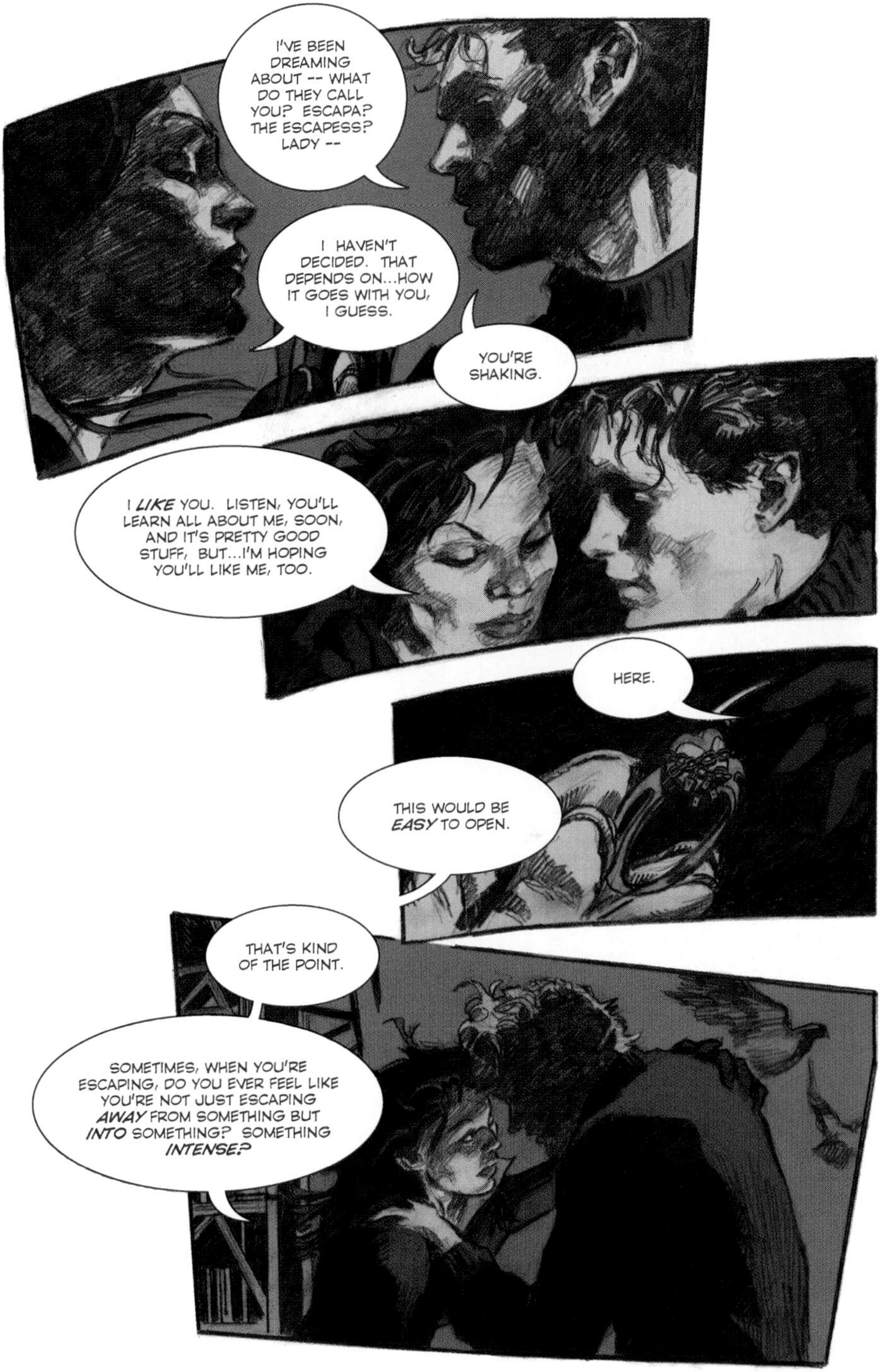
I'VE BEEN DREAMING ABOUT -- WHAT DO THEY CALL YOU? ESCAPA? THE ESCAPESS? LADY --
I HAVEN'T DECIDED. THAT DEPENDS ON...HOW IT GOES WITH YOU, I GUESS.
YOU'RE SHAKING.
I *LIKE* YOU. LISTEN, YOU'LL LEARN ALL ABOUT ME, SOON, AND IT'S PRETTY GOOD STUFF, BUT...I'M HOPING YOU'LL LIKE ME, TOO.
HERE.
THIS WOULD BE *EASY* TO OPEN.
THAT'S KIND OF THE POINT.
SOMETIMES, WHEN YOU'RE ESCAPING, DO YOU EVER FEEL LIKE YOU'RE NOT JUST ESCAPING *AWAY* FROM SOMETHING BUT *INTO* SOMETHING? SOMETHING *INTENSE?*

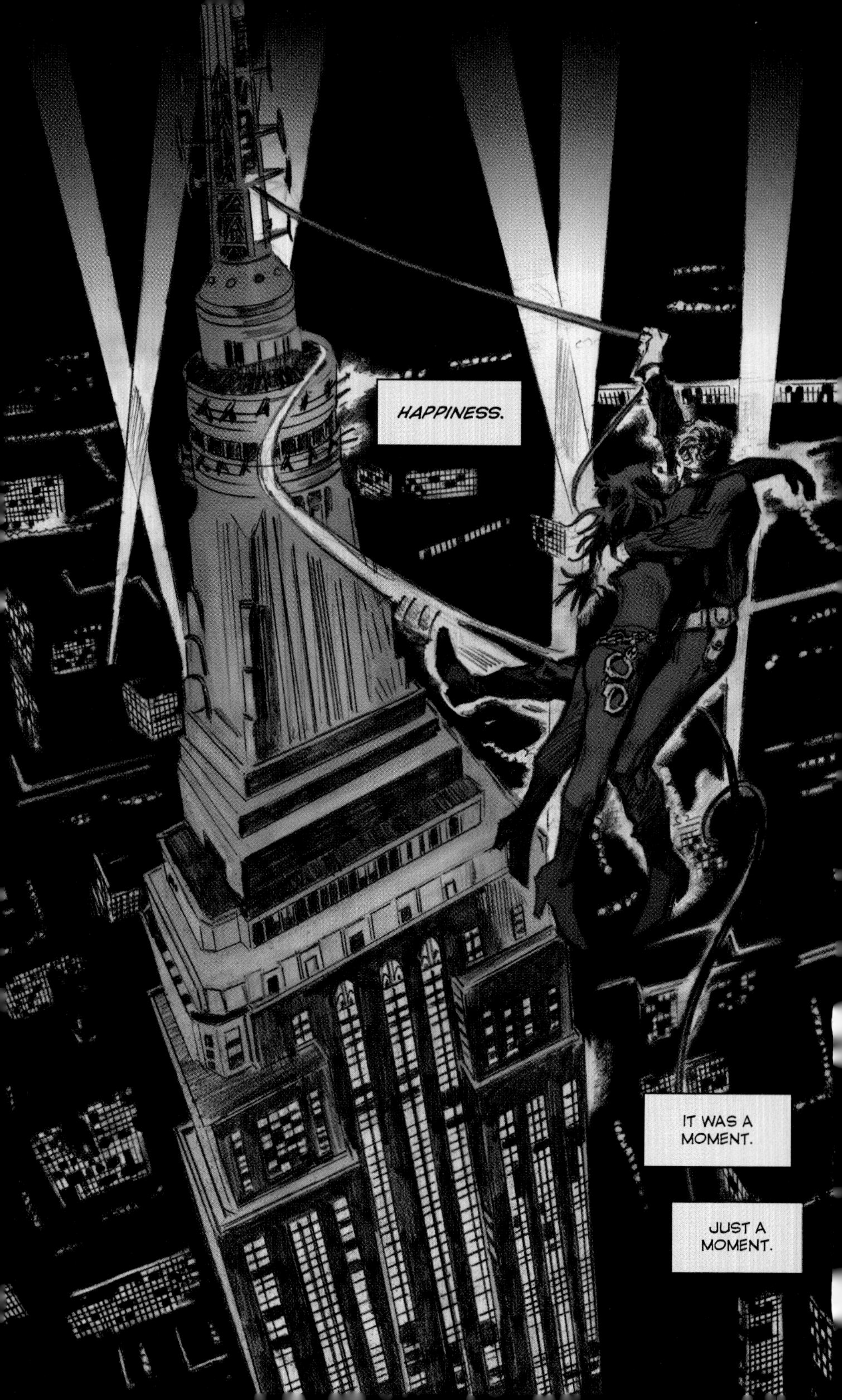
HAPPINESS.
IT WAS A MOMENT.
JUST A MOMENT.

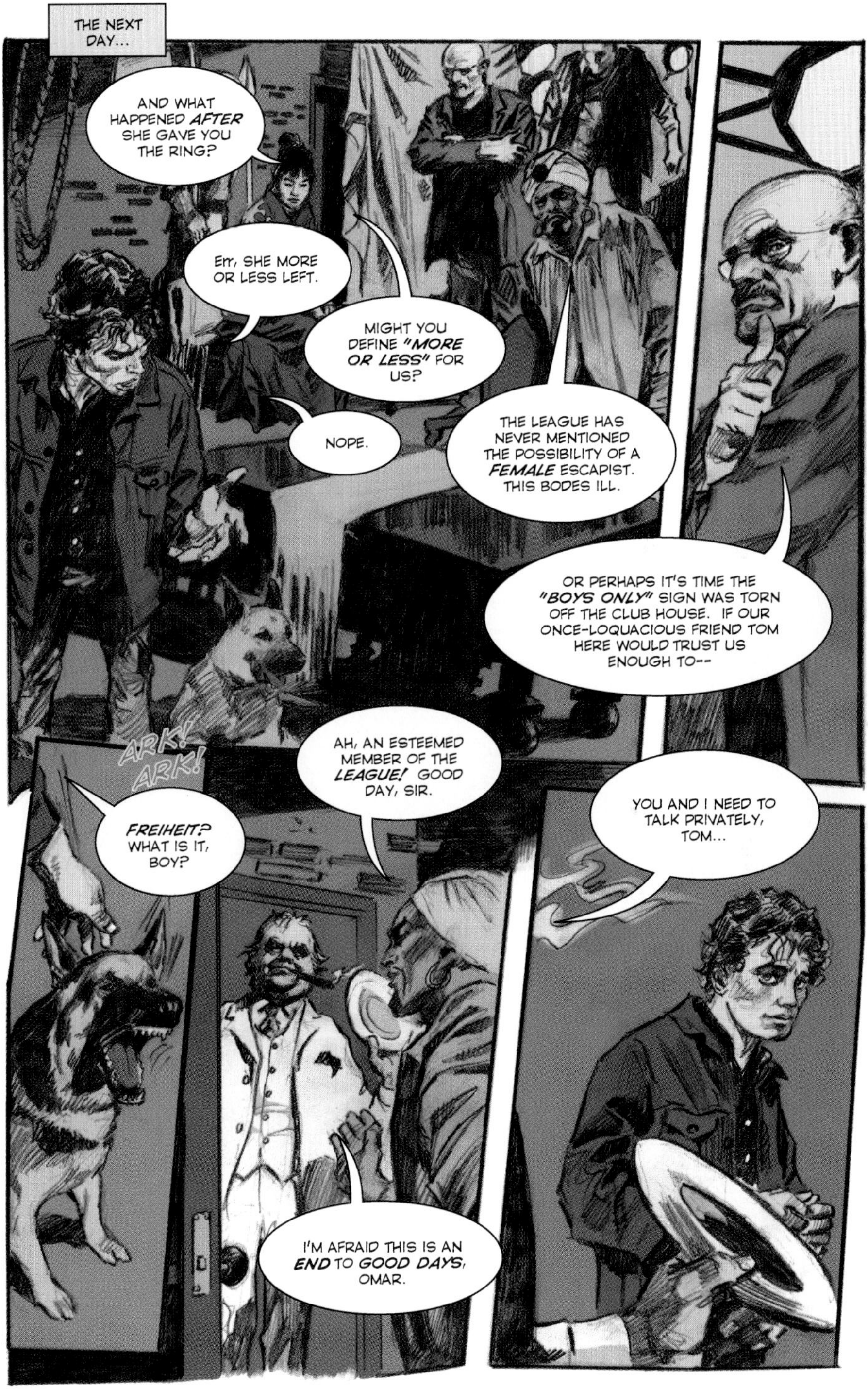
THE NEXT DAY...
AND WHAT HAPPENED AFTER SHE GAVE YOU THE RING?
Err, SHE MORE OR LESS LEFT.
MIGHT YOU DEFINE "MORE OR LESS" FOR US?
NOPE.
THE LEAGUE HAS NEVER MENTIONED THE POSSIBILITY OF A FEMALE ESCAPIST. THIS BODES ILL.
OR PERHAPS IT'S TIME THE "BOYS ONLY" SIGN WAS TORN OFF THE CLUB HOUSE. IF OUR ONCE-LOQUACIOUS FRIEND TOM HERE WOULD TRUST US ENOUGH TO--
ARK! ARK!
FREIHEIT? WHAT IS IT, BOY?
AH, AN ESTEEMED MEMBER OF THE LEAGUE! GOOD DAY, SIR.
I'M AFRAID THIS IS AN END TO GOOD DAYS, OMAR.
YOU AND I NEED TO TALK PRIVATELY, TOM...

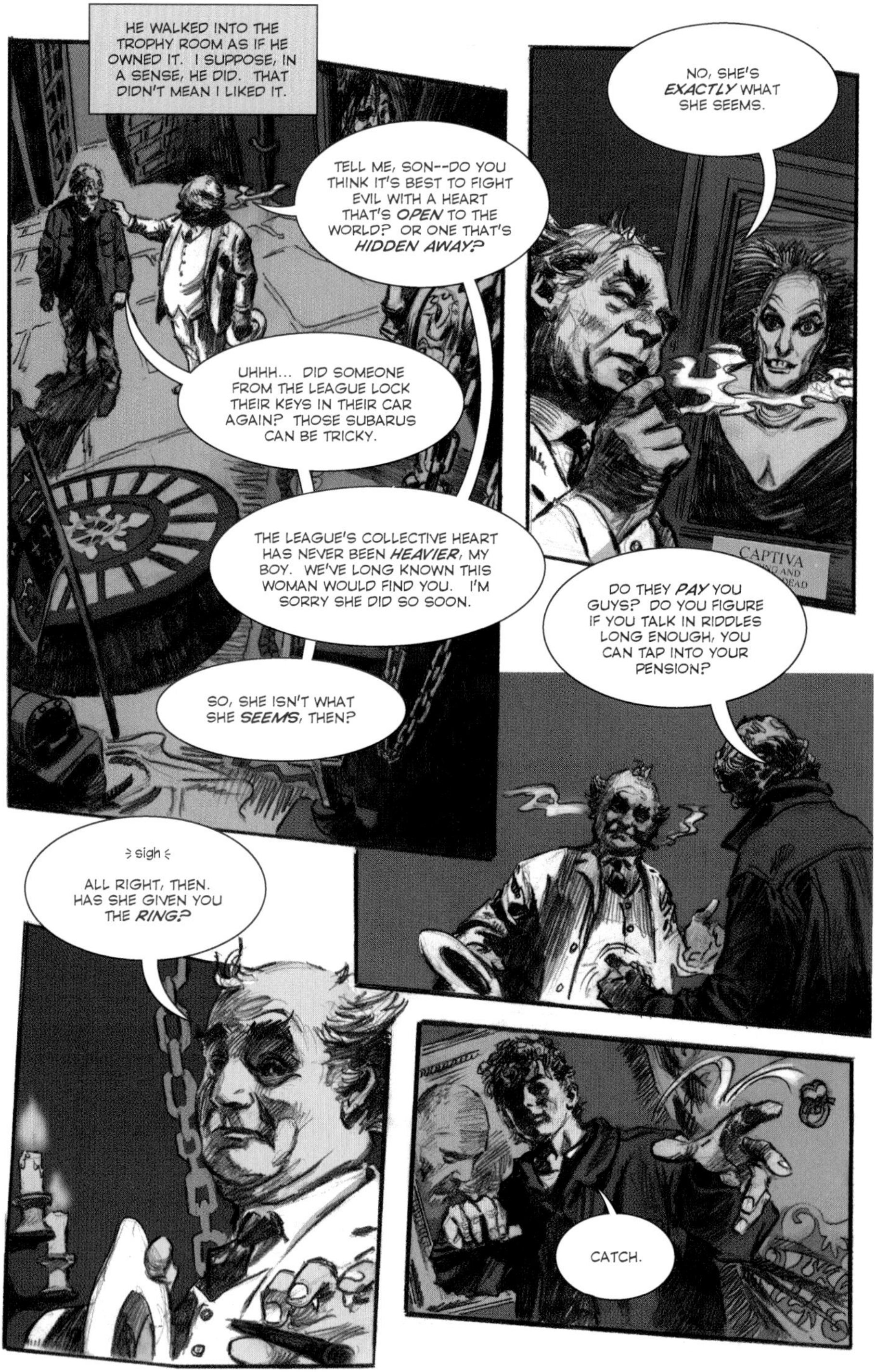
HE WALKED INTO THE TROPHY ROOM AS IF HE OWNED IT. I SUPPOSE, IN A SENSE, HE DID. THAT DIDN'T MEAN I LIKED IT.
TELL ME, SON--DO YOU THINK IT'S BEST TO FIGHT EVIL WITH A HEART THAT'S *OPEN* TO THE WORLD? OR ONE THAT'S ***HIDDEN AWAY?***
UHHH... DID SOMEONE FROM THE LEAGUE LOCK THEIR KEYS IN THEIR CAR AGAIN? THOSE SUBARUS CAN BE TRICKY.
THE LEAGUE'S COLLECTIVE HEART HAS NEVER BEEN ***HEAVIER***, MY BOY. WE'VE LONG KNOWN THIS WOMAN WOULD FIND YOU. I'M SORRY SHE DID SO SOON.
SO, SHE ISN'T WHAT SHE ***SEEMS***, THEN?
NO, SHE'S ***EXACTLY*** WHAT SHE SEEMS.
CAPTIVA
DO THEY ***PAY*** YOU GUYS? DO YOU FIGURE IF YOU TALK IN RIDDLES LONG ENOUGH, YOU CAN TAP INTO YOUR PENSION?
sigh
ALL RIGHT, THEN. HAS SHE GIVEN YOU THE ***RING?***
CATCH.

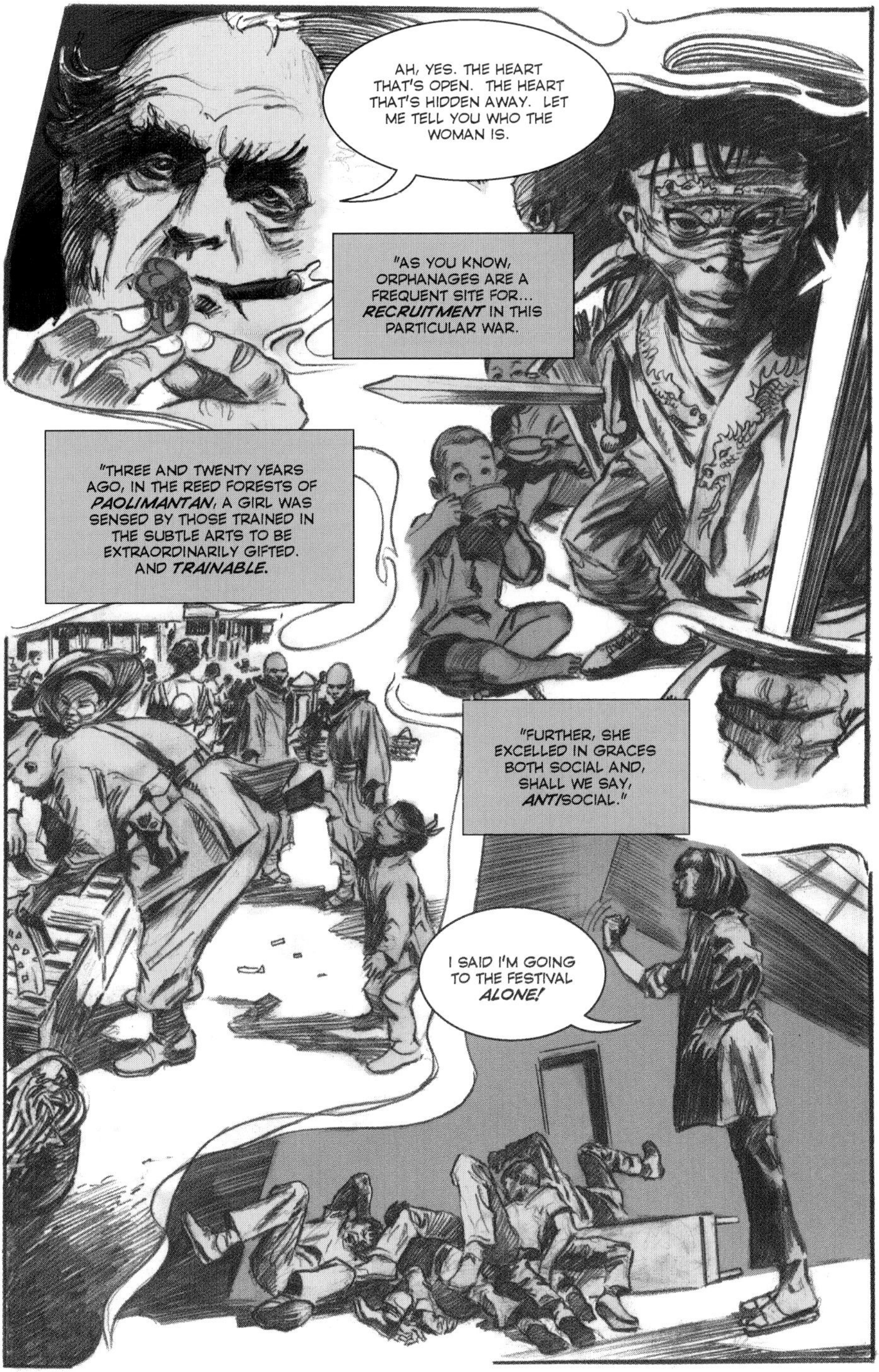
AH, YES. THE HEART THAT'S OPEN. THE HEART THAT'S HIDDEN AWAY. LET ME TELL YOU WHO THE WOMAN IS.
"AS YOU KNOW, ORPHANAGES ARE A FREQUENT SITE FOR... *RECRUITMENT* IN THIS PARTICULAR WAR.
"THREE AND TWENTY YEARS AGO, IN THE REED FORESTS OF *PAOLIMANTAN*, A GIRL WAS SENSED BY THOSE TRAINED IN THE SUBTLE ARTS TO BE EXTRAORDINARILY GIFTED. AND *TRAINABLE*.
"FURTHER, SHE EXCELLED IN GRACES BOTH SOCIAL AND, SHALL WE SAY, *ANTI*SOCIAL."
I SAID I'M GOING TO THE FESTIVAL *ALONE!*

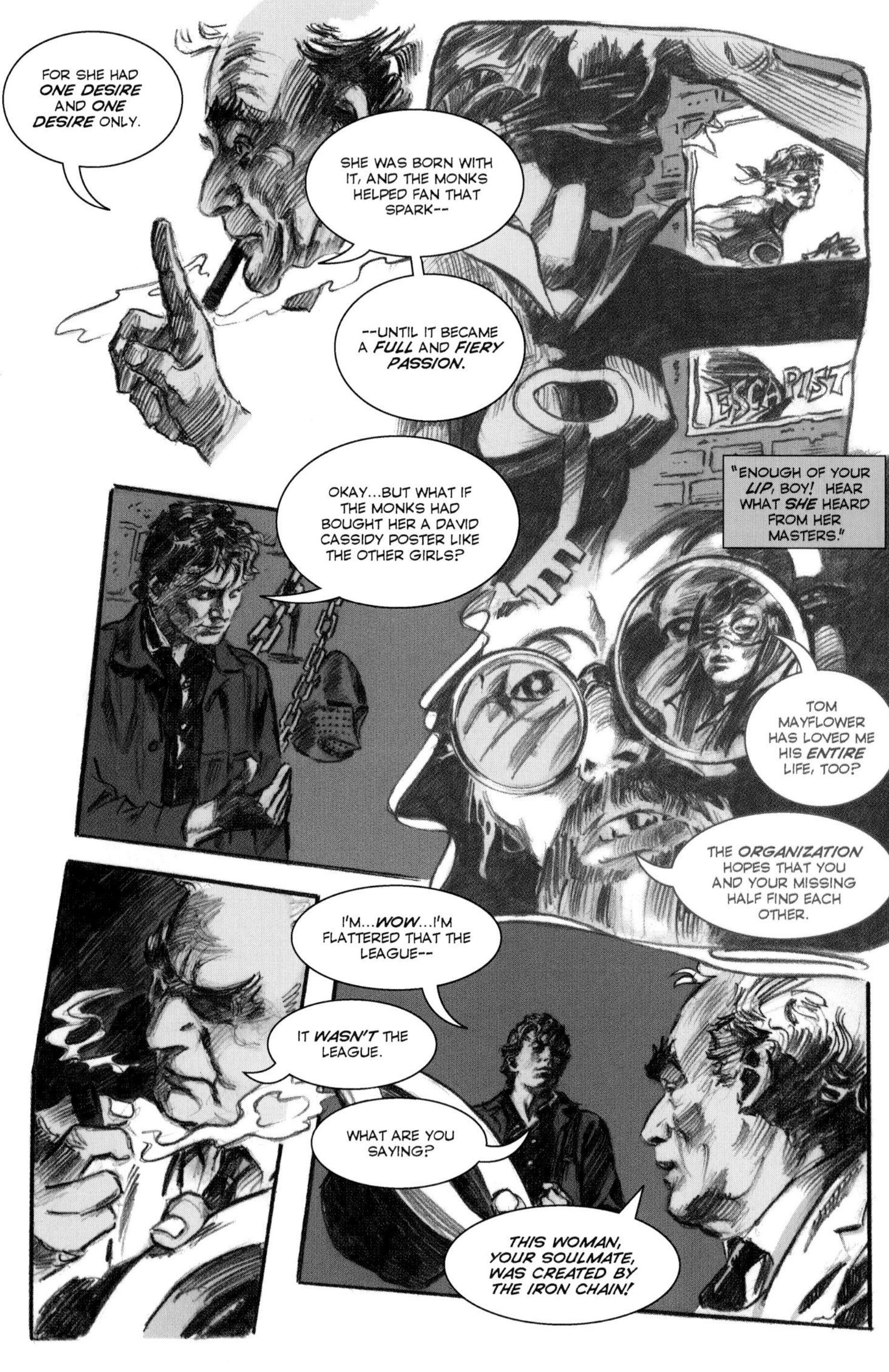
FOR SHE HAD ONE DESIRE AND ONE DESIRE ONLY.
SHE WAS BORN WITH IT, AND THE MONKS HELPED FAN THAT SPARK--
--UNTIL IT BECAME A FULL AND FIERY PASSION.
ESCAPIST
OKAY...BUT WHAT IF THE MONKS HAD BOUGHT HER A DAVID CASSIDY POSTER LIKE THE OTHER GIRLS?
"ENOUGH OF YOUR LIP, BOY! HEAR WHAT SHE HEARD FROM HER MASTERS."
TOM MAYFLOWER HAS LOVED ME HIS ENTIRE LIFE, TOO?
THE ORGANIZATION HOPES THAT YOU AND YOUR MISSING HALF FIND EACH OTHER.
I'M...WOW...I'M FLATTERED THAT THE LEAGUE--
IT WASN'T THE LEAGUE.
WHAT ARE YOU SAYING?
THIS WOMAN, YOUR SOULMATE, WAS CREATED BY THE IRON CHAIN!

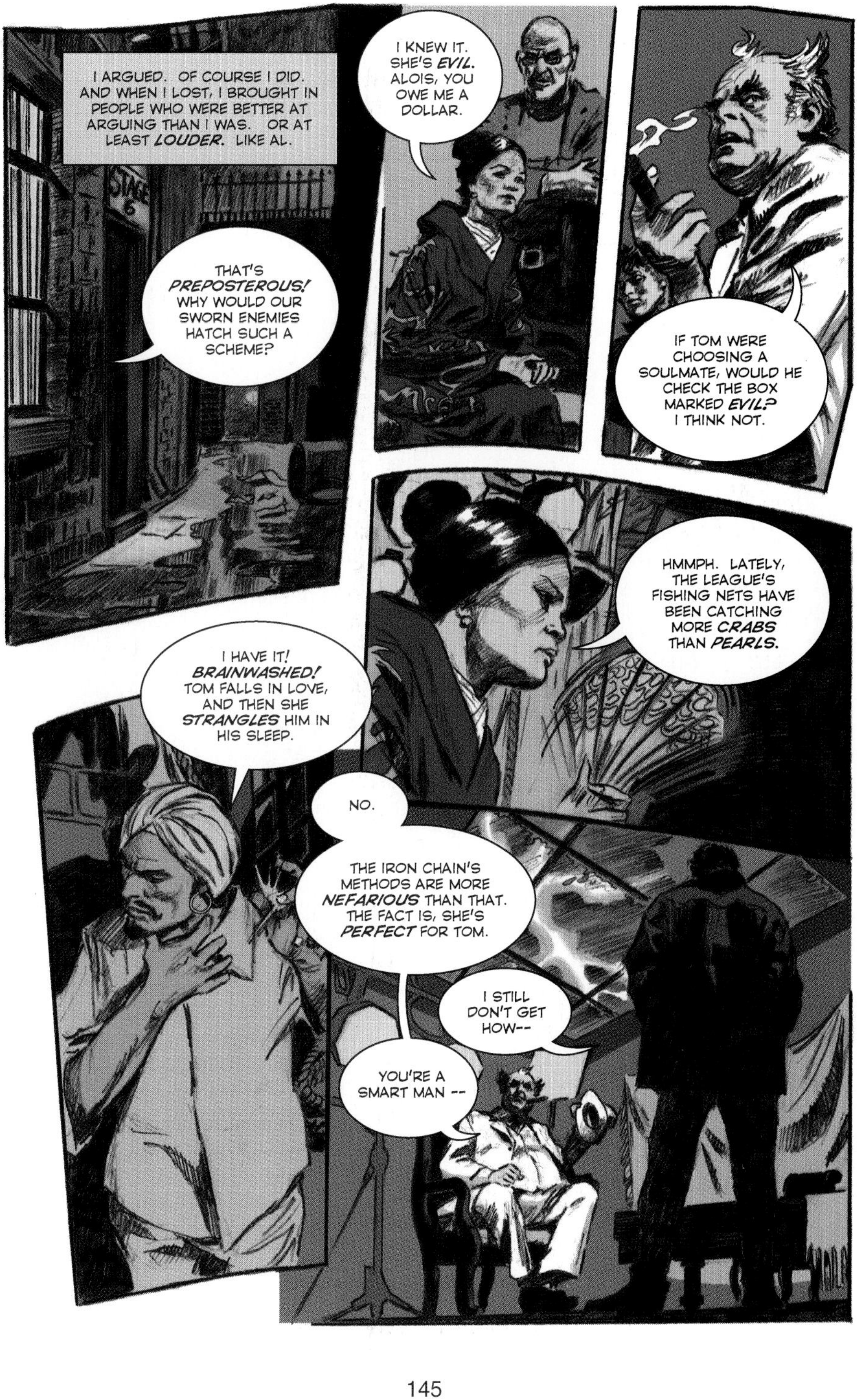
I ARGUED. OF COURSE I DID. AND WHEN I LOST, I BROUGHT IN PEOPLE WHO WERE BETTER AT ARGUING THAN I WAS. OR AT LEAST *LOUDER*. LIKE AL.
STAGE 6
THAT'S *PREPOSTEROUS!* WHY WOULD OUR SWORN ENEMIES HATCH SUCH A SCHEME?
I KNEW IT. SHE'S *EVIL*. ALOIS, YOU OWE ME A DOLLAR.
IF TOM WERE CHOOSING A SOULMATE, WOULD HE CHECK THE BOX MARKED *EVIL?* I THINK NOT.
HMMPH. LATELY, THE LEAGUE'S FISHING NETS HAVE BEEN CATCHING MORE *CRABS* THAN *PEARLS*.
I HAVE IT! *BRAINWASHED!* TOM FALLS IN LOVE, AND THEN SHE *STRANGLES* HIM IN HIS SLEEP.
NO.
THE IRON CHAIN'S METHODS ARE MORE *NEFARIOUS* THAN THAT. THE FACT IS, SHE'S *PERFECT* FOR TOM.
I STILL DON'T GET HOW--
YOU'RE A SMART MAN --

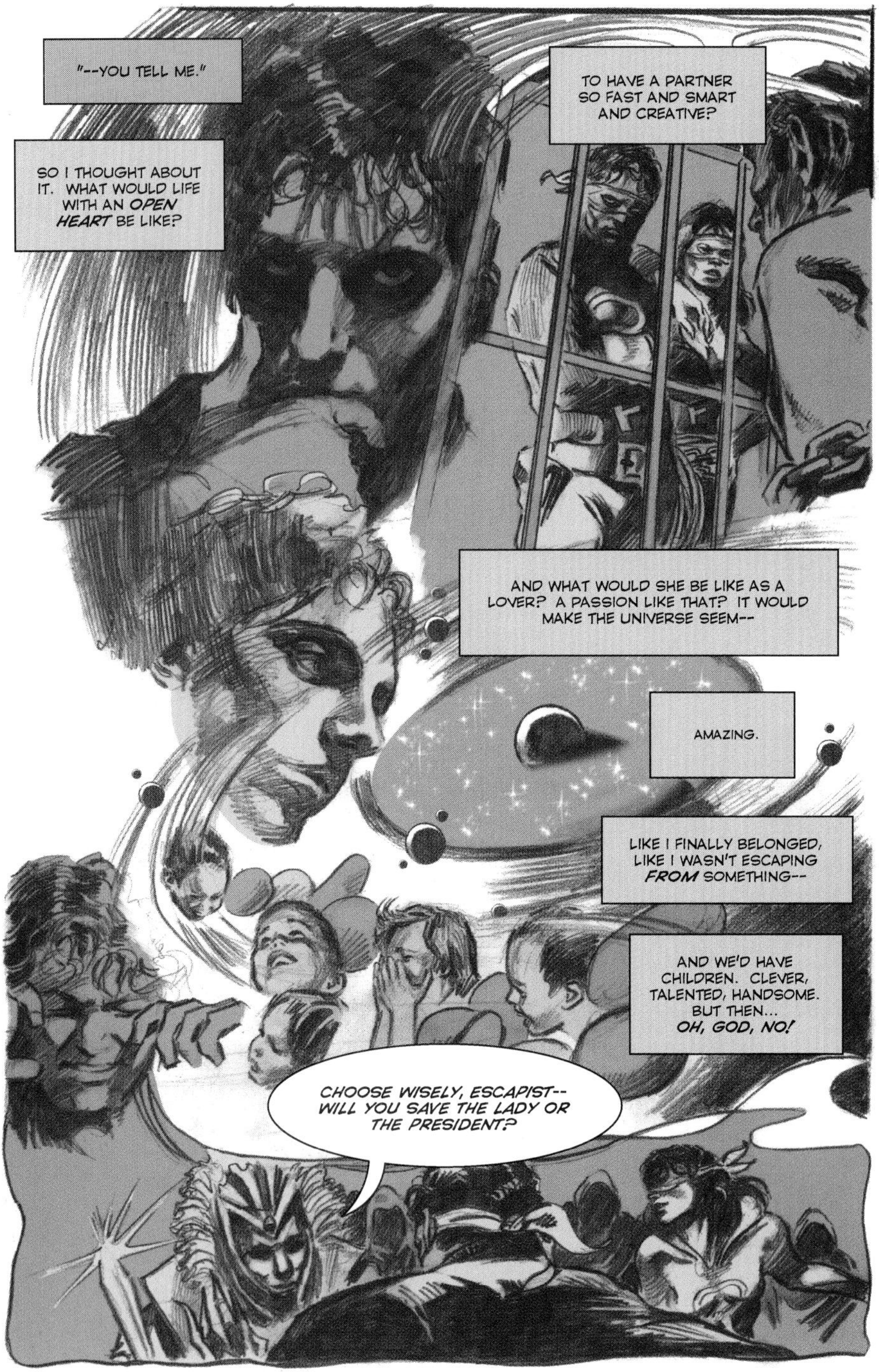
"--YOU TELL ME."
SO I THOUGHT ABOUT IT. WHAT WOULD LIFE WITH AN *OPEN HEART* BE LIKE?
TO HAVE A PARTNER SO FAST AND SMART AND CREATIVE?
AND WHAT WOULD SHE BE LIKE AS A LOVER? A PASSION LIKE THAT? IT WOULD MAKE THE UNIVERSE SEEM--
AMAZING.
LIKE I FINALLY BELONGED, LIKE I WASN'T ESCAPING *FROM* SOMETHING--
AND WE'D HAVE CHILDREN. CLEVER, TALENTED, HANDSOME. BUT THEN... ***OH, GOD, NO!***
CHOOSE WISELY, ESCAPIST-- WILL YOU SAVE THE LADY OR THE PRESIDENT?

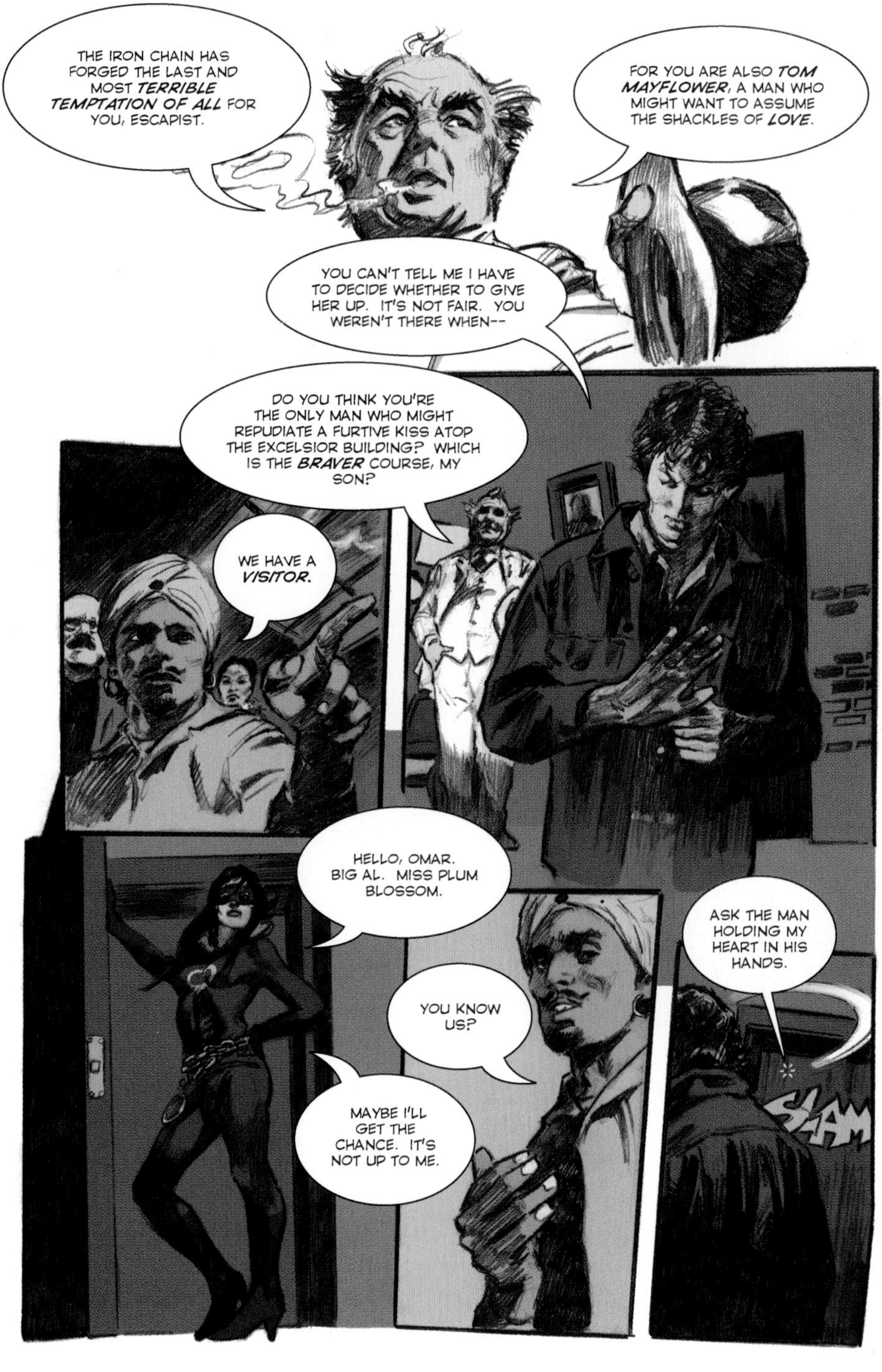
THE IRON CHAIN HAS FORGED THE LAST AND MOST TERRIBLE TEMPTATION OF ALL FOR YOU, ESCAPIST.
FOR YOU ARE ALSO TOM MAYFLOWER, A MAN WHO MIGHT WANT TO ASSUME THE SHACKLES OF LOVE.
YOU CAN'T TELL ME I HAVE TO DECIDE WHETHER TO GIVE HER UP. IT'S NOT FAIR. YOU WEREN'T THERE WHEN--
DO YOU THINK YOU'RE THE ONLY MAN WHO MIGHT REPUDIATE A FURTIVE KISS ATOP THE EXCELSIOR BUILDING? WHICH IS THE BRAVER COURSE, MY SON?
WE HAVE A VISITOR.
HELLO, OMAR. BIG AL. MISS PLUM BLOSSOM.
YOU KNOW US?
MAYBE I'LL GET THE CHANCE. IT'S NOT UP TO ME.
ASK THE MAN HOLDING MY HEART IN HIS HANDS.
SLAM

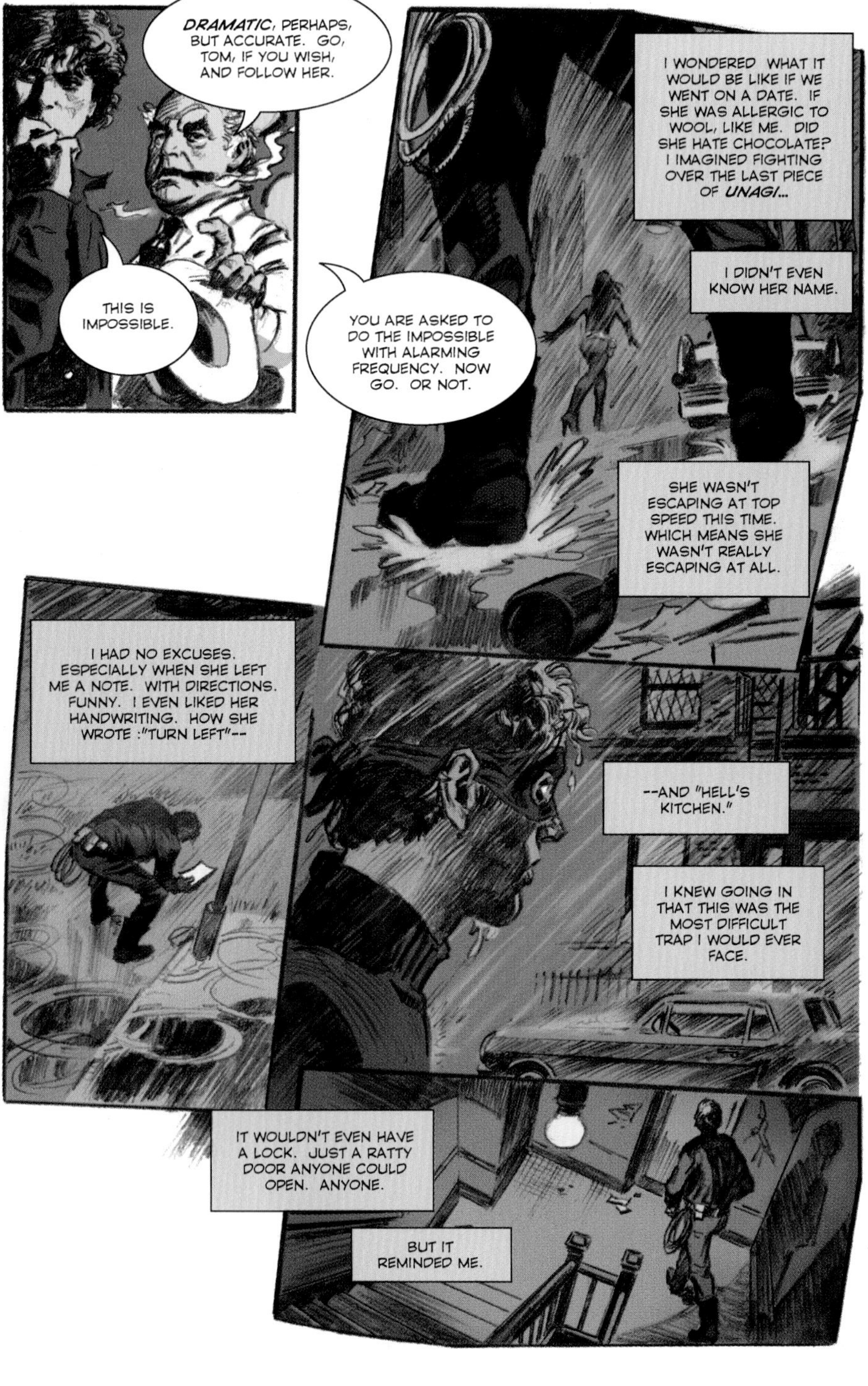
DRAMATIC, PERHAPS, BUT ACCURATE. GO, TOM, IF YOU WISH, AND FOLLOW HER.
THIS IS IMPOSSIBLE.
YOU ARE ASKED TO DO THE IMPOSSIBLE WITH ALARMING FREQUENCY. NOW GO. OR NOT.
I WONDERED WHAT IT WOULD BE LIKE IF WE WENT ON A DATE. IF SHE WAS ALLERGIC TO WOOL, LIKE ME. DID SHE HATE CHOCOLATE? I IMAGINED FIGHTING OVER THE LAST PIECE OF *UNAGI*...
I DIDN'T EVEN KNOW HER NAME.
SHE WASN'T ESCAPING AT TOP SPEED THIS TIME. WHICH MEANS SHE WASN'T REALLY ESCAPING AT ALL.
I HAD NO EXCUSES. ESPECIALLY WHEN SHE LEFT ME A NOTE. WITH DIRECTIONS. FUNNY. I EVEN LIKED HER HANDWRITING. HOW SHE WROTE :"TURN LEFT"--
--AND "HELL'S KITCHEN."
I KNEW GOING IN THAT THIS WAS THE MOST DIFFICULT TRAP I WOULD EVER FACE.
IT WOULDN'T EVEN HAVE A LOCK. JUST A RATTY DOOR ANYONE COULD OPEN. ANYONE.
BUT IT REMINDED ME.

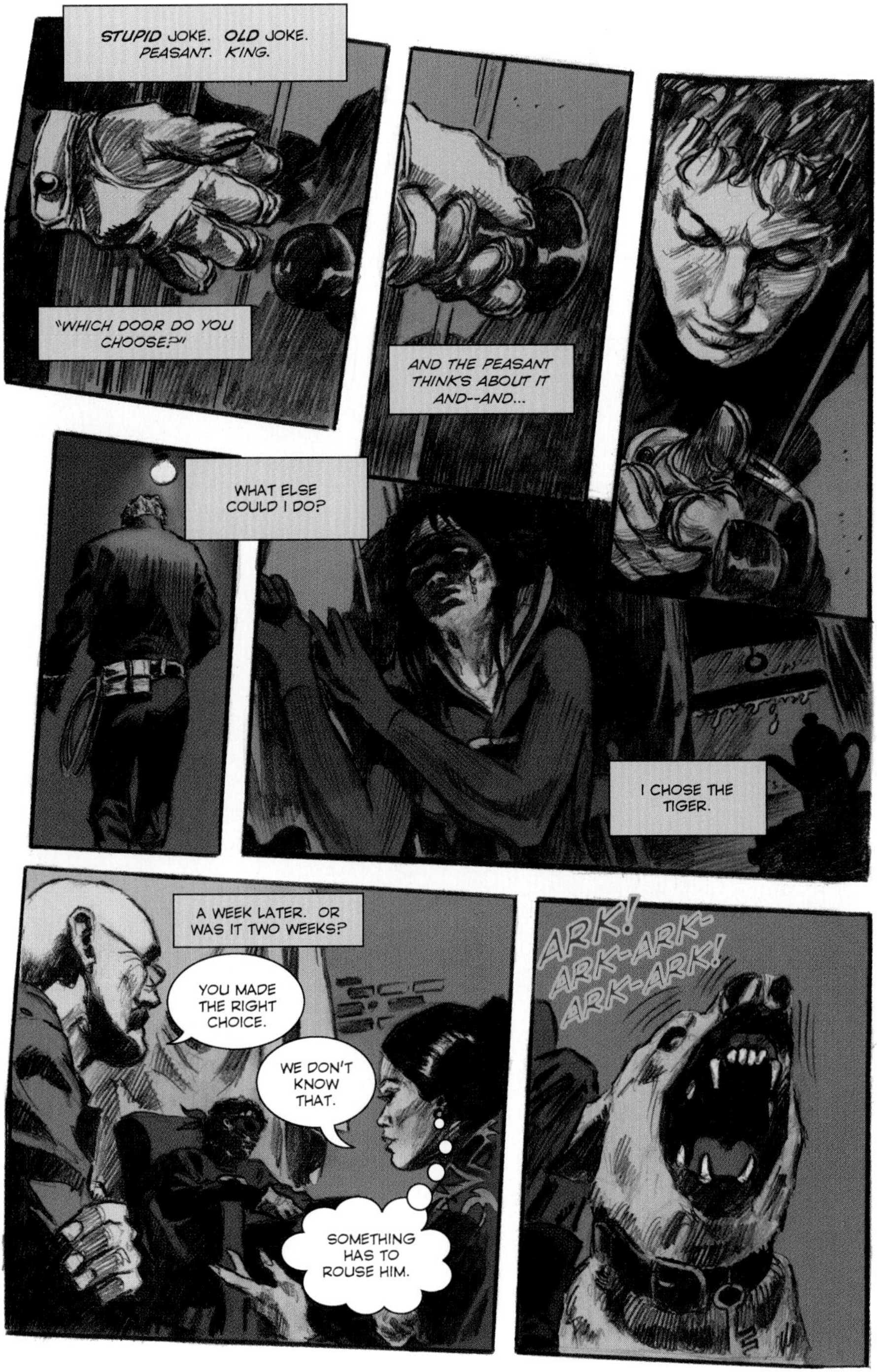
STUPID JOKE. OLD JOKE. PEASANT. KING.
"WHICH DOOR DO YOU CHOOSE?"
AND THE PEASANT THINKS ABOUT IT AND--AND...
WHAT ELSE COULD I DO?
I CHOSE THE TIGER.
A WEEK LATER. OR WAS IT TWO WEEKS?
YOU MADE THE RIGHT CHOICE.
WE DON'T KNOW THAT.
SOMETHING HAS TO ROUSE HIM.
ARK! ARK-ARK-ARK-ARK!

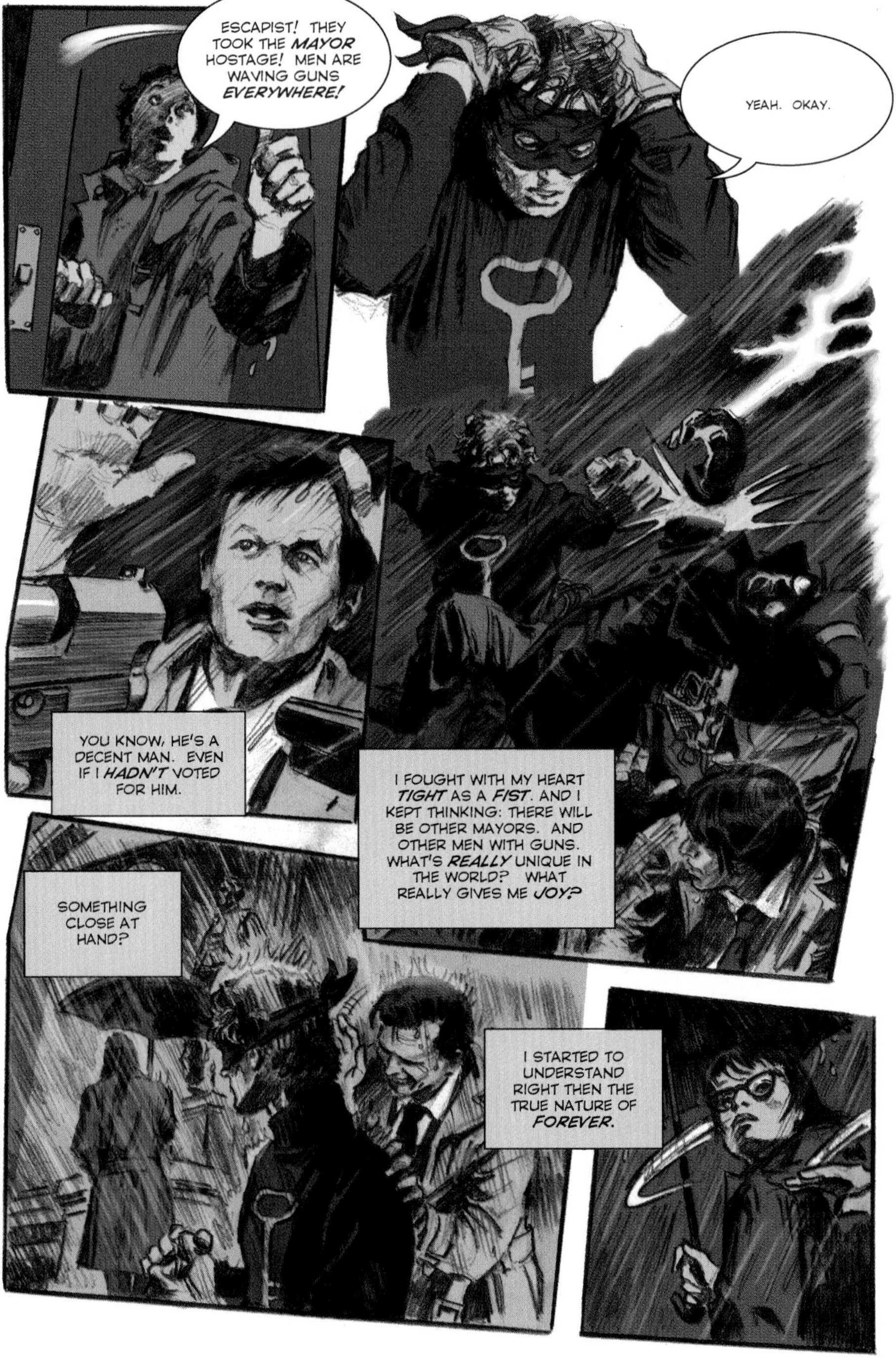
ESCAPIST! THEY TOOK THE MAYOR HOSTAGE! MEN ARE WAVING GUNS EVERYWHERE!
YEAH. OKAY.
YOU KNOW, HE'S A DECENT MAN. EVEN IF I HADN'T VOTED FOR HIM.
I FOUGHT WITH MY HEART TIGHT AS A FIST. AND I KEPT THINKING: THERE WILL BE OTHER MAYORS. AND OTHER MEN WITH GUNS. WHAT'S REALLY UNIQUE IN THE WORLD? WHAT REALLY GIVES ME JOY?
SOMETHING CLOSE AT HAND?
I STARTED TO UNDERSTAND RIGHT THEN THE TRUE NATURE OF FOREVER.

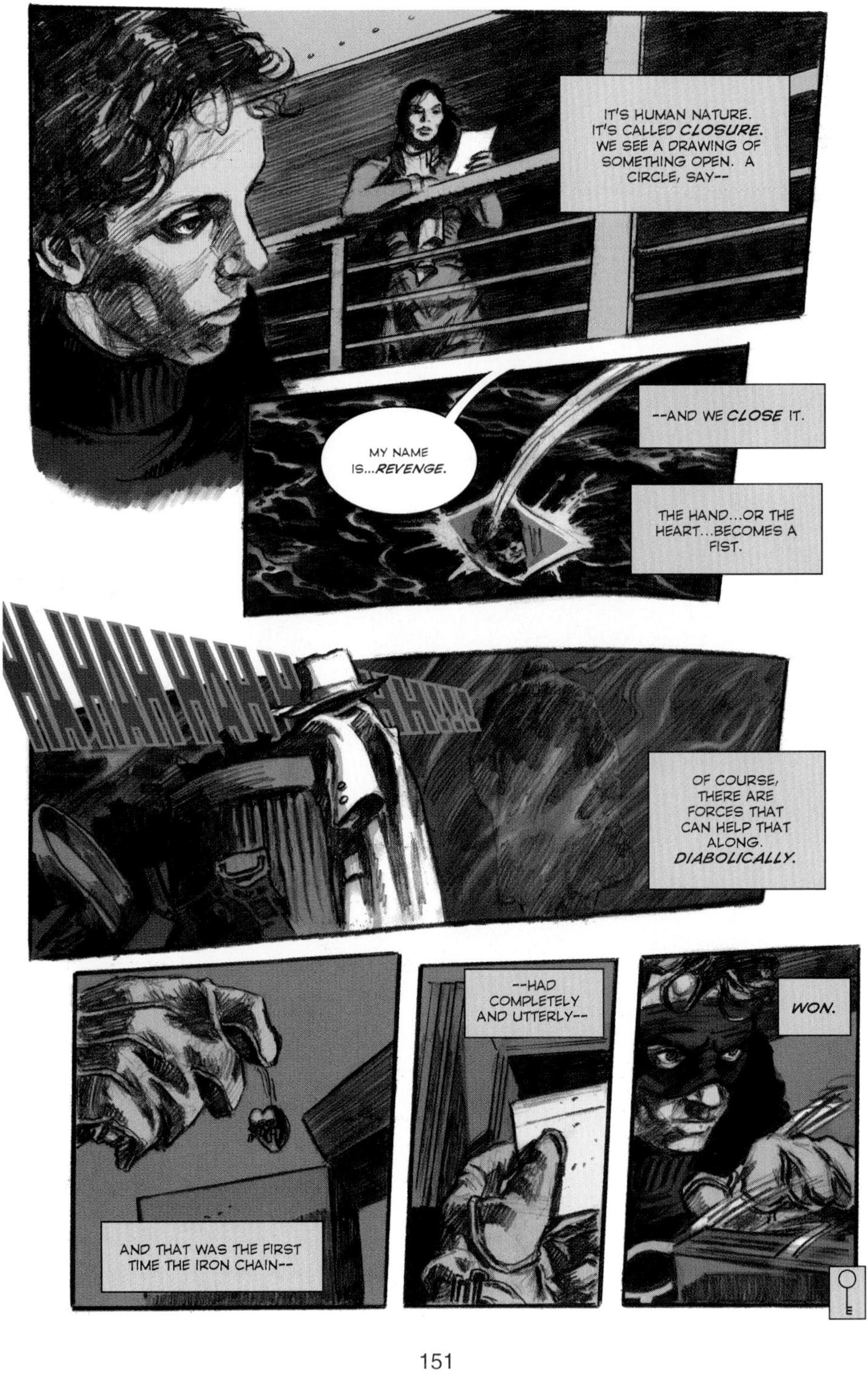
IT'S HUMAN NATURE. IT'S CALLED ***CLOSURE.*** WE SEE A DRAWING OF SOMETHING OPEN. A CIRCLE, SAY--
--AND WE ***CLOSE*** IT.
MY NAME IS...***REVENGE.***
THE HAND...OR THE HEART...BECOMES A FIST.
OF COURSE, THERE ARE FORCES THAT CAN HELP THAT ALONG. ***DIABOLICALLY.***
AND THAT WAS THE FIRST TIME THE IRON CHAIN--
--HAD COMPLETELY AND UTTERLY--
WON.

GALLERY

A Captivating Cornucopia of Illustrious Iconographies
Executed with Elegance
by an Assortment of Accomplished Artists

Eric Wight

Howard Chaykin

Chris Warner, *with color by* Dan Jackson

Jeff Parker

C. Scott Morse

Jae Lee

Dan Brereton

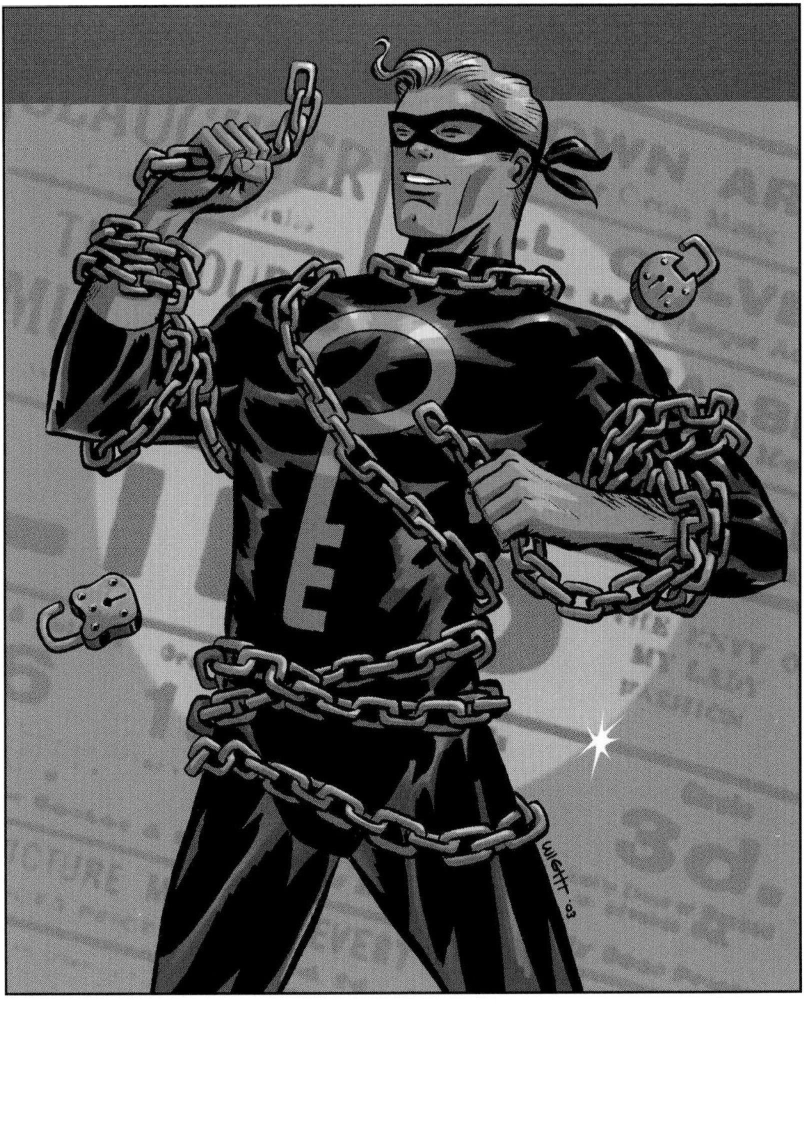
3d.

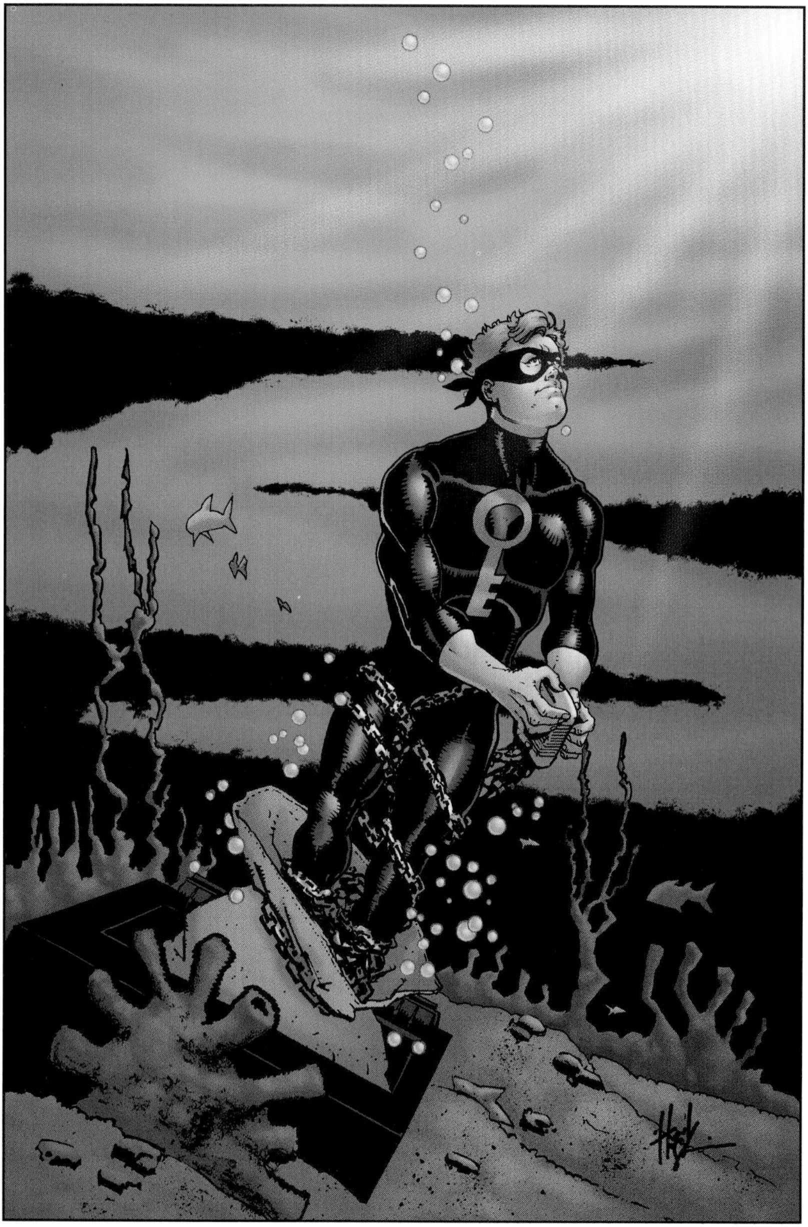

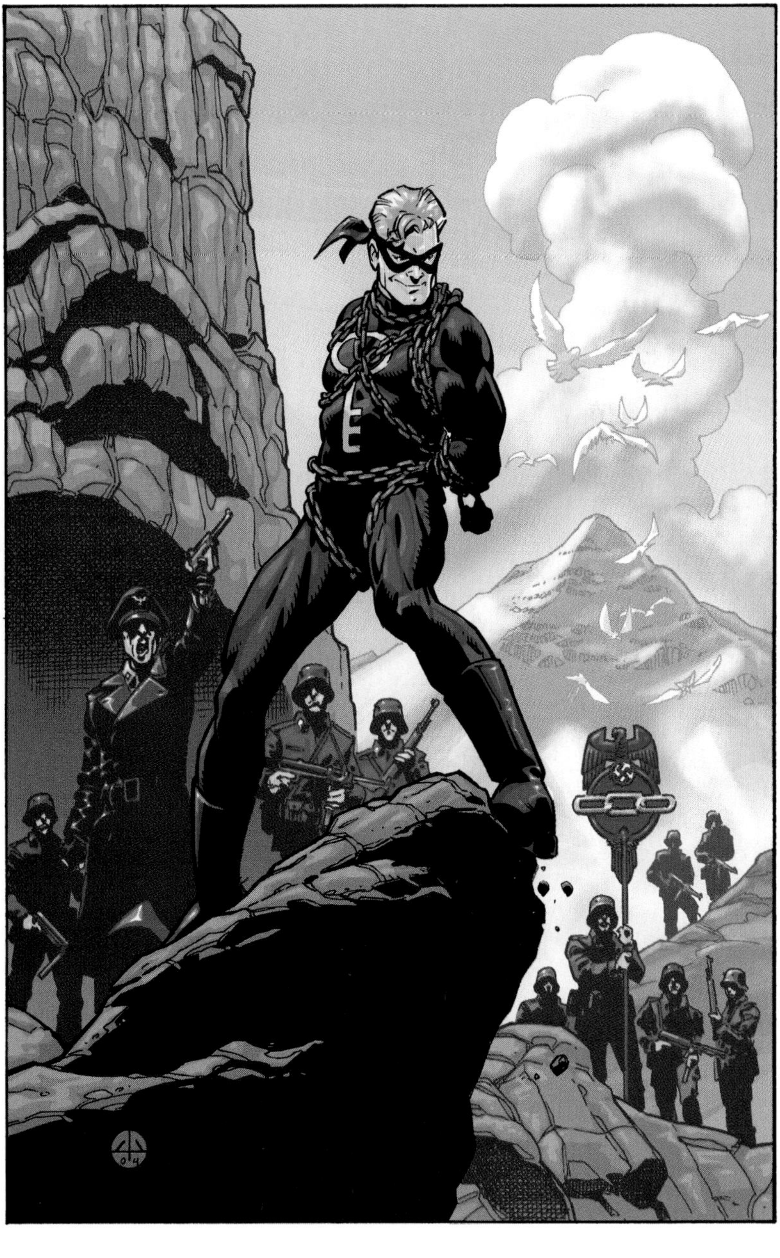

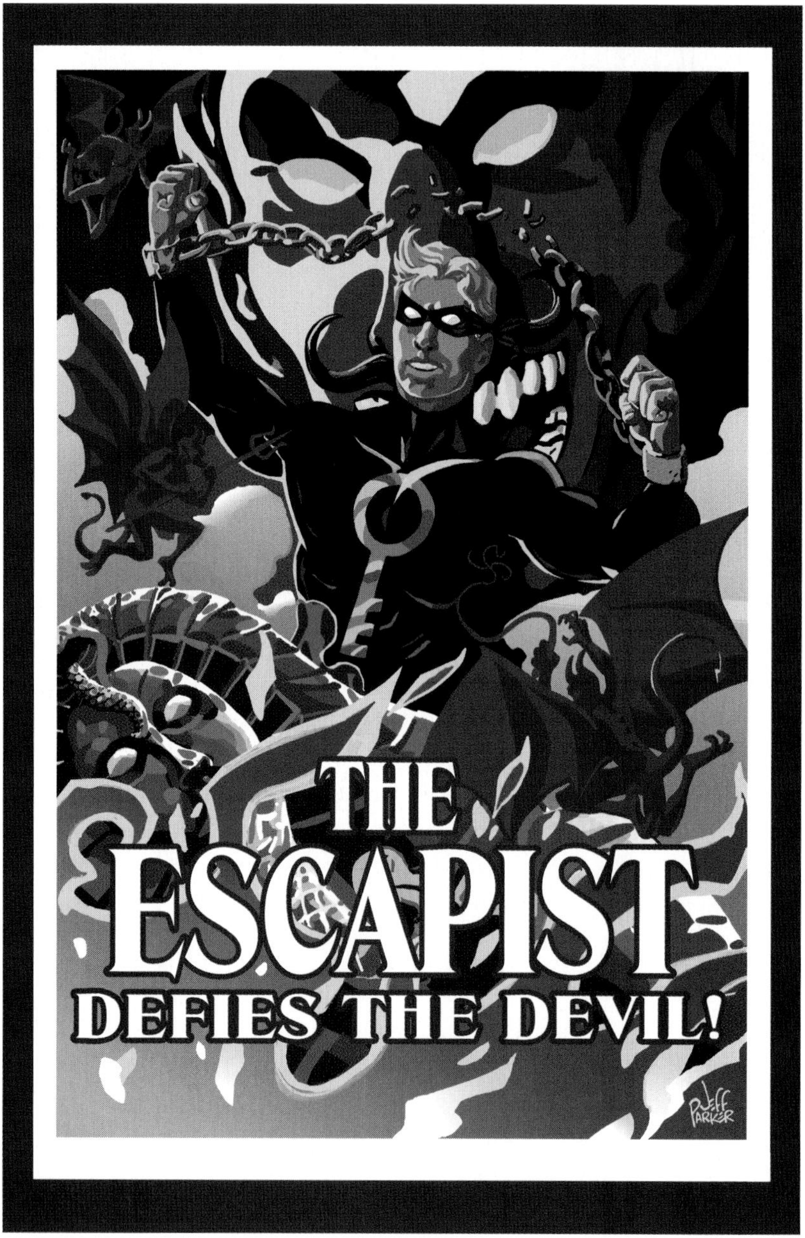
THE ESCAPIST
DEFIES THE DEVIL!
JEFF PARKER

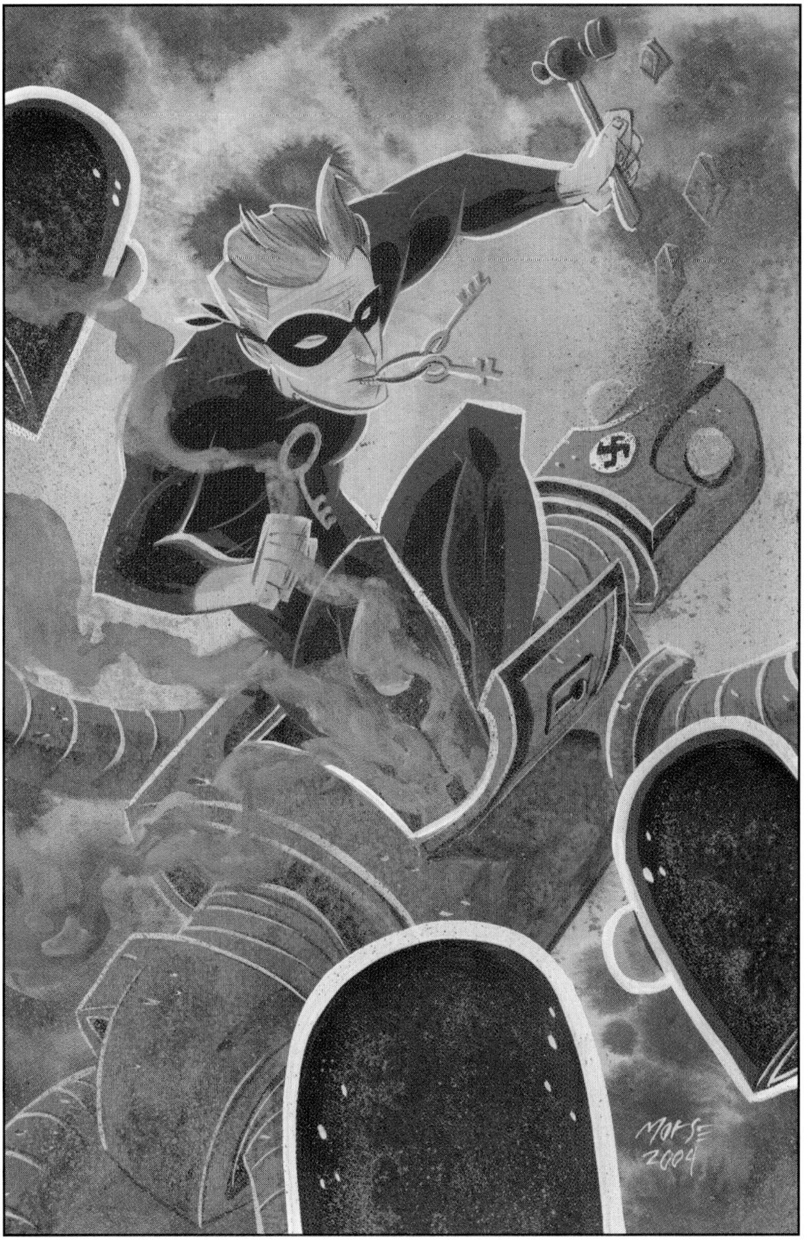
MORSE
2004

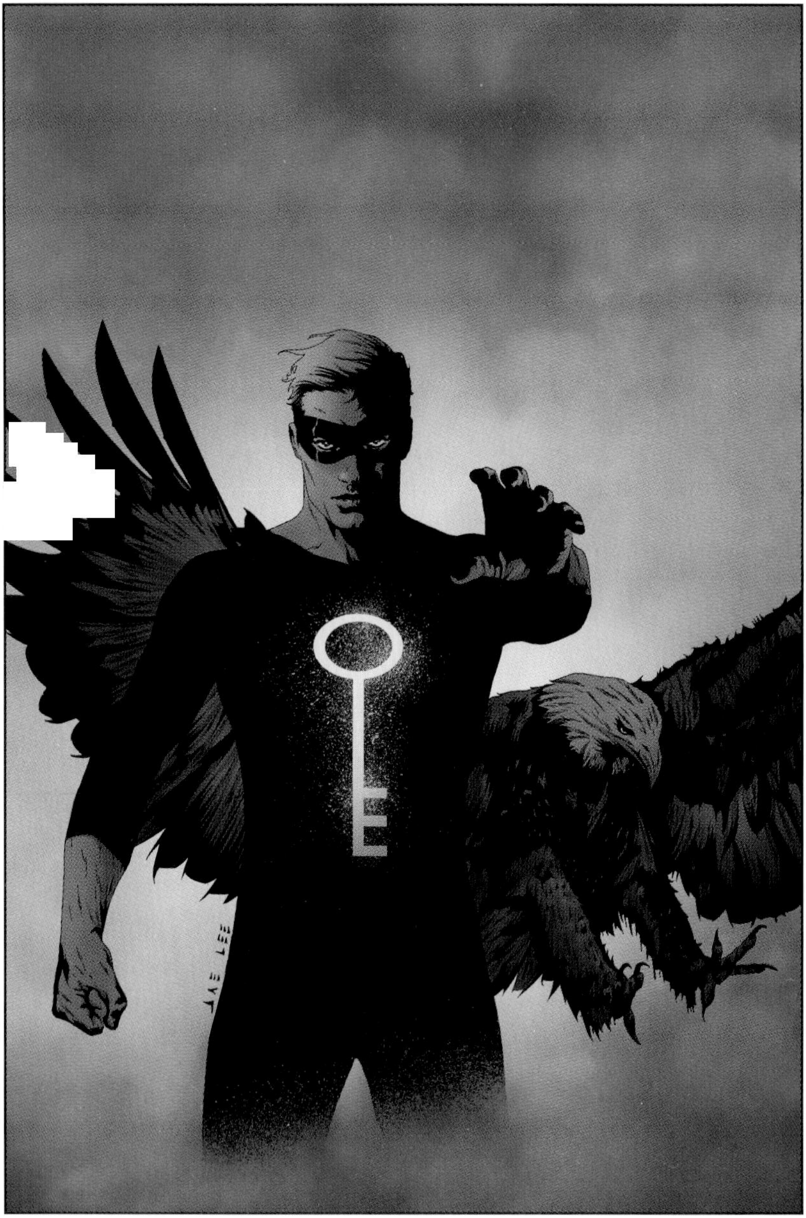

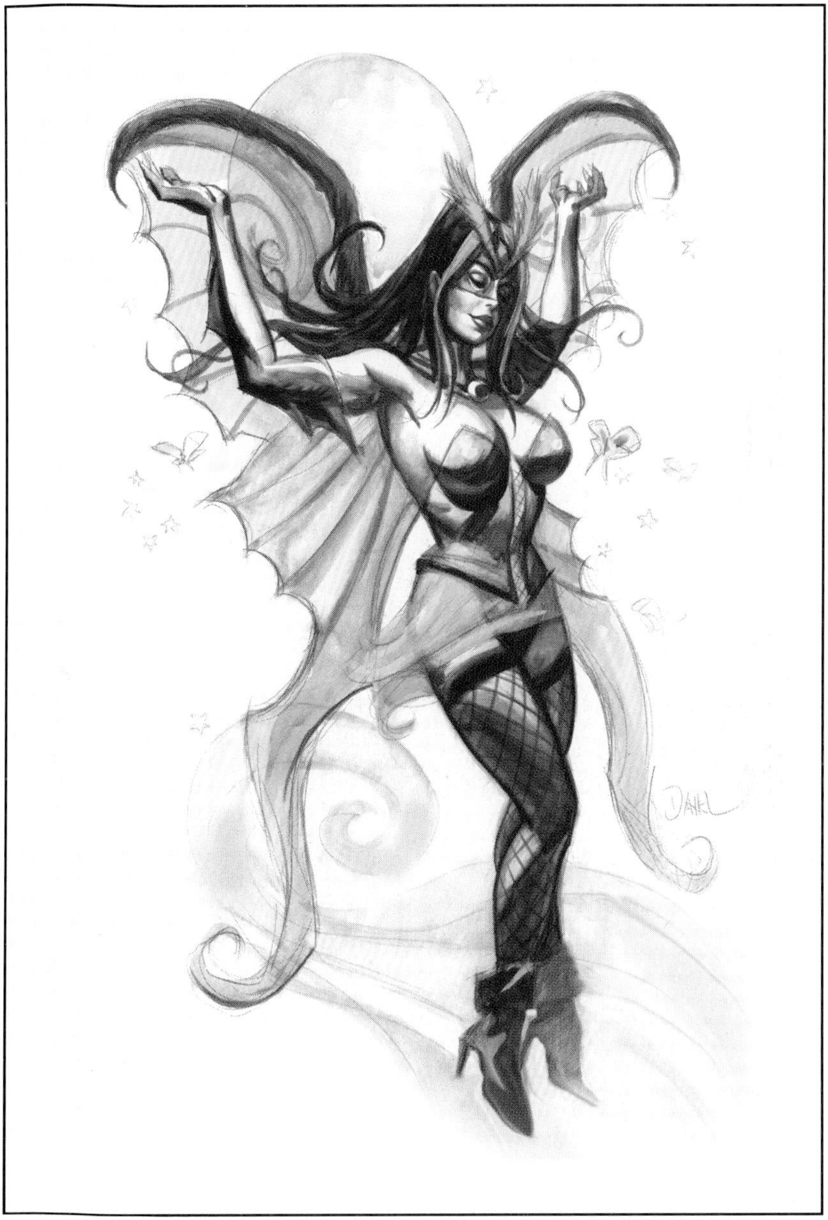

CREATOR BIOS

KYLE BAKER is the author of seven graphic novels: *You Are Here*; *Why I Hate Saturn*; *The Cowboy Wally Show*; *I Die at Midnight*; *King David*; *Kyle Baker, Cartoonist*; and *Undercover Genie*. His cartoons have appeared in such publications as *The New York Times, Esquire, The New Yorker, SPIN, Rolling Stone, Vibe, The Village Voice, MAD, Entertainment Weekly,* and *ESPN the Magazine.* This Eisner and Harvey Award winner recently wrote and directed *Looney Tunes* theatrical shorts for Warner Brothers.

MIKE BARON has won several Eisners for his work on the groundbreaking science fiction title *Nexus*, co-created with artist Steve Rude, and has been nominated numerous times for Best Writer in the Kirby, Harvey, and Eisner Awards. In addition to co-creating a number of other titles, Baron has also written for such mainstream comics as *Star Wars*, *The Flash*, and *The Punisher*. He lives in Colorado with his wife and pets.

DAN BRERETON is one of a bare handful of painters left in the industry who still does comics full time. Just barely out of art school, he burst onto the scene in 1989 with the award-winning *Black Terror* miniseries from Eclipse Comics and hasn't looked back since. In the last 15 years he's produced an amazingly prolific body of work, including his pet creation, *The Nocturnals*, and has been nominated many times for several different industry and fan awards. Brereton lives in the Sierra Nevada Mountains with his three kids.

MICHAEL CHABON is a novelist, short story writer, and comic book dilettante who lives in Berkeley, California.

HOWARD CHAYKIN is responsible for some of the most innovative and influential comics of the last two decades, including *American Flagg!*, *Time(Squared)*, *Black Kiss*, and *Power & Glory*.

Bronx native **GENE COLAN** has been a permanent fixture in the comics industry since 1946, and now his cinematic work is often published directly from pencils. Long associated with such popular characters as Dracula, Daredevil, Batman, Howard the Duck, Captain America, Wonder Woman, Sub-Mariner, Dr. Strange, Silver Surfer, and many others, Colan is comfortable illustrating numerous genres and has taught at both the School of Visual Arts in Manhattan and the Fashion Institute of Technology. Colan currently lives in Florida with his wife Adrienne.

GLEN DAVID GOLD has written screenplays, memoir, journalism, short stories, and a novel, *Carter Beats the Devil*.

One of the more popular artists in the industry, **JAE LEE** was born in South Korea in 1972. He has left his mark on such titles as *Namor, Spider-Man, Uncanny X-Men, X-Factor,* and his own creation, *Hellshock*. Lee has been nominated for an Eisner Award for Best Cover Artist; he worked on the Eisner Award-winning *Inhumans*; and his art for *Fantastic Four: 1234* was displayed at the Society of Illustrators exhibit in New York City. He has just completed *The Transformers/GI Joe* miniseries and is now active on *Batman: Jekyll and Hyde*. Lee currently resides in New York City.